The New Politics Congress

Other Books by the Same Author

Metropolitics and The Urban County, National Association of Counties, 1970.
Emerging Patterns in Urban Administration, Lexington Books,
     co-editor, 1970.
Science, Geopolitics, and Federal Spending, Lexington Books, 1971.
Pressures Upon Congress, Barrons, 1973.
Government Management Internships and Executive Development, Lexington
     Books, 1973.
Universities in the Urban Crisis, Dunellen and Company, 1974.
Organizing Public Services in Metropolitan America, Lexington Books, co-
     editor, 1974.

The New Politics Congress

Thomas P. Murphy
University of Maryland

Lexington Books
D.C. Heath and Company
Lexington, Massachusetts
Toronto   London

Library of Congress Cataloging in Publication Data

Murphy, Thomas P   1931–
   The new politics Congress.

     1. United States. Congress.   2. United States—
Politics and government—1945–   3. Political
participation—United States.   I. Title.
JK1051.M86   328.73′001   73-11664
ISBN 0-669-88187-2

Copyright © 1974 by D.C. Heath and Company

Published simultaneously in Canada.
Printed in the United States of America.
International Standard Book Number: 0-669-88187-2
Library of Congress Catalog Card Number: 73-11664

To Kevin, Mike, Tom, Dolores, and Danny

Contents

List of Figure and Tables

Preface

This book attempts to capture the spirit of the New Politics as an influence on Congress. New Politics, of course, has many definitions. To Mayor Richard Daley, it probably connotes long-haired Vietnam war protestors forcing their way into the 1968 Democratic Convention to block Hubert Humphrey's nomination, with the side effect of splitting the Democratic party so that Richard Nixon won the election. Daley's next remembrance would likely be the decision of the 1972 convention at Miami that his delegation was illegal and should not be seated.

George Meany views the New Politics as a conglomeration of women's libbers, welfare cheaters, homosexuals, and unknowledgeable youth being squeezed into the 1972 Democratic Convention because of the requirements of an unrealistic quota system, with a side effect of watering down labor's leverage at the convention.

To Eugene McCarthy in 1968, the New Politics was a movement of courageous Democrats willing to challenge President Lyndon Johnson's arbitrary decision making and machinelike domination of the Democratic party. McCarthy built his campaign on New Politics volunteers who went from New England town to town in a twentieth-century version of Paul Revere's ride in the cause of freedom.

To George McGovern, the New Politics was the road to the 1972 nomination, paved with associations with peaceniks and the youth culture. McGovern learned too late that packing a district convention or a primary contest with flocks of doorbell-ringing volunteers is not the same as appealing to Middle America and the traditional Democratic voters in the general election.

These conflicting perceptions of the New Politics involve some common themes. George Meany is just as interested as George McGovern in participating in the political process. Their differences involve who *else* should be participating, and how much weight should be given to their opinions. For better or for worse, submersion of the old-style politics of Democratic party stalwarts Daley and Meany led to the election and reelection of Richard Nixon.

The tone of the McGovern campaign incorporated all the basic themes of New Politics as defined in this book—broadened participation, an open political process, and the reduction of arbitrary decisions, as well as specific attention to the needs of the minorities in our society. McGovern, however, went wrong in overemphasizing the far-left wing of the New Politics movement and ignoring the middle strategy laid out by Scammon and Wattenberg in their book *The Real Majority*.

Despite the failure of George McGovern to capitalize upon the positive elements of the burgeoning New Politics movement, it was McGovern rather than the New Politics that really lost the 1972 election. Richard Nixon became the first President in history who failed to win either House of Congress during any part of his tenure as President. Congress during the Nixon years was in large measure a New Politics Congress. It contained more blacks, more Spanish-Americans, and more women elected on their own merits (as opposed to replacements for deceased husbands) than any Congress in history. It included many younger congressmen who beat less flexible but more experienced predecessors.

This involved more than liberal-oriented Congresses. There had been many such Congresses prior to the 1970s. The New Politics Congresses have moved a step beyond liberalism, by expanding the socioeconomic legislation while at the same time challenging the centers of power in America in the interest of improving the quality of life. This phenomenon is perhaps shown best in the consumer and the environmental legislation of the last decade. The movement has also included new legislation related to political participation.

Like any other movement, New Politics might have run out of steam by the 93rd Congress. More than he realizes, it was Richard Nixon who inadvertently set the stage for a further development of the New Politics Congress. If the themes of New Politics are to be fully realized, Congress must do more than pass legislation. It must establish itself as a powerful partner in making decisions regarding national priorities. Through his use of the veto power, the war power, and impoundment, Richard Nixon became a catalyst that caused Congress to look seriously at its institutional weaknesses. Congress is now dealing with each of the specific institutional challenges thrust upon it by President Nixon. If Congress succeeds in improving its procedures and in developing leadership appropriate to implement its responsibilities, it will truly be a New Politics Congress in power, as well as in spirit. If it fails, it will have no one to blame but itself.

My style of operation in undertaking a project of this magnitude is to mobilize the talents of graduate assistants, not only as footnote-chasers, researchers, and bibliography developers but also as chapter critics, and as a kind of Kitchen Cabinet. The cabinet for this volume included graduate assistants Glenn Gardner, David Kaminsky, Claudia Thurber, and Susan Wolf, as well as colleagues Robert Kline and Elizabeth Knipe.

Liz and Bob also contributed sufficiently to the development of several chapters to justify listing them as coauthors of chapters 6 and 15, respectively. Susie was especially helpful in gathering materials for chapters 1 and 2, and David performed the same task in chapter 11. Glenn did the interviews and tables necessary for chapter 1, and provided research assistance on chapters 5 and 10. Claudia was the only one to be called upon to read the whole manuscript. Judy Bair assisted on the final proofreading.

I received innumerable suggestions from colleagues, and should make specific mention of the help received from Dave Aylward, Michael Bromberg, Warren Cikins, Guy Hathorn, Lew Paper, Ben and Mavis Reeves, Clarence Stone, and David Walker.

As usual, the students in many classes have contributed substantially. Special mention should be made of Dan Fixell, David Garfinkle, Verna Harrison, Mark Pritchard, Bob Mazor, George Soohoo, and Bob Targ, all of whom were in my Government and Politics Internship Program.

Indispensable secretarial support came from Eleanor Futrell, who was also responsible for keeping the administrative processes of the Institute for Urban Studies in good shape. Eleanor was assisted on the project by Rosemary Minni Breen, Joyce Brooks, Annetta Howard, Rochelle Murphy, Willette Oliver, Charles Stokes, Carol Uhler, and Evelyn Yenias. Virginia Karas provided valuable administrative support. My wife, Marcella, and our children—Kevin, Mike, Tom, Dolores, and Danny—once again endured my weekend hours with good spirit or I might never have made it.

The New Politics Congress

**Part I
Changing Political Climates**

1 The New Politics

New Politics frequently has been identified with barefooted and long-haired anti-Vietnam demonstrators on the steps of the Capitol or with protesters filling the streets outside the Democratic or Republican convention halls. To the extent that those images connote the demand for broadened participation in the political bargaining process and more openness in public policy-making, they express the essence of the New Politics. In the long run, however, the greatest impact of the New Politics is taking place inside the Capitol and inside the convention halls. In short, the American political system can be responsive to the New Politics; the movement is working within as well as outside Congress and the Executive Branch.

The evolution of this New Politics is as much a response to a changing society as it is a force causing change in traditional institutions. Although definitions of politics differ, there can be no question that there is a difference between the old and the new versions, and that those differences are having an impact on our government, particularly on the Congress. Therefore attention must be focused upon the following questions: What is the "New Politics"? How does it differ from the "old politics"? What effect has this change had upon Congress?

Daniel Moynihan, Harvard professor, New Frontier Democrat, and domestic-policy advisor to Richard Nixon during his first term as President, offers a rather interesting assessment of the social ferment of the sixties and its root causes:

Most of the events that tore American society almost apart (or so it seemed in the 1960s) arose from conditions unique to the decade in which they had occurred. They had not ever existed before. They will not ever exist again. They involve the interaction of demographic and political-cultural changes.

The 1960s saw a profound demographic change occur in American society which was a one-time change, a growth in population vaster than any that had ever occurred before, or any that will ever occur again, with respect to a particular subgroup in the population—namely the persons from 14–24 years of age. This sudden increase in population interacted with a whole series of other events which originate, if you will, in the world of ideas.

In the best known example of the 1960s, people changed their minds about the requirements of justice and decent public policy concerning minority groups in American society, at just the moment when the size and location of those groups was dramatically changing. But this was not the only change. People changed their minds at just the point when the physical conditions of life, the ecological facts of how many people are around and where they are, were also changing. These changes interacted in such a way as to produce extraordinary discontinuities with the period immediately preceding and, I think, with the period that now follows.[1]

Many of the new congressmen of recent years have been more activist by nature and training than their predecessors. In his article, Moynihan went so

1

far as to suggest that the primary purpose of government is to help people move from age fourteen to age twenty-four. There is much truth in that comment; but receptiveness to change cannot be correlated exclusively to age. While many older congressmen and senators are resisting the New Politics, many senior congressmen, such as Representatives Tip O'Neill and John Blatnik, as well as Senators Phillip Hart and Harold Hughes, have become its active proponents. Hubert Humphrey's credentials extend back even further. Humphrey *was* the New Politics of the Cold War period.

The reasons for this mixed reception to the New Politics by established political figures in the Congress can in part be found in the changing constituency of the congressional district, and to a lesser degree of the states themselves. Senators and congressmen today must be responsive to a wide range of interests, none of which are exclusive, and many of which are conflicting. Added to this, however, are the problems presented by the peculiar character and pressures of the political craft itself in America.

The elected representative moves in an environment of ambiguity and uncertainty, as complex or as homogenous as the constituency he serves. The public is quite ambivalent about politics in general. A Gallup poll taken in June 1973 found that only 23 percent of the American public, or about one adult in four, would approve of a son making a career of politics. This response represents a decline from 36 percent who answered favorably in 1965. Moreover, the main reason given for opposing a political career is "the belief that politics is too corrupt" or that "it is difficult for a politician to stay honest."[2]

The 1973-74 Watergate investigation provided a vast number of Americans with insights to the potential effects of power on those holding it. Unfortunately, the revelation of political misconduct reinforces popular stereotypes regarding politics and the undesirability of a political career. Yet it should be noted that the perception of insincerity and fraud in many of society's institutions, including the political system itself, provided much of the impetus to the New Politics movement.

The 1960s, the decade that spawned the New Politics, was riddled with corruption in high places that fueled rebellion against authority. Ralph Nader successfully charged automobile and pharmaceutical companies with marketing defective, overpriced, and even harmful products to the public. Senator Daniel Brewster was convicted of bribery, Supreme Court Justice Abe Fortas resigned when some of his financial wheeling and dealing was exposed, and Bobby Baker, who had served as Lyndon Johnson's assistant in the Senate was sent to jail for a variety of corruption convictions. In short, the rules that business and government institutions were imposing on society became increasingly unacceptable to a young generation under pressure.

Old Roots to New Politics

The Constitutional Convention of 1787 in Philadelphia influenced the conduct of American politics in every decade that followed. The sixties and seventies were no exception. Indeed, many of the timeless points made at Philadelphia are especially relevant to the New Politics.

The national government of the United States is a republic. In the American context, "republic" translates into a national system in which individual citizens participate in shaping the uses of governmental power by electing their chief executives and legislators. Political scientists Austin Ranney and Willmoore Kendall, in equating a democratic republic with self-government, argue:

The representative assembly expresses the popular will better than any other known device for eliciting it, and therefore should be the fundamental organ of government—it should make the laws, supervise and hold responsible those who are charged with carrying out the laws and, in general do whatever the people it represents wish to do.[3]

This veneration of Congress or the representative assembly is reminiscent of certain opinions expressed during the Constitutional Convention of 1787. While there is agreement about the importance of Congress, the basis for representation within legislative assemblies, or for that matter at political conventions, still inspires sharp disagreement.

The 1787 resolution of the Continental Congress which created the Constitutional Convention, limited the purpose of that convention to revising the Articles of Confederation, and required that approval of the suggested revisions be authorized by the state legislatures. However, four days after the Convention began in Philadelphia, Edmund Randolph introduced his Virginia Plan, which proposed a fundamentally different form of government, to be ratified by the body of the people rather than by the states.

On representation the Virginia Plan provided

that the rights of sufferage in the National Legislature ought to be proportional to the Quotas of contribution [tax-payments] or to the number of free inhabitants, as the one or the other may seem best in different cases.[4]

An alternative to Randolph's Virginia Plan was proposed by William Patterson of New Jersey. The New Jersey Plan opposed representation in the national legislature based on population, which would have given the larger states dominance. Ultimately the Convention accepted Randolph's plan, and thus opted for a system of national supremacy based on sovereignty of the people, expressed through a bicameral Congress.

These timeless issues, resulting from the impact of majority rule, minority rights, checks and balances, separation of powers, and equitable representation, are at the heart of the New Politics. Although those issues did not originate in the sixties, the turbulence, frustrations, and unique configuration of the events that shook that decade amplified their expression to an extent unparalleled in the history of the Nation.

It should be clear that the roots of the New Politics are deeply embedded in our social fabric and can be seen surfacing at various times throughout our history. Franklin Roosevelt's new coalition of 1932 was, in his own time, a new politics of sorts; his coalition was to have a great impact upon the politics and directions of domestic policy that were to emerge in later generations.

The breakdown of that coalition in the late sixties was to provide the vacuum necessary for the success of the New Politics movement. However, a more verifiable antecedent to the New Politics of the sixties can be found in the civil rights movement.

While *Brown v. Board of Education* provided the first real "victory" for the civil rights movement in America, it was the encouraging rhetoric and attitude of "Camelot" that provided that fledgling movement with a proper climate for growth. The soaring rhetoric of the Kennedy Administration set the stage for much of what was to occur during the sixties. It raised the expectations of millions of Americans with its determined challenge "My fellow citizens of the world: ask not what America will do for you, but what together we can do for the freedom of man."[5]

It taught Americans to *question* tradition, to *question* the world as it was in seeking to move mankind toward the New Testament's "city on the hill":

The American people expect more from us than cries of indignation and attack . . . for the world is changing. The old era is ending. The old ways will not do.... Too many Americans have lost their way, their will and their sense of historic purpose.... It is time, in short, for a new generation of leadership—new men to cope with new problems and new opportunities. All over the world, particularly in the newer nations, young men are coming to power, men who are not bound by the traditions of the past, men who are not blinded by the old fears and hates and rivalries, young men who . . . believe the times demand invention, innovation, imagination, decision. I am asking each of you to be new pioneers on that new frontier.[6]

That spirit embraced the leadership of the country throughout the sixties. It was present in Martin Luther King's statements:

I am cognizant of the interrelatedness of all communities and states. I cannot sit idly by in Atlanta and not be concerned about what happens in Birmingham. Injustice anywhere is a threat to justice everywhere. We are caught in an inescapable network of mutuality, tied in a single garment of destiny.[7]

President Lyndon Baines Johnson contributed to the rhetoric and indeed to the spirit of the New Politics with his advocacy of the Great Society:

The Great Society is a place where every child can find knowledge to enrich his mind and enlarge his talents. . . . It is a place where the city of man serves not only the needs of the body and the demands of commerce, but the desire for beauty and the hunger for community. . . . It is a place where men are more concerned with the quality of their goals than with the quality of their goods. But most of all, the Great Society is not a safe harbor, a resting place, a final objective, a finished work. It is a challenge constantly renewed, beckoning us toward a destiny where the meaning of our lives matches the marvelous products of our labor.[8]

This atmosphere nourished the civil rights movement, which reached its high-water mark in 1963. Again, this resulted from the unique events that shook the sixties: the June "March on Washington," and the assassination of President Kennedy in November. It was that massive march and Dr. King's eloquent plea from the steps of the Lincoln Memorial for the extension of very basic human dignities to black people that prodded the Kennedy administration to its first *substantive* action in the field of civil rights.

The 1963 March on Washington by a quarter of a million people had two stated goals, one economic and the other moral. The political temper of the times put government force behind satisfying both goals, but fostered particular emphasis on the moral issue. The March marked a climax in the civil rights movement and most Americans now seemed to accept the legitimacy of black America's demands. It also established the use of the mass march as an effective route to social change.

The temper of the civil rights movement had begun to change. The unity and sense of common purpose that all too briefly characterized the early struggle for civil rights in America faded against the spectacle of burning cities during the "long hot summers" of 1965-67. Again, the frustrations that gave rise to these urban riots can be traced to some of the many ironic events which occurred during the sixties: the Johnson landslide of 1964, the resulting "Great Society Congress" (the 89th) of 1965-66, and the eventual shift of badly needed national resources from the Great-Society programs to the growing quagmire in Vietnam.

The 89th Congress represented a type of phenomenon that occurs rarely in the history of any nation. There have been three "landslide" presidential elections in this century—1932, 1964, and 1972. Only one President, however, has succeeded in obtaining the type of "coattail Congress" needed to pursue an ambitious legislative program. It was the infusion of many of these "one-term Congressmen" from 1965-66 that altered the balance of congressional power, destroying the old conservative—southern-Democratic voting bloc, and making Lyndon Johnson's Great Society possible. Yet what made the "Great Society" also, in part, contributed to its demise. So much was done, and so many expectations were raised—by the sheer *volume* of legislation passed—that expectation greatly outraced reality. Edward Banfield clarifies this disparity:

Improvements in performance, great as they have been, have not kept pace with rising expectations. In other words, although things have been getting better absolutely, they have been getting worse *relative to what we think they should be.* And this is because, as a people, we seem to act on the advice of the old jingle:

> Good, better, best
> Never let it rest
> Until your good is better
> And your better best.[9]

The frustrations thereby created began to permeate the fabric of American society in the sixties. Over 35,000 Americans were killed in Vietnam and the Johnson landslide of 1964 ended in humiliation when LBJ announced that he would not be a candidate in 1968. The "credibility gap," of which the press wrote frequently in the last Johnson years, only compounded a bad situation.

The confidence with which America seemed to be imbued during the early sixties was badly shaken. The "war of attrition" being waged in Vietnam had its domestic corollary in the civil rights movement. The "guns and butter" strategy of the Johnson administration was failing miserably, and mass protest against the war became the preoccupation of a large segment of the white American liberal group that had previously been occupied with the civil rights movement. "Civil rights" became associated more closely with "Black Power."

The frustrations that caused this change appeared in a variety of different forms, such as in the reassertion of "ethnic politics." Ethnic politics, though never dead, gained increasing prominence in these years, and although long a traditional part of the American political landscape, it must be considered a contributing factor to the budding New Politics. The blue-collar movement was sparked by what was perceived to be a "reverse bias" in the social policies of the national political system. The combination of special programs for the blacks, with whom other ethnic groups are mostly in competition, along with the attack of the general society on their values—church, family, and labor unions—made them feel anchorless.

In years past, whenever the new culture converged or clashed with the old, ethnic identity was sublimated in the eagerness to be *accepted* by a larger society of "Americans." That has changed. Now America's subparts have rejected assimilation in favor of ethnic and racial consciousness. Geno Baroni, director of the Center for Urban Ethnic Affairs in Washington, D.C., expressed the conflict in noting that ethnic Americans thought the way to become better Americans was to fly the flag on Independence Day, to talk about the Constitution, and to participate in parades on national holidays. The Irish also marched on St. Patrick's Day and the Italians on Columbus Day. Only recently did they note that white Anglo Saxon Protestants— WASPS—"never marched. Every day was their day."[10]

The new assertion of ethnic identity reflects the mood of the New Politics, the mood of the late sixties and seventies: confrontation, demand, and the feeling of a "right" to certain societal benefits replaced the emphasis upon conciliation, compromise, and the spirit of personal sacrifice for the good of the larger community that marked the beginning of America's adventure to "new frontiers."

Changes also occurred in the *style* of political intercourse: relevance, participation, openness became the bywords of the times. Distrust seemed to permeate the political system, so that the political values of the established order, once sacrosanct, were now challenged. That challenge was exemplified by the rejection of claims that public policy was valueless. It was now asserted that there were indeed values involved in the decision-making that shapes public policy, and those values, in turn, largely determined the distribution of society's wealth and benefits.

It was not surprising, therefore, that "citizen participation" became a key concept to be reconciled in the conception and implementation of domestic policies and programs. It was also no accident that this phenomenon both coincided with and reinforced growing demands for decentralization of government. Many people came to accept the notion, as one author put it, that "pluralist government systematically discriminates in favor of established stable bureaucracies and their special minority clientele . . . and against those minorities . . . who lack political and economic resources."[11]

Government, and the political process itself, became a battleground for social and economic advancement; they were viewed as an all-powerful weapon to redress the balance of social and economic inequities historically conferred upon particular subgroups within American society. With so much at stake during a period of social flux and change it is not difficult to understand why confrontation and conflict increased. Richard Nixon, while not cut in the mold of the "new politician," nonetheless perceived the changes and the confusion that accompanied them, and utilized both to his advantage by appealing to each group's self-interest.

The nation has turned nearly 180 degrees away from the early days of "Camelot," with its emphasis upon national unity, moral strength, and genuine cooperative effort in addressing the nation's ills. Personal commitment has somehow become translated into individual gain, and "ask not" has become "we demand." Robert Kennedy's abortive campaign of 1968 was perhaps the end of an era in which a nation seemed to discover, and lose, its sense of national purpose.

New Politics in the Seventies—The Maturation of a Movement

With the history of the New Politics in mind, attention must be focused upon the ways in which the new movement has sought to alter American society and one of its foremost institutions, the Congress. One way to answer that question is to identify the things that the new movement opposes and proposes.

The New Politics is anti-"sacred cow" programs. In its value system no government program on which public money is being spent should ever be exempt from analysis and questioning. There is a very sound strategic reason for this. Any new movement has things it wants to see accomplished, yet often the first barrier it will encounter is the lack of funds to accomplish these new objectives. Funds for new programs can come from only three sources—new revenues, increased output from existing revenues, or reallocation of the available resources. The latter is impossible without identifying some existing programs that are overfunded or at least of a lesser priority than the new programs being proposed.

Some would argue that the New Politics is antitradition. It is true that the New Politics assigns tradition a reduced weight in decision-making. The response seems to be that it should be analyzed for its lessons, but that when reason dictates a change in traditional policy or procedures it should not be permitted to block the change.

Perhaps one of the major targets of the New Politics in America is governmental secrecy. Citizens cannot be informed about problems and issues or indicate their preferences and priorities if the whole decision process, or at least the crucial part of it, is not accessible to the public. Special interests fare best in a closed system where there is limited knowledge and involvement. In such a situation, these interests will represent a higher percentage of the inputs, the knowledge, and the power at the bargaining table. The New Politics movement has therefore embraced public access to the political decision-making process as one of its primary goals.

Closely related to the demand for openness is a demand for broad scale participation in and access to the system. In some respects this is the most characteristic element of the New Politics. It started slowly with legal approaches, such as the extension of suffrage to women, the civil rights acts that opened up voting for minorities, and the court-ordered reapportionment of the sixties. These changes created the opportunity for the labor-led voter registration drives of the sixties. The ultimate impact has been increasing participation in politics by women, blacks, Spanish-speaking people, poor people, and other minorities in roles ranging from candidates to envelope stuffers.

These minorities have always lacked a voice in the decision process, since they often were less knowledgeable about how decisions were made and because they have lacked the financial resources or status to participate. Those who controlled the process had little interest in involving them because such involvement would just complicate their ability to control the outcomes. Big-city bosses in such places as New York, Chicago, Boston, and Kansas City were successful in mobilizing the ethnics and the poor during the days of ward politics because they were delivering votes that were uninformed but responded to bonds of loyalty, fear, or gratitude for favors.

One of the major triumphs of the New Politics was the Congressional Reorganization Act of 1970. This Act provided for more staff support for the minority members of committees and created the procedure of recording how each member voted in the Committee of the Whole upon the request of one-fifth of a quorum. Another major change was *not* among those proposed by the reorganization committee. A requirement for open committee votes was added by New Politics House members as a floor amendment. Previously, congressmen had the opportunity of satisfying special interests by introducing "softening" amendments or even voting against an action in the closed committee vote or in the anonymous Committee of the Whole vote and then voting their district interest during the House roll calls. Now this dual approach is very difficult on controversial issues.

The New Politics is more inclined to ask the "why" of proposed actions and their alternatives, rather than just "how" to get it done. The old political and administrative system reflected a middle-class tendency to subordinate policy questions. This served to strengthen the hand of efficient bureaucratic operators, a few of whom were really running private fiefdoms or were efficiently working toward the wrong goals.

The New Politics insists on expanding the accountability of elected officials. The old politics argued that accountability was determined in the election process. The position of the New Politics is that "the election process" is an empty phrase and an empty approach as long as the actions of congressmen in committees and on the floor remain secret, thereby keeping the voters uninformed of their representatives' performance.

The delay in reforming these secretive practices led to more radical demands by groups that felt excluded from the system. For example, the urban poor demanded more "community power" and participation. Citizens now feel they have a right to demand a voice in the implementation of public policy *beyond* that conferred through the participation of their elected representatives in public decision-making forums.

Thus, the internal congressional changes requiring more open decision-making help to fix the record of the incumbent. At the same time, the insistence that more attention be paid to policy rather than procedural questions helps to establish the representative's philosophy so that his record can be measured. By remodeling congressional procedure, the New Politics movement has put windows into the committee walls and new meaning into voting that takes place on the floor. This new exposure has directly influenced policy outcomes and has facilitated more meaningful accountability, not only at election time but also between elections as various issues are being considered.

This New Politics approach has been carried even further in the party process than it has in Congress itself. The impact has been felt more in the Democratic party because that party has traditionally been more responsive to minority groups and the philosophy of participation, and also because the out-party is necessarily more receptive to change as a means of improving its party fortunes. However, the Republican Party also found it necessary to respond to New Politics pressures by providing for broader party participation and more openness.

The New Politics and National Political Parties: The 1972 Conventions

The new participation was evident in both the Democratic and Republican 1972 national conventions. Both major parties were on public display as the internal factions tested their strength in contests of rules and delegate credentials. The significance of the 1972 conventions is that the rules of the game were new, reflecting New Politics pressures.

The New Politics of participation had established a beachhead in the Democratic Party during its convention in Chicago in 1968. There was an unusual amount of confusion on the convention floor, and violence in the streets and parks near the convention site. Although it lost in the confrontation with Chicago's police in the streets, inside the convention the left wing of the New Politics won a subtle victory. Theodore White describes the quiet passage of the resolution that mandated the Commission on Party Structure and Delegate Selection:

The words of the majority and minority reports of the Rules Committee floated almost unheard above the noise as the sound system squawked incomprehensibly through the fog, the smoke, the din. Had anyone cared to listen, he would have noted that the minority report, which favored the abolition of the unit rule system of voting, did not simply urge or recommend change; its language was stark. It "required" that the next convention conform to the stipulations laid down for reform. The minority report, if passed, would have binding effect on the convention of 1972, but few delegates were listening.[12]

The report passed 1350 to 1206. White concludes that either through innocence or inattention "they had voted for the most fundamental change in the party's long history." This was the first time either major party had ever given independent authority from a national convention to a reform commission, whose decisions on party structure and delegate selection would bind the next national convention as well as the state parties themselves.

The mandate for reform issued by the 1968 convention strongly influenced the delegate composition in 1972, and the McGovern-Fraser Commission was established to implement the reform resolution. A controversial feature of the new rules to increase participation and reduce arbitrary decisions emanating from the narrow confines of the traditional smoke-filled room was the creation of a quota system.

George Meany, President of the AFL-CIO and one of the traditional power brokers of the Democratic Party, questioned the outcome of the new rules. Meany, a former plumber in the bronx, looked over the 1972 New York delegation in Miami and commented, "They've got six open fags and only three AFL-CIO people on that delegation! Representative?"[13] Even some New Politics people had second thoughts. Speaking of the delegates, John Lindsay, the mayor of New York, who had recently switched from the Republican to the Democratic Party, said, "This party seems to have an instinct for suicide."[14]

The other old politics group that was squeezed out of the convention to create seats for the New Politics people was the elected officials. The number of delegates who were elected public officials dropped from 14 percent in 1968 to 10 percent in 1972. Table 1-1 shows how senators, representatives, and governors were affected. Congressman Wayne L. Hays of Ohio summed up his impression of the Reform Commission as follows: "The McGovern-O'Hara-Fraser Commissions reformed us out of the presidency and now they are trying to reform us out of the party."[15]

One might be tempted to charge the New Politics movement with using techniques characteristic of the old politics. In fact it was a new movement which pursued policies much different from those of the old-line, traditional Democratic coalition, but used similar techniques to achieve its ends. The new rules increased the number of women, youth, and minority delegates, just as the old rules favored public officials and big-city bosses.

The work of the McGovern-Fraser Commission has been a source of confusion to both the public and the experts. Even presidential election scholar Theodore White seems to have some misunderstandings. For instance, White cited the fact that if the twenty-eight-member commission had been a delegation to the 1972 convention, it would have had no chance of

Table 1-1

Governors, Representatives, and Senators as Convention Delegates

Delegate Senators	Total Senators	Delegate Representatives	Total Representatives	Delegate Governors	Total Governors	Total Votes at Convention
1972						
Rep. 48.9% (22)	(45)	44.1% (78)	(177)	80.0% (16)	(20)	1,348
Dem. 32.7% (18)	(55)	11.8% (30)	(255)	63.3% (19)	(30)	3,099
Gain or Loss over 1968						
Rep. 9.4%		+ 12.9%		− 12.3%		
Dem. 31.4%		− 25.0%		− 28.4%		
1968						
Rep. 56.8% (21)	(36)	31.2% (58)	(186)	92.3% (24)	(26)	1,333
Dem. 65.1% (41)	(64)	36.8% (91)	(247)	91.7% (22)	(24)	3,084

Source: Carol Casey, Research Coordinator for the Commission on Delegate Selection and Party Structure, Democratic National Committee; Oliver Cromwell, staff member of *Congressional Quarterly*; Josephine L. Good, Convention Director, Republican National Committee; and U.S. Bureau of the Census, *General Population Characteristics*, Final Report PC (1)-B1, United States Summary (Washington, D.C.: Government Printing Office, 1972).

being seated under the standards it was about to establish.[16] A close reading of the new rules, however, reveals that White is wrong. Quotas would be imposed if, and only if, a state did not take effective steps to try to insure that women, youth, and blacks were represented in reasonable proportions. Indeed, the famous challenge of Mayor Daley's fifty-eight delegates did not involve the rest of the Illinois delegation. Mayor Daley's delegation was vulnerable because of the violation of four guidelines. First, Daley's group had held a secret meeting to put together its slate, a violation of guideline C-3, which outlawed closed slate-making. Second, the Cook County Democratic leaders had endorsed Daley's slate of delegates, a violation of guideline C-4, which prohibits elected or appointed officials from making such endorsements. Finally, guidelines A-1 and A-2 were violated because Cook County had failed to take positive action to include sufficient women, youth, and minority members in the delegation. These latter challenges were avoidable since there is little doubt that Daley's choices would have been elected.[17]

West Virginia, on the other hand, was not challenged on guideline A-2, which deals with discrimination on the basis of age or sex. Hawaii, Maine, New Hampshire, South Dakota, Utah, and West Virginia, had *no* blacks in their delegations and were not challenged on guideline A-1, which deals with discrimination. There were twenty-four other state delegations that had a disproportionately low percentage of black members. Race was a factor in nine challenges. Five involving blacks in Georgia, Illinois, Maryland, and New Jersey and Indians in Oklahoma were successful.[18] Women made up 23 percent of the Maryland delegation, and only 6 percent of the West Virginia delegation, while only 4 percent of the Connecticut delegates were youths.[19] On face value, White's point seems rather damning, but after examining the actual numbers and percentages, as well as the intent of the new rules, his statement can be seen as another misunderstanding of the new rules.

What the New Politics rules did was to increase representation of black, female, and under-thirty delegates, by removing some of the procedural obstacles that had kept them off slates in the past. However, as is often the case, procedural reforms produced changes in substance, as is illustrated by table 1-2, which compares the delegates attending the Democratic and Republican national conventions held in 1968 and 1972. There were changes in both parties; however, the distinction between the advisory status of the Republican Party's Delegates and Organizations Committee, and the binding nature of the Democratic Party's Commission on Party Structure and Delegate-Selection, is evident in the impact the actions of the two panels had in altering the delegate composition between 1969 and 1972.

Despite many illusions to the contrary, the practitioners of the New Politics can be just as ruthless as those of the old. The New Politics majority in Miami was no less hardnosed than the Daley-Humphrey people had been in Chicago, four years earlier. In sizing up the New Politics-old politics debate, Jerome Donovan, executive director of the Credentials Committee in 1972, observed that the difference between New Politics and old politics largely depends on "whose ox is being gored."[20]

Table 1-2
Voting Delegates to National Conventions

Party	Total Delegates	Women Delegates	Percent of Population	Youth Delegates	Percent of Population	Black Delegates	Percent of Population
				1968			
Dem.	(3,084)	13.0% (402)	51%	4.0% (123)	6.1%	5.5% (169)	10.5%
Rep.	(1,333)	16.7% (223)	51%	2.0% (26)	6.1%	2.0% (26)	10.5%
				1972			
Dem.	(3,099)	37.9% (1,173)	51%	20.9% (649)	6.6%	15.1% (468)	11%
Rep.	(1,348)	29.8% (402)	51%	5.2%[a] (61)	6.6%	3.3% (39)[a]	11%
Dem.		+24.9%		+16.9%		+9.6%	
Rep.		+13.9%		+2.5%		+1.3%	

[a] of those responding, 1167 out of 1348

Source: Carol Casey, Research Coordinator for the Commission on Delegate Selection and Party Structure, Democratic National Committee; Oliver Cromwell, staff member of *Congressional Quarterly*; Josephine L. Good, Convention Director, Republican National Committee; and U.S. Bureau of the Census, *General Population Characteristics*, Final Report PC (1)-B1, United States Summary (Washington, D.C.: Government Printing Office, 1972).

McGovern's supporters now acknowledge that they deliberately lost the South Carolina challenge brought at Miami by the Women's Political Caucus.[21] McGovern wanted to avoid an appeal of the convention chairman's decision as to what constituted a majority for voting purposes. Convention chairman Larry O'Brien had ruled that, on all challenges, a majority of those present, eligible, and voting would constitute a majority. Had O'Brien's ruling been successfully challenged, so that an absolute majority of the convention would be required to carry the presidential nomination on the first roll call, McGovern would have needed more votes. This, in turn, might have jeopardized McGovern's nomination, since his staff expected defections by delegates elected in primaries who were not loyal to McGovern, and who were bound by convention rules only to support him through the first ballot.

Gary Hart, a top McGovern staffer, saw the key to winning the challenges at the convention as follows: "The whole thing is bottomed on floor discipline." Concerning the calculated loss of the South Carolina challenge Richard Stearns, another McGovern staff assistant commented, "When it really comes down to it, they [The Anybody But McGovern movement] had less guts than we had. We were willing to sell out the women, but they weren't willing to sell out a southern governor [Governor West of South Carolina]."[22]

One point that can be clearly drawn from the above is that while the New Politics pursues policies different from those of the old Democratic Party power structure, and while it serves a new clientele of women, youth, and blacks as well as traditional liberals, its techniques in the heat of battle can be just as coarse and gritty as those of the old politics.

The New Politics was also operating at the 1968 Republican Convention. That convention voted to start using "Roberts Rules of Order Revised" at future meetings of the National Committee, in place of the "Rules of the U.S. House of Representatives" and also established a committee to study discrimination because of race, religion, color, or national origin. In July 1971 that committee offered the National Committee ten substantive recommendations to open up participation in the Republican Party.[23] Most of its suggestions were accepted. However, unlike the Democratic Party, Republicans sharply rejected those proposals which would have established quotas. The 1972 Republican National Convention adopted a resolution that stated: "The Republican State Committee or governing committee of each state shall take positive action to achieve the broadest possible participation in party affairs, including such participation by women, young people, minority and heritage groups and senior citizens in the delegate selection process."[24] To be sure this movement did not pass unnoticed by Republican conservatives, New York's Senator James Buckley characterized the study group's actions as an attempt to "McGovernize the Republican Party."[25]

Both parties are still grappling with these issues. The McGovern success in exploiting the new rules to win delegates in precinct caucuses and the New Politics success in securing an increase in minority, youth, and female delegates had tangible effects on the outcome of both the 1972 Democratic

Convention and the election itself. While reform sentiment is still intense in certain sections of both parties, odds are that both parties will learn from 1972 and will be more careful about the backlash effects of their "reform" actions.

These changes also will tend to focus more party attention on the recruitment and selection process for members of Congress. It will result in a greater party focus on democratizing the congressional nomination process. Aided by the continuing increases in average education levels, this increased participation and openness should have substantial effects on determining the kinds of new congressmen who will be elected. This, in turn, will reinforce the pressures for a New Politics Congress. The New Politics impact already felt will be discussed in the chapters that follow.

2 Representing the New Constituencies

One of the most striking effects of the New Politics has been the opening up of opportunities for improved representation of the New Politics constituencies—the racial minority groups, the poor, the women, and the youth. The changes in the last decade have been nothing short of revolutionary. They have involved providing the vote to eighteen-year-olds, making formerly one-party southern Democratic districts competitive, creating new safe districts in central cities based largely on race, establishing women as viable candidates, and implementing the one-man, one-vote decision.

The overall impact of these changes has been to reduce the power of the Conservative Coalition of southern Democrats and conservative Republicans, to put the new black and women representatives into a channel of power which can lead to control of key congressional committees and subcommittees, and to subordinate rural power in Congress. It has also meant necessary and more frequent challenges for elderly congressmen. The House of Representatives has become especially diverse with the addition of black, Puerto Rican, Mexican-American, women, and younger congressmen who are anxious to have an impact without waiting for the seniority system to legitimize their influence.

In short, the change has been in *who votes*, who gets elected, and ultimately, the difference in the kinds of *values* represented that will in turn determine policy outcomes in Congress. All of these changes have occurred as a result of natural forces like the urban and suburban migration, the ideological split in the Democratic Party, the civil rights movement, the white backlash, Republican southern strategies, and the decline in the power of the party to name the candidate or determine the outcome of the election. The increase in split ticket voting and the new impact of the media in helping a candidate to become publicized through television have all helped to open up the political process to the new participants represented in the New Politics movement.

For decades the most powerful single force in the United States Congress was the Southern bloc. In both the House and the Senate aged southern representatives and senators rose to positions of power as chairmen of key committees. The most important contributing factor in this rise was the seniority system, which awarded chairmanships to the senior member of the dominant political party. Since 1932, the only time Republicans have had a majority in the House of Representatives was in 1947-48 and 1953-54. At no time since 1932 have the Republicans dominated the Senate. Seniority, therefore, was an especially significant power factor for any Democratic member of the House or Senate who represented a district or a state that was dominated by one party.

17

Until the rise of the New Politics, political analysts referred to the South as the "Solid South." It was solid because it consistently produced Democratic victories. In many districts no Republican candidate even appeared on the ballot. As a consequence, the Democratic representatives and senators from the south utilized the seniority system to secure committee and leadership positions beyond what the population of the South or the percentage of Southern Democrats in Congress would justify. The result was that a minority group within the Democratic Party often was able to control Congress. In the decades up to the 1960s the South was the chief beneficiary of the seniority system.

The disproportionate share of control and power in the hands of southern Democrats was further enhanced by frequent combinations with two other groups. Since the southerners were more conservative than the rest of the Democratic Party, they often formed coalitions with Republican conservatives from the North. Yet from the standpoint of *party* control of Congress, these southerners had a common basis of collaboration with the northern Democrats. Southern Democrats would not reap the benefits of the seniority system and have the leadership and committee control positions unless the Democratic Party controlled Congress. For the same reason, northern Congressmen with safe seats in the Democratic-controlled big cities were natural allies with these Southern congressmen. The southerners, therefore, had the best of both worlds: they were able to work with northern Democrats as party allies to control the Congress and its leadership positions for the Democratic Party, and with Republican ideological allies to shape the output of Congress in accordance with their conservative philosophies.

The southern and big-city districts were not the only safe seats in Congress, since most of the nonsouthern rural districts were traditionally dominated by Republicans. However, their impact was rather limited because their party so rarely controlled Congress. In this kind of system, the big losers were the congressmen who represented competitive northern districts. Even the Democrats in this group were relatively powerless, since they could not develop the seniority necessary to have influence. The total number of competitive districts in Congress was not very large and such representatives tended to be moderates. In the 435-member House of Representatives, the percentage of incumbents who won against opposition in general elections ranged from 87.75 percent in 1964 to 98.6 percent in 1968. Considering that 1964 was the year when many Republicans were caught up in the Johnson landslide, this is an extremely low turnover rate. [1]

Whenever the predominant national priority or emphasis is reversed, that change should be more quickly reflected in the House than in the Senate, because House members are elected every two years and so should be more alert and susceptible to change than senators, who have six-year terms. However, if the House of Representatives is to change, that change must be the result of change at the district level. With 435 congressional districts divided up among fifty states, these districts vary greatly in every respect: the average age, wealth, and education of the voters; the kind of industry and economic system; the religion, natural origin, and racial composition of the residents; the history and relative regional position of the locality.

When viewing the elected representatives in our Congress, one must not look merely at the clear-cut party divisions. The representatives are being affected by the differing patterns of change. New Politics has induced transformations not only in relative party influence but also in the levels of competition within each party. For example, many of the "safe seats" in the southern states of the 1950s changed hands as Republicans emerged as a more important force in those districts. Not only have the southern states seen this trend toward greater competition, but the entire nation has shown an increase in the number of candidates for office. Further, new campaign factors and approaches have made the whole election process more dynamic and less predictable.

The reasons for this greater level of competition are diverse. Redistricting along more equitable lines has caused an alteration in the congressional makeup. Rural areas are no longer overrepresented and suburban congressmen are now a majority of the total. The strength of new interest groups and their impact on the election of incumbents and challengers also has played a major role in stimulating that outcome. New societal mores, higher levels of educational attainment, and greater candidate exposure as a result of the technological advances in news coverage have contributed to making the public a more sophisticated and knowledgeable participant in the electoral process.

This was the scene in the early 1960s as the New Politics began to sweep America. The New Politics was the crystallization of a number of social forces unsatisfied with the status quo as represented by the Conservative Coalition's control of Congress. If the New Politics and the people they represented were to have an impact on decision-making at the national level, it was necessary that Congress be made more open and that its decisions be more sensitive to minority, and sometimes even majority, party attitudes.

The Upheaval in the Solid South

Traditionally many southern candidates for Congress ran unopposed either in the primary or the general election or both. For many years the South was a one-party region. However, a summary of the level of competition in Democratic primaries for southern congressional seats since 1960 shows that there is much more competition than is generally assumed. Still, not one southern state had both Democratic and Republican candidates in every congressional district over the twelve-year period. The year with the greatest number of contested seats was 1966, when two of the thirteen southern states—Kentucky and Oklahoma—had candidates entered in all scheduled primaries. Yet, even in this high-water year, more than 10 percent of the nominations in the eleven other southern states were settled without competition.

As of 1972 there were 121 congressional seats in the thirteen southern states, an increase of one since 1960. Over that twelve-year period, primary competition was substantially greater for Democratic than for Republican nominations in the South.

Even within the Democratic Party, southern primary contests were not as frequent as might be expected—only 360 (44 percent) of a total of 826 races from 1960 to 1972. More nominations were secured by default than by primary victories. Nevertheless, the pattern was not uniform and, as table 2-1 shows, some states demonstrated a high degree of competition between 1960 and 1972. In 82 percent of Kentucky's fifty scheduled primaries during those years, more than one candidate actively campaigned for the nomination. This number contrasts greatly with Virginia, where only 20 percent of the district nominations were contested.

Almost all of the southern districts provided at least one Democratic candidate. But even this was not true in all states. Here again, Virginia showed

Table 2-1
Democratic and Republican Primaries in the South 1960-72

	Total Primaries Scheduled	Number Primaries with No Candidate	Number and Percentage with One Candidate	Number and Percentage with More Than One Candidate	Percentage with One or More Candidates
Ala.	56 D	0 D	34 D (61%)	24 D (43%)	100
	0 R	0 R	no primaries held 1960-72		0
Ark.	30 D	0 D	18 D (100%)	12 D (40%)	100
	24 R	15 R	8 R (37%)	1 R (4%)	37
Fla.	83 D	5 D	57 D (67%)	24 D (29%)	94
	83 R	22 R	43 R (52%)	18 R (22%)	73
Ga.	70 D	0 D	34 D (49%)	36 D (51%)	100
	70 R	28 R	32 R (46%)	10 R (14%)	60
Ky.	50 D	0 D	9 D (18%)	41 D (82%)	100
	50 R	10 R	14 R (28%)	26 R (52%)	80
La.	56 D	0 D	18 D (32%)	38 D (68%)	100
	56 R	32 R	22 R (39%)	2 R (4%)	45
Miss.	36 D	0 D	14 D (39%)	22 D (61%)	100
	25 R	14 R	10 R (40%)	1 R (4%)	44
N.C.	78 D	1 D	46 D (59%)	31 D (40%)	99
	78 R	12 R	47 R (60%)	19 R (24%)	85
Okla.	42 D	0 D	12 D (29%)	30 D (71%)	100
	42 R	6 R	24 R (57%)	12 R (29%)	86
S.C.	42 D	4 D	29 D (69%)	9 D (21%)	92
	30 R	9 R	21 R (70%)	0 R (0%)	70
Tenn.	62 D	4 D	33 D (53%)	25 D (40%)	93
	62 R	18 R	32 R (52%)	12 R (19%)	71
Texas	161 D	2 D	103 D (64%)	56 D (35%)	99
	139 R	58 R	61 R (44%)	20 R (14%)	58
Va.	60 D [a]	5 D	43 D (72%)	12 D (20%)	92
	20 R	1 R	15 R (75%)	4 R (20%)	95
Totals	826 D	21 D	450 D (54%)	360 D (44%)	98
	682 R	228 R	329 R (48%)	125 R (18%)	66

[a] Virginia held no primaries in 1960

Source: *Congressional Quarterly* 1960-72 (Washington, D.C.: Congressional Quarterly Service).

the least competition. In five of its sixty scheduled Democratic primaries over the twelve-year period, not a single Democrat filed for the primary. Alabama, Arkansas, Georgia, Kentucky, Louisiana, Mississippi, and Oklahoma had at least one contender in every Democratic primary in every district.

The situation was somewhat different on the Republican side. A smaller percentage of Republican nominations were contested and in addition the Republicans run fewer primaries. This was due to two factors: some seats were forfeited to the Democrats without a contest, and many southern districts that had few registered Republicans designated their candidates through a convention.

No Republican primaries were held in Alabama between 1960 and 1972. In Arkansas primaries were held in twenty-four of thirty cases, but in fifteen of them there was no candidate. Only one of the thirty Arkansas districts had a contest for the Republican nomination. In the period from 1960 to 1972 the Republicans held 682 primaries for 826 seats. In 125 of these Republican primaries there was competition, but in 329 of the scheduled 682 scheduled primaries, only one candidate was entered. In 228 other Republican primaries there was not a single candidate on the ballot. The differing level of competitiveness among Democrats and Republicans for congressional nominations in an essentially one-party area was not surprising. Republican candidates were often businessmen or lawyers who desired the public exposure of engaging in a congressional contest but did not really expect to win.

Democratic party strength in the South traditionally had been so great that Republicans competed in only a small percentage of the contests, and succeeded in very few of those. Competition on the Democratic side was therefore more likely and the Democratic primary was usually a more significant contest than the general election in determining who would represent the district in Congress.

Moving from the primary to the general election, there was no recognizable increase in southern interparty contests for Congress over the 1960-72 period. That is, the Democrats generally run a candidate in almost every congressional district in the South and the Republicans bypass a certain percentage of these elections each year. There is no real change in the percentage of elections forfeited by Republicans in 1960-72. What has changed is the outcome of the elections that *are* contested.

Republican congressional candidates in the South were especially successful in 1964, 1966, and 1972. Two of these years were presidential election years, with Barry Goldwater running in 1964 and Richard Nixon in 1972. The prospects of Republican presidential candidates doing well in the South presumably convinced more qualified southern Republicans to run for Congress.

These thirteen states had 120 congressional seats in 1960, 119 from 1962-70, and 121 in 1972 tested. Between 1960 and 1972, Florida gained seven seats through reapportionment and Texas two; Alabama and Arkansas each lost two seats and Kentucky, Mississippi, North Carolina, and Tennessee each lost one. The Democrats were handed one-third of the total seats over the twelve-year period. The greatest number of forfeits occurred in 1960, when sixty-three Democrats were unopposed by Republican congressional candidates, but even in 1972, the year with the second lowest number of forfeits, the Republicans gave up thirty-two seats without a contest.

This forfeiture rate was much higher than that in the rest of the nation. Although having an average of 120 of the 435 congressional seats, these thirteen southern states had between 70 and 91 percent of all the unopposed elections since 1960. Only in 1966 did other regions have a larger share of the unopposed winners, but even in that year 44 percent of the unopposed seats were located in the thirteen southern states. Table 2-2 shows how the different southern states have contributed to this effect.

Mississippi, Arkansas, Georgia, and Louisiana have consistently had more than half of their congressional seats uncontested in the general election,

Table 2-2
Elections Won Without Competition from the Other Major Party

Total 1972 Congressional Districts		72	70	68	66	64	62	60	Total Unopposed	Total Seats	Percent Unopposed
Ala.	7	1 D	4 D	2 D	2 D	2 D	0	7 D	18	54	33
Ark.	4	1 D	3 D	2 D	2 D	3 D	2 D	4 D	17	28	61
Fla.	15	0	3 D	1 D 1 R	0	6 D	2 D	3 D	16	90	18
Ga.	10	6 D	5 D	7 D	2 D	5 D	8 D	9 D	42	70	60
Ky.	7	0	2 D	1 D	0	1 D	2 D 1 R	3 D	10	49	20
La.	8	6 D	7 D	5 D	2 D	4 D	6 D	3 D	33	56	59
Miss.	5	2 D	4 D	4 D	2 D	4 D	5 D	3 D	24	35	68
N.C.	11	2 D	1 D	2 D 1 R	0	2 D	3 D	0	11	77	14
Okla.	6	1 D	1 D	0	0	1 D	2 D	0	5	43	11
S.C.	6	1 R	2 D	1 D	3 D	4 D	4 D	5 D	20	43	46
Tenn.	8	1 R	1 D	1 D	0	2 D	5 D	6 D 1 R	17	61	28
Texas	24	11 D	12 D 1 R	11 D	7 D	0	5 D	16 D	64	166	39
Va.	10	2 D	1 D	2 D 1 R	4 D	2 D	4 D	4 D	21	70	30
Total in 13 Southern States	121	34	47	43	24	36	49	65	298	842	36
Total, U.S.		45	66	62	54	44	53	71	389	3045	13

Note: D—Democrat elected, no Republican candidate; R—Republican elected, no Democratic candidate
Source: *Congressional Quarterly Almanac, 1960-73* (Washington, D.C.: Congressional Quarterly Service).

with the totals over the twelve-year period running 68, 61, 60, and 59 percent respectively. At the other end of the spectrum, the states with the greatest amount of competition were Oklahoma, North Carolina, Florida, and Kentucky, where the percentage of unopposed seats ranged from 1 to 20 percent. In comparing 1972 with 1960, all but three of the thirteen states have reduced the number of uncontested seats in the general election. However, by 1972 Louisiana had taken the leadership in uncontested seats away from Mississippi, Georgia, and Arkansas. In that year six of the eight Louisiana seats were uncontested.

The percentage of Republican successes in southern congressional elections has advanced even faster than the increase in the number of seats for which they have competed. This outcome has been enhanced substantially by the success of Republican presidential candidates since 1964, as well as by the third-party movements that periodically upset the power balance in those states. As a consequence 36 of the 121 southern seats now have Republican representatives—an increase from only nine Republican seats in those states in 1960. Table 2-3 shows in which states the transition has occurred.

The net gain of twenty-seven House seats since 1960 has resulted in the Republicans actually taking control of several delegations. For example, seven of Virginia's ten seats and five of Tennessee's eight are held by Republicans. Only seven southern states had even one Republican congressman in 1960, and by 1972 each of the thirteen had at least one, a very drastic change in the power relationships. In fact, some Republican southern districts have even become "safe" districts, in that the winner received over 55 percent of the popular vote. In two cases, it was the Democrats rather than the Republicans who failed to field a candidate.

Table 2-3
Trend in Southern Republican Members of House of Representatives

	1960	1962	1964	1960-72 1966	1968	1970	1972	Gain 1960-72
Ala.	0	0	5	3	3	3	3	3
Ark.	0	0	0	1	1	1	1	1
Fla.	1	2	2	3	3	3	3	2
Ga.	0	0	1	2	2	2	1	1
Ky.	1	2	1	3	3	2	2	1
La.	0	0	0	0	0	0	1	1
Miss.	0	0	1	0	0	0	2	2
N.C.	1	1	2	3	4	4	4	3
Okla.	1	1	1	2	2	2	1	0
S.C.	0	0	0	1	1	1	2	2
Tenn.	2	3	3	4	4	4	5	3
Texas	1	2	2	2	3	3	4	3
Va.	2	2	2	4	5	6	7	5
Total	9	13	20	28	31	31	36	27
Net gain		4	7	8	3	0	5	27

Source: *Congressional Quarterly Almanac,* 1960-72 (Washington, D.C.: Congressional Quarterly Service).

The dramatic character of this change is illustrated by looking at the percentage of competitive districts in the South as a percentage of the total number of national competitive districts. In 1972 only 16.9 percent of all the competitive districts in the country were located in these thirteen southern states, which had 27 percent of the total seats. From 1960 through 1972, the South had an average of 14 percent of the national total of seats for which there was competition.

Another view of the Republicans' increased strength is provided by Professors Wolfinger and Heifitz, who note the downward trend in the number of southern Democrats receiving 65 percent of the vote for the House.[2] Between 1946 and 1964, 79 percent of all the southern seats fell into this category. But in 1964, the year of Barry Goldwater's presidential bid, only 36 percent could show such results. In 1972 the comparable figure was 51 percent.

National Turnover and Incumbency Patterns

It is also interesting to examine national changes in the rate of return of incumbents to Congress. The number of incumbents not returning to the House between 1960 and 1972 has ranged from thirty-nine in 1968 to ninety-one in 1964. The average is sixty-five members, or 15 percent of the total membership of the House of Representatives. This is not a large amount of turnover for such a competitive arena as politics. The stability reflects the number of noncompetitive nominations and unopposed elections to the House of Representatives. However, an analysis of the causes for the nonreturn of the incumbents shows that there are some differences related to presidential years and perhaps some developing trends.

Table 2-4 depicts the reasons that incumbents were not returned to the House in seven elections. Primary defeats were quite important in 1970 and 1972 and perhaps this is a trend related to the New Politics. In addition,

Table 2-4
House of Representatives—Incumbents Not Returning

	Total	Retired	Redistricted	Primary Defeats	General Defeats	Senate Try	Other
1972	71	22	16	6	15	10	2
1970	58	10	3	10	11	16	8
1968	39	12	6	3	5	8	5
1966	74	6	17	3	39	3	6
1964	91	21	4	5	45	5	11
1962	64	11	21	7	14	8	3
1960	62	19	0	5	25	6	7
Total	459	102	67	39	134	56	42

Source: *Congressional Quarterly Almanac,* 1960-72 (Washington, D.C.: Congressional Quarterly Service).

retirement was more than twice as high in 1972 as in 1970. A high percentage of the twenty-two retirees in 1972 felt threatened in the primary.

Redistricting contributes most powerfully to the defeat of incumbents in the election just after the completion of the decennial census of population. In the 1960s there was an additional election, or two where redistricting was a major factor. This abnormal intervention resulted from the one-man, one-vote decision by the Supreme Court in 1962 in *Baker v. Carr*, which caused many states to redistrict that otherwise would have waited until 1972 before doing so.

It is noteworthy that the number of retirements has been highest in presidential years, both numerically and as a percentage of the total nonreturns of incumbents. This reflects to some degree the anticipated effects of riding on presidential coattails. In the spring of 1974, for example, an unusually large number of Republicans announced that they would not be candidates in November. Many of them admitted that the Watergate scandals were a major factor in their decision.

Despite the drastic change in the South in both competitiveness and party fortunes in election outcomes, total turnover is very low. This stability is attributed by many to television and other media which help publicize the names of incumbents. Similarly, the high cost of campaigning is a deterrent to new competitors for Congress. Campaign expenditures are less of a problem for an incumbent who has a staff paid with federal money, both Washington and district offices, and the benefits of free postage and publicity to buttress his campaign.

In the thirteen southern states, 73.1 percent of all the House seats *have not* switched parties since 1954. In the West, 60.9 percent of all House seats *have* shifted in party at least once during those same years.[3] In future years this differential is likely to narrow considerably.

There is a substantial change in the number of districts where the winning candidate received less than 55 percent of the total vote and where an opposing candidate received at least 45 percent. From 1960 to 1964 there was a steady increase in the number of such competitive districts—from 75 to 82 to 116. Since the Johnson landslide in 1964, which made many formerly safe seats close contests, there has been a steady decline in the number of seats falling within this range. The number reached a high of 78 in 1966, with 69 in 1968, 58 in 1970, and 53 in 1972. Over this twelve-year period the median change in seats was 80 per Congress, and the mean change was 77.

In the same period, there were five states where the contest was never decided by less than 10 percent in a single race: Vermont, Rhode Island, Mississippi, Hawaii, and Nevada. On the other hand, the most competitive states were Iowa and Kansas, where a high percentage of general elections fell into the competitive range each year. Within the South, the states with the greatest competition over the time period considered were North Carolina, Tennessee, and Oklahoma.

Another factor in the turnover question is the incumbent who does not return because he competed for higher office. There has been some increase in the percentage of congressmen attempting to secure election to the Senate. For example, the number making this attempt varied from three in 1966 to sixteen in 1970. Twenty-one of the 56 former House members trying to reach the Senate between 1960 and 1974 have been successful. This move toward Senate seats has been even higher in the South than nationally. Those states have a lower population base, and therefore a congressman has a better chance of becoming known statewide than in such states as New York, Pennsylvania, or California.

The figures also show that when there is a big sweep in one year, so that districts traditionally controlled by one party are taken by the other party, the coattail effect is likely to disappear in a pendulum reaction in the following election. The Johnson landslide in 1964 and the Republican recovery in 1966 is the most recent example.

Senate Trends

While it is slower to respond to the new trends, the Senate too is pushed by increasing competition for office. Once again, the most dramatic changes have occurred in the South. In 1960 all of the Senate seats in the thirteen southern states were Democratic. By 1972 ten of the twenty-six Senate seats were held by Republicans. The Republicans gained one southern Senate seat in every election between 1960 and 1970. In 1968 and 1972 they gained two seats. However, none of these states has yet elected two Republican senators simultaneously. Nineteen southern senators left the Senate between 1960 and 1972. Nine of the nineteen were defeated for reelection—six in primaries and three in general elections. Eleven of the nineteen changes occurred in 1970 and 1972.[4]

The Republican inroads in the South have been directly related to the presidential elections. The so-called "solid South" provided 50 percent of its votes to the Democratic candidate for president in 1948 and 31 percent in 1968, when George Wallace outpolled Hubert Humphrey in the South. Even the first southerner in the twentieth century to run for president, Lyndon Johnson, carried only 49.5 percent of the southern votes, whereas his non-southern total was 63.5 percent and total percentage of all votes cast was 61.0 percent.

The Youth Vote

Another of the changing factors in the makeup of who votes for congressmen has been the lowering of the median age of the electorate. Several trends have been in progress. First, in presidential elections, the percentage of eligible voters who have cast their ballot has declined steadily from 64 percent in 1960 to 54.6 percent in 1972.[5] Since 1946, when the effect of low birth rates during World War II was reversed by the postwar baby boom, young people have constituted gradually increasing percentages of the total American population. By the mid-1960s, postwar babies were reaching voting age. The impact of this trend was substantial as the median age of voters declined to 46.7 in 1968.[6]

In 1971, Congress passed the twenty-sixth Amendment to the Constitution and in less than four months, thirty-eight states ratified it so that it became effective in time for the 1972 elections. The new Amendment not only lowered the voting age to eighteen in all federal, state, and local elections, but also reduced residency requirements to thirty days and suspended literacy tests in all states.

The youth vote was expected to have a substantial impact; 11.5 million new voters aged eighteen to twenty were enfranchised. In addition to the age change, the residency clause encouraged high turnout of these new voters. Youth were the most mobile group in the country, and so were more affected by restrictive residency clauses than other groups in the population.

The potential of these changes was so great that in 1972 the George McGovern campaign was built on the assumption that if a sufficient number of the young could be induced to register, he would receive a disproportionate share of their votes and could win the presidential election. This theory was partially based on the idea that the new voters, the most educated generation of all time, are more liberally oriented than their predecessors. The assumptions were also supported by the belief that Richard Nixon was not an acceptable candidate for the young voters.

As it developed, the youth vote did not make any difference in the outcome of the 1972 election. Only 48.3 percent of the newly franchised voters appeared at the polls, and only 51 percent of those aged twenty-one to twenty-four voted. Although this had the effect of reducing the median age of the electorate to forty-four years, it did not change the emphasis sufficiently to turn the election over to the young. The greatest turnout, as is traditionally the case, occurred among the old voters. Seventy-one percent of those forty-five to sixty-five and 68 percent of those sixty-five to seventy-four voted. As a result of the low youth vote, total turnout dropped to 54.6 percent from 61.8 percent for the previous presidential election year.[7]

Even if a higher percentage of the youth had voted, the outcome would not have been changed. A study by Peter Hart, Inc. revealed that the voting preferences of youth as well as of the older voter are influenced by the level of education.[8] There were two different youth constituencies in 1972. The college constituency behaved the way McGovern expected them to, but the so-called invisible constituency of working-class youth apparently supported President Nixon, watering down the impact of the college students. The following breakdown of the status of those aged eighteen to twenty is instructive, since it shows that less than half of the new voters are in school:

4.0 million are in college
 .9 million are in high school
4.1 million are employed
 .1 million are in hospitals or prisons
 .8 million are in the armed forces
1.5 million are housewives[9]

The youth vote was not a bloc vote, but was as potentially diverse as the total vote. Further, apart from the Nixon-McGovern choice, table 2-5 indicates that youth are increasingly registering as independents. Since party identification usually results in a high sense of loyalty and turnout, the presence of relatively weak party identification among youth is one explanation for the low turnout. This nonidentification also creates a potential constituency for a New Politics candidate of either party.

The other element involved in the increasing youth vote and the higher average level of education which characterizes that vote is the tendency toward more ticket-splitting. This is a favorable factor for New Politics in the future. A good example of the ticket-splitting and liberal voting of the college students occurred at the University of Massachusetts, where Nixon received 25.6 percent of the vote and McGovern 74.6 percent. At the same time the Republican candidate for the Senate, Edward Brooke, a black, received 74.2 percent of the vote against his Democratic opponent. A similar result was obtained at Southern Illinois University (Carbondale), where Nixon received 26.9 percent of the vote and McGovern 73.1 percent, while Republican Senator Charles Percy received 65.1 percent of the vote in his contest. In fact, in the thirty-one university districts covered in a University of California survey, Nixon won only five (University of Miami, Tulane University in New Orleans, Colorado State University, The University of Northern Colorado, and Brigham Young University in Utah). At Brigham Young, Nixon received 79 percent of the vote, Schmitz 15, and McGovern 6.[10]

With respect to the potential of the student vote to affect Congressional elections, thirty-one of the thirty-three states that were electing senators in 1972 had populations aged eighteen to twenty-four that exceeded the margin by which the incumbent was elected. In fifteen of those thirty-three states, the number of newly enfranchised voters was at least three times as large as the last margin of victory. In one specific case drawn from this sample, Senator Joseph R. Biden, a twenty-nine-year-old candidate, defeated an incumbent, Republican J. Caleb Boggs. Biden won by a vote of 3162, while the number of new voters was 68,000. Nixon had won in Delaware in 1968 with a plurality of 7520 but in 1972 he won by 48,000.[11]

Table 2-5
Party Identification Among Youth

Year	Percentages		
	Republican	Democrat	Independent
1966	26	35	39
1967	29	29	42
1968	19	38	44
1969	23	33	44
1970	18	30	52
1971	19.7	32.9	57.4
1972	19.3	41.9	38.8
1973	14.2	43.1	42.7

Source: *Gallup Poll Index*, June 6, 1970. p. 21: Unidex Poll of Campus Opinion, Released September 27, 1973; and Republican National Committee.

On the House side, there were 280 House districts where the number of young voters was larger than the total by which the present representatives won election.[12] In seventy-one districts the number of new voters was three times greater than the most recent winning margin. The point is that even if all these young voters did not vote against incumbents, and there is no automatic reason why they should, their very presence in such large numbers in these districts created a whole new set of political pressures in support of the New Politics.

The New Congressmen

These new patterns of competition in the South and the changing competitive nature of contests for the House and the Senate have attracted a different breed of candidate. This alone would have had some effect in bringing more New-Politics-oriented congressmen into Washington. However, this trend has been supplemented by the move toward more diversity which resulted from the expansion of the right to vote and the election of more minority and female representatives. Chapter 3 will deal more specifically with these developments.

3

Blacks, Spanish-speaking Americans, and Women in Congress

Development of a two-party system in the South, the lowered average age of voters, and increasing educational levels of voters created substantial political change. They had the effect of opening up the political process. While these are relatively recent events, even more current are the advances made by blacks, Spanish-Americans, and women in the polling booth since the dawn of New Politics.

Election of Black Congressmen

It seems hard to believe now, but there was not a single black member of Congress in the first twenty-eight years of the twentieth century. In the entire history of the United States there had been only twenty black representatives and two black senators, all of whom held office in the thirty years following the Civil War. All twenty-two were Republicans representing southern states. The two senators were from Mississippi; eight of the House members were from South Carolina; four from North Carolina; three from Alabama; and one each from Florida, Georgia, Louisiana, Mississippi, and Virginia.[1]

After these Reconstruction-era black Republicans left office, there was a black political vacuum. In 1928 Oscar DePriest of Illinois—also a Republican—was elected to the House. After serving three terms, he was replaced in 1935 by the first black Democratic congressman, Arthur Mitchell. Except for DePriest, no black Republican has served in the House in the twentieth century. When Mitchell left office in 1942, two new black congressmen were elected—William Dawson in Mitchell's Chicago district and Adam Clayton Powell in New York's Harlem district. For twelve years, until Detroit sent Charles Diggs to the House in 1955, they were the only black members of Congress. In 1959 Robert Nix of Philadelphia was elected to a House seat.

The long drive for black representation in Congress essentially began with the passage in 1870 of the Fifteenth Amendment, which guaranteed the right to vote to black men over the age of twenty-one. Although they were favored by the Republicans in the Reconstruction South, blacks experienced great difficulty in voting there as a variety of schemes were used to disenfranchise them.

Essentially, four major actions were to occur that would change the situation. First came an urban migration of blacks, following World War II. Then the civil rights movement resulted in making the vote available to blacks in greater numbers than ever before. The one-man, one-vote decision of the Supreme Court put more of the congressional seats in the cities, where

31

blacks were clustered. The postwar educational revolution resulted in the availability of more qualified blacks able to compete for political positions.

Prior to the one-man, one-vote ruling, gerrymandering of districts was the means used to enhance the power of the few at the expense of the many. This was generally done to penalize the urban areas in favor of the rural areas, since most state legislatures, which were responsible for the redistricting, were dominated by rural interests. In many states the upper house of the legislature consisted of an equal number of representatives for each county, on the model of the United States Senate. As a consequence, the urban interests were grossly underrepresented in the state legislatures which determined congressional district boundaries. At the time of the one-man, one-vote decision in 1962 many states had not redistricted in years or even decades.

Redistricting was necessary when there was a change in the number of House seats assigned to the state. That occurred only when a state's population increased so much that the decennial reapportionment by Congress resulted in the assignment of one or more new seats or when its population declined relative to other states so that it lost one or more seats. While the urban migration tipped the balance of population more and more to the metropolitan areas, it did not necessarily change the pattern of representation in the state. In general this protected the rural Republican seats at the expense of Democratic central cities. As blacks concentrated in cities, they lost opportunities for representation.

Additional changes took place after the civil rights acts were pushed through Congress in the 1960s. New Politics influenced the labor unions and promoted the funding of voter registration drives that were able to tip the political balance in numerous districts and states by registering more black voters.

Table 3-1 shows the impact of a voter registration drive in eleven of the thirteen southern states by the Voter Education Project, which was funded by the Ford Foundation. The project precipitated an increase of 212,000 new black voters in the eleven states, despite substantial outmigration of blacks during the period. Even here, though, there was ample opportunity for increasing black political clout. The figures show that an average of 66 percent of the blacks were registered to vote, compared with 83 percent of the whites in the eleven states. Nevertheless, a number of key congressional districts would have the votes to elect a black or a pro-black white candidate merely by increasing the registration of blacks.

The Voting Rights Act of 1965 made other dramatic changes in the strength of the black vote. It outlawed certain literacy tests and other procedural barriers to black voting, created a procedure to review changes in the election laws of five southern states with poor black voting participation, and empowered the attorney general to appoint federal voting registrars in counties where less than half of the voting age blacks were registered.[2] The law had a five-year life, and was extended for another five years when it expired in 1970.

A 1972 report on black electoral power by the Joint Center for Political

Table 3-1

Voter Registration in the Southern States (Spring-Summer, 1970)

State	White Voting Age Population[a]	Black Voting Age Population[a]	Whites Registered	Percent White VAP Registered	Blacks Registered (1968 figure in parentheses)		Percent Black VAP Registered
Alabama	1,353,058	481,320	1,300,000	96.1	308,000	(273,000)	64.0
Arkansas	850,643	192,626	683,000	80.3	138,000	(130,000)	71.6
Florida	2,617,438	470,261	2,465,000	94.2	315,000	(292,000)	67.0
Georgia	1,797,062	612,910	1,610,000	89.6	390,000	(344,000)	63.6
Louisiana	1,289,216	514,589	1,137,000	88.2	318,000	(305,000)	61.8
Mississippi	748,266	422,256	650,000	86.9	285,000	(251,000)	67.5
North Carolina	2,005,955	550,929	1,598,000	79.6	302,000	(305,000)	54.8
South Carolina	895,147	371,873	656,000	73.3	213,000	(189,000)	57.3
Tennessee	1,779,018	313,873	1,570,000	88.3	240,000	(228,000)	76.5
Texas	4,884,765	649,512	3,599,000	73.7	550,000	(540,000)	84.7
Virginia	1,876,167	436,720	1,472,000	78.4	265,000	(255,000)	60.7
Totals	20,096,735	5,016,100	16,740,000	83.3	3,324,000	(3,112,000)	66.3

[a] VAP—Voting Age Population, 1960 Census

Source: *Congressional Quarterly Weekly Report*, June 24, 1972 (Washington, D.C.: Congressional Quarterly Service Inc.), p. 2952

Studies at Howard University stated that "the concentration of blacks in major cities, together with the impact of the Voting Rights Act of 1965, has put within reach the capacity to overcome their historical powerless status and to operate in the political system from a position of strength."[3] That concentration is clearly indicated in table 3-2. As shown, the clustering resulted from a two-way movement—an actual outmigration of whites accompanied by an inmigration of blacks.

The most recent wave of new black Democratic congressmen resulted from the judicial and legislative policies of the 1960s. In 1962 Augustus Hawkins was elected in Los Angeles and in 1964 John Conyers in Detroit. In 1968 the first black congresswoman, Shirley Chisholm of Brooklyn, was elected. William Clay and Louis Stokes were also elected that year and they were joined in 1970 by Ralph Metcalfe, Ron Dellums, Charles Rangel, Parren Mitchell, and George Collins. In 1972 Andrew Young, Barbara Jordan, and Yvonne Burke were elected. Rangel defeated Powell, who had been censured by the House for misusing his chairmanship for personal gains, and Ralph Metcalfe replaced Dawson, who had retired. George Collins died in an airline crash at Chicago in December 1972 after he had been reelected. A special election to select a new congressman was won by Cardiss Collins, his widow, in June 1973.

Congress authorized the election of a nonvoting delegate from the District of Columbia in 1970. Walter Fauntroy emerged victorious in a Democratic primary in January and in a special election held in March 1971. While having no floor vote, Fauntroy does have a vote in the District of Columbia Committee to which he is automatically assigned. He played a major role in securing approval of the home-rule bill for Washington, D.C.

Due to the gradual addition of new black representatives and the fact that Powell is the only black elected since 1942 who has ever been defeated, there

Table 3-2
Racial Composition of Core City and Suburbs
of Ten Selected SMSAs, 1960-70

	Percent Change in Black Population		Percent Change in White Population	
	Core	Suburban	Core	Suburban
Atlanta	36.8	165.4	−20.0	67.3
Baltimore	29.1	33.6	−21.4	48.5
Chicago	35.7	67.22	−18.6	33.9
Cleveland	14.8	392.4	−26.5	23.4
Detroit	37.0	28.3	−29.1	27.8
Houston	47.2	18.3	25.4	147.8
Los Angeles	51.7	93.1	4.7	14.4
New York	53.3	12.4	−8.9	15.0
Philadelphia	23.5	32.2	12.9	21.5
St. Louis	18.6	56.0	−31.6	30.7

Source: U.S. Bureau of the Census, *Census of Population: 1970*, Vol. I (1970 data); 1960 black migration in/out of core derived from tables 3 (SMSAs) and 4 (Cities), *County and City Data Book 1967*.

has been a continual increase in the number of black representatives. No black representative elected in the twentieth century has been replaced by a nonblack. The process is summarized in table 3-3. The House of Representatives had fifteen black members in the 93rd Congress. The first black senator in the twentieth century, and the only one ever elected from the North, Republican Edward W. Brooke of Massachusetts, was elected in 1967. It is noteworthy that every black elected to the House since since 1934 has been a Democrat, while no black Democrat has ever been elected to the Senate.

Of the total black delegation in the 93rd Congress, California had three black congressmen; Michigan, New York, and Illinois had two; and Pennsylvania, Missouri, Ohio, Georgia, Texas, Maryland, and the District of Columbia each had one. *Every* black member was from an urban district. On a city basis the breakdown was as follows:

New York—Rangel, Chisholm
Los Angeles—Hawkins, Burke
Chicago—Metcalfe, C. Collins
Detroit—Diggs, Conyers
Philadelphia—Nix
St. Louis—Clay
Cleveland—Stokes
Atlanta—Young
Baltimore—Mitchell
Houston—Jordan
Berkeley—Dellums
Washington—Fauntroy

At the time of the election for the 88th Congress in 1962, five congressional districts in the United States had a black population in excess of 50 percent.[4] Hawkins, Dawson, Nix, and Powell represented four of these districts. The only black district not represented by a black was the 2nd District in Mississippi, where blacks made up 59 percent of the population but where the Republicans did not field a candidate and the Democratic candidate was white.

As a result of redistricting during the 1960s, three new districts were created with a black majority in Brooklyn, Cleveland, and St. Louis. These seats were won in the next election by Shirley Chisholm, Louis Stokes, and William Clay. Until the 1970 election therefore, the only blacks elected from districts which did not have a black majority were Diggs and Conyers of Detroit. The Diggs district had a 49.7 percent black population and the Conyers district was 41 percent black. Since 1970 five of the six districts with first-time black representatives—Dellums, Collins, Mitchell, Young, and Jordan—were districts that did *not* have a black majority. The sixth district was that of Yvonne Burke, which was officially 51 percent black, but was experiencing a trend of black inmigration and white outmigration.

The recent growth of black strength in Congress is the direct result of the increasing migration of blacks to the big cities of the North, the movement

Table 3-3
Growth of Black Caucus

								Young
								Jordan
								Burke
							Fauntroy	Fauntroy
							G. Collins	C. Collins
							C. Mitchell	C. Mitchell
							Dellums	Dellums
						Stokes	Stokes	Stokes
						Chisholm	Chisholm	Chisholm
						Clay	Clay	Clay
					Conyers	Conyers	Conyers	Conyers
				Hawkins	Hawkins	Hawkins	Hawkins	Hawkins
				Nix	Nix	Nix	Nix	Nix
			Diggs	Diggs	Diggs	Diggs	Diggs	Diggs
		Powell	Powell	Powell	Powell	Powell	*Rangel*	Rangel
		Dawson	Dawson	Dawson	Dawson	Dawson	*Metcalfe*	Metcalfe
De Priest	*A. Mitchell*							
1929-34	1935-42	1943-54	1955-58	1959-64	1965-68	1969-70	1971-72	1973-74
71st-73rd	74th-77th	78th-83rd	84th-85th	86th-88th	89th-90th	91st	92nd	93rd

Note: Italics show first term of new member of Congress

Source: *Congressional Directory*, 1929-74, and *Biographical Directory of the American Congress, 1774-1971* (Washington, D.C.: U.S. Government Printing Office, 1972).

of the white population to the suburbs, and of the *Baker v. Carr* decision, which strengthened the power of the urban areas. This effect was greatest in states that had overrepresented their rural population in Congress. Now that the districts had to be essentially equal in population and also had to be of contiguous territory. The existence of a ghetto area made it difficult to avoid establishing districts with black majorities. It then fell to the local black leadership to insure that there would be a viable black candidate.

Until 1970 the 1st District of Mississippi was the only one having a black majority and not having a black representative. After the 1970 Census, Mississippi redistricted and its 37 percent black population, the highest percentage of blacks in any state, was more evenly distributed. After the redistricting, three of the five districts had large black populations of 46, 43, and 41 percent.

During the 93rd Congress, fifty-five of the 435 congressional districts had a black population of 30 percent or more, twenty-two had over forty percent, and sixteen had over 50 percent. Blacks represented thirteen of the fourteen districts in which the black population outnumbered the nonblacks. The only one not represented by a black congressman was the 10th District of New Jersey, which is represented by Peter Rodino, the chairman of the House Judiciary Committee. The district is 51.8 percent black and 5.8 percent Puerto Rican, so that 57.6 percent of the district is nonwhite.[5] Table 3-4 shows the 33 districts that have a substantial minority population, including the twenty-two with black populations in excess of 40 percent.

In another approach to analyzing potential black electoral power, the Joint Center for Political Studies at Howard University analyzed congressional districts in which the black voting age population was at least double the congressman's 1972 margin of victory. Fifty-one such districts were identified, including twenty-five districts where the winner had less than 55 percent of the vote, so that the district could be classified as a competitive rather than a safe district.[6] Only one of the twenty-five, the 5th District of Georgia, was currently represented by a black, Andrew Young. Even though black voters are not the majority in these districts, their congressmen would be under some pressure to be responsive to black causes.

The growth in black representation is not yet complete. As indicated above, there are a number of congressional districts without a black congressman that already have a majority black population or where the blacks tend to have a greater turnout. If the urban migrations continue, many other urban districts will develop black majorities. On a strict percentage basis, the 25 million blacks in America constitute roughly 12 percent of the national population. That proportion of the 435 seats in the House of Representatives would amount to fifty-two seats. Since Blacks currently hold fifteen, it is clear that there will be significant additional growth in black representation in Congress. However, the New Politics should also result in the election of some blacks in predominantly white districts where the candidate's race is not as important as his policy positions.

Table 3-4
1972 Congressional Districts with Minority Populations over 40 Percent

State	District	Representative	Percent Black	Percent Spanish-Speaking	Percent Other Minority	Total Percent Minority
Ill.	1	Metcalfe[a]	88.9	—	—	88.9
N.Y.	12	Chisholm[a]	77.1	13.5	—	90.6
Md.	7	Mitchell[a]	74.0	—	—	74.0
D.C.	—	Fauntroy[a]	72.1	—	—	72.1
Mich.	1	Conyers[a]	70.0	—	—	70.0
Ohio	21	Stokes[a]	66.3	—	—	66.3
Mich.	13	Diggs[a]	65.8	—	—	65.8
Penn.	2	Nix[a]	65.0	—	—	65.0
N.Y.	19	Rangel[a]	58.7	17.3	—	76.0
Ill.	7	Collins[a]	54.9	16.6	—	71.5
Calif.	21	Hawkins[a]	54.2	21.1	2.7(J)	78.0
Mo.	1	Clay[a]	53.3	—	—	53.3
N.J.	10	Rodino	51.8	5.8	—	57.6
Calif.	37	Burke[a]	50.7	9.3	3.4(J)	63.4
Tenn.	8	Kuykendall	47.5	—	—	47.5
Miss.	2	Bowen	45.9	—	—	45.9
Ga.	5	Young[a]	44.2	—	—	44.2
Miss.	4	Cochran	43.1	—	—	43.1
S.C.	6	Young	42.2	—	—	42.2
N.Y.	21	Badillo[b]	41.7	43.8	—	85.5
Texas	18	Jordan[a]	41.6	18.6	—	60.2
Miss.	3	Montgomery	40.4	—	—	40.4
Ill.	2	Murphy	39.7	5.2	—	44.9
N.Y.	14	Rooney	23.2	24.6	—	47.8
Calif.	5	Burton	17.5	17.4	9.7(C) 4.4(F)	48.0
Fla.	14	Pepper	15.0	41.0	—	56.0
Texas	20	Gonzalez[b]	10.8	59.7	—	70.5
Calif.	38	Roybal[b]	3.9	49.5	—	53.4
N.Y.	23	Peyser	3.4	47.6	—	51.0
Texas	16	White	3.3	50.2	—	53.5
Texas	15	de la Garza[b]	—	75.0	—	75.0
N.M.	1	Lujan[b]	—	48.9	3.4(I)	52.3
N.M.	2	Runnels	—	31.1	10.7(I)	41.8

[a] Black congressman or congresswoman
[b] Spanish-speaking congressman
(J) Japanese
(C) Chinese
(I) American Indian
(F) Filipino
Source: U.S. Congress, *Biographical Directory of the American Congress 1774–1971* (Washington, D.C.: United States Government Printing Office, 1973) and Congressional Quarterly, *Congressional Districts in the 1970s* (Washington, D.C.: Congressional Quarterly Service, 1973).

Black Power in the House

Winning elections to Congress is only a first step; becoming influential in Congress is another matter. In 1969 the emerging black congressional group organized the Black Caucus. William Clay of Missourri, one of the most vocal of the group, expressed what he feels is the "Emerging New Black Politics." According to Representative Clay, this philosophy:

1. Rejects the theory of appeasement of the White Majority;
2. Builds a new politics of confrontation;
3. Stresses leadership—the true fundamentals consists of a personal commitment to the concept of justice and equality at any cost. It also consists of a relative degree of political independence. There is also the attribute of political integrity.[7]

He goes further and says that it replaces the philosophy that what is good for the nation is good for the minorities; instead it argues the belief that what is good for the minorities is good for the nation.

4. In this sense, it is a practical and selfish philosophy We must take what we can and give what we must.
5. Political independence. This politics is abrasive; it depends on retaliatory techniques. There are no liberal friends. If there are liberal friends their relationships must be based on different roles.[8]

Beginning in about February of 1970, the Black Caucus made numerous attempts to meet with President Nixon, who avoided the meeting. In response, the Black Caucus, with the exception of Robert Nix, boycotted the 1971 Nixon State of the Union address because of his "consistent refusal to hear the pleas of the Black Americans." The group charged the President with "pitting the rural areas against the cities, the rich against the poor, black against white, and young against old." Their statement went on to charge that he had failed "to give moral leadership necessary to guide and unify this nation in time of crisis."[9]

Finally, on March 25, Nixon met with the Black Caucus, which delivered a list of sixty recommendations affecting the 25 million black Americans. Declaring themselves to be congressmen-at-large, they argued that these actions were necessary steps "to demonstrate commitment to the goal of equal rights for all Americans" and called for a response by May 17, the anniversary of the *Brown v. Topeka Board of Education* Supreme Court decision, which outlawed segregation in schools.[10]

The recommendations supported a national welfare system, preservation of the Office of Economic Opportunity, expanded aid to education, release of impounded money voted by Congress for public housing in the suburbs, appointment of more black judges and federal district attorneys, more aggressive manpower training and public employment programs, a guaranteed minimum family income of $6500, and more aid to minority business. Other points dealt with international affairs and included a call for reduction of military expenditures, withdrawal from Vietnam, and more aid for African countries.

The Nixon response was issued on May 18 in a 115-page paper which claimed general agreement with most of the goals presented by the Caucus, including expanded economic opportunity, welfare reform, and revenue-sharing. He specifically rejected the $6500 minimum income proposal as fiscally irresponsible, and also indicated that he did not intend to reestablish OEO as an operating agency with continuing programs. He disagreed that revenue-sharing for education would be detrimental to minority students.

The Caucus was not satisfied with the reply. Charles Diggs, the Chairman, said he was deeply disappointed. William Clay called the "White House document . . . a charade, nothing more than the documentation of existing Administration actions."[11]

The activities sponsored by the Black Caucus have included a National Policy Conference on Education for Blacks. The well-attended conference in 1972 covered controversial questions such as the impact of integration and separate education for black children. Other events sponsored included an African-American National Conference on Africa, which attempted to set some priorities for black development in Africa and to deal with the problem of freedom for blacks in South Africa; a national strategy session in March 1973 on the impact of presidential budget cuts and impoundments; and Caucus hearings conducted by Ron Dellums on the Bureaucratic Accountability Act of 1973. This bill sought to remedy problems caused when the federal government does not follow laws enacted by Congress, and stresses protection of individuals' rights in their dealing with the federal government. All the members of the Congressional Black Caucus cosponsored this bill.

The Caucus has had a reasonably good professional staff, primarily paid from the proceeds of an annual fund-raising dinner. The 1973 dinner raised over $250,000. In addition, members of the Black Caucus have contributed funds for the Caucus staff operations and some money has been made available by foundations.

In 1973, Louis Stokes, then Chairman of the Caucus, reflected on its development:

Initially there were a number of misconceptions as to the role and responsibilities of the Congressional Black Caucus. Some felt that the Caucus was trying to replace traditional civil rights groups. Still others felt the Caucus was trying to become the national forum or clearinghouse for a host of problems and issues confronting Black Americans.

Admitting to some confusion within the Caucus as to its proper role, Stokes reported that in 1973, the decision made was that if the Caucus was "going to make a meaningful contribution to minority citizens and this country, then it must be as legislators."[12]

A major source of future black power in Congress has an institutional basis. A black once elected has been able to count on staying in office. The only exception was Adam Clayton Powell, whose behavior was in blatant disregard of his own constituency as well as of the rules of the House. This black tenure phenomenon has had an interesting impact on the seniority process. The formerly supersafe districts of the South represented by Democratic conservatives are increasingly threatened both by Republicans and by the ability of black Democrats there to tip an election, by voting for the Republican candidate or by running an independent candidate. This occurred in a number of Alabama districts in 1968 and the Republicans capitalized on it. At the same time, seats located in the black ghettos have become safe seats because of their stability. Powell and Dawson both rose to powerful committee chairmanships in the House, and this process is now working heavily in the blacks' favor. Charles Diggs became Chairman of the House Committee on the District of Columbia in 1972.

An analysis of the committee assignments blacks have had since the election of Dawson and Powell in 1942 shows a strong preference for the Education and Labor Committee, which Powell chaired for several years. Five different black congressmen have served on that Committee, including three of the sixteen members of the Caucus (Hawkins, Clay, and Chisholm).

Likewise, the District of Columbia Committee, chaired by Diggs, has four black members, including Fauntroy. This Committee is important to the Black Caucus because of Washington's large black population. Some of the other blacks were drafted to serve because of the need to involve more friends of home rule on the Committee. Some, including Shirley Chisholm, flatly refused to serve on the Committee.

William Dawson, the first black ever to serve on the Government Operations Committee, became its chairman in 1955, a position he held until his resignation in 1970. John Conyers and George Collins joined that committee in 1969. The Foreign Affairs Committee has also been a popular committee for black Congressmen. Diggs, Nix, Dellums, and Stokes have served there. Diggs is chairman of the Subcommittee on African Affairs and Nix heads the Asian and Pacific Affairs Subcommittee. In 1973, Ron Dellums became the first black to be appointed to the Armed Services Committee, despite the chairman's protest that he was an antiwar militant. Louis Stokes was the first black ever appointed to the powerful Appropriations Committee. No black has yet served on the two other powerhouse committees—Ways and Means and Rules. Shirley Chisholm has set her sights on the Rules Committee but was bypassed in 1973. There were no vacancies on Ways and Means in the 93rd Congress.

The Judiciary Committee taking up the question of presidential impeachment in 1974 included John Conyers, Charles Rangel, and Barbara Jordan. Black members also serve on the committees on Banking and Currency, House Administration, Interior and Insular Affairs, Commerce, Merchant Marine, Post Office and Civil Service, Public Works, and Science and Astronautics. The only standing committees in the House without a black, in addition to Rules and Ways and Means, are Veterans' Affairs, Standards of Official Conduct, and Agriculture. These omissions, partly deliberate, reflect Caucus priorities.

Nevertheless, committee assignments can be a controversial matter. When

Shirley Chisholm first came to Congress she was assigned to the Agriculture Committee. Pointing out that there is more to Brooklyn than the fact that "a tree grows there," she demanded to be taken off the Committee. She was finally placed on the Veterans' Affairs Committee, but later transferred to the Education and Labor Committee. Barbara Jordan sought assistance from former President Johnson when she joined the Congress in 1973. LBJ called Wilbur Mills, Chairman of the Committee on Committees, to advise him that Ms. Jordan wanted a seat on the Judiciary Committee. She not only got it but was given seniority over the four other freshmen assigned to that Committee.[13]

The legislative interests of black Congressmen have tended to be just as diverse as those of other Congressmen, except that there is general accord on bills that are clearly black-related. Ron Dellums, for example, who represents the Berkeley district, sponsored so many bills in his first term relating to California's ecological condition that he was accused by some blacks of not being interested in black problems. His first bills covered the following subjects: air pollution control, regulation of strip mining, beach conservation, pesticides, noise abatement, reclamation projects, automotive emission research, the Sequoia National Park, the Alaska pipeline, fish and wildlife preservation, and water pollution control.

Charles Rangel of Harlem has a district so heavily black that all his district-related legislation is black oriented, with heavy emphasis on drug control, welfare, subsidized housing, weapons control, and health legislation. Likewise, during her first term, Shirley Chisholm sponsored bills related to antipoverty legal services, smoking on public corners, drug abuse, social security, unemployment, veterans' health and allowances, mass transportation, welfare, child development, recidivism, pretrial detention procedures, and government manpower training programs.

However well organized the Black Caucus might be, fifteen votes are not going to be able to control a legislative body with 435 members. To secure more strength and to promote common interests, the Black Caucus has shown some disposition to collaborate with other minority groups in the House. For example, there is some collaboration with the five Spanish-speaking representatives and with the two Asian-Americans who represent Hawaii in the House. Partly because of the need to secure more strength through coalitions, the Black Caucus has sometimes worked with the sixteen-member Women's Caucus in the House. Shirley Chisholm's involvement with the women's movement in the House is another reason for that relationship, and the election of Yvonne Burke, Cardiss Collins, and Barbara Jordan means that one-quarter of the Women's Caucus members are black.

Spanish-Americans and Asiatics in Congress

While blacks have become more politically active and group conscious, Spanish-speaking Americans have been moving simultaneously in the same direction. The nation's second largest minority group has 4.5 percent of the national population and totals just over 9 million, including about 5 million of Mexican ancestry and 1.5 million with family ties to Puerto Rico.

The 93rd Congress included five Spanish-speaking Americans in the House and one in the Senate. New York, Los Angeles, Miami, and San Antonio are cities having large Spanish-American populations. New Mexico, California, Florida, New York, and Texas are the states with the largest Spanish-American populations.

In 1932, Dennis Chavez of Albuquerque became the first Spanish-American elected to Congress when he won one of New Mexico's two House seats. After two terms he was appointed a United States Senator by the Governor of New Mexico. His House seat was won by John Dempsey, a non-Mexican, but in 1942 Antonio Fernandez of Sante Fe won the seat. When Fernandez died in 1957, Joseph Montoya, also from Sante Fe, was elected to replace him. Montoya held the seat seven years and was elected to the Senate in 1964. Senator Chavez died in 1962, after twenty-seven years in the Senate, and a non-Mexican, Edward Mechem, was appointed to serve the last two years of his term. Manuel Lujan of Albuquerque was elected to the House in 1968. Consequently, since 1932 one of New Mexico's two House seats has been held for all but four years by Mexican-Americans, and except for the 1962–64 period one of its two Senate seats has been held continuously by a Mexican-American since 1935.

The first Mexican-American congressman from Texas, Henry B. Gonzalez of San Antonio, has demonstrated an independence from the minority caucus on some policies. San Antonio's prime industry is Defense Department-related and he consistently opposed legislation to end the Vietnam War. At the same time he has denounced the Mexican-American Youth Movement (MAYO) for stereotyped thinking. Gonzalez was first elected to Congress in 1961 to fill an unexpired term and has been reelected six times since then.

Edward Roybal, another Mexican-American, has represented a blue-collar district in Los Angeles since the 1962 election. Eligio de la Garza of the 15th District of Texas was elected to Congress in 1964 and has been re-elected four times. He represents an agricultural district including the nine southernmost counties in Texas.

In 1970, the first Puerto Rican was elected to Congress. Herman Badillo's district is composed of parts of Manhattan and the Bronx in New York City. It is a new district designed to cluster the Puerto Rican population into one district, but it has almost as many blacks as Puerto Ricans. Together they total 85.5 percent of the district population.

No Cubans have been elected to Congress, but the Miami area has heavy Cuban concentrations and sometime soon it is likely to send a Cuban-American to Congress. Congressman Claude Pepper's district in Miami has a 41 percent Spanish-American population along with a 15 percent black population. All of the Spanish-speaking representatives and senators except Manuel Lujan have been Democrats.

Hawaii is the only state that has produced a large number of congressmen of Asiatic descent. When Hawaii was admitted to statehood in 1959, the first two senators elected were Hiram Fong and Oren Long, a Caucasian. Daniel Inouye was elected to the House seat in 1959 and held it until he was elected to the Senate in 1962. Spark Matsunaga replaced Inouye in the House and is still there. Thomas Gill was elected to the other House seat in 1962 and was replaced in 1964 by Patsy Mink, who has served continuously since then. None of Hawaii's House or Senate seats has changed hands since 1964, and all are held by Asiatic-Americans. The three Democrats—Inouye, Matsunaga, and Mink—are all of Japanese ancestry, while Fong, who is Republican, is of Chinese descent.

Women in Congress

More women were elected to the House of Representatives in 1972 than in any year since 1960. That year also showed a dramatic increase in the number of women office-seekers, the greatest number of all time.[14] These factors point to a change in congressional makeup and an increase in the recognition of women as viable candidates for office. Rather than coming into office as the surrogates for their late husbands, the recently elected congresswomen have won on their own merits. Interestingly, only one woman, Emily Taft Douglas of Illinois, who served as a House Democrat from 1945 to 1947, has ever preceded her husband to Congress. Senator Paul Douglas of Illinois served from 1949 to 1967.

Since they were granted the right to vote in national elections in 1920 through the Nineteenth Amendment, women have played an important role in the election process. The first woman ever elected to Congress was Jeannette Rankin. Elected from Montana in 1916, she was one of 56 members of the House of Representatives who voted against American entry into World War I in April 1917. During her second term in the House twenty-four years later, Miss Rankin was the only member of Congress to vote against the declaration of war against Japan.[15]

Rankin was a constant advocate of women's liberation in the years leading up to the mid-1960s, when her movement flourished. Throughout her years in Congress she was an advocate of equal opportunity for women before the idea was popularly accepted.

Since Jeannette Rankin's first election in 1916, eighty-one women have served in Congress. These women have gained their seats by election to the House of Representatives and Senate, or by appointment to the Senate. In recent years there has been a substantial rise in the number of female candidates. The seventy candidates in the 1972 elections represented a jump from forty-seven candidates in 1970. Thirty-four of the seventy were major party nominees. Most of the minor party candidacies were based on issue orientations especially appropriate for women office-seekers.

The minor parties had an important project besides running members for Congress. In 1972 their efforts included the nomination of women for the offices of president and vice president. Linda Jenness was the presidential nominee of the Socialist Workers Party in eighteen states. In three additional states her name was barred because at thirty-one she was too young to hold the office if elected. In these states, Evelyn Reed was her replacement. Another woman, Genevieve Gunderson, appeared as the vice-presidential nominee of the Socialist Labor Party.

From a quantitative standpoint, there was a steady increase in the number of women in the House from 1919 to 1962. After a decrease in the 1960s, the total is increasing again. Table 3-5 shows not only the numerical totals, but also, and more important, the number of women elected directly rather than as replacements for their deceased husbands. The practice of nominating widows for their husbands' seats often has been followed because it is convenient for the party. By electing the widow of a well-known congressman, an interparty squabble may be avoided. In most cases the widow dropped out when the next election occurred and the seat was rewon by a male.

Table 3-5
The Increase in Nonwidow Representatives

Congress	Years	Widows Replacing Husbands	Nonwidows	Total Women
93rd	1973-74	3	13	16
92nd	1971-72	1	12	13
91st	1969-70	1	9	10
90th	1967-68	2	9	11
89th	1965-66	2	8	10
88th	1963-64	4	7	11
87th	1961-62	8	9	17
86th	1959-60	7	9	16
85th	1957-58	6	9	15
84th	1955-56	7	9	16
83rd	1953-54	7	5	12
82nd	1951-52	5	5	10

Source: Congressional Quarterly, *Guide to the U.S. Congress* (Washington, D.C.: Congressional Quarterly Service, 1971), pp. 1a-175a. and *Congressional Directory,* 93rd Congress, 2nd Session, 1974.

Recently, the women in Congress have developed their own power bases. Only three women in Congress are widows of previous representatives. Two of the three, Corrine Boggs and Cardiss Collins, were elected in 1973 to fill their husband's unexpired terms. However, the third, Leonor Sullivan, is a veteran congresswoman who has been elected in her own right ten times since entering the House. Thirty-one of the eighty-one women elected to Congress through June 1974 have been widows replacing their husbands. The 1972 proportion of widows (three of sixteen) is much lower than the historical average.

Women in Congress have educations that compare well with those of their male counterparts. Along with rundowns of their home states and committee assignments, table 3-6 shows the educational level of the women representatives in the 93rd Congress. Fourteen of the sixteen are Democrats. As these women accrue seniority on committees, they probably will exercise more power than the women who preceded them. This change in the status of women in Congress is another result of the New Politics. Their election is made possible by the greater willingness of voters—both male and female— to consider a woman for what was formerly viewed as a man's job.

The women holding the top positions in the House are of course those with the most seniority. Ms. Sullivan of St. Louis, who is in her eleventh term, is the second woman to chair a congressional committee—the House Committee on Merchant Marine and Fisheries. She also chairs the Subcommittee on Consumer Affairs of the House Committee on Banking and Currency. The first woman to chair a congressional committee was Mary T. Norton who served as Chairwoman of the House Committee on the District of Columbia. In 1941 she became Chairwoman of the House Labor Com-

Table 3-6
Women in the 93rd Congress

Name	Party State	Widow	Times Reelected	Committee Memberships	Education Level
Abzug, Bella	D–N.Y.	no	1	Public Works; Govt. Operations	LL.B.
Burke, Yvonne B.	D–Calif.	no	—	Public Works; Interior	LL.B.
Boggs, Corrine	D–La.	yes	—	Banking and Currency	B.A.
Chisholm, Shirley	D–N.Y.	no	2	Education and Labor	M.A.
Collins, Cardiss	D–Ill.	yes	—	Government Operations	attended college
Grasso, Ella	D–Conn.	no	1	Education and Labor; Veterans' Affairs	M.A.
Green, Edith	D–Ore.	no	9	Appropriations	B.A.
Griffiths, Martha	D–Mich.	no	9	Ways and Means; Joint Economic Committee	LL.B.
Hansen, Julia B.	D–Wash.	no	7	Appropriations; Interior	B.A.
Heckler, Margaret	R–Mass.	no	3	Banking and Currency; Veterans' Affairs	LL.B.
Holt, Marjorie	R–Md.	no	—	Armed Services	LL.B.
Holtzman, Elizabeth	D–N.Y.	no	—	Judiciary	LL.B.
Jordan, Barbara	D–Texas	no	—	Judiciary	LL.B.
Mink, Patsy	D–Hawaii	no	4	Education and Labor; Interior	LL.B.
Schroeder, Patricia	D–Colo.	no	—	Armed Services; Post Office and Civil Service	LL.B.
Sullivan, Leonor K.	D–Mo.	yes	10	Merchant Marine and Fisheries; Banking and Currency	attended college

Source: *Congressional Directory*, 93rd Congress, 2nd Session, 1974.

mittee. Martha W. Griffiths, a Michigan Democrat in her tenth term, is the only woman ever to serve on the powerful Ways and Means Committee. She influenced the decisions to increase Social Security benefits. She has also been mentioned as a possible Supreme Court nominee. Edith Green, an Oregon Democrat, has been a major influence in the House Education and Labor Committee, and in 1973 became the first woman to serve on the powerful Appropriations Committee. To take the position she had to leave the Education and Labor Committee, where she chaired a subcommittee. Patsy Mink chairs the Interior Subcommittee on Mines and Mining.

Emerging as the best-known congresswoman is Shirley Chisholm, who at the 1972 Democratic Convention received the highest number of nominating votes for president ever given to a woman. That brought her widespread attention and made her one of the most influential black women in the nation. She also is distinguished as the first black woman elected to the House.

The five new congresswomen elected in 1972 share a common element other than their sex—all are recognized to be New Politics additions to the House of Representatives. All appear to have a strong commitment to social issues and all are actively in accord with the provisions of the Equal Rights Amendment.

Democrat Elizabeth Holtzman (of New York) is a perfect example of a challenge to the male-dominated establishment. In 1972 Ms. Holtzman defeated Emanuel Celler—a veteran of fifty years of congressional service who was also Judiciary Committee Chairman. Celler, who blocked the Equal Rights Amendment for decades, was replaced on his own committee by Ms. Holtzman, a thirty-one-year-old lawyer. Another "unbeatable," Republican James McKevitt, was defeated by Pat Schroeder of Denver, who used a grassroots campaign to win in 1972. Ms. Marjorie Holt of Maryland also outpolled a male and won a seat in the House.

Ms. Chisholm was joined in the House in 1972 by two other black women with impressive accomplishments. Texas Democrat Barbara Jordan became the first black woman ever elected to the House from the South. Prior to coming to Washington Ms. Jordan had served in the Texas State Legislature. Yvonne Brathwaite Burke of California also had unusual accomplishments to her credit. Besides serving as deputy presiding officer of the 1972 Democratic Convention, which provided her with national exposure, Ms. Burke made headlines late in 1973 when she became the first member of Congress to bear a child while in office.

While gaining a seat in the House of Representatives, women lost an important post when Senator Margaret Chase Smith lost her reelection bid in 1972. She began her career of more than twenty years in 1940 through a special House election caused by the death of her husband. After several reelections, she was elected to the Senate in 1949. At the time of her defeat, she was the ranking Republican member of both the Senate Armed Services Committee and the Aeronautical and Space Sciences Committee, and the second ranking Republican on the Appropriations Committee. Senator

Smith is the only woman who has sat in both chambers, and can boast of serving more years in Congress than any other woman in history.

Few women have served in the Senate. Senators Smith and Arkansas Democrat Hattie W. Caraway (1931–45) were the only two women to be reelected. Rebecca Felton served one day in 1922 and nine women have been sworn into the Senate since. One additional woman, Gladys Pyle, a Republican from South Dakota was appointed but never sworn in, because Congress was not in session between her appointment in 1938 and the expiration of her term a month later in 1939.

For a brief time in 1954 Margaret Chase Smith was joined in the Senate by two other women—Eva Bowring and Hazel Abel, both Nebraska Republicans appointed to fill out short terms. However the strongest women's presence in the Senate occurred in the 1960s when Margaret Chase Smith and Maurine B. Neuberger, a Democrat from Oregon, were both present as elected senators serving full terms. Senator Neuberger succeeded her husband who died in 1960 but she was beaten for reelection in 1966.[16]

The Changing Racial and Sexual Composition of Congress

The open attitude of the New Politics, as well as its indifference to stereotypes, has surely contributed to the diversification of Congress. The political atmosphere of change is related to the presence of increasing numbers of blacks, Spanish-speaking, Asiatic, and female members of Congress. A glimpse at table 3–7 should show how drastic the change has been—and how much more change is still possible.

Table 3–7
Racial and Sexual Composition of Congress

	1920	1930	1940	1950	1960	1965	1974
House of Representatives							
Women	0	7	9	9	16	10	16[a]
Blacks	0	1	1	2	5	6	16[a]
Asiatics	0	0	0	0	2	2[b]	2[b]
Spanish-speaking	0	0	1	1	1	4	5
Total nonwhite males	0	8	11	12	24	22	39
Senate							
Women	0	0	1	1	1	2	0
Blacks	0	0	0	0	0	0	1
Asiatics	0	0	0	0	2	2	2
Spanish-speaking	0	0	1	1	1	1	1
Total nonwhite males	0	0	2	2	4	5	4

a including four black women
b including Patsy Mink
Source: Roscoe C. Brown and Harry A. Ploski, *The Negro Almanac* (New York: Bellewether Publishing Company, 1967), pp. 453–54; Congressional Quarterly, *Congressional Districts in the 1970s* (Washington, D.C.: Congressional Quarterly Service, 1973); U.S. Congress, *The Congressional Directory,* 1920–74; and *The Congressional Quarterly Weekly Report,* July 10, 1970, p. 1747.

That 4 percent of the U.S. Senate and 8 percent of the House of Representatives consists of nonwhite males is not of itself likely to cause any major changes in national policy. There are very few issues that would cause all these people to unite and vote as a bloc against the white males. In some respects their constituencies differ, and regional or other interests may be more important to them than race or sex.

However, on New Politics votes involving economic or social policy or affecting urban constituencies, there has been a tendency for the black, female, Spanish-speaking, and Asiatic-background congressmen to vote on the same side. In a close vote their number is now sufficient to tip the balance. On votes involving civil rights or discrimination, their bloc voting and their intensity of feeling make a force to be reckoned with by their colleagues.

Another source of their strength is the fact that most of the minority and women members of the House are Democrats and members of the Democratic Study Group (DSG), a subgroup of the Democrats in the House. There they constitute about 20 percent of the total. To the extent that the DSG can influence the Democratic Caucus, which is capable of dominating the House of Representatives, their potential power is much greater than their numbers might indicate.

4 Freshman Power in the House of Representatives

To a large extent Congress determines what a president can accomplish during his administration. One of the fallouts of the 1973 confrontations between Richard Nixon and Congress was an effort to neutralize congressional power. Since 1960, as a new breed of freshman legislators in both parties has been elected and reelected, there has been more concern with power and how it is used in the House of Representatives. The high rate of turnover since 1960 and the impact of new political and social forces have been felt in the form of basic changes in the structure and activity of the House of Representatives.

The reactions of congressmen, especially in the 89th (Great Society) and 90th Congresses, provide much data on the classic representation questions, such as whether a politician is to vote according to what he believes or according to what he thinks his constituents want.[1] Faced with this question of political philosophy, Edmund Burke told his constituents in Bristol that a member of Parliament was elected to contribute his judgment to the best interests of the empire and the nation—whether or not those judgments coincided with those of the constituents.[2]

A related ethical question in voting is whether to support a position because it is the position of one's political party. Burke gave us one of the famous definitions of a political party as "a body of men united, for promoting by their joint endeavors the national interests, upon some particular principle in which they are all agreed."[3] He assumed that the members of the political party would agree upon essential principles. But as the American political parties have developed, they have placed the major emphasis on the first part of Burke's definition rather than on the latter part, so that each major party includes a whole range of views on principles as well as procedures. This means that the congressman is often faced with pressure to vote in support of his party's position, even when he disagrees with it.

It would be difficult to secure universally applicable judgments on these questions, as much of the answer would depend upon the nature of the votes. At one end of the spectrum of possibilities are simple pragmatic decisions on procedural questions, yet at the other end are the votes involving broad moral issues. Fixing the responsibility of the politician in these extreme cases is easy. However, most issues lie between these two poles and may involve complex combinations of procedural and substantive issues with moral impact. To complicate the process further, it must be noted that whatever decision the legislator takes is public record and ready ammunition for his opponents.

While freshmen are especially vulnerable on this point, even entrenched political leaders are not immune. An example of the problems involved is

51

presented by the voting pattern of Senator Lister Hill, a Democrat from Alabama. Aided by the realities of one-party voting in his state, Hill rose in seniority to become recognized as an outstanding chairman of the Senate Committee on Labor and Public Welfare, which handled the major legislation on medical research in the 1950s and 1960s.

At one point Senator Hill was voted one of the most liberal southern senators by the various organizations that rate congressmen on a liberal-conservative scale for the benefit of their followers. These ratings receive broad publicity in the public press. While Senator Hill's rating was cause for joy in New York, it almost cost the Alabama senator his reelection in 1962. After that scare, he changed his voting pattern so that he was later rated in accord with the most conservative southern senators. If he had failed to switch he would have sacrificed what he was accomplishing as chairman. In the 89th Congress Democratic Senator Ross Bass of Georgia was rated the most liberal southern senator. He failed to cover his tracks as Senator Hill did, and was denied renomination by his own party in 1966.

A more dramatic example of political courage involved Congressman Charles Weltner of Georgia, who had also been a progressive influence in the House. Nominated for a third term by the Democrats and already campaigning for reelection, Weltner withdrew from the race in October when Lester Maddox, the former Atlanta restaurateur who went out of business rather than serve Negro customers, won a runoff election for the Democratic nomination for governor. Many Maddox opponents planned to give only token support to him, but Weltner was not content with that route. He indicated that the Democratic Party rules required that he support the Party's candidate for governor and that his conscience would not permit him to do this.

It would be difficult to assess the impact of Weltner's action on the people of Atlanta, but his selflessness received much publicity and in the November election Maddox received 46.88 per cent of the vote in a three-way race. His Republican opponent, Congressman Howard Calloway, received 47.07 percent, but with heavy support in Atlanta. Maddox became governor only after the Supreme Court, in a 5-to-4 decision, ruled that the Georgia legislature could constitutionally decide who would be the next governor.

J.F.K.'s Congressional Problem

While it is important that congressmen have strong political ethics, votes are required to change policy decisions. For example, although John F. Kennedy was elected President in 1960, that year the Democrats lost twenty seats in the House of Representatives. In addition, many southern Democrats went on to vote with the Republicans on substantive matters, including goals presumably agreed upon in the Democratic party platform.

Faced with major obstacles in pushing through the legislation needed to redeem his campaign pledges, President Kennedy decided to work toward securing congressional cooperation. He had Larry O'Brien develop the most systematic program for presenting the Administration's view that had been seen on Capitol Hill since the early days of the Roosevelt Administration. Although the power advantage of the Republican Southern Democratic alliance was such that even a well-organized approach to the 88th Congress could not guarantee legislative success, Kennedy's chances were vastly improved by O'Brien's work.

First, the Kennedy strategists challenged the old guard in the person of "Judge" Howard Smith of Virginia, the Democratic chairman of the House Rules Committee. For many years, Smith had used his position on the Rules Committee to keep liberal legislation from reaching the floor of the House. If unchecked, he would have demanded amendments that would have weakened the Kennedy legislation, or might even have prevented the program from coming to a vote. Kennedy's strategy was to diminish the power of Smith's vote by enlarging the Rules Committee. In this move, the 1960 freshmen Democrats' voting supported the President 13 to 5, giving him the very narrow margin by which the measure finally passed. This was only the first of several Kennedy "must" measures that were saved by the Democratic freshmen.

Another example was Kennedy's feed grains price-support bill, which won 209 to 202: the freshmen voted 14 to 3 in favor of it. The minimum-wage bill, however, lost 216 to 203, despite an eleven-vote plurality from the Democratic freshmen. While the rest of the Republicans had opposed the President by a ratio of below 6 to 1 on this issue, the Republican freshmen voted against him 36 to 2. Thus it was the Republican freshmen who torpedoed Kennedy's minimum-wage bill—a lesson that President Johnson had reason to ponder later in dealing with the 90th Congress.

The Great Society Congress

The Eighty-ninth Congress provides useful information regarding the behavior of a relatively large group of aggressive politicians operating under extreme pressure. Table 4-1 shows how much larger a freshman group than normal was elected in 1964. Of the seventy-one new Democrats elected to the House of Representatives in the 1964 Lyndon Johnson victory over Barry Goldwater, fifty-one took their seats from Republicans. These new Democrats, who owed their election both to Johnson's image as a man who could get things done and to Goldwater's trigger-happy shoot-from-the-hip image, proceeded to write a new chapter in political ethics as well as in political action.

These Democratic freshmen, helped into office by the heavy vote for President Johnson in 1964, felt that they had a mandate to go "all the way with L.B.J." They not only supported him with a distinctively higher degree of regularity than other Democrats, but also provided the total margin of victory on a number of his key measures in a Congress logically billed as "the Fighting Eighty-ninth." Significant legislation, much of it with a history dating back to Harry Truman, was enacted. Great strides forward were

Table 4-1
Freshmen in the House of Representatives, 1961–74

Congress	Total Members		Vacant	New Freshmen[a]		Old Freshmen[b]		New Freshmen Reelected in Succeeding Congress	
	Dem.	Rep.		Dem.	Rep.	Dem.	Rep.	Dem.	Rep.
87th (1961–62)	260	174	3	29	38	1	5	25	29
88th (1963–64)	254	178	3	39	37	1	1	35	25
89th (1965–66)	294	139	2	72	20	4	1	44	15
90th (1967–68)	248	186	1	17	49	0	11	17	47
91st (1969–70)	244	188	3	26	24	2	0	25	20
92nd (1971–72)	255	180		32	26	3	0	26	22
93rd (1973–74)[c]	243	192		27	43	2	0		

Note: All figures based on close of session.

[a] Never served in a previous Congress

[b] Served in a previous but not the immediately previous session

[c] 93rd Congress to September 30, 1973

Source: U.S. Congress, *Congressional Record*, 1961–74.

made in the areas of housing, immigration, civil rights, economic development, urban affairs, and the alleviation of poverty. Many of these involved questions of societal conscience.

They proceeded knowing that most of them would face extremely difficult reelection campaigns, owing to: (1) the absence of the President on the 1966 ticket; (2) the normal off-year attrition suffered by the party in control of the presidency (an average of forty seats lost in each of the past seven elections); (3) the fact that they represented normally Republican, or at best marginal, districts; (4) the fact that many of the defeated Republicans vowed to run again in 1966, expecting to be able to claim that the new Democrats were Johnson puppets; and (5) their margin of victory had been extremely small. Forty-one of these Democratic freshmen won by less than 55 percent of the vote, thirty-two by less than 53 percent.

These Democrats from marginal districts knew that if they supported the President and his program, they would find themselves running for reelection in two years on the basis of the President's program but without the benefit of the President's name on the ballot. Equally crucial in many of these marginal districts was the absence of presidential candidate Goldwater's name from the ballot.

Traditionally, congressmen from marginal districts have worked overtime to establish a record of independence from the Administration. They need the independent vote to win, and in an off-year election this vote is not captured by a rubber-stamp congressman.

Yet independence was difficult in the face of the barrage of legislation requested of the Congress; the President's own proclivities for making his preferences known directly to individual legislators; the political debts owed to President Johnson by his former colleagues in the House and Senate; and his own use of the new lobbying systems set up by President Kennedy's staff. In addition, and perhaps paramount, most of the Democratic freshmen felt a strong personal commitment to carrying forward the social philosophy of the Kennedy-Johnson program.

The Democratic freshmen of 1964 received more lavish attention from the President than any previous group of freshmen had enjoyed. President Johnson knew that their narrow margins of victory would put the freshmen under great pressure to establish independent voting records in Congress. Yet he also knew that their support was essential to the success of his legislative programs. Accordingly, he took steps to solidify their positions with their constituents so that they could, in turn, give full support to him without fear of retaliation at the polls. For example, instead of releasing the presidential campaign staff after the 1964 election, President Johnson had the Democratic National Committee (D.N.C.) retain a large number of specialists to provide services to the Democratic forces in Congress, with special preference for the freshmen. One service enabled a congressman to phone press releases and statements to the D.N.C. while debates and decisions were still hot. Through its communications network the D.N.C. was then able to speed these items to radio stations and newspapers in the congressman's district—and provide him with some instant image-building among his constituents.

Other Administration efforts to provide individual support to the new House Democrats included invitations to visit the White House in small groups, so that the President could become personally acquainted with them and with their problems. These meetings were often followed by press releases and meetings with Administration officials in charge of programs of interest to the congressmen's districts. And, of course, the Johnson Administration did not fail to impress upon the freshmen the ways in which the Federal Government could aid local projects dear to the hearts of the voters in their home districts.

The Republicans later charged that the 1964 Democratic freshmen were too successful in obtaining their share of the pork barrel. They alleged that this was possible only because the freshmen "sold" their votes to Lyndon Johnson. But another explanation, advanced by the successful freshmen on their own behalf, was that their success was due to their Republican predecessors' neglect of the matters on which they themselves had been able to get action.

Early in the first session, Vice President Humphrey was assigned the task of guiding the new freshmen in the techniques of being Congressmen. The "ombudsman" function in particular was both a burden and an opportunity for the new Democrats who were willing to cooperate with the Administration. As a Senator, Humphrey had complained loudly that the ombudsman role of intervening with the federal bureaucracy on specific constituent problems interfered with his legislative functions. Nevertheless, it was the Vice President who met with the freshmen every three or four weeks early in the 1965 session to help them adjust to Washington, and to their ombudsman role in particular.

Fresh Air in the Committee Room

A very practical problem faced by a freshman congressman is that of building a good record in a very short period of time, when his power within the Congress is at its lowest point. Lacking seniority, subcommittee chairmanships, and the other positions that make it relatively easy for a senior member of Congress to be given attention by the press and other news media, the freshman must generate involvement almost artificially. If he does a yeoman job of homework on the committee, a benign chairman may grant him some opportunity to share the limelight as well as the work.

Committee assignments can have a major impact on a congressman's re-election possibilities. The right committee assignments give him additional knowledge of problems relevant to his district, access to the administrative officials who deal with these problems, and a chance for some publicity on matters meaningful to his constituents. Partly due to the positive efforts of the Administration to help them as much as possible, the vast majority of freshmen in the 89th Congress were able to secure their first or second choices of committee assignments, despite the fact that many of them wanted assignments usually reserved for senior members.

Eleven of the freshmen from rural areas were assigned to the House Agriculture Committee. This turned out to be a rather mixed blessing for Chairman Harold Cooley of North Carolina, who was later challenged by Democratic first-termer Joseph Resnick of New York on the question of sugar allotments, an area long considered part of Cooley's personal fiefdom.

Seven freshmen joined the Armed Services Committee chaired by Mendel Rivers of South Carolina. Rivers, another chairman from the old school, was to sharply challenge the defense management decisions of Secretary of Defense Robert McNamara in the course of the 89th Congress. These freshmen presented a potential source of support to such independent Democrats on the Committee as Otis Pike and Sam Stratton of New York, who frequently challenged Chairman Rivers. In one of his first speeches in the House, freshman Democrat Floyd Hicks of Washington spoke out against Chairman Rivers. Twenty months later Rivers was in Tacoma with Hicks, ostensibly to look at the local defense installations and contractor facilities. When a skeptical reporter asked if he wasn't really there to help Hicks's campaign, Rivers replied, "Well, you could say I'm not here to hurt him." Clearly the hard committee work done by freshmen such as Hicks had won Rivers's respect.

Representative Adam Clayton Powell, Chairman of the Committee on Education and Labor, was assigned five freshmen members, all of whom played a key role in the move made in the summer of 1966 by the other committee members, such as Sam Gibbons, John Brademas, and Edith Green, to limit Powell's authoritarian control of their activities. Although this action was publicized as having racial overtones, it should be obvious that the tendency in the Congress was to limit the autonomy enjoyed by senior chairmen, most of whom were conservatives from the South who had attained their seniority because they represented safe districts. The effort to contain Powell's far-ranging activities was actually quite analogous to the previous rebellion against Cooley of North Carolina, Rivers of South Carolina, and Tom Murray of Tennessee. Chairman Murray of the Post Office and Civil Service Committee was also forced to establish subcommittees and delegate decision-making responsibility to them.

Even when freshmen are responsible for drafting or filing major bills, they sometimes find that if hearings are to be held on the bill it will probably have to carry the chairman's name as the sponsor. One major breakthrough in this area was made by Democratic Congressman Richard Ottinger of New York, who successfully introduced a Hudson River conservation bill. Ottinger was not even a member of the Interior and Insular Affairs Committee, which had to consider the bill. In addition, the Administration was not especially interested in the bill, apart from its water-pollution aspects, because of fears of upsetting Republican Governor Nelson Rockefeller, who had a strong conservationist image. In addition, his family money and influence had been helpful to Lady Bird Johnson's Beautification Program, as well as to numerous natural-resources projects across the country. Success in this area by a freshman congressman who happened to represent the Governor's home district would have been quite embarrassing to Rockefeller, since he wanted to take the lead on such items.

No department in the Executive Branch can testify to Congress on a bill without clearance from the White House as represented by the Office of Management and Budget (OMB). In this case, OMB (then still the Bureau of the Budget) delayed approval of the Department of the Interior's favorable report to Congress on Ottinger's bill. Governor Rockefeller made the mistake of appealing directly to the President to kill the bill, but the letter was publicized in the newspapers. The Bureau of the Budget then released the Interior report, and the bill was passed as an Administration bill bearing Ottinger's name.

The Margin of Victory

Because of their effective organization, the freshmen Democrats were even more valuable to the Administration on the House floor. The Democratic freshmen of 1964 are the largest number of Democrats to have ever taken the seats of senior Republicans. Moreover, what Democratic losses there were in 1964 were almost all sustained in the South, where Goldwater's candidacy created an unusual wave of support for the Republican Party. Since most of the defeated southern Democrats would have voted the same way as the Republicans elected in their places, that shift had no real effect on the Great Society domestic programs.

The extent to which the Republican-southern block was able to coalesce is clear in the voting patterns on ten of the closest key issues put before the 89th Congress:

Eighteen of the twenty newly elected Republicans did not support the President on a single one of the ten votes; the other two voted the Democratic position one time out of ten.

Seven freshman southern Democrats—three of them from the President's own Texas delegation—voted against the President on more than half of the ten votes.

Two of the southern Democrats did not support the President on any of the Great Society programs.

In contrast, the Democratic freshmen,—with the exception of the seven southern Congressmen, may be credited with the successful record of the 89th Congress. Early in the first session of the 89th Congress, the new Democrats again challenged the Conservative Coalition of Republicans and southern Democrats that had often stymied the Kennedy legislative program. The Democratic freshmen helped push through a change in the House Rules that made it possible to bypass the Rules Committee if it did not grant a ruling on a bill within twenty-one days. This meant that the Conservative Coalition could no longer keep liberal legislation from reaching the floor of the House by arbitrarily refusing to grant a ruling. The freshman Democrats—including forty-four out of the forty-eight who had taken seats held by Republicans in the 88th Congress—provided President Johnson with a plurality of fifty-five votes on the rules-change vote—and still the measure passed by only twenty-two votes.

The Department of Housing and Urban Development was created by a vote of 217 to 184, or a margin of thirty-three votes. Since the freshman Democrats voted 59 to 10 in favor of it, they again contributed the full margin of victory. The freshman Democrat votes also made the difference on medicare, rent supplements, repeal of the "right to work" section of the Taft-Hartley Act (a move that later died in a Senate filibuster), the poverty program, and other key legislation of the 1965 session. Unquestionably the Great Society legislative programs passed by the 89th Congress would have been defeated without their support. Table 4-2 documents ten of the key votes.

This is not to say that they never opposed the Administration. When the situs-picketing bill was being pushed by the House Democratic leadership in 1966, for example, the freshmen resisted. In a special meeting they requested with the leadership, they argued that they had taken a political gamble by supporting the repeal of Section 14 (b) in 1965 despite the fact that many of the states have right-to-work laws. After the freshmen went out on a political limb, the Administration did not succeed in securing passage of the bill in the Senate. The freshmen advised Majority Leader Carl Albert that they resented having to take a position on the situs-picketing bill before it was known whether or not the Senate would go along with it. The bill was never brought to the House floor.

Sometimes the drive to avoid being tagged as a rubber stamp by the Republicans had a comic aspect. While one suburban freshman from a formerly Republican district was being interviewed, his administrative assistant entered and excitedly announced the sad news that the agriculture bill the freshman had voted against the previous day was not an administration-sponsored measure. The congressman responded, "Damn it—we missed again and we won't have many more opportunities."[4]

Reelection Realities

In early 1965, the political strategy of the freshmen from the marginal districts was reflective of the presumably stronger Republican position in the off-year election of 1966. The conduct of the freshmen in regard to presidential support was of primary interest. In effect, Johnson would be on the ballot with them even though he was not running, due to the extensive legislation produced by the popular mandate of the 1964 election.

But the Johnson program had mixed success, due in large part to the economic drain of the war in Vietnam. Many programs were oversold, such as the war on poverty. Charges of mismanagement in the Job Corps and the Community Action Program, delays in implementing the urban-affairs program, and violence in the cities put the President's supporters on the defensive. The economic issues became a liability for Democrats in 1966, whereas in 1964 the economic environment had favored them.

In the late summer President Johnson let it be known that he would campaign in all fifty states before November, a move literally unprecedented

Table 4-2
Ten Great-Society Votes of the 89th Congress
Total Vote

	Margin P = Passed D = Defeated	Total		Dem.		Rep.		Freshmen Votes Dem.[b]		Rep.	
		For	Against	Pro	Con	Pro	Con	Pro	Con	Pro	Con
Bypassing of Rules Comm. under 21-day rule	P–22	224	202	208	79	16	123	62	7	0	20
Republican alternative to medicare[a]	D–45	191	236	63	226	128	10	7	64	20	0
Establish Dept. of Housing and Urban Development	P–33	217	184	208	66	9	118	59	10	0	18
Amendment to delete rent supplements from Authorization bill[a]	D–6	202	208	72	204	130	4	10	55	20	0
Republican amendment to delete supplemental appropriations for rent supplements[a]	P–23	185	162	86	160	99	2	16	48	17	0
Republican amendment to Antipoverty bill to cut funds & retain governor's veto[a]	D–49	178	227	57	214	121	13	6	61	19	1
Repeal of right-to-work laws (Sec. 148)	P–18	221	203	200	86	21	117	61	8	1	18
Republican amendment to delete rent supplements from supplemental appropriation bill for fiscal 1966[a]	D–8	190	198	65	192	125	6	15	53	18	0
"War on Poverty" Appropriation Increase	P–54	210	156	195	51	15	105	54	4	0	16
Amendments to Foreign Assistance Act of 1961[a]	D–2	191	193	70	189	121	4	13	54	18	0

a Indicates Nay vote supports President's position
b Includes all 70 freshman Democrats, including 20 whose seats were held by Democrats in the 89th Congress
Source: Thomas P. Murphy, "The Extraordinary Power of Freshmen in Congress," *Transaction*, March 1968, p. 36.

for an off-year election. However, as the polls showed his popularity continuing to decline, he concluded that the magic carpet that his name represented to his party in the 1964 election would best be transformed into an Oriental rug in 1966. And so he undertook a seventeen-day Asiatic trip.

The Democrats of the class of 1964 believed in the Great Society. In 1966, as election time drew near, many of them moved closer to the Republican position on economic or other issues—especially when Johnson did not need their vote. The Democratic plurality on noncontroversial issues was large enough to permit considerable "antiAdministration" voting useful in building up an image of independence. However, when the tough issues were on the floor the freshmen shouldered their share of the load and took the political heat that often followed. This loyalty is best illustrated by their support, in the closing days of the Congress, of the Demonstration Cities bill, which was so necessary to the implementation of the program of the Department of Housing and Urban Development. It won by a vote of 142 to 126. Thirty-two of the fifty-one freshmen who had taken Republican seats were still in Washington despite the imminence of the election. They voted 29 to 3 for the bill, once again providing the total margin of victory.

Despite this display of political courage, twenty-two of these freshmen did not return to Washington in 1967. On November 8, 1966 they paid the price for their support of the Great Society program. The irony is that in all but a few cases it was not their voting records that defeated them. They were simply swept up in the tides of a Republican year, as well as the reflex reaction to 1964.

In 1966, the voters seemed to be responding to something more intangible—they were expressing a mood of uneasiness and frustration regarding Vietnam, the economy, and violence in the cities. In addition, it would have taken a near-miracle to reelect Democratic freshmen from some of the traditionally Republican districts that reacted against Barry Goldwater in 1964 by voting for Democrats for Congress. In 1966 the situation was different, since there was growing disenchantment with President Johnson.

When interviewed before the election virtually all of these freshmen intimated that they would vote the same way again—even knowing it might bring their political careers to an untimely end. Although each of them clearly hoped to be among the survivors on election day, they also believed that they would be vindicated if most of their group could be reelected. In later conversations, some of the defeated representatives stressed the positive fact that twenty-five of the Democratic freshmen who took Republican seats in 1964 were returned to office. They also pointed out that in most cases the Republicans had to switch to a more liberal type of Republican candidate to defeat them, so that loss of support for the programs they voted into law would not be as great as the election returns indicated.[5]

Winners and losers alike, these freshmen left their mark on the Congress, its processes and leadership, leading qualified professional analysts to predict that Congress would never be the same. Despite the odds against their reelection, they also demonstrated that political courage can be good politics, thus providing strong encouragement to the developing New Politics movement of which they were a part.

Republican Freshmen and the 90th Congress

The 90th Congress presents a marked contrast to the hyperactive 89th. The 90th Congress, faced with racial conflict of revolutionary dimensions, bitterly divided by the commitment in Vietnam, and with a Republican-controlled freshman class, concentrated on wielding the ax to trim Administration programs. Particularly in the area of urban legislation, the forty-eight Republican freshmen had a controlling voice in dictating policy—and they were aided by many Democrats reluctant to support a tax increase without some compensatory reductions in federal spending.

In 1967 it had seemed that the Democrats might feel properly chastised and, faced with a smaller majority in the House, regroup under the President's leadership in the interests of self-preservation. But this did not occur in the 90th Congress. In fact, the liberal Democratic Study Group, which had been a major element in the organization and record of the 89th Congress, didn't function at all during the first session because the members could not find anyone to accept the chairmanship.

Though reduced in number, the sophomore survivors, who exerted such power as freshmen in the 89th Congress, continued to be a bulwark of support to the Administration. The 1966 crop of Democratic freshmen, however, seemed to have other ideas. Of the ten urban issues recorded in table 4-3, the Democratic freshmen and the Republican freshmen voted against the President on three, whereas the forty-one Democratic sophomores who first joined the Congress in the 1964 Johnson landslide continued to give the President lopsided support. On only five of the ten votes did the Democratic freshmen vote with the Democratic sophomores. As for the other two votes, the Democratic freshmen split their votes evenly on the ninth, but on the tenth vote (the Teacher Corps bill) they opposed the President when both the Democratic sophomores and the Republican freshmen supported him— a truly remarkable situation.

The motion to kill the Model Cities appropriation was defeated by twenty votes: The G.O.P. freshmen voted 37 to 10 for the cutback. The squeeze on rent supplements was approved, with the Republican freshmen voting 41 to 7 for reducing the appropriation. But President Johnson's Appalachian Development bill passed by twenty-one votes, despite the fact that the Republican freshmen voted against it 34 to 14. In this instance, Democratic party discipline, bringing votes of 11 to 3 from the Democratic freshmen and 31 to 7 from the Democratic sophomores, saved the Administration's bill.

At the end of September 1967, the Republican-sponsored motion for recommittal of continuing appropriations joined the fiscal battle against the Administration. It was passed by twenty votes: the Republicans, including all forty-eight freshmen, voted as a bloc for the motion. Just six days later, however, a Democratic motion to prevent further delay of continuing appropriations was passed by eight votes. The Republicans again voted as a solid bloc in opposition, but this time the Administration succeeded in getting nine Democrats, seven from the South (including the influential Wilbur Mills of Arkansas), to switch their votes. Had the Administration been able

Table 4-3
90th Congress House Votes on Urban Legislation (as of 9/5/67)

	Margin P=Passed D=Defeated	Dem. Pro	Dem. Con	Rep. Pro	Rep. Con	Freshman Votes Dem. Pro	Freshman Votes Dem. Con	Freshman Votes Rep. Pro	Freshman Votes Rep. Con	Democratic Sophomore Votes Pro	Democratic Sophomore Votes Con
Rat Control (1)	D— 31	154	59	22	148	6	8	6	41	33	5
Delete Model Cities Approp.[a]	D— 20	52	178	141	35	5	9	37	10	5	34
Cut Back Rent Supplements[a]	P— 61	69	159	163	12	8	6	41	7	10	29
Disapproval of DC Reorg. Bill[a]	D— 84	50	180	110	64	7	7	25	21	6	33
Elementary School Aid	P—172	195	42	99	80	10	4	35	13	35	4
Not Renew Teacher Corps[a]	D—111	63	162	83	95	9	5	14	34	7	32
Appalachian Development Bill	P— 21	154	45	35	123	11	3	13	34	31	7
Rat Control (2)	P— 54	159	63	68	110	5	9	18	30	32	5
Recommit Continuing Appropriations[a]	P— 20	34	182	168	0	6	8	48	0	3	36
HJ Res. 853 (Continue Appropriations)	P— 8	213	25	0	180	9	5	0	48	36	3

[a] Indicates Nay vote supports President's position.
Source: Thomas P. Murphy, "The Extraordinary Power of Freshmen in Congress," *Transaction*, March 1968, p. 37.

to peel off ten votes from the northern Republican freshman bloc in the first place, the original recommittal motion would have been defeated without recourse to soliciting vote-switching from the southern Democrats. These two votes illustrate the newfound effectiveness, at least in fiscal matters, of G. O. P. party discipline, as well as the peril to Administration measures presented by Republican bloc voting.

The defeat of the first rat-control measure was accomplished by a solid 41 to 6 Republican freshman vote against the bill (which threatened to immortalize the 90th as the "Rat Congress"). When a second rat-control bill passed by fifty-four votes, it was because thirty-eight Republicans switched their votes. The Democratic vote was virtually unchanged.

In late September 1967, the fiscal battle began in earnest. Twenty-eight G. O. P. freshmen sent a letter to the House Speaker urging a six-day, extended-hour work week and asking for "some procedural improvements in the House of Representatives."[6] This incident later made national headlines, when Democrat Charles Vanik of Ohio pointed out that twelve of the petitioners were absent for a roll-call vote on the same day the letter was sent. On October 10, a package of bills intended to deal with the issue of organized crime was submitted by twenty-three freshman Republicans. They charged that organized crime was preying on the urban poor.

These events illustrate two significant points. First, members of the freshman bloc, in this case the Republicans, are sufficiently aware of their potential power to take concerted action; and second, the party leadership can take advantage of this potential either to propose or to oppose legislation. In the 90th Congress, the keynote was opposition.

The Administration, faced with a large deficit stemming from the staggering costs of the Vietnam War, had enough trouble holding the line on established programs without trying to initiate new ones. As with the rent supplement and model cities bills, the Senate reverted to its traditional role as a court of last appeal for the restoration of House cuts. But the fiscal conservatism in the House is logical: the entire membership of the House was up for reelection in 1968, whereas only one-third of their Senate colleagues were.

Republican and Democratic Prospects

The legislative record that the G. O. P. put before the voters in 1968 was largely negative. It showed opposition to Administration proposals, but few constructive counterproposals. Republican negativism at the congressional level, however, stood in sharp contrast with the behavior of state and local Republican leaders. Eight Republican governors, headed by Nelson Rockefeller, rather than simply running against Johnson programs, proposed a sixty point program of their own for dealing with the urban crisis.

The voice of moderate Republicanism, which was stilled at the 1964 Republican convention, made itself heard at the state and local levels in 1968—but, with the exception of a few senators, it was noticeably silent on Capitol

Hill. Of course, the battle for the Republican Party was eventually decided by the county chairmen at Miami. But the party's schizophrenia was already evident in the contrast between its negative congressional record and the positive public pronouncements of Governors Romney and Rockefeller or with the vigorous public policies of Republican mayors like New York's John Lindsay, who tried to resolve his dilemma by becoming a Democrat.

Some Democratic governors, in contrast to the Republican governors, initiated "Governors' Revolt" after the 1966 election, attempting to exert a more conservative influence on their national party leadership. This effort, which took the form of pressure for greater federal dependence on state governments—for example, and for federal-state tax-sharing plans—had the support of the Democratic freshmen in the 90th Congress. By supporting this move toward conservatism, the new freshmen came into conflict with the Democratic sophomores—those freshmen from the class of 1964 who were reelected in 1966.

This record of conservatism among new House Democrats is at least partially due to the fact that the twenty-six Democratic freshmen of 1964 who were defeated in 1966 represented the liberal wing of the party. Had they not been defeated, the record of the 90th Congress might have been far different. Nevertheless, some of the key freshmen from the 89th and 90th Congresses have survived a number of election tests and still provide much of the New Politics leadership to the House.

Increased Freshman Power

Whatever the outcome of the congressional and presidential races, several elements are enhancing the power of freshman congressmen. Important precedents were set by the freshman delegations of the 89th and 90th Congresses. Both delegations, one heavily Democratic and the other heavily Republican, had enough votes to determine the outcome of major issues.

This power was due in part to the size of the freshman delegations— seventy-four Democrats in the 89th and forty-nine Republicans in the 90th. There were a total of fifty-three Democratic and Republican freshmen in the 91st Congress (1969-70), fifty-eight in the 92nd, and seventy in the 93rd. What is important is that the larger freshmen groups mobilized this power with a view toward group interest.

This increase in their potential power and the psychological changes making them willing to use it have allowed freshmen to successfully challenge many House traditions. They rejected the idea that freshmen should be seen and not heard. Keeping quiet, they argued, is not the way to be reelected. They supported and even led revolts against prestigious committee chairmen. In short, the House of Representatives will never be the same.[7]

One basic reason for this new aggressiveness among freshman Congressmen is the greater competition for House seats. This greater competition means that winning candidates are probably better qualified than their predecessors; and it means that an elected congressman, to be reelected, must try to achieve more for his constituents as well as become better known to them.

This increasing competition for congressional seats has at least two causes:

1. The growing number of election districts unsafe for either party. In recent House elections, both Republicans and Democrats invaded districts once earmarked for the opposition. These forays aided by the declining power of the old-time party machines, have turned many safe districts into marginal ones. The Democratic machine in lower Manhattan and in some parts of the South, for example, can no longer count on electing a listless party regular if they face energetic opposition. Likewise, the precedent-setting election of six Democrats in Iowa's seven-member delegation in 1964 has made that state much more competitive.

2. The growing political power of the suburbs. The suburbs are becoming larger and more politically heterogeneous due to the migration of liberal middle-class Democrats from the urban core. They will become even more powerful politically, because reapportionment and redistricting on a one-man, one-vote basis will increase their representation.

In short, the spread of the two-party system to some traditionally Democratic northern cities, to the Democratic South, and to the farm states (once traditionally Republican), together with the new power of the politically divided suburbs, is increasing competition for public office. This in turn may be breeding a more vigorous type of congressmen.

The higher level of voter education may be another cause of freshman assertiveness. The unqualified congressional candidate may find it more and more difficult to mislead people into voting for him. This too would tend to increase the level of competence and performance among new congressmen—and so be another element contributing to the growth of freshman power.

But whatever the origins of the new freshman power, it may still face one major limitation. A new kind of interdependence between presidential and congressional elections may be emerging. When large numbers of freshman candidates upset opposition-party incumbents, these switches usually occur in marginal districts. But the victorious new congressmen may soon make a jolting discovery: while their votes can make the difference in passing or defeating the President's programs, their own fate at the polls, because of the marginal nature of their districts, may well be in the President's hands. In an age when the mass media have created the cult of the presidential personality, so that the public may identify all party candidates with the man who leads the party, the voters, even in a congressional election, may really be voting for or against the President. If so, the political fortunes of the nation's congressmen will vary—directly or inversely, depending upon their party affiliation—with the fortunes of the man in the White House.

**Part II
Internal Congressional Changes**

5

New Politics in the House of Representatives

The values most closely identified with the New Politics movements—increased and meaningful participation, nonarbitrary decision-making, and openness—have been increasingly apparent in the House and in the party caucuses since 1960. Considering the tendency of the 1972 Democratic convention to reduce the participation of House members in party decisions, it is interesting to review how operative New Politics has been in the House.

In the Federalist papers, James Madison commented, "If angels were to govern men, neither external nor internal control on government would be necessary."[1] However, in setting the foundations of government administered by men over men one "must enable the government to control the governed and in the next place oblige it to control itself."[2] Externally the legislative, executive, and judicial branches were consciously constructed to check each other.

But Madison's theoretical checks between branches would have to operate in a dynamic atmosphere where, as it developed, partisan forces constantly work to create one party or branch more equal than another. Whether legislators elected by a diverse society would form a body possessing inherent democratic safeguards for minority interests quickly became a practical question. It remained to be seen whether a Congress set up with such attention to representation could in fact govern.

Early in the twentieth century the Democratic Caucus adopted a rule that requires members to support the Caucus position on matters of party policy or principle if two-thirds of those present and voting (amounting to a majority of the whole Democratic membership) at a Caucus adopt such a position.[3] The only exceptions relate to constitutional questions and commitments made to the constituency prior to the election. The existence of such a procedure has the potential for abuse. Theoretically, a majority of one party that is less than a majority of the House can control a House decision through this process. That majority, though, could be a progressive or a reactionary group. The process itself is neutral, and the effect of its usage depends upon the values of the majority at any particular time.

Since the House leadership generally holds the pivotal position regarding House procedures, the historical pattern of House reformers has been to challenge procedural rules rather than the leadership that applies them. Essentially, this has been done because of the greater chance of success.

Prior to the New Politics movement, which blossomed with John. F. Kennedy's election, there were two major twentieth-century changes in those procedures. The first was an assault on the powers of House Speaker Joseph P. Cannon, who was using the House rules to support his personal legislative preferences and to impede those of progressive Democrats and Republicans.

69

This revolt against "Cannonism" began with the adoption in 1909 of the Calendar Wednesday Rule, which allowed committee chairmen or specified members to call up bills without clearance from the Rules Committee.[4] Progressives heralded this as a major reform, enabling the House to consider bills favored by a committee but opposed by the leadership. As a practical matter, the rule change failed to meet its supporters' expectations.

Later in 1909, a group of insurgents, including thirty Republicans led by George Norris of Nebraska and John Nelson of Wisconsin, successfully defeated the normally perfunctory motion to adopt the rules of the preceding Congress. The insurgents proposed the following rule changes:

1. End the Speaker's authority to appoint committee members and chairmen;
2. Remove the Speaker from the Rules Committee;
3. Enlarge the Rules Committee from five to fifteen members.

Initially, these aims were defeated, but in March of 1910 all were realized, and the Rules Committee was expanded to ten members.[5]

A second and more sweeping reform effort was the Legislative Reorganization Act of 1946. This act fathered such necessary innovations of increasing staff resources and reducing the number of House standing committees from forty-eight to nineteen and Senate standing committees from thirty-three to fifteen.[6] The 1946 Act was a product of the Joint Committee on the Organization of Congress, which was cochaired by Senator Robert M. La-Follette, Jr. and Representative A. S. Mike Monroney. While these changes were all procedural and concerned the relationship of the members to the leadership, they had an impact on the division of labor in the House and on participation, decision-making, and openness.

New Politics in the Kennedy Congress

With the election of John F. Kennedy in 1960, the Democrats regained the presidency after an eight-year lapse. The opportunity for providing new national leadership seemed at hand, as one party was in command of both the executive and legislative branches of the government for the first time since 1952. In addition, a large number of New-Politics-oriented intellectuals and liberals descended upon Washington in response to the Kennedy charisma.

The House of Representatives in 1961 was dominated by Speaker Sam Rayburn, Majority Leader John McCormack, Rules Committee Chairman Howard Smith, Appropriations Committee Chairman Clarence Cannon, and Armed Services Committee Chairman Carl Vinson. All might be classified as basically conservative, and all except McCormack had southern origins. On the Republican side of the fence, Charles Halleck of Indiana was the Minority Leader and Les Arends of Illinois was the Whip. The Republicans tended to align themselves with the conservative Democratic elements in the House, thus creating the so-called Conservative Coalition, a formidable power bloc confronting Kennedy's legislative program. What developed was a discouraging uphill legislative fight between Congress and the advocates of the New Frontier. Key Administration items like a tax cut, medical care for the aged, and funding for education were not popular in the House.

But it was also in the House of Representatives that the roots of what was to be called the New Politics developed.

In 1961 Kennedy's attempt to make Congress respond was launched in the House with a fight to enlarge the House Rules Committee. The House Rules Committee is essentially the gatekeeper or traffic cop for the House, which handles five times as many bills as the Senate. Bills introduced in the House each year are put into the legislative hopper and then referred by the Speaker's office to the respective legislative committees. Once a legislative committee has completed work on a bill and the bill is ready to be sent to the floor of the House, a rule is requested on the bill from the Rules Committee.

Here is where the gatekeeper function of the Rules Committee comes into play. Since the House calendar is always crowded, the Rules Committee holds the bill until, in its judgment, the calendar is sufficiently clear to accept new legislation. Prior to putting the bill on the calendar, the Rules Committee considers the procedures that it will recommend be used on the House floor while this particular bill is under consideration. For instance, it determines whether debate should be limited, and whether the bill can be amended or not. The bill is then put on a calendar with the recommended conditions to be followed during its consideration. Finally, the House must approve the committee's ruling before considering that particular bill.

In 1961, the Kennedy Administration, with the support of House Speaker Sam Rayburn, deemed it necessary to the success of its legislative program to enlarge this very conservative Rules Committee from twelve to fifteen members. At stake in this effort to expand the committee was the issue of what groups were going to share the power of the Rules Committee. While numerically under Democratic control, the majority of the Committee represented the Conservative Coalition of southern Democrats and conservative Republicans. The Committee was dominated by its Chairman Judge Howard Smith of Virginia, who knew how to use his powers to the utmost. Rayburn spearheaded the successful fight to add two liberal Democrats to the Committee and won with a margin of five votes—217 to 212.[7]

Even though the Rules Committee was expanded, political scientist James Robinson noted that the "larger-sized committee had not made much 'objective difference' in the conduct of House business, and the weight of the committee's power seems not to have been altered much and in fact it continued to bargain with legislative committees about the form of the bill in exchange for a rule."[8]

For example, in 1961, the House Education and Labor Committee reported a clean bill extending and expanding the National Defense Education Act of 1958 (NDEA). However, Majority Leader McCormack wanted assurances that private and Catholic schools would also benefit from the bill.

The Rules Committee voted to withhold floor action and delay the bill. Adam Clayton Powell, the chairman of the Education and Labor Committee, tried to discharge the NDEA bill through the Calendar Wednesday procedure, but did not secure the necessary votes.[9]

The Rules Committee also bargained with House legislators concerning House bills going into conference with the Senate. In 1966, in order to get an education bill released for conference, Chairman Powell and Edith Green, who led the House conference, had to promise Rules Committee chairman William Colmer that under no circumstances would they accept certain portions of the Senate version of the bill.[10]

Another anti-New Politics tactic the Rules Committee increasingly used after its expansion of 1961 was the closed rule. When a bill is approved for floor consideration under such a rule, there can be no amendments. It must be voted upon in the form in which it passes through the Rules Committee. This procedure reduces the options available to the House, increases the negotiating power of the Rules Committee, and creates a less open and participatory decision-making environment.

Leadership changes occurred in the House as a result of Sam Rayburn's death in November 1961 and John McCormack's succession to the post. Moving up in leadership positions were Carl Albert, who became Majority Leader, and Hale Boggs of Louisiana, who replaced him as Majority Whip. Albert was a former Rhodes scholar of a less conservative bent than Rayburn; McCormack was from liberal- and New-Politics-oriented Massachusetts, which suggested that New Politics positions might now have a better political environment.

However, McCormack lacked Rayburn's control of the House Democrats. The House of Representatives during the Kennedy Administration was likened by some to a headless horseman. Not only was the leadership unable to control power brokers like Clarence Cannon, the aged Appropriations Committee Chairman, and Howard Smith, representing the Rules Committee, but it was also being embarrassed by the more moderate and liberal side. Many of these Democrats were unhappy with the Kennedy Administration in general and, as the 1962 off-year elections drew near, the mood became one of truculence and in some cases bitterness toward the President. They felt he was not sufficiently helpful to them in their reelection campaigns. Many liberal members also believed that Kennedy's legislative program lacked political appeal. Medical care for the aged just did not have much political mileage in 1962. As a result of this mood, legislation such as the Free Trade bill, which had been expected to pass easily in 1962, became the subject of bitter debate.[11] Many Republicans bucked their leadership and strongly opposed it.

Another underlying cause for this dissatisfaction was the feeling of some that the President had accelerated the decline of congressional stature by ignoring the legislative branch as a policy-making arm of the government. This feeling of neglect was very well illustrated in Armed Services Committee Chairman Carl Vinson's tangle with Secretary of Defense Robert McNamara over funding for the RB-70 manned bombers. Vinson believed very strongly that the U.S. should build this bomber, but McNamara and his advisers did not consider it wise to do so. Vinson drafted legislation that mandated the President to spend the necessary funds for the bombers—a precursor of the Nixon-Congress struggle over presidential impoundment. A head-on clash was averted, with each side compromising to some extent.[12] However, it was unlikely that Vinson would have attempted such a confrontation with the Administration if he had been consulted more frequently. During the Eisenhower years Vinson had exercised considerable power and now believed that he was being ignored by the Kennedy Administration. There were other chairmen who felt the same way.

They also believed that the President was making overly extensive use of executive powers in promoting civil rights and in rolling back the steel prices without consulting Congress. In doing so Kennedy was taking advice from the liberal intellectuals associated with his Administration. The press did not help when it billed these people as charismatic types coming into Washington to save the nation from outmoded congressmen. Some of the New Frontiersmen did not hide their disdain for the intellectual powers of the legislators. Powerful congressmen were made to feel like fifth wheels, and so they exercised what power they had in the legislative area to delay the Kennedy legislative program.

Members of the House were also unhappy with the lobbying tactics used by the Administration. For example, a large number of Administration officials converged on the House to lobby for a controversial farm bill. Extensive dissatisfaction was expressed by House members over this type of pressure and the leadership requested the Administration not to repeat such tactics. However, other Administration lobbying efforts were also under fire. One congressman received ten phone calls from various Administration officials urging support of a bill that already had his support. Members were also reporting not-so-subtle threats that such items as post offices would not be approved in their districts if they did not vote for a bill.[13] Discontent with these Administration tactics manifested itself in bottled-up legislation, bitter partisan fights on the floor, and criticism of both the leadership and the Administration.

Realizing the President's inability to gain the cooperation of his own party, Republicans became more vocal in their opposition. Procedural fights within Congress were also responsible for delaying passage of important legislation. A power struggle between Senator Carl Hayden of the Senate Appropriations Committee and Representative Cannon as to where Senate-House Conference meetings on appropriations bills were to be held and who was to preside had prevented action on any appropriations bills for several months in mid-1962.

The 88th Congress convened in January of 1963 with what one reporter termed an "apathy hangover."[14] President Kennedy decided to concentrate on one important bill, tax relief, which he deemed vital to the economy. While the 1962 elections did not really change the face of the House, new undercurrents of revolt were beginning to surface. The election of two southern liberals to the House Ways and Means Committee was one. Instead of electing the controversial and conservative Phil Landrum of Georgia, the increasingly New-Politics-oriented Democratic Caucus revolted and approved the more liberal and acceptable Pat Jennings of Virginia and Ross Bass of Tennessee. This was a shock to the Democratic leadership, which had promised the assignment to Landrum.[15]

Serious dissatisfaction also was being registered in the Republican ranks. The younger members—including Melvin Laird of Wisconsin, Gerald Ford of Michigan, Charles Goodell of New York, Robert Griffin of Michigan, and Albert Quie of Minnesota—were challenging Charlie Halleck's leadership. To assuage them, Halleck appointed Laird to the House Republican Policy Committee and also began to consult more frequently with them. However, at the beginning of the 88th Congress, the Party Conference meeting, in a slap at Halleck's leadership, voted to replace Conference chairman Charles Hoeven with Gerald Ford. The younger Republicans complained that Halleck was too negative and had failed to promote any GOP alternatives to Kennedy legislation—a theme that became even more important to House Republicans during the Johnson Administration.[16] However, Halleck faced a dilemma. On the one hand he had the more liberal group, who wanted Republican-style legislation on medicare, urban mass transit, aid to education, and other "liberal" causes, and on the other the powerful ultra-conservative Republicans who wanted no government programs in these areas.

One of the first results of the "alternative legislation" push by the younger Republicans was the introduction in February 1963 of a broad civil rights bill. It was similar to Judiciary Chairman Celler's bill, but the Republicans were seeking to embarrass the Kennedy Administration by submitting their own proposal. But despite these legislative maneuvers, a lethargic atmosphere gripped the Congress, particularly the House, and major legislation remained in committees.[17]

The Johnson Honeymoon

The assassination of John Kennedy in November 1963 stunned the House of Representatives. The legislation that had been bottled up in committees came pouring out. President Johnson, taking advantage of this, pushed Congress almost unmercifully. By his personal involvement in congressional matters he kept the heat on the decision-makers. Whatever methods the new President used, they were effective. A civil rights bill passed that was stronger than any Kennedy had ever offered and appropriations bills that had been tied up for months were finally passed. It was almost as if Congress was attempting to make amends to the dead President.

After the initial shock of Kennedy's death had worn off, Johnson's skill in handling the Congress and his personal devotion to the details necessary for passage of legislation through complicated parliamentary maneuverings kept Congress moving. The 88th Congress closed without any reversals for the Democratic leadership. The stage was set for the Great Society Congress.

The Democratic Caucus as the beginning of the 89th Congress addressed itself to a number of issues. With its ranks swelled by some sixty-five freshmen, Democrats had the largest majority since 1937. Reform was the password, and one of the most important reforms as far as the liberals were concerned was to establish the twenty-one-day rule.

Upon instructions from the Caucus, Majority Leader Carl Albert introduced H. Res. 8 on the first day of the 89th Congress. According to H. Res. 8, a member recognized by the Speaker on the floor of the House could request a bill to go to conference, and upon a majority vote of the House, his request would be honored. Another provision in the resolution stripped the House Rules Committee of the power to refuse to send a House-passed measure to conference with the Senate. Heretofore a bill had needed the unanimous consent of the House or a rule from the Rules Committee to send it to conference. Passage of this resolution would curtail Rules Committee autonomy and its ability to undermine majority rule.[18]

A successful effort had been made in 1949 to institute the twenty-one-day rule, but the rule did not last more than one session before going down to defeat at the hands of a revitalized Conservative Coalition. This time Carl Albert floor-managed the resolution, and together with Speaker McCormack collected the necessary votes to enable its passage. It passed by a vote of 224 to 204, with 16 of 139 Republicans voting for it. Within the Democratic Party, northern Democrats voted 185 to 4 for it, and 23 southern Democrats voted for it while 75 voted against it. The new Minority leader Gerald Ford and Judge Howard Smith, Chairman of the Rules Committee, argued against the establishment of the twenty-one-day rule in 1965 just as they had in previous years.[19]

The influx of liberal first-term Democrats into the 89th Congress is credited with breaking the back of the Conservative Coalition. According to *Congressional Quarterly,* in 1965 the Coalition obtained its lowest percentage of victories (33 per cent) since scores were first measured in 1957.[20]

Table 5-1 figures are the percentages of victory when the Coalition was mobilized on a measure.

Johnson made superb use of the advantages of the overpowering majority of liberal Democrats to obtain an unprecedented amount of legislation concerning education, aging, health, and aid to urban areas. Much of it had been around the halls of Congress for a long time. But important new legis-

Table 5-1
Conservative Coalition Victory Percentage, 1961-65

Year	Total %	Senate %	House %
1961	55	48	74
1962	62	71	44
1963	50	44	67
1964	51	47	67
1965	33	39	25

Source: *Congressional Quarterly Almanac,* (Washington, D.C.: Congressional Quarterly Service, 1965), p. 1083.

lation like the Antipoverty bill was also passed that clearly bore the LBJ brand.

The New Politics contingent also took advantage of their numbers to establish a Joint Committee on the Reorganization of Congress, chaired by Senator A. S. "Mike" Monroney of Oklahoma. After much argument, liberal backers of the committee in the House accepted the guidelines for the committee, even though they prohibited review of rules and parliamentary procedures, practices, and precedents of the Senate and House. While this was quite restrictive, liberals decided that half a loaf was better than no loaf at all and agreed to the guidelines in order to get the Joint Committee established. Members of the committee from the House side were Ray Madden of Indiana, Jack Brooks of Texas, and Ken Hechler of West Virginia. Republicans included Thomas Curtis and Durwood Hall of Missouri and Robert Griffin of Michigan.[21]

One of the most unusual legislative efforts in the 89th Congress was Wilbur Mills's face-saving efforts concerning medicare legislation. When his Ways and Means Committee was enlarged over his strong objections with two more liberal Democrats, and since he could no longer count on defeating the bill on the floor in this largely liberal House, Mills was ready to concede a bill. He was determined, however, to put his own stamp on it (H. R. 1). Meanwhile, John Byrnes of Wisconsin, ranking Republican on the Ways and Means Committee, introduced a bill that went far beyond H. R. 1 as proposed by the Administration. Mills held hearings on the proposals, and even Administration officials admitted that Byrnes's proposal was a good one. So Mills dumped the Administration's bill and adopted the Republican proposal, which passed after some further amending.

In his efforts to get legislation passed, Lyndon Johnson created unlikely alliances of big-city Democrats and midwestern farm conservatives, particularly in the House. For instance, big-city Democrats agreed to assist in the passage of a complex wheat-cotton bill in exchange for support of a bill providing aid to mass transit.

One of Johnson's finest hours was the utilization of Phil Landrum of Georgia, a conservative and a ranking member of the House Education and Labor Committee, as House floor manager for the War on Poverty bill. Adam Clayton Powell, the Committee chairman, who normally would have managed the bill, stayed in the background. Johnson also enlisted the support of the AFL-CIO, which to say the least disliked Landrum. The effort was successful. Landrum was palatable to the conservative element, and with the powerful support of the labor lobby, the bill passed the House.[22]

While the legislative accomplishments of the 89th Congress are legendary, that Congress is also notable for the way the liberals used the complicated House parliamentary procedures to defeat the Conservative Coalition in its attempt to overturn the Supreme Court's school prayer decision through a constitutional amendment. Liberals also defeated the Coalition's attempt to pass a law curbing court-ordered reapportionment of the states.

Congressmen like Adam Clayton Powell, wishing to capitalize on the predominantly liberal Congress, wanted to develop their own legislation. Powell announced that his powerful prolabor subcommittee was going to hold hearings on the thirty-two-hour week and consider a minimum annual wage of $2,100. This displeased both the leadership and the Administration, as it went far beyond what anyone else was prepared to do at that time.[23]

Others like Henry Reuss of Wisconsin were proposing adoption of new rules, including one permitting a floor vote on bills stranded in committees. Richard Bolling of Missouri was calling for a reshaping of the power structure in the House and the removal from committee chairmanships of those who opposed the Administration's programs. His main target was the southerners, who gained their chairman posts on the basis of seniority. Nevertheless, the energetic 89th Congress closed without any drastic reforms in procedures or changes in the seniority system.

Many reasons are advanced for the floodtide of legislation that was produced in the 89th Congress and no one explanation suffices. Years of spadework had gone before it. The educating processes begun in the late fifties and nourished in the Kennedy Administration regarding such legislation as civil rights, federal funding of education, and medicare finally bore fruit. The persistent prodding of the Congress in the early sixties by the Kennedy Administration, plus Johnson's consummate skill and meticulous attention to detail—coupled with a large liberal majority in the House—finally resulted in this massive outpouring of legislation.

The Post-Great Society Congress and the Republican Resurgence

The 1966 off-year election was a problem for the New Politics freshmen Democrats who came in on Johnson's coattails. Predictably, the Republicans picked up forty-seven seats in the House and pushed liberals into a little more conservative position. The resulting change in committee ratios hurt the Administration's chances for easy passage of its legislation. Many of these new Republicans were young and in the activist spirit of Gerald Ford. An interesting sidelight here is that Richard Nixon campaigned heavily and quite successfully for many of the Republican freshmen in 1966, emerging as a major Republican spokesman for his efforts.

The Republican leadership announced that excessive federal spending on the part of the Democratic Administration was causing inflation. Their principal theme was going to be that the budget must be reduced. However, Minority Leader Gerald Ford and Conference Chairman Melvin Laird were also working to strengthen the Party's power base in the House, with an eye toward the national elections in 1968. Ford concentrated on building a Republican legislative program, while Laird used his position as chairman of the Republican Conference to garner assistance from various sources in developing a legislative program for the Party. The result of their efforts was a forty-four-point legislative program that even won praise from the liberal *Washington Post*. One of the forty-four points was that a law should be passed requiring full disclosure of campaign finances.[24]

Laird also co-opted the concept of revenue-sharing for the Republican Party, and even persuaded Everett Dirksen to endorse it. Laird attacked LBJ's East-West trade proposal. Using information developed by one of his collegial think tanks, he stated that the proposal was not timely and that the open Soviet support for North Vietnam would cause the American people to oppose it.

Republican leadership in the House shifted ideologically as Laird swung to the right and Goodell to the left. Ford occupied the middle, and always insisted that one of the key party strategies should be that the Republicans stand on their own and not just vote with the Southern Democrats.

Democrats were experiencing some of the same discontent that enveloped the Republicans in 1965. However, it did not result in a wholesale turnover of the leadership. The New Politics Democrats were particularly unhappy. They were committed to LBJ's legislative program and they wanted it to pass, but felt unable to communicate with Speaker McCormack. They used Majority Leader Carl Albert as their pipeline and held strategy sessions with Administration people. One result of their pressures on the leadership was a promise by Colmer of the Rules Committee that he would not unduly hold up legislation in the Rules Committee.[25]

One of the frustrations of the liberals was the seeming inertia of senior Democrats in key positions. For instance, William Dawson of Illinois, chairman of the Government Operations Committee, sat on the Intergovernmental Cooperation Act, which would have benefited his own constituency. Emanuel Celler, while continuing his strong efforts in the civil rights field, totally neglected antitrust legislation. Seventy-four-year-old Ray Madden of Indiana, senior member of the Legislative Reorganization Committee and senior member of the Rules Committee, was another source of dissatisfaction. The Legislative Reorganization Act had been passed in the Senate in 1967. However, when the bill (S 355) reached the House, Speaker McCormack referred it to the Rules Committee. It was argued that the bill changed House rules, and since it contained a number of amendments added by the Senate that had not been considered by any committee, some study of the bill was needed before it went to the floor of the House. Liberals thought that Madden, who held positions on both committees, should expend more effort to get the bill to the floor. The House did enact several provisions of S 355 separately, but the bill itself died in the House Rules Committee.

The frustrated liberals were too fragmented to truly wield power, and their Democratic Study Group (DSG) was becoming suspect in some quarters. According to one observer in the House, its original mandate to set a middle course between ideological purity and legislative pragmatism had been subverted by the operator types, and the DSG had been turned into little more than a tool of the White House for whipping people into line. Some vanguard House liberals, keeping their DSG membership, formed a special alliance to promote their own special causes.

The Democratic Caucus at the beginning of the 90th Congress also had to deal with flamboyant Adam Clayton Powell. Powell's abuses of House rules and procedures had become so obvious and so well chronicled by the press that the Caucus was compelled to discipline him. The leadership did not want any severe punishment, but the main body overrode them and opted for stripping Powell of his chairmanship of the Education and Labor Committee. Liberals in the Caucus hoped that this punishment would prevent any challenge on the floor of the House to Powell's taking his seat. By voting with other members in the Caucus to strip Powell of his chairmanship, liberals hoped to gain enough votes to block Colmer from being named chairman of the Rules Committee. The strategy was unsuccessful and Colmer returned to the chairmanship.

The perennial issue of the twenty-one-day rule was revived. With the advent of more Republicans in the Congress in the election of 1966 the dominant liberal element receded, and the twenty-one-day rule was repealed in 1967 by a vote of 233 to 185 in the House.[26] The Conservative Coalition was clearly back in force in 1967. It won 73 percent of the roll calls where a majority of the voting Northern Democrats opposed a majority of the voting Southern Democrats.[27]

Johnson's key legislation faced a challenge from the newly revived Conservative Coalition. Important legislation, including aid to education and housing, faced threats of deep cuts by the Republicans and conservative Democrats. The Administration was parrying that with a request for income tax increases, a request basically repugnant to congressmen anyway, and even more so in light of what the conservatives considered excessive federal spending. Advocates of Johnson's legislation were being left more to their own devices than in previous years. Vietnam was demanding an increasing amount of the President's attention as well as a greater portion of the national budget. New Politics advocates found themselves caught in the squeeze between the riots in the cities, the war in Vietnam, and the battle over the tax surcharge. They began to branch out on their own and mold the legislation to their liking. Republican activists Quie and Goodell led the efforts of Republicans to introduce alternative legislation.

Perhaps one of the outstanding examples of Johnson Administration loss of influence over the legislative branch was the Elementary and Secondary Education Amendment of 1967. Republicans led by Quie proposed a "block grant" amendment to the bill that would give money to the states in lieu of traditional direct categorical grants to localities. This amendment was opposed by a large group of powerful lobbies, including the National Education Association, the NAACP, the school superintendents of large cities, and religious organizations. Aided by Administration forces and New Politics congressmen interested in increasing urban as opposed to state control, the lobbyists succeeded in defeating the amendment.

However, Edith Green, Oregon Democrat and member of the Education and Labor Committee, received support from Republicans and Southern Democrats for her amendments placing all control of Titles II and V of the bill in state education departments. Johnson had attempted to dissuade her from introducing these amendments, but had been unsuccessful. The amendments survived the Senate over stiff opposition. After prolonged squabbling in the House and Senate, the largest school assistance bill in the nation's history was passed.[28] The scope of the bill far exceeded the original Administration requests, but the Administration chose to support the changes rather than fight them. The bill became one of the major accomplishments of the 90th Congress and the Johnson Administration.

The most serious challenges to the President, though, were the demands of Republicans and dissident Democrats for deep budget cuts in return for passage of the tax surcharge. By a vote of 254 to 143 the House in October 1967 passed a resolution supporting a spending cut of one-third in the antipoverty and foreign affairs bills.[29]

The antipoverty legislation survived the cut due to some fancy legislative strategy on the part of the liberal Democrats in the House who floor-managed it. They agreed that cuts were necessary in the bill, and included a key provision giving local officials control over the money. This kept the Southern Democrats in line and cut the ground out from under Republicans Quie and Goodell, who had proposed an overhaul of the antipoverty legislation and counted on the Southern Democrats to go along. Quie and Goodell even lost Ford's backing at the key moment, and most Republicans elected to oppose or to compromise rather than to vote on a totally different bill.[30] Quie and Goodell's activism, exerted in efforts to propose alternative legislation to Johnson's suffered a blow from which it never really recovered.

New Politics congressmen who had supported LBJ's program now found it increasingly more necessary to take new initiatives in domestic legislation. They took the lead in pushing open housing legislation; Representative Leonor Sullivan pushed consumer legislation; Senator Mondale teamed with Representatives Thomas Foley and Neal Smith in securing a strong federal meat inspection law; and Senator Warren Magnuson and members of the House Judiciary Committee pressed for federal studies of auto insurance. The leadership gap left by LBJ on the domestic front was rapidly being filled by New Politics congressmen, so that the conservatives considered it a plus that they forced the Administration to cut its budget in return for a tax surcharge.

The New Politics and a Republican President

With the opening of the 91st Congress in 1969 the Democratic majority in the House was substantially smaller than in the 90th. There were 243 Democrats and 192 Republicans. As the number of Republicans in the House increased, the strength of the Conservative Coalition rose. The Coalition won 71 percent of House roll-call votes in 1969. It had again become a powerful force.[31] However, it was now in a different position. With a more conservative President its role switched to supporting an Administration instead of obstructing it.

The Democratic Caucus had many issues to resolve at the opening of the 91st Congress. One of the most divisive was the seating of Adam Clayton Powell, who had been ousted in 1967 from his seat in the House. The Caucus voted to reinstate Powell, and this was finally accomplished on a roll-call vote on the House floor, but he was fined $25,000. John Conyers of Michigan, one of the senior black congressmen, actively worked with the leadership of both sides to have Powell reinstated. The New Politics group supported the reinstatement, but largely as a gesture to the Black Caucus.

Under a Democratic President, the House Democrats were presented with a legislative program compatible with New Politics. Now with a Republican in the White House they found themselves in the position with which House Republicans had long been familiar—that of having either to support the opposition's legislative program or to develop alternatives. The liberals wanted to develop alternatives, but were facing formidable internal difficulties in the House. They lacked a real leader. John McCormack presided but he allowed the committee chairmen to call the legislative signals. The seniority system gave committee chairmen a disproportionate amount of control over legislation and also worked to reward Democrats from safe districts— the South and the big cities. Despite all the talk about New Politics and responsiveness to the demands of the day, the relatively few liberals who had acquired some power were reluctant to challenge or upset the system.

Morris Udall of Arizona, a long-time DSG member, challenged John McCormack for the Speaker's positon in the 1969 Caucus. He had counted on the votes of the disaffected liberal wing of the party, including the members of the Democratic Study Group. However, the DSG did not publicly take sides in the contest. Its strategy was to use the opportunity to negotiate with McCormack for some changes in the system. One of these was a successful effort to pressure McCormack to hold monthly Caucus meetings.

The Democratic Study Group, while suspect in some quarters, did unite the liberals to win an important legislative victory over the Appropriations Committee. For the first time in legislative memory the Appropriations Committee lost a major battle on the floor of the House as the DSG successfully organized labor and education lobbyists to pressure the House to add $894.5 million to an education money bill.

However, the very next day after that heady victory, the New Politics group lost an important battle to delete from an appropriations bill language designed to slow school integration in the South. Without the horde of lobbyists around, many liberal Democrats did not show up for the vote and the language was retained.[32] This inability of the liberals to maintain a consistent voting front to counteract the Conservative Coalition was one of their biggest failings. Only a taskmaster like President Johnson could keep them in line to vote.

However, the liberal Democrats found President Nixon on their side in the fight to retain the office of Economic Opportunity for eighteen more months. Minority Leader Gerald Ford, taking a rare stance in opposition to the Nixon Administration, backed a plan to turn over control of federal antipoverty programs to the states. He was assuming that the Conservative Coalition would assist him but he discovered too late that a sizable minority of Republicans had balked at the plan and joined with the liberal Democrats to defeat the proposal. This occurred even after the White House had all but given up the battle for the retention of the OEO.[33] Liberal and conservative

Republicans were now divided, which made it possible for the New Politics group to secure passage of several civil rights bills that the administration opposed. When this was followed by the New Politics victory on the education segment of the HEW appropriations bill, the Republicans realized that they too had organizational problems.

In terms of procedural reform, one of the most important pieces of legislation passed in the House of Representatives in 1970 was the Legislative Reform Act. Having languished in the House for three years, it finally passed by a vote of 326 to 19.[34] Scheduled to take effect in 1971, the Reform Act included two provisions that would have long-reaching effects.

The most important provision concerning the House as a Committee of the Whole was the requirement that votes on important amendments during floor debates be recorded, if a certain number of members so requested. There were four methods of voting in the House. In a recorded or roll-call vote, each member's name is called and he answers "Yea," "Nay," or "Present." Only in overriding a presidential veto does the Constitution require the "yeas" and "nays" to be recorded. Three less formal and unrecorded voting methods were by voice, by standing, and by passing through tellers.

Prior to the Legislative Reorganization Act of 1970, no recorded roll calls could be requested in the Committee of the Whole, where many major test votes are taken before bills are considered by the full House. For the first time, when the Reform Act became effective in 1971, votes would be recorded individually or a teller vote taken, if twenty members so requested. This fifth voting procedure is called "teller vote with clerk," because votes pass between the teller clerks, who record names as well as votes. It ended a 181-year tradition of nonrecorded voting in the Committee of the Whole of the House of Representatives. Two obvious effects were an increase in the number of members who would turn out to vote in the Committee of the Whole, and a curbing of the practice of voting one way in a legislative committee and taking the opposite stand in public.

The second provision in the Reform Act that became the subject of intense House debate was the provision to guarantee the minority party members on standing committees one-third of each committee's staff allocation. Heretofore, committee chairmen had decided unilaterally who would be allowed to have staff. In most cases the minority party members had little bargaining power and fared badly. For example, in the mid-1960s one committee chairman with twelve professional staff positions allocated eleven to the Democrats and one to the Republicans. Even that one was a Boston Irish Democrat selected by the chairman. A notable exception to this high-handed treatment was the House Education and Labor Committee, where the minority acknowledged that they received fair treatment.

This provision was the subject of some heated debate on the House floor in 1970. Frank Thompson, a Democrat from New Jersey, noted that while the staffing requirement might be fair for one committee it might not be considered fair for another.[35] Republican Congressman James Harvey from Michigan stated that the minority party has never had the staff necessary for the job that they were sent to Washington to do.[36]

James Cleveland, a Republican from New Hampshire, cited an example of the treatment minority party members receive from committee chairmen. The minority party members of the Public Works Committee had requested permission to hire an economist to help them with the details of the Appalachian Development Act and the Public Works and Economic Development Act that were before the committee. According to Cleveland, the committee chairmen refused the request even though the case for hiring the economist was a good one. [37]

The New Politics forces made some gains in their efforts to challenge the seniority system. Speaker John McCormack, under a combination of pressures from his own party, announced in midseason that he would retire at the end of the year. The leadership finally permitted the Caucus to establish the Organizational Study and Revision Committee chaired by Julia Butler Hansen of Washington, to review the problems related to the seniority system and propose recommendations. (This is discussed in detail in chapter 7.)

Nevertheless, Nixon did not fare badly at the hands of the New Politics forces in the 91st Congress. While Congress cut the military budget and banned presidential deployment of troops, it approved the postal service organization, a voluntary draft, and the revenue-sharing legislation which was important to the New Federalism.

Carl Albert was elected Speaker in January 1971 and Hale Boggs was promoted to Majority Leader. The off-year elections of 1970 gave the Democrats a net gain of eight seats, almost all of which were New Politics activists. The list included Father Robert Drinan of Massachusetts, Paul Sarbanes of Baltimore, three new women members—superliberal Bella Abzug of New York, Ella Grasso of Connecticut, and conservative Louise Day Hicks of Massachusetts—and three new black members—Ronald Dellums of California, Parren Mitchell of Maryland, and George Collins of Illinois. In addition, Charles Rangel of New York ousted Adam Clayton Powell in a primary and won the election, while Ralph Metcalfe replaced William Dawson, who retired. The first congressman of Puerto Rican descent, Herman Badillo, was elected from New York City. Several of the defeated Republicans were conservative leaders, including William Ayres, the ranking Republican on the House Labor Committee of Ohio, who lost to antiwar liberal John Seiberling.

The chairmanship of the House Republican Conference was hotly contested. John Anderson of Ohio, the moderate incumbent, was challenged by Samuel Devine of Ohio, a member of an informal group called the Republican Regulars. Consisting of about sixty of the most conservative Republicans in the House, this group had been organized early in 1969 expressly to exert pressure on the Nixon Administration. The Devine group contended that Anderson was no longer a conservative, because he had provided the liberals with the deciding vote in the fight to release open housing legislation from the Rules Committee. Anderson countered that he had supported the Administration far more than Devine and also had received a distinguished service award from the American Conservative Union in 1968. Anderson won in a very close (89–81) vote. [39]

The Democratic Caucus also considered several important changes in rules and procedures. The controversial twenty-one-day rule, which had been repealed in 1967, came up again in 1971 when the Democratic Caucus instructed William Colmer, chairman of the Rules Committee, to introduce a resolution for a modified twenty-one-day rule. (This rule actually was a thirty-one-day rule, as it provided for a ten-day grace period before a request for the twenty-one-day discharge could be brought up.) Colmer of course openly expressed opposition, and noted that "the Rules Committee had been the whipping boy for certain people of a certain philosophy and for the ultra-liberal press."[40] Carl Albert introduced the resolution on the House floor; Colmer argued it would abolish the Rules Committee and voted against its passage.

In large measure the facts were in Colmer's favor. During the previous four years only four of 493 requests for rules were refused. According to Colmer, the committee performs three functions: it cooperates with the leadership of the House; it provides a cooling-off period; and it serves as a buffer between the Speaker and membership of the House. Colmer objected to eliminating the Rules Committee's basic function and returning the power to the Speaker. As he put it: "Talk about democracy. This is nothing else but Cannonism, you are going back 60 years if you do that."[41]

The Colmer Resolution (H.Res. 5) also contained a section to eliminate the minority staffing provision in the Legislative Reorganization Act of 1970. However, B. F. Sisk of California, a member of the Rules Committee, introduced an amendment allowing a separate vote on the twenty-one-day rule.[42] This gave the moderate and liberal Republicans a chance to vote affirmatively on the twenty-one-day rule without jeopardizing the minority staffing provision. However, the twenty-one-day rule was killed on the House floor. The Republicans also lost the vote on the retention of the minority staffing provision, primarily because the Democratic Caucus had bound its members to vote against it. In this case New Politics supporters suppressed their ideological position in the interest of their party.

The Democratic Caucus had also passed a resolution limiting subcommittee chairmanships. This had some immediate effects. For instance, Congressman Hebert of Louisiana, chairman of the Armed Services Committee, had to give up several subcommittee chairmanships on that committee. Overall it meant that forty more Democrats would become chairmen of some of the 137 House subcommittees.

Some committee chairmen sought to evade the effects of the reform measure. A New Politics leader, Chet Holifield of California, who was chairman of the Government Operations Committee, consolidated two of the most active subcommittees—Executive Reorganization and Military Operation. John McMillan, chairman of the House District Committee, struck back at those who opposed his chairmanship by passing over eight eligible chairmen for the new District of Columbia Reorganization Subcommittee and picking a congressman he believed would support him.[43]

The implementation of the recorded teller provision of the 1970 Reorganization Act had almost immediate results in 1971. Its effect was most apparent in the fight over the appropriations for the Supersonic Transport plane (SST). The renewal of these appropriations had been receiving stiff opposition in the Congress, but the Administration and powerful lobbies, such as the AFL-CIO, were pushing very hard for passage. Members in the House, though under tremendous pressure from pro- and anti-SST lobbying groups, realized that public opinion opposed the measure and voted against continuing the appropriations after March 1971. It is believed that the recorded vote made possible by the new rules was the deciding factor in the contest.

The recorded vote substantially weakens the carrot-and-stick power that committees hold. Their ability to grant favors to other members or withhold them is unspoken, but ever present. It is a factor during the consideration of bill amendments on the House floor. Nonrecorded voting often made it possible for committees to entice a majority to their side. Logrolling deals are more difficult to manipulate now that the House members must justify the merits of their votes on important amendments. Some of the committee power is now shifted to the floor of the House, as the recorded vote forces more meaningful voting on the floor on matters normally decided in committee. It also reduces committee advocacy of special interests. However, one of the most noticeable results of the recorded vote provision is that the floor of the House, once conspicuously empty even during the consideration of important legislation, has become well populated with congressmen, who realize their vote will be on record.

Another procedure used by the House committees to protect their interests and to prevent their legislation from being altered on the floor was the closed rule. No amendments could be voted to legislation sent to the floor of the House under closed rule, and the Rules Committee under Judge Howard Smith used it frequently. The Ways and Means Committee traditionally uses this procedure with complicated tax and tariff laws. However, in more recent years it has been seeking such treatment for social security and other legislation not in the tax law or tariff category.

The opposition to the war in Southeast Asia was a continuing theme in the House. Public sentiment against the war was rising, forcing many congressmen to openly oppose it. Republican Congressman Pete McCloskey of California was preparing to run against Nixon in 1972 on an antiwar platform, and was receiving some noticeable support from well-heeled antiwar people. Even several long-time hawks switched to the dovish side. Congressmen John Flynt of Georgia and Thomas Downing of Virginia were ardent supporters of the U.S. position in Vietnam, but they voted against the Administration's bill to extend the draft. However, one of the most impressive switches was Dan Rostenkowski of Chicago. A member of Mayor Daley's machine, and formerly a hawk, Rostenkowski became most vocal in his opposition.

Amendments and resolutions to set deadlines for the President to withdraw from the war were being presented in the House throughout the year. Congressmen came under great pressure from lobbies such as Common Cause and various end-the-war groups. The antiwar lobbyists were successful in causing the majority of Democrats in the House to go on record in favor of a fixed pullout date in Vietnam. Here too the recorded vote put House members under tremendous pressure and contributed to the New Politics responsiveness.

The Conservative Coalition went down to defeat on the SST appropriation in 1971, but otherwise compiled its highest percentage of victories in both the House and the Senate in eleven years. *Congressional Quarterly* attributes some of this success to the recorded teller vote, which provided the Coalition an opportunity to defeat a variety of liberal amendments to certain types of legislation, such as the military draft extension and the annual defense procurement authorization.[44] The recorded teller vote was a weapon that both sides could use, but the more disciplined unified Conservative Coalition utilized it more effectively.

On the legislative front the 92nd Congress passed a great many environmental protection bills, despite the opposition of such people as Wayne Aspinall, the powerful chairman of the House Interior Committee. They also approved two constitutional amendments giving the right to vote to eighteen-year olds and assuring equal rights to women.

There were an abnormal number of retirements before the 1972 elections, due to increased retirement benefits and reapportionment. Many senior congressmen of both parties announced that they would not run for reelection. The House Republicans lost senior members such as William L. Springer of Illinois, William McCullough of Ohio, Thomas Pelly of Washington, John Jarman of North Carolina, John Byrnes of Wisconsin, Frank Bow of Ohio, and H. Allen Smith of California.[45]

Probably one of the most important retirements from the Democratic leadership's point of view was that of William Colmer, Chairman of the Rules Committee. Succeeding him, if reelected, would be Ray Madden of Indiana, a liberal Democrat and strong supporter of Carl Albert. Age was an issue in the elections, too. Eighty-three-year-old Congressman Emanuel Celler of New York was defeated in the primaries by thirty-year-old Elizabeth Holtzman. Eighty-one-year-old George Miller, Chairman of the House Space Committee, and seventy-four-year old John McMillan, Chairman of the District Committee, were also defeated in primaries. However, Wright Patman, seventy-eight, survived a strong challenge by a forty-six-year-old stockbroker. The high turnover in 1972 encompassed some sixty defeated incumbents and almost one hundred newcomers, but struck more heavily than usual at those in very senior positions.

The 1972 election brought a massive victory to the President, but his coattails were not strong enough to bring the Republicans the needed forty seats to gain control of the House. They picked up twelve of the forty, but eight of their gains were in the South, where they won two seats in Mississippi and one each in Virginia, South Carolina, Florida, Louisiana, Tennessee, and Texas. Indications were that the South was slowly becoming a two-party region. Blacks gained three congressional seats with the election of Andrew Young from Atlanta, Barbara Jordan from Texas, and Yvonne Burke from California. Since most of the southern seats lost to Republicans had been held by conservative Democrats, the New Politics gained as much as the Republicans did.

The Reform and Confrontation Congress

The most notable result of this extraordinary turnover was the shift in committee lineups and leadership positions in the 93rd Congress, which began in 1973. Peter Rodino of New Jersey succeeded Emanuel Celler as Chairman of the Judiciary Committee. At the time no one was aware that the most important piece of business before the Committee would be consideration of the impeachment of Richard Nixon.

Ray Madden replaced William Colmer as Rules Committee Chairman. An Albert supporter, Madden can be relied upon to do the Speaker's will. In fact the Rules Committee in 1973 has been described as "such a liberal sieve that it is regularly being overruled by a more conservative House."[46]

James Haley of Florida succeeded Wayne Aspinall as Chairman of the Interior Committee. This gave the conservationists hope, as Aspinall had in their minds been a major stumbling block. With John Byrnes gone from the Ways and Means Committee, the Administration lost a strong supporter in that Committee and in the House.

Majority Whip Thomas "Tip" O'Neill of Massachusetts was named Majority Leader, to replace Hale Boggs, who was killed in an Alaskan plane crash in 1972. O'Neill, known as the "politician's politician," is a tough, forceful leader with long experience in politics. He is one of the liberals on the Rules Committee, where he has served since 1955. O'Neill considers the recorded teller vote one of his greatest accomplishments. As a liberal and a reformer he qualifies as one of the New Politics breed. Observers believe he has brought a strength which had been lacking to the Democratic leadership in the House. John McFall of California, another liberal, was selected to replace O'Neill as Majority Whip, so that for the first time the top three leaders of the House Democrats were all supportive of the New Politics.

The 93rd Congress responded to this leadership with two substantial changes for which New Politics was responsible. The Democratic Caucus in several meetings between January and the end of February voted favorably on a proposal requiring committee chairmen to win their positions by a majority vote of all House Democrats. The reform was adopted on January 22 by a Caucus vote of 117 to 58.[47] Chairmanships were no longer automatic and if requested by 20 percent of the Caucus, a secret ballot vote on each chairman would be held. No chairman was ousted but seniority alone was no longer an automatic guarantee of a chairmanship within the House Democratic Party and future accountability of the committee chairmen was greatly enhanced.

Philip Burton of California, who was scheduled to become chairman of the Democratic Study Group in March, proposed a modification in the closed rule procedure of the Rules Committee. Burton proposed that four days before a committee chairman or designee can request a closed rule prohibiting germane amendments, he must give notice in the *Congressional Record.* If during the four-day period fifty Democratic Caucus members address a written request to submit a particular germane amendment to both the chairman seeking the closed rule and the chairman of the Rules Committee then the Caucus as a whole (not the Rules Committee alone) decides if the amendment will be allowed. Under this procedure the closed rule can be circumvented. The proposal was successfully voted upon in the Democratic Caucus and included in the "Addendum" of the Caucus Rules, number 17. This reform reduced the closed rule oligarchy of the Ways and Means and Rules Committees.

Al Ullman, acting as chairman of the Ways and Means Committee in the absence of Wilbur Mills, was the first to utilize this new rule, in October 1973. He requested a modified closed rule on the Trade Reform Act of 1973. The bill was scheduled for floor debate the last days in October. Ullman was granted a modified closed rule. However, before the bill was brought to the floor international events became such that the leadership hastily postponed floor action on the legislation until November.[48] While the new rule safeguarded the rights of the membership outside the Ways and Means and Rules Committee circle, it also gave the leadership the flexibility it needed in a crisis.

The other significant change involved the openness of committee meetings, including meetings to draft legislation—generally called mark-up sessions. A proposal requiring that all committee sessions be open to the public unless a majority of the committee's members vote in public to close a session was sponsored by Dante Fascell of Florida, Bob Eckhardt of Texas, and Thomas Foley of Washington. It had the backing of 150 members of the Caucus, the Democratic Study Group, and such groups as Common Cause and Americans for Democratic Action. The measure passed the Democratic Caucus on January 21 and was brought to the House floor on March 7, 1963.

A modifying amendment was offered by Democrat Samuel Stratton of New York allowing the executive department spokesmen to be present during closed committee sessions. Although Fascell and other sponsors of the bill were strongly opposed to it, the House passed the measure with Stratton's amendment 370 to 27.[49] Republicans, led by Whip John Anderson, maneuvered to attach an amendment providing for minority staffing to the measure, but were unsuccessful.

The effect of this new rule on committee hearings was immediate. With the exception of Ways and Means, Appropriations, and the Armed Services Committee, few have closed their meetings. However, Common Cause conducted a survey of bill-drafting sessions from March 7, when the new law was adopted, through June 15, and found that while 238 bill-drafting sessions where the final legislative trades take place were open, 47 were closed to the public and the press. Ten House committees, including Foreign Affairs, Judiciary, Public Works, and Banking and Currency, reported holding no secret sessions of any kind. However, the House Appropriations Committee and all but one of its subcommittees have held their bill-drafting sessions in secret. The one exception was the subcommittee headed by the House Majority Whip John McFall of California, which handles Transportation Department appropriations.[50]

Until June 16, the Ways and Means Committee had held all its bill-drafting sessions in secret, but on June 18 it voted 15 to 10 to close the initial mark-up meeting on President Nixon's important foreign trade proposals.[51] Then the Committee recessed rather than adjourned subsequent trade bill mark-up sessions to continue the secrecy so that it would not technically violate the requirement for a public vote whether a session will be open or closed. It sharply reversed itself in October 1973 however with the historical decision to open up its bill mark-up sessions to the public.

Another major reform was slowly gaining shape in the House. A special House committee was set up by Speaker Albert in 1973 and chaired by Richard Bolling of Missouri, with the purpose of updating the legislative machinery in the House, machinery that had not been changed since 1946. The Bolling Committee produced a working draft of proposals that would, if enacted, have far-reaching effects in the House.

To facilitate procedural efficiency, Bolling would change virtually every standing committee in the House. The powerful Ways and Means Committee would lose its jurisdiction over trade and tariff proposals to the Foreign Affairs Committee. All health insurance and medicare legislation would be referred to a reconstituted Commerce and Health Committee, and unemployment compensation to a newly constituted Labor Committee. But Ways and Means would gain jurisdiction over food stamp bills from the Agriculture Committee, and bills concerning foundations would also be referred to it.

Another proposal included in the Bolling package is the creation of an Energy and Environment Committee, which would gain jurisdiction over a variety of legislation including clean air, solid waste, and noise pollution, presently the jurisdiction of the Commerce Committee, and radiation, now the jurisdiction of the Joint Committee on Atomic Energy. The Public Works Committee would be assigned jurisdiction over transportation legislation. The Science and Astronautics Committee would be concerned with most of the research and development programs.

The Internal Security Committee would be abolished and its duties assigned to the Judiciary Committee; and the Merchant Marine and Fisheries and Post Office and Civil Service Committees would also be abolished. The Education and Labor Committee would be divided, and the new Labor Committee would gain jurisdiction over some legislation now in other committees. The House Rules Committee would be made a court of appeals over jurisdictional disputes, such as the tug of war between Ways and Means and Education and Labor over which should write a pension reform bill.[52]

The Bolling Committee has also drafted a resolution providing that in election years organizing caucuses of the two parties would be held soon after the November election day so the House can get right down to legislative work when it convenes in January. Other proposals included the expansion of professional staffs, assuring the minority party one-third of the staff, and ending all proxy voting in committees by absent members. While these proposals were working drafts, Congressman Bolling conceded that they will cause some discomfort to senior members, whose power will be somewhat diminished if the proposals are implemented.

And he was correct. On May 9, a deeply divided Democratic Caucus met to decide the fate of the reform proposals. Leading the opposition was Wilbur Mills whose Ways and Means Committee would be stripped of much of its power if the reforms were approved. Other committee chairmen were also unhappy with the treatment they would receive. This opposition, coupled with those liberals who believed that the proposed reforms would fragment the most powerful liberal center in the House—the Education and Labor Committee—while doing nothing to curb the powers of the most conservative committees—Appropriations, Armed Services and Rules, combined to force the Caucus to delay final approval of the reforms. The Caucus referred the matter to the Organizational Study and Revision Committee chaired by Julia Butler Hansen. This Committee had previously been involved in reforms concerning the seniority system and committee secrecy.

Reforms concerning the budget process were begun and may be ready to implement in the 94th Congress. In terms of procedural reform, the 93rd Congress may well be one of the most effective in history. But in terms of dealing with the President, the 93rd Congress was one of confrontation, aggravated by the Watergate scandal, the firing of Archibald Cox, the indictment of Vice President Agnew, and the Nixon impeachment inquiry. The President was in a weakened position, but he continued to exercise his veto power and to impound appropriated funds that he believed inflationary or that were for programs he opposed. (Congress's counterattack on impoundment will be discussed in chapter 10.)

The amount of legislation enacted was not large, but included the opening of the highway trust fund to purchase mass transit equipment, home rule for the District of Columbia, and federal aid for emergency medical care and for health maintenance organizations. One of the most important developments in the House was that the majority finally came around to oppose the Indochina war.

While the doves in the House had been active and vocal, they could never in previous years muster a majority to threaten the President with drastic action if he did not cease hostilities. But finally in May 1973 the dam broke and the House threatened a cutoff of funds to run the government if the President did not halt the bombing in Cambodia. The fact that the pendulum finally swung to the side of the doves can be attributed to the influx of antiwar congressmen and women, and to the House leadership's indication that it opposed any further U.S. participation in the war in Indochina. Tip O'Neill particularly had been strongly opposed to the war for some time, and he was a major force in the House's turnaround and in the enactment of the war powers bill designed to prevent a President from leading the nation into any more Vietnam-type wars without approval of Congress. (This will be discussed further in chapter 10.)

The Evolving House

Reviewing the House under the Kennedy, Johnson, and Nixon Administrations, in terms of liberals versus conservatives and the advent of what has come to be named the "New Politics," one sees a seesaw, with conservatives up and liberals down during one Congress and the trend reversed in the next.

The turning point for the liberals came in 1964 with the Johnson landslide. The impetus was slowed somewhat by the 1966 off-year elections, but the seeds had been planted. As the Vietnam War began to occupy most of the President's time, members of the House and the Senate found themselves to a certain extent on their own. They were defending Great Society programs against the onslaught of conservatives and Republicans and, with the advent of the Nixon Administration, they were fighting holding actions to preserve the gains of the mid-sixties, and to continue and increase funds for those programs. This has led to the impoundment of funds and veto encounters with President Nixon.

But perhaps in the House the most important long-range gain in terms of reform was the recorded teller vote. A tool that could be used by both sides, it might prove to be the most important New-Politics-initiated reform in fifty years. No longer can members vote one way and talk another. No longer can they hide behind the nonrecorded vote on important issues. Some may argue that this makes them more vulnerable to pressure groups; but it also gives the constituents the opportunity to judge members on the basis of actions and not just words.

The office of the Speaker has become a more powerful one since McCormack retired and Carl Albert succeeded him in 1971. While Albert has been criticized by conservative members of the House for supposedly bending to the wishes of liberal members, he has managed to consolidate power in the Speaker's office.

The one big thorn in the side of the younger Democrats has been the seniority system. In 1973, with the advent of the selection of committee chairmen by vote in the Caucus, some of this dissatisfaction was alleviated. But the seniority system has survived because no one has proposed an alternative that is satisfactory to those who have "arrived" and those who are "waiting in the wings."

New Politics congressmen have subjected the Nixon Administration's legislative program to severe scrutiny. They have fought tough battles against increases in defense budgets, foreign aid, and renewal of SST appropriations, and have sought to expand programs on the domestic front, especially in the health area. Congressmen like Les Aspin, a former McNamara "whiz kid," have made their mark. Aspin has singlehandedly taken on the Department of Defense (DOD) and its spending policies. He has forced the DOD to account for its usage of tax dollars.

The New Politics congressmen have differed with the President over priorities, but in these confrontations the President has exposed and exploited fully the one great weakness in the legislative flank—the lack of sufficient monitoring of the federal budget. The Congress, and particularly the House, has been forced to seriously consider reforms of the procedures used in considering the budget.

If Congress, and especially the House, where the appropriations originate, eventually effects this badly needed reform, then the balance of power between the legislative and executive branches will perhaps be moved back toward the pre-1932 position. However, the House will always be the principal battleground for conservative-liberal battles, since its members are elected only for two-year terms and are most likely to respond to the latest influences in the electorate. Likewise the pressure for strong and effective action on the international scene will continue to provide strong justification for a powerful executive.

Congress has felt the impact of the presence of a new breed of congressman. Increased numbers of black, Spanish-speaking, and women members have changed the face of the House. Congressmen are also coming into the House at a younger age. At the same time the educational level of the members is continuing to climb. All these elements combine to mean increasing pressure for participation, more openness in the legislative process, more use of problem-solving approaches. They also mean less attention to House traditions, seniority and other artificial, although very effective determinants of power.

6

The New Senate

Thomas P. Murphy and
Elizabeth A. Knipe

The United States Senate has been described as the greatest deliberative body in the world. Seen as the more elite body of Congress, because of its smaller size and longer terms, the Senate is highly visible. Charged with the major responsibilities of dealing with foreign affairs and confirmation of presidential appointments, the Senate has recently assumed the role of a springboard for presidential aspirants.

The Senate has also been the center of power for the Conservative Coalition, with its domination of committees and the leadership. This domination has slowly deteriorated in the past twenty years, and today the Senate can be considered even more liberal than the rest of the country. However, freshman Senator James Buckley, elected on the Conservative Party ticket in New York, stated in an interview that the Senate

is also a place where the rules of civility are still observed and the rights and independence of each individual still respected. It is a place where many of the major decisions affecting the shape of our times are made; a place where even the least of its members may have a hand in making them.[1]

Lyndon Baines Johnson—Majority Leader, 1955-61

A tall Texan, who left a deep and permanent brand not only on the Senate but on the nation, Lyndon Baines Johnson first joined the Senate Democratic Leadership as Democratic Party Whip in 1951. In 1953, the first year of President Eisenhower's term, he was elected Minority Leader of the Democratic Party under a Republican president. He had a unique opportunity to be the leader of the "constructive opposition," a role he played to the hilt until he left the Senate in 1961, after six years as Majority Leader.

Known as a conciliator and a seeker of consensus, Johnson built the position of Majority Leader into one of the most powerful in Washington. Under his guidance the Senate passed some landmark legislation in the fifties and established the groundwork for the explosion of liberal legislation that was to come in the sixties while he was President.

Johnson was considered by the more outspoken liberals in the Senate to be basically a southern conservative, yet he was responsible for the passage of the pioneer 1957 Civil Rights Act. Faced with a majority of two after the 1956 election, when Democrats numbered forty-nine and Republicans forty-seven, the Majority Leader had to effect a sensitive conciliation of liberals and conservatives in order to secure passage of the Act.

The liberals, led by Senator Clinton Anderson of New Mexico, challenged

93

Rule 22, which stated that two-thirds of the Senate must vote to invoke cloture on a filibuster. They said that unless this rule were modified, civil rights legislation would never be passed. They were unsuccessful in their challenge, but Johnson stood fast. He broke the filibuster against the civil rights legislation by extending the length of the sessions and literally, physically exhausting those who were filibustering. The 1957 Act was the first piece of civil rights legislation to pass the Senate since 1875. Although it was a disappointment to many of its supporters, it was a beginning. The bill established a Commission on Civil Rights and empowered the U.S. Attorney General to seek injunctions when individuals were denied the right to vote.

The 85th Congress, which ended in 1958, was probably the last Congress in which Johnson's leadership went unchallenged. During the 1958 elections, Johnson, backed by Speaker of the House Sam Rayburn, announced the Democratic legislative programs for the 86th Congress. This included an education bill to fund a wide range of science programs, scholarships, and fellowships for advanced study; a program to bolster farm income; a housing bill to increase FHA loans and build public housing; and a public works program. There was mixed success with this proposed program, but it laid the groundwork for the future.

The elections of 1958 brought an influx of younger, ambitious, and definitely more liberal senators into the Senate. They included Bartlett and Gruening of Alaska, Dodd of Connecticut, Hartke of Indiana, McGee of Wyoming, Engle of California, Muskie of Maine, McCarthy of Minnesota, Williams of New Jersey, Keating of New York, Young of Ohio, and Moss of Utah. Those who might be considered on the conservative side were Byrd of West Virginia, Prouty of Vermont, and Randolph of Virginia. William Proxmire of Wisconsin, who in those days was considered a flaming liberal had come to the Senate in a special election in 1957 after the death of Senator Joseph McCarthy. These senators joined forces with such outspoken but previously outnumbered liberals as Albert Gore, Joseph Clark, Jacob Javits, Hubert Humphrey, John Pastore, and Paul Douglas. With added numbers to their ranks, they posted a serious challenge to the Majority Leader.

The biennial challenge to the filibuster was renewed by the liberals, but they were defeated in their attempts to substantially overhaul Rule 22 by permitting cloture with a majority of at least three-fifths of the Senate. However, a bipartisan leadership group pushed through a slight revision of the rule which the southern bloc did not really fight. The changes were basically designed and put through by Johnson, who seized the initiative from the liberals. The 1959 changes in Rule 22 allowed cloture to be invoked by two-thirds of those present and voting (rather than two-thirds of the full membership, as it had been before 1959), and applied the cloture rule to debate on motions to change the Senate rules. The change also amended Senate Rule 32 by adding the language: "The rules of the Senate shall continue from one Congress to the next Congress unless they are changed as provided in these rules."[2] Despite this, liberals later continued to argue that the Senate has a constitutional right to manage its rules by majority vote at the beginning of a session and that the amendment to Section 32 should not be in effect at that time.

The Majority Leader introduced four civil rights bills in the first session of the 86th Congress. These included a bill to create a community relations service—an independent federal agency to mediate civil rights disputes; a bill to make interstate shipment of explosives in so-called "hate bombings" a federal offense; a bill to give general subpoena rights to the federal government in voting rights cases; and a bill to extend the Civil Rights Commission.

Nevertheless, his method of leadership was attacked by the liberals. Senator William Proxmire spoke out early in 1959 with a sweeping indictment of LBJ's methods which only Wayne Morse of Oregon endorsed. Joseph Clark of Pennsylvania voiced the opinion that perhaps more frequent meetings of the Democratic Conference might be useful. In his defense, Senator Richard Neuberger stated that "LBJ holds 98 caucuses a day with individual senators to work out party positions."[3] Proxmire objected to this technique and wanted Johnson to consult more with the Conference as a whole.

In April of 1959, Joseph Clark released a letter he had written to the Majority Leader complaining that the younger Democrats were frustrated because they were unable to participate in questions of party policy. Clark, however, was more critical of the Democratic Conference procedures than of the Majority Leader.[4]

Johnson replied to the mounting chorus of critics during a debate with Gore on rising interest rates. He opposed a move by Gore to freeze interest rates on GI housing loans and argued with Gore on the Senate floor as to whether Gore should submit the bill to the Senate Banking and Currency Committee. In the course of a heated exchange with Gore, Johnson stated that there is no "one man rule" in the Senate. "I do not know how one can force a Senator to do anything."[5]

But the liberals kept pressuring Johnson for more Conference meetings. Early in 1960 the Majority Leader agreed that he would call a Conference meeting any time a fellow Democrat requested one. The liberals, led by Paul Douglas (and including McNamara, Clark, Humphrey, and Proxmire), were interested in establishing a legislative program for the election in 1960. Like Johnson, Senators Humphrey and Stuart Symington, who were among the liberals pushing for more participation in decision-making, had their eye on the presidential race. However, Johnson retained his control of the Democratic Policy Committee, which was established to spell out the campaign issues for the Democrats.

The liberals wanted LBJ's wings clipped for a number of reasons. Most of them came from the midwestern and eastern states and were outnumbered in terms of seniority and control of committees. They believed that the Conference Committee could be their most effective weapon in the Senate and would be useful in pushing legislation they favored, such as federal aid to education and broader minimum wage coverage. They also felt that if a liberal Democratic president was elected he should not deal with the Majority Leader on equal terms, but rather that the Senate Democratic Conference should be the policy-making body in the Senate, with the President and the Majority Leader deferring to its wishes.

It is to be noted that the criticism of Johnson was coming from liberals who had been in the Senate for a few years. The Majority Leader had treated the freshmen group well by giving them choice committee assignments—in fact two freshmen, Hartke and McCarthy, were named to the prestigious Senate Finance Committee. Johnson also set a procedent by assigning freshman Democrat Gale McGee of Wyoming to the Appropriations Committee. This was just one of the many examples of how Johnson divided the opposition and secured support for his programs.

At the Democratic Convention in Los Angeles, Senator John F. Kennedy was nominated as the Democratic candidate, and after much politicking and indecision on all sides, he named Lyndon B. Johnson as the vice-presidential candidate. With the election of a liberal Democratic president, Democrats in the Congress, particularly the more liberal ones, looked forward to productive years in terms of legislation in the sixties.

Mike Mansfield and Hubert Humphrey, 1961–65

The opening of the 87th Congress in January 1961 saw the election of Mike Mansfield of Montana to replace Johnson as Majority Leader. Hubert Humphrey was elected whip and George Smathers of Florida became chairman of the Conference. On the Republican side, the new minority leader selected to succeed the retiring William Knowland was Everett Dirksen, and the new whip was Thomas Kuchel of California. Comparisons between LBJ's and Mansfield's styles of leadership in the Senate were inevitable. Mansfield was quiet to the point of self-effacement, and had no talent or wish to wheel and deal as his predecessor had done. He was inclined to give the senators their head and let them run at will. Why was Mansfield picked? He had served as Party Whip under LBJ and so was in line of succession, and there was no one else who was acceptable to the liberals, the southerners, and the Kennedy Administration. So, for better or worse, Mansfield became the Majority Leader. He was to be overshadowed by an ebullient Humphrey serving as Whip, a magnetic President Kennedy, and the brooding presence of a now silent Vice President Johnson.

After Mansfield's election, a bipartisan group of liberal Senators launched another attack on Rule 22. They hoped to push through an amendment allowing cloture by majority or at least three-fifths of those present and voting. After seven days of debate, Mike Mansfield moved to refer the issue to the Rules and Administration Committee, of which he was to become chairman. The Mansfield motion barely carried on a 50 to 46 roll-call vote.[6] Liberals were bitter with the lack of support both from the Kennedy Administration and from Mansfield himself, whom they considered one of their group. Much to their disappointment, Mansfield did not bring the issue up again until the September adjournment rush, where the motion to change Rule 22 to cut off debate by a three-fifths vote was soundly defeated.[7]

Liberal Democrats were also angry with Mansfield's committee assignments. Kennedy supporters Muskie and Clark did not receive desired committee assignments and McCarthy of Minnesota was switched from the Public Works Committee to the Agriculture Committee. Meanwhile, Dodd of Connecticut, a freshman and a supporter of Johnson, was assigned to the prestigious Foreign Affairs Committee instead of Joseph Clark.

Mansfield's leadership image was that of a benevolent father. He was not inclined to push legislation through the Senate as Johnson had done. However the Kennedy Administration found Senate Whip Hubert Humphrey of Minnesota to be an enthusiastic and effective supporter of its program. He was particularly effective in mediating between the Administration and the Senate on the complicated education legislation, which involved a controversial section on funds for parochial schools. He played a key role in persuading the Administration to moderate its proposed farm legislation so that it would be more acceptable to the Senate, and then he convinced the conservative chairman of the Senate Agriculture Committee, Allen Ellender, to introduce the bill. He also persuaded liberals not to challenge the nomination of Texan John Connally for Secretary of the Navy, and the conservatives not to challenge the nomination of Robert Weaver as federal housing chief. In a sense, Humphrey was wheeling and dealing in the old Johnson manner.

Humphrey himself was changing. After losing the 1960 Democratic presidential nomination to Kennedy, he had come back to exercise his talents as a leader within the Senate. Despite the fact that his political philosophy was somewhat to the left of those who held the power, Humphrey had always been part of the Senate inner group. He understood the Senate's clubbiness and did not challenge its inner workings as did Proxmire, Clark, and Douglas. This meant he was in a position to work with both liberals and most of the conservatives. However, no one person filled the void left by Johnson. The power that had once resided in the Majority Leader now was spread among powerful Senators such as Robert Kerr of Oklahoma and Richard Russell of Georgia, as well as Humphrey and Mansfield. Kerr in particular was in a unique position. He was second in seniority on the Finance Committee where ultraconservative Harry Byrd of Virginia was chairman. He also served as chairman of the Senate Aeronautical and Space Sciences Committee and chairman of the Rivers and Harbors Subcommittee of the Public Works Committee, which had control over much of the pork-barrel legislation so dear to the heart of senators. Long held in check by Johnson, Kerr was now freer to wheel and deal. Russell of Georgia exerted a more subtle influence behind the scenes as a leader of the powerful southern bloc. Generally, he was a strong supporter of the Administration.

Despite the euphoria that usually exists for the first six months of a new presidential term, the Congress and particularly the Senate approached the Kennedy legislative program with caution. Holdover legislation from previous years, including aid to depressed areas, an increase in minimum wage, and an omnibus housing bill with emphasis on low-cost housing for low-income groups were passed, as did some new legislation including bills to establish the Peace Corps and the Alliance for Progress. But Kennedy's plan to reorganize the Executive Branch was vetoed in the Senate; his tax legislation was put aside, the proposal for higher postal rates did not pass, and the farm bill was buffeted about and finally defeated. Angered by charges that the Congress was a rubber stamp for the New Politics President, senators also began reacting to the Administration itself.

Probably the most notable incident in the second session of the 87th Congress in 1962 was the feud between Senate and House Appropriations Committees, which kept the Congress in turmoil. The dispute centered on the questions of the Senate's right under the Constitution to initiate appropriation bills and to add to House-passed appropriations measures funds for items either not previously considered by the House or considered and rejected. The issue was drawn by a dispute over where Senate-House conference committees on appropriations bills should meet and by whom they should be chaired. Key figures in the bitter feud were eighty-three-year-old Representative Clarence Cannon, chairman of the House Appropriations Committee, and eighty-four-year-old Senator Carl Hayden, chairman of the Senate Appropriations Committee. The feud held up final action on appropriations bills for three months. This was one of the few times that Johnson stepped out of his vice-presidential office and exercised his influence in the Senate. He helped mediate an end to this feud in July, but another dispute broke out late in the session over agricultural research funds. This too was resolved, but one the Senate's last acts before adjourning was to adopt a resolution asserting its "coequal power with the House to originate appropriations."[8]

Liberal Senators Gore and Kefauver attempted to use the filibuster in an effort to prevent the passage of an Administration bill to authorize creation of a quasi-private corporation (COMSAT) to own and operate a commercial communications satellite system. Several liberal Democrats denounced the bill as a giveaway of public resources spent to finance National Aeronautics and Space Administration research programs and mounted a filibuster against it. After the bill was debated for five days, the leadership filed a cloture petition and gained the necessary votes to invoke it. One reason those opposed to COMSAT were unsuccessful with their filibuster was that they organized too late to prevent passage of the legislation.

When the 88th Congress convened in January 1963, Senate liberals once again lost their biennial battle to ease the cloture requirements of Rule 22. Although the vote to ease cloture requirements fell ten short of the two-thirds required, it marked the first time in five attempts over the past ten years that proponents of a rules change had registered even a majority but Vice President Johnson ruled that a two-thirds vote was needed to invoke cloture. Thirty-six Democrats and eighteen Republicans voted for loosening the cloture requirements in Rule 22, while twenty-seven Democrats and fifteen Republicans voted against it. Once again Johnson departed from the impartiality of the vice presidency to help shelve this latest effort by the liberals to ease the cloture requirements.[9]

Another action that Mansfield supported was the bill to establish a Joint Congressional Committee on the Budget. For the sixth time since 1952 the Senate approved such a proposal, which had never passed the House, where the House Appropriations Committee opposed it. In 1963, in the first session of the 88th Congress, there were even more unprecedented delays in the passage of appropriations bills.

However, the reformers in the Senate were active in that session. Led by Senator Clark of Pennsylvania, they proposed various changes in Senate Rules, and also pushed for the establishment of a joint committee to study the organization of the Congress. This proposal was debated by the Senate late in the session but died when a filibuster was threatened on amendments to broaden the scope of the committee. Two other rules proposed and finally adopted in 1964 included one to permit Senate committees to meet through the "morning hour"—that is, up to the first two hours of the legislative day—and one to establish a three-hour period after the morning hour during which debate must be germane.[10] The intent of the germaneness rule was to speed passage of pending bills by preventing speeches on irrelevant matters until later in each day's session. This change had the effect of eliminating extraneous debate during consideration of floor debate without violating the Senate traditions. The rule also allowed committees to work while the Senate was in session without securing unanimous consent of the Senators.

The entire nation was jolted by the assassination of President Kennedy in November 1963. The accession of Johnson to the presidency radically altered the whole tone of the legislative efforts of the Executive Branch, as well as the attitude of the Senate toward those efforts. Johnson was back in his element, utilizing every tool in his power to expedite passage of legislation. Johnson viewed Congress as the potential means of accomplishing his ends, whereas Kennedy considered Congress an obstacle to be overcome or ignored. This contrast in attitudes toward the Congress accounts to some degree for the lack of success the Kennedy Administration had with its legislative program. Johnson fell heir to legislation that had been in the hopper for some time, much of it initiated by Kennedy's New Frontier movement, but he also understood the workings of the legislative body better than any recent president and was able to capitalize on this. In terms of nurturing the New Politics leanings of Congress, Johnson was a positive force. His "consensus-seeking" style of operation led to more participation and a departisanization of legislative proposals. This fits in well with the New Politics orientation toward problem-solving.

Mansfield, Dirksen, and President Johnson

The surge of legislative activity after Kennedy's assassination was phenomenal. Johnson was again in command of the Senate, but from the Oval Office instead of his suite in the Capitol. Legislation that had been bottled up for three years came pouring out, prodded by a demanding President and the shock waves of the assassination. Aid to higher education, mass transit legislation, and the poverty program were moving in committees. Within twelve weeks of Johnson's swearing in, the House had passed the 1964 Civil Rights bill and the Senate tax cut.

Majority Leader Mansfield was little more than an expediter of the large amount of legislation that flowed through the Senate. While subjected to criticism from his own peers for his very low-key approach to the leadership, Mansfield's style of operation was probably best suited to the high-powered style of President Johnson. Gone were the days when a Majority Leader could present his own "State of the Union Message" and set his own legislative goals. Now the legislative goals of a strong Democratic president took precedence and the Majority Leader did little more than echo his wishes. This suited Mansfield and Johnson well, but quite a few liberal senators wanted Mansfield to be more forceful. Many were unhappy that he let Minority Leader Dirksen set the tone of the Senate.

Everett Dirksen was to play a unique role in the Senate during Johnson's presidency. Nicknamed the "Wizard of Ooze," the white-haired senator from Pekin, Illinois was to rise to heights unprecedented for a minority leader. President Johnson in his constant seeking of the consensus for his legislation cultivated Dirksen, and a close and loyal friendship developed between the two men. The Minority Leader wholeheartedly supported the President, sometimes to the detriment of his own party's goals. His support particularly for the President's Vietnam policies was such that the President could rely on him far more than he could on some senators from the Democratic side of the aisle. On numerous occasions he provided the handful of swing Republican votes needed to put out Johnson's legislation. Because of this support, Johnson observed a hands-off policy concerning Dirksen's efforts throughout the late sixties to overturn the Supreme Court's one-man, one-vote ruling. One reporter, fascinated with Dirksen's machinations, commented on the Minority Leader's flexibility on issues and his ability to switch positions rapidly. "Sometimes it serves his party's interests, sometimes his nation's interests, but it always serves Dirksen's interests."[11] Johnson was careful to take good care of Dirksen patronage needs.

The best Johnson years were 1965 and 1966. The 1964 elections returned him to the White House with a huge majority. He brought with him an overwhelming majority in the House and Senate. Democrats in the Senate outnumbered the Republicans sixty-eight to thirty-two. Freshmen entering the Senate on that tidal wave included Robert F. Kennedy of New York, Joseph Tydings of Maryland, Ross Bass of Tennessee, Joseph Montoya of New Mexico, Fred Harris of Oklahoma, and Walter Mondale of Minnesota. But they were just the latest liberal wave in the Senate. Abraham Ribicoff, George McGovern, Gaylord Nelson, and Edward Kennedy all had been elected in the 1962 off-year elections.

Johnson shaped his legislation to gain the widest political support possible in the Congress. The result was a cornucopia of legislation that included medicare, immigration reform, expanded aid for higher education, rent supplements for low-income families, the establishment of a Department of

Housing and Urban Development, aid to Appalachia, and amendments to the 1964 Poverty Bill, which doubled the first year's authorization. Some of the legislation had been part of the Democratic platform for years, particularly aid to education and medicare. In many ways this first session of the 89th Congress was a culmination of many years of labor by the liberal wing of the Democratic Party, as well as by Lyndon Johnson himself. Throughout the fifties, as Majority Leader, he had advocated much of the legislation.

Perhaps the most important accomplishment of this first session, and the outstanding example of Johnson's consensus-building technique, was the enactment of the Elementary and Secondary Education Act of 1965. Previous bills to provide general aid to education had always foundered over the issue of aid to church-supported schools. So, before the bill was sent to the Congress, Johnson directed that Administration officials meet with two of the major education lobbies, the National Education Association and the National Catholic Welfare Conference. A new approach was developed under which aid would be given to *children*, whether in public or private schools, with particular emphasis on poor areas. The lobbyists then supported the bill, and it withstood major challenges in both the Senate and the House.

From the Senate's viewpoint, the landmark Voting Rights Act of 1965 was a turning point, as it marked the descent of the power of the Conservative Coalition in the Senate. In 1964 the Senate liberals produced enough votes to close off the filibuster on the 1964 Civil Rights Act. It was the first time in the history of Rule 22 that cloture was successfully involved to close off debate on civil rights legislation. The Voting Rights Act, which was then passed, was the most comprehensive legislation extending the right to vote in ninety years.

Senator Joseph Clark in commenting on the filibuster as an institution, noted that it forces the proponents of legislation to go to a lot of extra trouble if they truly want the legislation to pass. He also made the point that the filibuster comes when the Senate is considering legislation dealing with what he termed "new frontiers of public policy."[12] During the New Politics era the COMSAT legislation, the 1964 Civil Rights Act, and the 1965 Voting Rights Act were landmark pieces of legislation which activated the filibuster and promoted extensive debate.

It is interesting to compare the way Johnson and Mansfield handled filibusters. Johnson used a "wear-down" strategy on those filibustering, but it also was wearing on those who wanted the legislation passed. During the period Johnson was Majority Leader it was probably the only strategy he could use, given the dominance of the Senate by southerners and midwestern conservatives. Mansfield allowed the Senate to keep gentlemen's hours, so to speak, but three filibusters against COMSAT and the Civil Rights and Voting Rights Bills respectively were eventually broken. The New Politics Senate was now in ascendance, as the number of liberals in the Senate had increased to the point where they could garner enough votes to succeed with cloture.

With regard to the internal functioning of the Democratic Party in the

Senate, the opening of the 89th Congress in 1965 saw the election of Senator Russell Long of Louisiana to the position of Majority Whip to replace Hubert Humphrey, who was now the vice presidential candidate. An attempt was made by several of the more liberal members of the Democratic Conference to have the membership of the Democratic Steering Committee enlarged by four members, preferably with senators of a liberal outlook. They were defeated in this attempt, but Mansfield assuaged their feelings by assigning two members of their group, Senators Pat McNamara and Eugene McCarthy, to the Committee.

President Johnson still had retained momentum from the first session of the 89th Congress. While he was rebuffed on efforts to secure a repeal of section 14 (b) of the Taft-Hartley Act, he did get Congress to enact a "truth-in-packaging" law, establish a new federal Department of Transportation, vote more funds for rent supplements, and establish the Teacher Corps. A strong auto and highway safety bill was passed, as was a far-reaching anti-pollution measure. One of the most important outputs was a $900 million Demonstration Cities plan for intensive attack on urban blight. However, the wave of riots in the cities and the rise of militant black-power advocates helped defeat any Administration efforts to gain passage of open housing laws.

The Congress was also finally forced to turn inward and look at its own procedures and methods for handling legislation and dealing with the conduct of its members. A Legislative Reorganization Committee was finally established and Senator A. S. "Mike" Monroney and Representative Ray Madden were appointed co-chairmen. The committee reported its recommendations for congressional reform on July 29, 1966. Bills embodying the recommended reforms were introduced on the floors of both houses, but no action was taken during the remainder of the 89th Congress.

The problem of ethics and conduct was a matter of major concern in both houses. Adam Clayton Powell was under fire from members of his own Education and Labor Committee for his flamboyant disregard of the rules and norms governing committees and their chairmen. The Senate, still smarting from the aftereffects of the Bobby Baker scandal, was confronted by columnists Drew Pearson's and Jack Anderson's accusations against Senator Thomas Dodd for misuse of campaign funds. The Senator requested the not-yet-activated Senate Select Committee on Standards and Conduct to investigate the charges. Hearings were held in June and July 1966 but no action was taken against the Senator at that time.

With the 1966 off-year elections came a resurgence of the Republican Party. The Republicans had campaigned successfully on the issues of inflation, Vietnam, crime, and the alleged "credibility gap" between what the Administration said it was doing and its actual performance. As a result they gained three new seats in the Senate. New Republican faces included Charles Percy, of Illinois who defeated Paul Douglas; Everett Dirkson's son-in-law Howard Baker of Tennessee; Mark Hatfield of Oregon, who defeated Maureen Neuberger; Edward Brooke of Massachusetts, who gained the retiring Leverett Saltonstall's seat; and Clifford Hansen of Wyoming. Interestingly, most of these Republicans also fit the New Politics description.

The Senate devoted the first session of the 90th Congress, which opened in 1967, to two proposals—consideration of the Legislative Reorganization bill (S. 355) and Majority Whip Russell Long's plan to finance presidential election campaigns. Debate on S. 355 was extended largely due to Senator Joseph Clark's efforts to utilize the bill as a vehicle to enact amendments which would change many of the Senate's rules and procedures. Clark's principal amendments included elimination of the filibuster, restriction of outside employment of Senate employees, a requirement that Senators and employees file financial statements, prohibition of joint ventures between Senators and lobbyists, and prohibition of the receipt of fees of more than one hundred dollars by senators from lobbyists. All of these points were sensitive ones in light of the Bobby Baker scandal and the recent Dodd indiscretions. Senator Monroney, floor manager of the bill, managed to have most of Clark's amendments tabled on the ground that they dealt with Senate rules alone and went beyond the scope of the bill. The Reorganization bill passed the Senate in March of 1967 after eighteen days of debate and thirty-one roll-call votes.[13] The House leadership was unhappy with many provisions in the bill and Speaker McCormack sent it to the Rules Committee, which assured its demise.

The Senate spent five weeks in seesaw debate over Long's plan to finance presidential election campaigns through federal subsidies. Mansfield, usually a patient and mild man, was angered by Long's insistence on tying up the Senate with his pet bill. The capricious Long exacerbated the dispute that year by sending a newsletter to his constituents in which he listed his disagreements with President Johnson and Majority Leader Mansfield. Mansfield then attempted to circumvent Long by appointing four assistant Whips to do Long's work, and to get the Senate on the legislative track.

The nagging problem of ethical conduct also sidetracked the Senate. In June Senator Dodd was censured for his conduct "which is contrary to accepted morals, derogates from the public trust expected of a Senator and tends to bring the Senate into dishonor and disrepute."[14] Senator Edward Long of Missouri also came under attack when *Life* magazine charged that he had used his office to render assistance to jailed teamster Jimmy Hoffa, and had accepted payment for that assistance. The Senate Ethics Committee investigated the charge and exonerated Long, but he lost to Thomas Eagleton in his next primary.

While these internal events occupied the Senate, the President's legislative program suffered, despite the fact that it was a modest one compared to previous years. The Senate ratified the outer-space and U.S. Soviet consular treaties, and approved the establishment of the Public Broadcasting System, but funds for existing programs such as foreign aid, model cities, and rent supplements were scaled down considerably. They became victims of the crossfire between the President and the Congress over the tax surcharge.

Republicans in particular were telling the President that if he wanted the tax surcharge, he would have to cut his spending requests deeply. Johnson, under attack from the left on Vietnam and from the right over his spending policies, was in a weakened position. His great majority in the 89th Congress had been diminished in the elections of 1966, and he no longer commanded monolithic support from the Democrats in Congress.

The bitter fight over the budget and tax surcharge extended into 1968, when the President finally won congressional approval for the surcharge—but only after he agreed to a spending ceiling for fiscal year 1969 which required cuts of up to six billion dollars in his budget. He also reluctantly agreed to limitations in federal employment.

The strident opposition to the President and his domestic and foreign legislation seemed to mellow somewhat in 1968. Possibly his surprise announcement that he would not run for reelection had something to do with it. He was successful in getting some key legislation passed including a major housing bill for low-income groups, and the important open-housing legislation that had run into so much opposition in the previous Congress passed easily. Several health and education programs were extended with little controversy, and programs that had suffered severe cutbacks in 1967, such as Model Cities and the Poverty Program, were voted increased appropriations.

However, the President was dealt a humiliating blow in the Senate with the rejection of the nomination of Abe Fortas as the Chief Justice of the Surpreme Court. There were mixed motives in the unprecedented attack on Fortas. It was definitely a political move on the part of the Senate Republicans who wanted Johnson's successor, who they hoped would be a Republican, to nominate a candidate for the Chief Justice. Dissatisfaction with the liberal view of the Supreme Court on the part of a number of moderate and conservative Senators also played a role. These motives along with some unfortunate actions on the part of Fortas during his tenure as an Associate Justice combined to defeat the nomination.

Again in 1968 the Senate was the spawning ground for presidential hopefuls. The shock of Johnson's statement that he would not run was brief. The field was now clear for Senators Robert Kennedy and Eugene McCarthy who battled it out in the primaries. Vice President Humphrey did not enter any primaries, but he was the choice of the Democratic regulars. The tragic assassination of Robert Kennedy changed the whole picture once more and left Humphrey and McCarthy alone in the ring. Humphrey was nominated by an embattled party and chose as his running mate Senator Edmund Muskie of Maine.

Even with a deeply divided Democratic Party, Humphrey still managed to run a close second to Richard Nixon. The Democrats maintained a 58 to 42 majority in the Senate, but the Republicans gained five new seats for a total of forty-two, the largest number they had held since 1956.

New Republicans included former Senator Barry Goldwater, who won retiring Carl Hayden's seat in Arizona; Charles Mathias, who defeated Senator Daniel Brewster in Maryland; and Richard Schweiker, a moderate, who defeated Joseph Clark in Pennsylvania. Conservative Edward J. Gurney of Florida defeated former Governor LeRoy Collins for retiring Democratic Senator George Smather's seat. Other Republicans winning seats previously held by Democrats were Henry Bellmon of Oklahoma, who defeated A. S. "Mike" Monroney; Robert W. Packwood, a moderate who defeated Wayne Morse; and William Saxbe, a moderate who won a tough campaign for Frank Lausche's seat. Conservatives Marlow W. Cook and Robert Dole won seats held by retiring Republicans in Kentucky and Kansas. Freshmen Democratic Senators included liberals Alan Cranston of California and Harold E. Hughes of Iowa, who somewhat balanced the loss of liberals Clark and Monroney. The overall New Politics orientation was not seriously hurt by 'he changes, however, as Mathias and Schweiker became liberal levers in the Republican Party.

The New Politics Senate and the Nixon Administration

The 91st Congress convened in 1969 with the Democrats in command of Congress and the Republicans in command of the presidency. Nixon was the first president in over a century not to have a majority in the Congress in his first term. With the country taking a more conservative swing in the election of a Republican President, the Senate was still moving to the liberal side. The first indication was the defeat of southerner Russell Long by Ted Kennedy of Massachusetts for the post of Majority Whip. Kennedy announced his candidacy when Muskie decided not to challenge the powerful Long of Louisiana for the job. In secret balloting in the Democratic Conference Kennedy triumphed by a vote of 31 to 26.[15]

In an interview after his defeat, Long said he had gone to the meeting thinking he had twenty-nine votes—just enough to win—but found he had "miscounted." He was very candid about the reasons he had lost. The primary reason, he believed, was that Senator Kennedy had used his vote-getting capability on the campaign trail to swing senators to his side. Long denied that he had used his position as Chairman of the Senate Finance Committee to hold out promises of tremendous goodies to wavering colleagues. Of course, he stated, he and Kennedy "used everything we had .... Everything we could lay our hands on."[16] Kennedy's surprise upset of Long led to much speculation concerning the possibility of his becoming the new Majority Leader and perhaps the next Democratic nominee for the presidency.

Liberal Republicans were also unhappy with their leader Everett Dirksen. This unhappiness was expressed in the election of Hugh Scott as Minority Whip over conservative Roman Hruska, the personal favorite of Dirksen, in a close vote of 23 to 20.[17] His rejection by the Republicans signaled problems for the "Wizard of Ooze."

The position of Minority Leader had become a more difficult one with the swelling number of Republicans in the Senate and the inevitable divergence of viewpoints. With a member of their own party in the White House for the first time in eight years, the Republican Minority Leader became a key figure in assisting passage of the Administration's legislation. Everett Dirksen had led his troops well throughout the dark days when the Republicans were a small minority. His genius was that he was able to maintain tight control over the outnumbered Senate Republicans, and to translate this control into amendments and compromises on many pieces of legislation that otherwise would have been jammed through without concession to Republicans.

Dirksen's death in September 1969 left the Republicans with a large leadership gap. The fight for Minority Leader was a hotly contested one between Hugh Scott, Roman Hruska, and Howard Baker of Tennessee. Baker was backed by such party elders as Barry Goldwater, who believed the party should strike a youthful note, but Scott won. Baker then opposed Robert Griffin of Michigan for the post of Minority Whip and lost again, this time by a vote of 23 to 20.[18] Hugh Scott became the first eastern-establishment liberal to hold a Republican leadership post in the Senate.

Hugh Scott's political philosophy and voting record differed sharply from Dirksen's. For instance, in the 90th Congress Scott supported the Conservative Coalition 44 percent of the time. In the same Congress he had supported President Johnson's positions 64 percent of the time. The Americans for Democratic Action gave him a 57-percent rating and Dirksen a 7-percent rating concerning their positions on "liberal" issues in that Congress.[19]

Just as the Democrats experienced a drop-off in discipline when Mansfield replaced Johnson, Republican Senate discipline also relaxed during Scott's tenure. *Congressional Quarterly* noted that during Dirksen's short tenure under a Republican president, the Nixon position was defeated on only one vote that could have been reversed by full Republican support. Under Scott, the Republican Senate support of Nixon on roll-call votes dropped considerably.[20] Also, while Dirksen had opposed the Administration's nomination of John Knowles for Assistant Secretary for Health and Scientific Affairs he had never criticized its policies in public. In contrast, Scott disagreed publicly with the Administration over the tactics it used to promote passage of personal income tax exemption increase. He voiced a hope for a cease-fire in Vietnam and openly opposed amending the Voting Rights Act of 1965. He was not in favor of the so-called "southern strategy." Scott was also unhappy with the lack of communications between the White House and the Senate, and stated so publicly.

Dirksen never had a close working relationship with Scott when Scott was the Minority Whip. Scott, however, believes in shared leadership. He has delegated considerable responsibility to Robert Griffin and also appointed six regional whips to serve under Griffin. This idea of his was rejected by Dirksen in early 1969. The six regional whips included both conservatives and liberals—Senators Edward Brooke, Charles Percy, Edward Gurney, Jack Miller, Clifford Hansen, and Mark Hatfield. Also, Scott has allowed the chairman of the Senate Republican Conference to hold weekly press briefings in the Senate press gallery, a function Dirksen had reserved for himself.[21]

With accession of a Republican President, the Senate Democrats had to fill the void left in policy-making. Mansfield attempted this by boosting the membership of the Democratic Policy Committee from nine to thirteen and expanding the role of the Committee from just scheduling legislation for floor action to that of a full-fledged legislative review committee. The Committee, for example, became the vehicle through which the Democrats decided that they would not allow the passage of a surtax unless it was accompanied by tax reform measures. The Committee also, in the name of Democrats in the Senate, endorsed a 15-percent social security increase, and decided to hold up Senate consideration of the appropriations for the Department of Health, Education and Welfare to gather support in an effort to override the threatened presidential veto.[22]

Under Mansfield's guidance the Democratic Policy Committee has developed into a leadership group of the Democrats in the Senate. Between 1969 and 1971, the Committee passed seventeen resolutions, all but one of which dealt with the Vietnam War. The resolutions were then presented to the full Democratic Conference for ratification. The far-reaching nature of the resolutions and the relative ease with which they were adopted was a surprise to many of the Democrats. Senator Hart, a member of the Policy Committee since 1959, stated that, "under Mansfield's leadership we have moved quickly and it is all to the good."[23]

Early in the 91st session liberals attempted again to modify Rule 22. However they were defeated again by a vice president's ruling. Outgoing Vice President Humphrey ruled that a simple majority could invoke cloture on a motion to take up a change of rules. After much debate and parliamentary maneuvering, Humphrey's ruling was reversed, but the liberals still lacked sufficient votes to relax the cloture rule.

This first session was a seesaw one for the new President. The Administration kept a relatively low profile and there were few direct confrontations with the Congress. Nixon won a razor-thin victory over a proposal to kill the Anti-Ballistic Missile Program, and he gained approval of a draft-lottery system. The Administration's controversial Philadelphia Plan, to ensure minority hiring by contractors on federal construction, was also retained. However, the Senate, in a long and bitter fight led by Birch Bayh, defeated the President's nomination of Clement Haynsworth to the Supreme Court by a 45 to 55 vote after a three-month-long Administration effort to secure nomination.[24]

The second session of the 91st was marked by prolonged clashes with President Nixon over foreign policy and spending. Again the Senate was a battleground, with Senator Fulbright holding hearings on Vietnam. A large number of Senate doves used the hearing and the floor of the Senate to criticize the President's efforts. The debate over the repeal of the Gulf of Tonkin Resolution was perhaps one of the most interesting. Senator Fulbright had been planning to introduce a resolution calling for the repeal of the Gulf of Tonkin Resolution late in the session. However, Republican Senators led by Robert Dole of Kansas offered a resolution for repeal early in the debate over the Cooper-Church amendment. It was a surprise move on their part, and they hoped to steal the credit for repeal from Fulbright. When the resolution was introduced on the Senate floor, Fulbright moved to have it tabled. He and several other Senate doves, including Eugene McCarthy, wanted the Tonkin Resolution on the books a little longer to give them a vehicle to mount attacks against the policy. However, most of the Senate voted against Fulbright's motion, and voted for Dole's resolution. Many Senate doves sympathetic to Fulbright's position were placed in an awkward situation and voted for Dole's resolution for fear they would be misunderstood by their constituents. Fulbright introduced his repeal resolution later in the session, and the Senate voted again to repeal the Gulf of Tonkin Resolution of 1964.

The introduction of the controversial Cooper-Church amendment caused the Senate to debate the whole spectrum of the Administration's Asian policy. The measure would have prohibited the use of any funds to retain U.S. forces in Cambodia unless the Congress enacted legislation to authorize such operations. For seven weeks late in the year the Senate debated this resolution. Another controversial amendment tacked onto the defense appropriations bill was the "end-the-war amendment" authored by Senators McGovern, Hatfield, Cranston, Hughes, and Goodell. While neither amendment was successful, the Senate doves used the opportunity to air the whole foreign policy situation and the presidential power to conduct it.

In what seemed to be a duplicate of the Haynsworth scenario, the Senate rejected the Administration's second nominee to the Supreme Court, G. Harrold Carswell of Florida. The final vote on the floor of the Senate was a significant one since Senator Marlow Cook, a Republican from Kentucky, who had led the battle for the nomination of Haynsworth, voted against Carswell. Four southern Democrats—Fulbright, Spong from Virginia, Gore from Tennessee, and Yarborough from Texas—also voted against the nomination. Gore and Yarborough, already in trouble in their states, were not assisted by their Nay votes for Carswell.

On the domestic side of the fence the "New Politics" senators were intent on trying to push costly alternatives to Nixon's proposals. McGovern was planning more generous legislative alternatives to Nixon's welfare program; Hartke was proposing large increases in anticrime grants; and Muskie planned extensive hearings on air and water pollution with an eye toward more comprehensive legislation.

The principal quarrel with the President was over spending priorities. Congress sliced funds from his military, foreign aid, and space requests, and added money to numerous domestic programs, notably education, health, manpower training, and pollution. It enacted a spending ceiling for fiscal year 1971, the third year it had done so. Nixon responded by vetoing health measures, among others. He also sought to have the secondary-education programs consolidated and a variety of housing programs streamlined. But the Congress in response added funds to these programs, kept them separate, and in some cases established new programs.

Despite the extended debates over the Carswell nomination and the various end-the-war amendments, the second session of the 91st Congress was one of the most productive in recent years in the area of domestic legislation. Congress established a government postal corporation, wrote major air and water pollution measures, extended the 1965 Voting Rights Act, and passed legislation allowing eighteen-year-olds the right to vote in the upcoming election. It also enacted the first occupational safety and health bill in history.

The 1970 off-year elections were unusual in that the Administration campaigned heavily for some Republicans and against others. One of their key targets for elimination was Charles Goodell of New York. In the previous year Goodell had taken a decided turn to the left and had become overwhelmingly associated with antiwar factions in the Senate. He had traveled around the country speaking to various groups and had gained considerable publicity for himself. In the process he also gained the disfavor of the Administration and of the New York State Republican Party. Faced with stiff opposition in the campaign from Democrat Richard Ottinger and Conservative James Buckley, Goodell did not get the support he needed from the Republican Party to mount an effective campaign. This plus a conservative swing of the voters in New York State defeated him in the 1970 elections. James Buckley of New York, the Conservative Party candidate, won the three-way race and announced that he would caucus with the Republicans.

Yarborough, a liberal Democrat, did not even get to the election campaign. He was defeated in the primary. William Brock, a Republican, won Gore's seat in a close election, and Lloyd Bentsen, a wealthy Texan and a moderate, ran a tough race against Republican George Bush to win Yarborough's seat. Joseph Tydings lost to conservative J. Glen Beall in Maryland, and Robert Taft, Jr. defeated Howard Metzenbaum in Ohio for retiring Senator Young's seat. Moderate Republican Lowell Weicker won Senator Thomas Dodd's Connecticut seat, defeating both the Reverend Joseph Duffey running on the Democratic ticket and Senator Thomas Dodd running on an independent ticket. The Republicans gained two seats, bringing their total number to forty-five as opposed to fifty-five for the Democrats.

There were more leadership changes in sight in the 92nd Congress. Senator Robert C. Byrd of West Virginia was elected Majority Whip over Edward Kennedy by a vote of 31 to 24.[25] Byrd's victory was the result of a long and careful campaign. He had been managing many of the Whip's functions such as marshalling votes, handling party activities, and filling in for Kennedy during the latter's extensive absences in the 91st Congress due to Chappaquiddick, his father's death, and his reelection campaign.

On the Republican side of the aisle, Howard Baker again challenged Hugh Scott for the minority leadership. Scott won by a vote of 24 to 20. Baker had not intended to run, but Senators Cooper of Kentucky and Young of North Dakota prevailed upon him to oppose Scott and Hruska nominated him. This illustrated the support Baker had from the more conservative wing of the party.[26]

The biennial attack on Rule 22 was mounted early in the session. However, southern Democrats, led by Senators Ervin, Eastland, and Ellender, mounted a three-week filibuster. They offered various compromises to the opposing forces, which were rejected, and in the end the liberals did not succeed in making any substantive changes. Prior to the filibuster they thought they had between fifty-five and sixty firm votes for modification of the rule. The filibuster was successful, and the liberals lost their votes.[27]

In response to a detailed memorandum from Senator Fred Harris of Oklahoma, the Democratic Conference at the beginning of the 92nd Congress adopted several reforms. Harris had suggested that Senate Democrats confer as a body once a week or at least once a month, and that these meetings be public. He wanted the Democratic Conference to have the power to pass judgment upon individual committee assignments that are voted upon by the seventeen-member Democratic Steering Committee. He also wanted the Conference to empanel a special committee on reforming the seniority system and on creating prospective guidelines for party loyalty.[28]

In response to Harris's push for reforms, Mansfield agreed to convene the Democratic Conference whenever any of its fifty-five members requested a meeting. Mansfield established the precedent that the Conference might nullify by majority secret ballot any committee assignment and retain the power to name committee chairmen. He also set up a special three-man committee, headed by Harris, to study both seniority and party loyalty.[29]

It was a historic move on the part of Mansfield, and a triumph for the liberal senators like Proxmire, the now defeated Gore, and Douglas. As far back as 1957, all of them had been calling for regular meetings of the Conference with specific agenda to consider the legislative program. New Politics senators could count these concessions as some of the most important reforms ever made in the Senate.

But perhaps the most far-reaching move by Mansfield was to confer on the Conference the power to remove committee chairmen. Mansfield claimed that the Conference is "empowered to decide all questions of committee membership, including chairmen, ratios, distribution and the basis on which assignments are made."[30] This was the first major tinkering with the seniority system since Lyndon Johnson established the Johnson Rule, whereby all Democratic senators are to have a seat on one major committee before any Democrat is assigned to a second major committee.

The Republicans finally voted their own version of this rule in 1971, stating that no senator shall be the ranking minority member of more than one standing committee in the Senate. The Republicans also established committees to study the seniority system. The five-member Republican Committee consisted of Senators Bennett, Boggs, Hansen, Packwood, and Taft.

In March 1971, the Senate rejected a major challenge to the seniority system by tabling a resolution introduced by Fred Harris and Charles Mathias that would have permitted the selection of committee chairmen on some basis other than seniority. The resolution provided that in making committee assignment "neither party conference shall be bound by any tradition, custom or principle of seniority."[31]

Reforms that liberal New Politics senators had long desired concerning the internal operations of their party mechanisms were being quietly implemented. But they found themselves engaged in a series of bouts with the President over presidential vetoes of legislation and impoundment of funds, as well as in efforts to limit the President's power to involve the United States in war.

With the reelection of President Nixon in 1972 by a huge majority, there was grave concern in the Senate over the power of the President. But Democrats maintained control of the Senate and increased their majority by two to fifty-seven. Three seemingly well-entrenched Republicans were upset, including J. Caleb Boggs of Delaware, who lost to young Joseph Biden; Margaret Chase Smith, who was defeated by liberal William D. Hathaway; and Gordon Allott of Colorado, who lost to Floyd Haskell, an opponent of the war in Vietnam. If it had not been for Republican victories in four southern states (Virginia, North Carolina, Oklahoma, and Texas), the Democratic majority in the Senate would have been much larger. Other freshmen Democratic senators in the Class of 1972 included outspoken liberal war opponent James Abourezk of South Dakota and moderate Dick Clark, who defeated Jack Miller of Iowa. The Democrats, particularly in the Senate, were ready to battle the President over such things as impoundment of appropriated funds, the war in Southeast Asia, and the setting of priorities.

However, if the Congress and particularly the Senate was going to challenge the President and recoup some of its "lost power," it would have to reorganize its procedures. Concern was such that early in 1973 senators and congressmen invited twenty well-known professors of law, government, history, and economics to discuss what could be done about the Congress and its efforts to recover some of these lost powers. Concern was expressed by members of Congress over the control of federal spending. Most of the professors who attended the meeting, including Charles O. Jones of the University of Pittsburgh, concluded that there was no constitutional crisis. Jones stated that "Part of the price of Vietnam is an urge to cut the presidency back to size not only in his war-making powers which is defensible but in his domestic leadership."[32] Concerning the impoundment issue, several of the professors suggested that the Congress get a handle on the budget so the President cannot charge them with fiscal irresponsibility. Congress should also "fix" the Anti-Deficiency Act of 1905, which gives the President the right to reserve funds. In general the professors suggested that the problem was not a matter of cutting the President down but of building the Congress up. Several senators, including Edward Kennedy and Harold Hughes, did not share this view. They believed that the Congress had been pushed into a corner where it was useless to the people, and that it badly needed to regain some of its constitutional powers.[33]

This mood governed the Congress's attitude towards President Nixon throughout 1973. Linked with this was a sense of helplessness and inability to cope, particularly with the federal budget. With the President exercising his veto power on one level and impounding funds on another, and criticizing the members as "spendthrifts," senators and congressmen began to look seriously at the outdated methods utilized to review the federal budget.

In July the Senate Government Operations Committee approved a bill to reform the authorization-appropriation system in the Senate. There was considerable debate over the bill and Senators Muskie, Percy, and Brock, among others, strongly opposed the plan as it came out of the Committee. Muskie presented an alternative plan that he claimed would give the Senate more flexibility and would not concentrate the power into one super Joint

Committee. Muskie was expressing the fears of the liberals that this Joint Committee would be dominated by the elder conservative members of the House and Senate who were still strong on the Finance and Appropriations Committees. While nothing was resolved concerning this matter in the first session of the 93rd Congress, the reform of congressional methods of dealing with the federal budget was under way.

The Watergate scandal weakened the President and sidetracked the clash with Congress over the federal budget. One result of this weakened position was the passage of a bill in July severely restricting presidential war powers. It was approved by a lopsided vote in the Senate. Senator Eagleton offered amendments to make it even more restrictive, but was voted down. Although the House vote was very close, the Senate overrode the presidential veto of this bill with plenty of votes to spare. It was the only one of nine Nixon vetoes overriden in that session.

The Senate also passed bills that would require Senate confirmation of future nominees for the positions of Director and Deputy Director of the Office of Management and Budget, Executive Director of the National Security Council, and Executive Director of the Domestic Council. The legislation passed the House of Representatives, but was vetoed by the President.[34]

In terms of internal reform, the issue of open versus closed committees was the subject of heated debate. The Senate's senior members teamed up on March 6, 1973 to defeat an antisecrecy proposal that would have required Senate committees to hold meetings in public unless a majority voted at each meeting to close its doors. The amendment to the rules of the Senate, offered by William V. Roth, Jr., a Republican from Delaware, was beaten on a 38 to 47 roll-call vote. The Senate then voted 91 to 0 in favor of a milder proposal endorsed by the Rules and Administration Committee that would have granted each standing committee the right to set up its own rules concerning public meetings.[35]

The debate on Roth's amendment covered a wide range of issues, but national security and the public image of the Congress were the central themes. Supporters of Roth's proposal claimed that Congress had reached a low point in its reputation and needed reform to make it more responsive. Critics countered that the amendment would place America in danger by revealing state secrets in open meetings. In the end the reformers lost, but the vote was very close.

An Overview

Recognition that a problem exists is usually a first step toward a solution. In the case of Congress in general and the Senate in particular, the public polls should provide sufficient basis for recognizing that some change is necessary to regain public confidence. Despite all the Watergate uproar and the consequent drop in the President's popularity and in the public's confidence in his Administration, the public in 1974 was still rating Congress even lower than it rated the President. Since the Senate is the more visible of the two houses, this low rating in the polls was not to be taken lightly.

The paradox is that in the face of the low esteem in which the public holds Congress, every presidential nominee since 1960 with the exception of Richard Nixon was a senator. His Senate service ended in 1953 and so he was not a member of the modern Senate. In a sense this may be part of the problem in the Senate. Lyndon Johnson accumulated so much power that he left a major gap when he became Vice President.

No one person has taken Johnson's place. Instead, genial Mike Mansfield has been the leader, and many of the other significant Democratic senators—Humphrey, McGovern, Muskie, Jackson, Bayh, McCarthy, Harris, Mondale, and Eagleton—have been jockeying for position as future presidential candidates. This internal competition made it difficult for the Democrats to coalesce even for the purpose of maximizing the political potential of Watergate.

Internal reforms of the mechanisms within the Senate have come slowly. While there was a Democratic president, the Senate Democrats felt little need to reform their methods of operation. The move toward New Politics policy positions began in the early 1960s. However, not until the election of a Republican president were efforts made to adopt New Politics procedural reforms as well. Internal reforms like the expansion of the Democratic Policy Committee, the relaxation of the seniority rules, and establishment of more openness in committee hearings have all come during the Nixon presidency. Another view might be that those reforms could not have come until the New Politics Democrats had sufficient seniority and status.

At the same time, in recent years the Democratic majority in the Senate has been busy defending the domestic and civil rights legislative gains of the sixties from Nixon's new priority and value approaches. This is at the heart of the impoundment controversy, which will be taken up in chapter 10.

In his classic book on the Senate, *Citadel: Story of the U.S. Senate,* William S. White wrote of the "Inner Club" that existed in the Senate in the fifties. The unifying theme of the Club was a sense that being a senator was almost as great an honor as being president.[36] The hectic pace of social and political change in the Senate in the sixties has broken down the Inner Club, and in a sense the New Politics senators have become a new club. While the style of operation is somewhat less exclusionary, there is no changing the fact that the one-hundred-seat Senate with its six-year terms is still one of the most exclusive clubs in the world. The Senate may effect all the internal reforms it wishes, but the prestige and importance of being a United States Senator, and the sense of the Senate's significance in the scheme of our government, is of greater consequence. If this is lost, all the internal reforms really won't have much meaning.

7

New Politics and Congressional Party Organization

The two political parties and their party machinery within the Congress have necessarily been affected by the New Politics. The basic goal of a party within Congress is to provide itself with the leadership to make a legislative record in the Congress that will convince the electorate that it should vote for that party's candidates in the upcoming election. Toward this end, the majority party seeks to control the legislative process, pass popular legislation, and block unacceptable bills. The leadership's test is to produce the necessary votes to achieve these purposes.

Party machinery designed for enforcement of majority party goals pivots on the Speaker of the House, who leads the majority party and also serves as the Chamber's presiding officer. His power is great and his office is the only congressional office identified in the Constitution. He has extensive input into legislative strategy, development of the legislative programs, and the committee assignments given to members of his party. Under the House rules he exercises his judgment in referring bills to committees and has the parliamentary power to recognize members on the floor during the debates. The House Majority Leader serves as the Speaker's bridge to his party and is responsible for the Party's legislative program.

There is no Senate counterpart to the Speaker of the House, as the majority party leadership and presiding officer functions are separate. The Vice President, who may not even represent the majority party, presides over the Senate although he is rarely present. Usually the President pro tempore of the Senate, the senior senator of the majority party, presides, but the job is not especially sought after and the chair is often occupied by freshmen senators. The Senate Majority Leader possesses most of the Speaker's powers and is the most powerful senator. He is responsible for creating the party record and determining party strategy.

There are also minority leaders in both houses and they have comparable leadership tasks, although their powers and opportunities are more limited than those of the Speaker or the Senate Majority Leader. The whips are responsible for keeping the congressmen and their staffs informed as to the legislative program for the week and presenting to them the party position on the major issues. They are also responsible for determining the presence or absence of their members for a vote. In addition, they function as an intelligence-gathering unit for the leadership, briefing them on the voting inclinations of the party members.

The whip organization in the House is elaborate and organized along regional lines. For instance, the Republican Whip is formally appointed by a vote of the Republican Party Conference, which meets at the beginning of a new Congress. He in turn appoints four regional whips for the East, the

Midwest, the South, and the West. He also selects fifteen assistant whips from these areas. The Democrats use a different method to select their whip. The Majority Floor Leader appoints the whip, and fifteen to seventeen assistant whips are selected on a regional basis by state delegations.

Party Caucuses, Conferences, and Committees

The principal governing body of each party in the House and Senate is the Party Conference, or Caucus, as the House Democrats call it. The Conference meets at the beginning of each new Congress to consider an agenda, which usually consists of election of members to leadership posts and consideration of party policy, procedures, and legislative programs.

Elections for leadership posts on the Democratic side of the House have tended to be cut and dried, while the Republicans have had several hotly contested elections. In 1959 Charles Halleck of Indiana ousted Joe Martin for the minority leadership post, and Halleck in turn was dumped in 1965 by Gerald Ford in a close 73 to 67 vote. Ford's support spanned the spectrum of Republican ideology and he maintained his post until President Nixon named him to the vice presidency in the fall of 1973. John J. Rhodes was elected by the Conference to succeed Ford.

Lesser posts have been equally contested in Conference meetings. Melvin Laird faced stiff opposition from Peter Frelinghuysen of New Jersey for the post of presiding officer of the Republican Conference in 1965. Frelinghuysen then fought for the position of Minority Whip to replace Leslie Arends, the incumbent. With the support of the more conservative elements Arends was reelected, but it was a tough fight.

Battles for leadership posts on the Democratic side in the House have not been as dramatic. In 1969 Morris Udall challenged John McCormack for the Speakership, but was defeated by a large margin. When McCormack announced that he would retire in 1970, it was expected that Carl Albert, the Majority Leader, would be elected. When this occurred at the beginning of the 1971 session, Hale Boggs, the Majority Whip, was nominated for the Majority Leader position and was challenged by Udall and B. F. Sisk of California, but Boggs was able to overcome the opposition.

On the Senate side the Democrats have experienced several challenges for major leadership posts. In 1968, Senator Kennedy of Massachusetts, in a surprise move, successfully challenged Russell Long of Louisiana for the post of Assistant Majority Leader, and in 1971 Kennedy in turn was successfully challenged by Robert Byrd of West Virginia.

The policy committees in the House and Senate were established in an effort to coordinate party strategy and tactics concerning legislation. Membership on these policy committees is achieved in varying ways. In the Senate, members of the Democratic Policy Committee are appointed by the Majority Leader, with ratification by the Democratic Caucus. New members are appointed only when vacancies occur through death or failure to gain reelection.

The Senate Republican Policy Committee, presently chaired by Senator Tower of Texas, consists of fifteen senators chosen by the Republican Conference at the beginning of a new Congress from a list presented to them by the Minority Leader after much consultation with leaders in the Party. Members of the Policy Committee also include the Minority Leader, the Whip, and the Chairmen of the Committee on Committees and Campaign Committee, all of whom serve as ex officio members. Elected members of the Policy Committee serve two-year terms; thus there is some circulation of membership among the various factions and geographical interests of the Party.

The Republican Policy Committee on the Senate side is a more active group, with the staff resources to perform useful research and publicity work. The Committee also hosts a luncheon every Tuesday, open to all senators. This has proved to be very useful and informative to the Republicans in the Senate.

In the House, the Democratic Steering and Policy Committee is chaired by the Speaker of the House, and has two vice chairmen, the Majority Leader and the Chairman of the Democratic Caucus. There are twelve elected regional members and eight members appointed by the Speaker, including the Majority Whip and four deputy whips. The Steering and Policy Committee is considered to have nominal existence only, and its record shows that it has done little to enhance party unity or resolve divisive party issues.

The Republican Policy Committee, consisting of twenty-seven members, is reconstituted by a resolution passed by the Republican Conference at the beginning of each Congress. The Minority Leader, the elected Chairman of the Conference, the Whip, the Secretary and Vice President of the Conference, the Chairman of the Research Committee, the Chairman of the Congressional Campaign Committee, and the ranking member of the Rules Committee automatically become members. Republicans from eight geographical areas of the country are elected by the Conference to serve on the Policy Committee. The Leadership also invites three congressmen from the more recent Congresses; e.g., two members from the 92nd and one member from the 93rd were elected by their respective clubs to serve in 1973–74. The Minority Leader also selects seven members from important standing committees and areas or states not represented.

The Policy Committee meets every Tuesday. When they plan to make a statement on a piece of pending legislation they invite members of the committee having jurisdiction over that legislation to meet with them to help draft a statement. The Committee also has several subcommittees concentrating on various policy areas.

In each house, the parties have set up a committee that assigns members to committees. In the Senate, the Democrats call this the Steering Committee and the Republicans call it the Committee on Committees. Senator Mansfield, the Majority Leader, chairs the Steering Committee and chooses the members who will serve. Members are selected after consultation with the Assistant Majority Leader and other party leaders, to ensure equitable geographical representation. If a senator is a member of the Policy Committee he cannot serve on the Steering Committee. The Steering Committee follows the "Johnson Rule," since no Democratic senator can be assigned to a second major committee until all the others have one such membership. Even freshmen senators get at least one good assignment.

The Senate Republican Committee on Committees chairman and members must have the approval of the Conference. Their names are presented to the full Conference prior to the beginning of a new Congress by the leadership. The Republicans generally follow the same procedure as the Democrats in appointing freshmen senators to major committees.

In the House, the Democratic Committee on Committees consists of the Democratic members of the Ways and Means Committee and is chaired by the Ways and Means Committee chairman, or its ranking minority member if the Republicans have a House majority. Committee assignments have been based on seniority, but New Politics congressmen have been slowly easing that hard-and-fast criterion.

The House Republican Committee on Committees is chaired by the Minority Leader. Members of the Committee are selected by the leadership with the approval of the full Conference.

Assigning members to committees is not always a smooth procedure, particularly if it develops into a power struggle, as it did in 1965 when the new Minority Leader, Gerald Ford, attempted to have his choice, Charles Goodell of New York, named to the Republican vacancy on the Ways and Means Committee. He was thwarted by the Committee on Committees, which selected conservative James Batten of Montana. Three of the men on the Committee on Committees—Arends of Illinois, Utt of California, and Fulton of Pennsylvania—carried too much weight for Ford to overcome. Their state delegations were among the largest and their vote carried Batten through the Republican Conference.[1]

Liberals in the Democratic Caucus in 1971 saw one of the former Democratic Study Group chairmen, Donald Fraser, lose a seat on the Ways and Means Committee to conservative Joe Waggoner of Louisiana. In this case the Democratic Caucus voted to seat Waggoner on that Committee.

In 1970, the Democratic Caucus had voted to establish the Committee on Organizational Study and Revision, chaired by Julia Butler Hansen of Washington. The Committee reported to the Caucus in 1971 the following recommendations for selection of members to committees:

1. That the Committee on Committees recommend to the Caucus nominees for chairmen and membership on the committees. Such recommendations need not follow seniority.
2. That the Committee would make recommendations to the Caucus concerning one committee at a time if demanded by 10 or more members. Nominations could be debated and voted upon separately.
3. If a nomination was rejected, the Committee on Committees would submit more nominations.
4. No member could be chairman of more than one legislative subcommittee.[2]

The Caucus adopted the recommendations. The Republican Conference also voted to reform its selection of committee members. Under the new procedure the Committee on Committees selects the nominees, but the Conference votes for each nominee on a secret ballot. "This would make Republican committee members leaders and not just survivors."[3]

Congressional campaign committees in each House are designed mainly to render campaign assistance to party members. They provide financial aid for public relations expenses such as newsletters, questionnaires, and radio tapes, but not for travel expenses. Staff resources are available to help members with some of the public relations problems they may encounter.

In outlining the structure of the Congressional party machinery, from the Speaker and floor leaders through the whip organizations and the various conferences and committees, it is obvious that the party leadership possesses a number of bargaining advantages with which it can seek to develop party cohesion and produce a good party record. Despite their controls over the party machinery, party leaders maintain party harmony primarily through persuasion.

Four patterns of majority party leadership have emerged in this century. The most common is leadership by the Speaker, who plays a major part in the determination of party strategy and tactics. On occasion he will yield this power to majority leaders, as did William Bankhead between 1937 and 1940 when he assigned Sam Rayburn to the role of chief strategist.[4] A third relationship occurs when the Speaker shares his authority with his chief lieutenants. John McCormack, who succeeded Rayburn as Speaker, shifted to this type of pattern by involving Majority Leader Carl Albert and Whip Hale Boggs in tactical decision-making. The fourth pattern of leadership is rarely seen. It occurred in the early years of the New Deal when House Democrats deferred entirely to the President. While the evidence is not conclusive, the highly centralized patterns, where a single figure dominates the party machinery, seem to produce the best legislative results. Leroy Rieselbach states that up until 1959, the Republicans were disorganized and without structured purposeful leadership. Since 1959, the Republicans have developed a shared-leadership pattern.[5]

In the Senate the same patterns are evident; allowing for the differences in size and the absence of the elaborate organization existing in the House. Lyndon Johnson is the best example of a strong majority leader dominating party strategy. He did so with a strong inner group of Senate friends, including Everett Dirksen, the Minority Leader, with whom he frequently made deals for support. As indicated in chapter 6, Senator Mike Mansfield does not dominate the Senate majority in the same way, since he tends to share the leadership with his top assistants. During the Nixon presidency the Republicans, on the other hand, found themselves in the unique situation of being a minority party in the Senate while their party controlled the Executive Branch. Thus, they became spokesmen for the President in the Senate—backing his legislative program and endeavoring to get it passed.

The outstanding characteristic of these various formal organizations of the political parties in both houses is the domination by the leadership. The leadership in the House and Senate is reluctant to allow the control to move out of their hands. The state delegations hold meetings and serve useful purposes, but these groups are generally nonideological. They are also controlled by senior members, who are referred to as delegation deans. With this in mind it is easy to understand why congressmen, particularly members of the House, turn to such groups as the Democratic Study Group or the Wednesday Group to develop leverage. There is a need for the members who are not part of the leadership to feel they have some influence on an input to the legislation being offered for their consideration. There is also a very important need to communicate with other members of similar views, and again this is more important in the House than in the Senate. Nevertheless, there are "class" groups in each House as those beginning their service come together to learn the ropes and share their problems.

The Senate Groupings

There is no Democratic counterpart to the DSG in the Senate, although there is a small Republican Wednesday Group there. Senators do not face the constant pressure of reelection every two years. Senators also have larger staffs, and are already members of a group that is small enough to facilitate closer relationships.

However, Senators sometimes have formed informal groups, such as the "Inner Club" discussed in chapter 6. In a 1969 article entitled "Goodbye to the Inner Club," Nelson W. Polsby argued that Majority Leader Lyndon Johnson was one of the most steadfast promoters of the whole idea of the Inner Club.[6] For instance, Senator Joseph S. Clark described a lunch that Johnson gave for Clark's "class" of freshmen Democrats in 1957. Each guest was presented with a copy of White's book *Citadel,* and during the lunch Johnson encouraged them to read it as if it were a basic textbook. Polsby contends that the Inner Club was in essence the façade for Johnson's centralization of the political power in the Senate into his own hands.[7] Since Lyndon Johnson left the Senate, his type of centralized power has not reappeared.

Over the years the Senate has been dominated largely by the southern senators. It has a very established way of doing business, including many rules and courtesies, all designed to enable it to function and to keep friction at a minimum. Nevertheless, because of the media attention the Senate receives and because of its special role in foreign relations and in confirming presidential appointees, the Senate has become a springboard for presidential candidates, especially among the Democrats, whose last four candidates were senators. Whether this has been harmful to the Senate as a deliberative body is another story. Interestingly, when the precedent-setting resignation of Vice President Agnew occurred, House Minority Leader Gerald Ford was jumped over the top Republican senators as Agnew's replacement. Nixon's long-time friendship with Ford, and the fact that the House, not the Senate, has the power to vote articles of impeachment of the President, were special factors influencing Nixon's decision.

The Democratic Study Group

As suggested, the 435-member House is too large to operate as informally as the Senate. The best organized and most influential group in the House is the Democratic Study Group (DSG), an offspring of the New Politics movement. It was born as Dwight Eisenhower, the first Republican President since 1932, was concluding his second term in the White House. The liberal Democratic members of the House of Representatives had previously made several attempts to develop greater cohesion, and that led to the election of a large number of new Democrats in 1958.

Both parties were anxious to improve their position for the upcoming 1960 elections. Although they were members of the majority party, the liberal Democrats felt somewhat leaderless. Sam Rayburn was Speaker of the House and the levers of control were in the firm grasp of chairmen from southern and border states. Republican control of the White House resulted in more domination of Congress by the Conservative Coalition of Republicans and southern Democrats. In addition, on many issues the southern Democrats made deals with the northern Democrats who represented big-city districts where party machines created a virtual one-party situation. Majority Leader John McCormack of Massachusetts was personally a liberal, yet this did not strengthen *their* hand because he had become Speaker. Rayburn had selected him for his talent in getting along with the diverse groups in the Democratic party, and not for any penchant for challenging them ideologically.

Given such a political environment, the newer Democratic representatives with liberal leanings faced a dilemma. They were generally closer to the developing groundswell related to such emotional issues as civil rights and the urban crisis. Further, they tended to be from districts that were more competitive than those represented by members of the conservative coalition. While the big-city and southern Democrats were concerned with power and patronage, the new liberal congressmen were also concerned with issues. They needed to influence the decision process to establish a record for their reelection to the House. The difference in values, concerns, and constituencies between these new members and their Democratic seniors was an unsettling factor in itself. However, the new members' potential impact also was limited by the traditions and the institutions of the House. As a result even as a group they had much less power than their numbers should have justified.

Many of the key votes were taken in the Committee of the Whole House, usually after lengthy and rambling discussions. Activist congressmen were impatient with such sessions, and so they had a poor attendance pattern on these nonrecord votes. That factor, along with the natural tendency of the House Democratic leadership to respond to the existing organized party leadership—the committee chairman and the whips—meant that the newer group had little influence in voting or in trying to serve as power brokers.

It is virtually impossible for any representative, especially one who is still learning his job, to develop full information concerning the vast variety of items upon which he must vote. Consequently the representative is generally driven to take cues from representatives who are more knowledgeable. This immediately reduces to a rather small number the persons from whom one could take cues; it generally means that cues are taken from a member of the committee handling the legislation. It may also mean that the best cue-maker available might not have a policy position totally acceptable to the junior member.

The New Politics concern with an open discussion of issues was evident in planning for the new House organization as well as in its early functioning. To some extent the problem was created by the traditional House Democratic preference for limiting Caucus meetings to nonprocedural matters. In his *History of the House of Representatives,* George B. Galloway reported that the Democratic Caucus did not hold a single meeting on a substantive issue between 1953 and 1960, while during that same time period the House Republican Conference met at least forty times on such issues.[8]

As a consequence, the liberal group grew frustrated at its inability to assist in the establishment of more activist social policies consistent with the 1956 candidacy of Adlai Stevenson and the forthcoming 1960 candidacy of John F. Kennedy. It would be no exaggeration to say that the Legislative Reorganization Act of 1970, as well as other House procedural reforms, had their roots in the late 1950s. That was when this group of younger congressmen with New Politics leanings started to make systematic moves to counter the influence of the Conservative Coalition.

Though there had been spasmodic attempts by liberals to coalesce on key votes in prior years, the first systematically organized initiative occurred in January 1957, after President Eisenhower defeated Adlai Stevenson for the second time. A group led by Eugene McCarthy, Lee Metcalf, and Frank Thompson prepared and distributed a Liberal Manifesto immediately prior to the President's State of the Union Address. McCarthy wrote most of the document, but Metcalf prepared the portion on resources, Chet Holifield the piece on atomic energy, and John Blatnik the section on public works.

The document was circulated among House Democrats considered likely to sign it. Members of the leadership as well as committee chairmen were not invited to endorse the program since it was assumed that they would resent the challenge to the elected party leadership or would be in a difficult position to respond affirmatively. Despite this assumption, four chairmen came forward voluntarily to join the other seventy-six signers. As a courtesy the document was shown to Speaker Rayburn several days before it was made public.[9]

While twenty-one states were represented among the signatories, there was a heavy representation from northern and western urban areas. For example, New York City provided thirteen of New York's fourteen signatures, Chicago all eight of those from Illinois, and Detroit the eight from Michigan. Philadelphia provided five, Los Angeles and San Francisco three each, and Pittsburgh two. These seven cities alone provided forty-three of the eighty signatures. Support might have been higher except that the broad scope of the policy items included in the Manifesto dissuaded some potential signers, even though they might have supported a majority of the items in the program.

During the 85th Congress, which began in 1957, the liberal Democrats established a whip system to improve group turnout and cohesion on key votes. This group held periodic meetings, usually in the office of Eugene McCarthy, with twelve members of the whip group serving as an informal executive committee. The whips were John Blatnik, Chet Holifield, Ray Madden, Lee Metcalf, John Moss, Melvin Prince, Henry Reuss, George Rhodes, James Roosevelt, Frank Thompson, Stewart Udall, and Sidney Yates. For about a year the group cooperatively hired a staff director and a stenographer, who were paid out of the clerk allowances of several of the leading members.[10]

The election year of 1958 proved to be very significant for the growth of the potential Democratic Study Group. First, its chairman, Eugene McCarthy, ran successfully for the Senate. Second, the group offered some technical assistance to approximately eighty-five Democrats running for Congress. More than fifty of these candidates requested help and thirty-five were eventually elected to the 86th Congress. This group provided much of the numerical strength necessary to the success of the DSG, which was yet to be formally organized.

As the new Congress opened, the behavior of the House Rules Committee in blocking legislation was designated the prime target. Speaker Sam Rayburn was following a conservative course, and yet it was much less conservative than the rest of the House leadership would have wanted. In turn, there were situations where Rayburn was able to use a quasi-organized group to support things he wanted. The group therefore was careful to consult periodically with Rayburn. Richard Bolling, a Rayburn protégé and a key member of the Rules Committee, intervened on their behalf as situations required.

Since the election caused some significant membership changes on the Rules Committee, the group sent Chet Holifield and John Blatnik to meet with Speaker Rayburn on the subject. One approach would have been to push for a reinstitution of the twenty-one-day rule used in the 81st Congress as a means of bypassing the committee. Another possibility was to use the increased proportion of Democratic membership in the House as the basis of a change in control. The party ratio on the Rules Committee could have been revised or its total size increased so that a sufficient number of additional members friendly to the Democratic liberals could have been added. Rayburn was unable to agree to either of these proposals, but promised instead that he would personally insure that the Rules Committee would not block legislation. In making this commitment he was relying upon his relationship with Minority Leader Joe Martin of Massachusetts, who controlled several key Republican votes on the Committee. Only days after the meeting with Rayburn, the Republican Conference suddenly dumped Martin as minority leader and replaced him with Charles Halleck of Indiana. Halleck appointed two strong conservatives to the Rules Committee and would not agree to any ratio changes or changes in the size of the Committee that would strengthen the power of the Democratic liberals. This added to the pressure by the liberal Democrats for more extensive changes.[11]

In April 1959 the group adopted the name the "Congressional Study Group," as a means of avoiding its growing "young Turk" image. However, the group took a considerable beating in its efforts to defeat the Landrum-Griffin Labor Act of 1959, because of poor preparation and organization. It became apparent that Speaker Rayburn would be unable to deliver on his commitments. Various liberals reacted in different ways to this. Some started to respond in a punitive way against legislation supported by the Conservative Coalition. This backfired in several situations, and the leadership of the Congressional Study Group decided that the lack of formal organization and discipline was contributing to the fragmentation of liberal efforts.[12]

New legislation on housing, civil rights, area redevelopment, medical care for the aged, aid to education, and minimum wages was defeated on the House floor or died in committee. Despite having the largest Democratic majority in the House since the New Deal, John Blatnik noted that "between January and September 1959 liberals lost 10 of 11 key roll call votes. They had no way to match the power, teamwork, and drive of the conservatives."[13]

A new planning committee was organized to establish a more formal organization. It recommended that a much larger policy group be established, which would also have the function of providing whip services. After these recommendations were accepted, the group changed its name to the Democratic Study Group (DSG), and proceeded to invite many Democrats to join the organization. The September 1959 letter of invitation from the temporary chairman, Lee Metcalf, noted:

We all realize that there will be basic conflicts between individual beliefs and among the interests of the districts which we represent. But these may be resolved in a freer discussion of each other's problems than we are able to get from floor debate. No individual participating will be asked to bind himself to a group decision.[14]

It was agreed that the membership of the DSG would be kept secret. Although the members themselves would know who belonged, no membership roster would exist as such or be available to the press or the public. In fact, there are three different ways of categorizing "membership"—those who pay the $100 dues, those on the whip lists, and those on the mailing list. DSG claimed 80 members in 1959 and 165 in 1973. The high water mark for the DSG membership was during the 89th Congress, when it reached 175 following the Johnson landslide.[15]

The success of the DSG membership and organization drive is startling. A 1962 study by the National Committee for an Effective Congress declared that of the 263 Democrats in the House, 110 were from southern and border one-party states and sixty were from boss-controlled one-party Democratic districts in the big cities. These big-city Democrats often traded votes with the southern Democrats, sometimes giving the conservative coalition its margin of victory. This meant that there were only ninety-three members out of 263 not under control of either one of those two groups.[16] Obviously not all of the remaining ninety-three Democrats were liberals, yet only three years later DSG claimed 175 actual members. The liberal upsurge was possible because of the increased turnover and increased representation of urban and suburban districts after the 1960 Census required reapportionment of House seats. The very existence of the DSG also gave some of the big-city Democrats an alternative to their southern alliance.

To forestall charges of divisiveness in the Democratic party, the DSG established a geographic balance in the membership of its executive committee, implying that the organization had a geographic rather than an ideological base. Geographic and regional groupings of House members were common, but it was considered inappropriate for ideological groups or factions to organize themselves. They also used the term "Democratic" to offset the faction charge, and took the position that there was nothing wrong with having Democrats who represented various regions meet to study the issues.

When the DSG officially came into existence in September 1959 it selected Lee Metcalf as permanent chairman. In practice, the policy committee was replaced by a series of task forces established to deal with a number of problem areas. The policy group therefore concentrates on the whip functions. When Lee Metcalf followed Eugene McCarthy's path by running successfully for the Senate in 1960, Chet Holifield was selected as the new chairman.

The nine task forces operating in 1960 were reasonably successful, since the DSG was able to be aggressive and to propose party positions. However, after Kennedy became President and established his own task forces on most of these same matters, this format was dropped. The DSG did not want to be in the position of proposing something inconsistent with what a Democratic President was proposing. The task force model was readopted in 1963 because Kennedy suffered serious defeats in the foreign aid area the prior year, and because the movement to secure civil rights legislation was beginning. It has continued to the present, with the number of task forces increasing gradually from two in the 88th Congress to five in the 90th.[17] Then, with the loss of the White House to the Republicans in 1968, the DSG was placed on the defensive as far as domestic policy was concerned. It responded by doubling its task forces to eleven and expanding its staff in the 91st Congress.

In 1961 the DSG attempted to discipline five Democrats who had supported Nixon against Kennedy, by removing their seniority and revising their committee assignments. One prime target of this attempted purge had been Representative William Colmer, whose removal from the Rules Committee would have turned that group over to the control of liberals. Speaker Rayburn blocked this move, claiming that it was an ex post facto attempt, since no specific warning of the penalty for not supporting Kennedy had been given before the election.[18]

The Rules Committee continued to be a major stumbling block. Chairman Howard Smith of Virginia had life-and-death power over legislation. Before a bill can be considered on the House floor, the Rules Committee must decide how much time to allocate for a debate and whether or not the bill can be amended. Even after legislation passes the House, the Rules Committee can refuse to send it to a House Senate conference if there are legislative differences to be resolved. The liberal members of Congress were upset that such power was in the hands of a conservative committee. Although the Democrats had eight of the twelve members on the Rules Committee, Chairman Smith and Representative Colmer consistently voted with the four Republicans against any kind of liberal legislation.

Once again, Blatnik, Holifield, and Henry Reuss of Wisconsin confronted Speaker Sam Rayburn about the Rules Committee problem. While he again refused to go along with a purge of Colmer, this time the Speaker agreed to support an enlargement of the Committee from twelve to fifteen members. After a tough fight on the House floor, the Speaker and the DSG won, in an extremely close 217-to-212 vote. The DSG claimed that it picked up 150 of the votes, and the victory was sealed when 22 Republicans voted for it.[19] The issue of party loyalty arose again in 1964, as many Southern Democrats were pressured to support Barry Goldwater. On October 2, 1964, DSG Chairman John Blatnik inserted a loyalty warning in the *Congressional Record*. While affirming the DSG's belief in the freedom of Democrats to support a presidential candidate acceptable to them, the statement signed by the DSG executive committee added:

We feel that the new Administration and the American public are entitled to expect that the progressive Democratic programs will be implemented by Congress. It must not be thwarted by a repudiated minority holding legislative positions of power which permit them to frustrate the mandate for progress. We do not feel that members who openly support candidates from other parties should be welcomed back into the Democratic fold on an equal basis with loyal Democrats.[20]

In spite of the warning, two Democrats, Albert Watson of South Carolina and John Bell Williams of Mississippi, openly supported Goldwater. When the Democratic Caucus met in January 1965, the DSG insisted on a firm response. In a precedent-setting action these two Congressmen were stripped of their seniority. Watson, a freshman, had little seniority, but Williams had been in Congress for nine terms and was next in line to be Chairman of the Interstate and Foreign Commerce Committee.

The DSG also succeeded in securing a Caucus agreement for some tough new rules. One new rule required the Rules Committee to discharge bills it held over twenty-one days upon receipt of a House petition. Another rule permitted the Speaker to recognize a motion by a committee chairman to send to conference a bill which had passed both Houses. Adoption of these rules enabled the DSG to break the Rules Committee's stranglehold on liberal legislation.

Over the years the DSG had promoted the development of a policy group within the Democratic Caucus. This was in line with the liberals' New Politics and issue orientation. Previously, the southern and big-city machine Democrats had been content to let the leadership wrestle with policy questions, as long as their own political needs were met. The result was a generally inconsistent or negative party approach to major policy questions.

Following the death of Sam Rayburn in 1961, the DSG proposed a policy committee to the newly elected Speaker, John McCormack. The thought was not very revolutionary, since the Republicans already had an equivalent organization. Nevertheless, McCormack objected to a resolution that changed the policy committee with advising and consulting on proposals and party policy and which would have provided it with an office, staff, and space. He finally agreed to a resolution that would create a steering committee rather than a policy committee, to "cooperate and consult with the Democratic Leadership on measures reported by the appropriate legislative committee."[21] The resolution was passed by the Democratic Caucus on March 14, 1962 by a vote of 124 to 66.[22] McCormack was accused of trying to rally the Democratic machine vote in the Caucus to oppose such a steering committee, and then giving up the attempt in the face of the bad publicity it produced.

In the 93rd Congress the Committee was reconstituted as a Steering and Policy Committee with twenty-three members: the Speaker, the majority leader, the Caucus chairman, twelve members elected from equal regions, and eight members appointed by the Speaker. It was given the power to make recommendations to the Committee on Committees regarding nominees for chairmen of House committees.[23] Speaker Carl Albert included a number of DSG members among his eight appointees.

In its first major effort to bolster its growing power, the DSG offered to assist Democratic nominees in the 1964 elections for the House. Richard Bolling was selected to direct a special Campaign Committee. The DSG provided money and/or research support to eighty-five Democratic candidates for the House. Seventy-four of these candidates, two-thirds of whom were newcomers, were elected with substantial assistance from the Johnson landslide. Just as the 1958 election had resulted in a large group of liberal Democratic freshmen making the DSG's organization feasible, the 1964 election meant an influx of many new DSG members. Now the DSG had actual control of the Democratic Party Caucus for the first time, as well as enough votes to beat the conservative coalition on the House floor.

The turnout of liberals for votes in the Committee of the Whole House improved under prodding by the DSG whip system. However, this was still occasionally a problem, and became more serious after 1966 when the DSG membership fell back a bit. Consequently the DSG worked successfully for a rule change whereby teller votes would be recorded. After this rule went into effect in the 92nd Congress, attendance averages increased from 150 before the recording process was begun to 385 in the first year thereafter.[24]

Three political scientists have attempted to determine whether the DSG has succeeded in its primary goal of mobilizing the potential strength of liberal Democrats. Defining a nonunanimous roll call as one where at least 10 percent of those voting opposed the majority, they studied 100 nonunanimous roll call votes from eight Congresses between 1965 and 1970. The analysis showed that DSG liberals had much more cohesion than southern Democrats and Republicans, and that with the single exception of the 91st Congress (1969-70), the trend was toward even greater DSG cohesion, as compared with these other groups. DSG members, drawn almost exclusively from northern and western states, also had significantly higher cohesion scores than non-DSG members who were also nonsouthern.[25]

One additional point considered by the political scientists was the impact of Vietnam on cohesion within the Democratic Study Group. As indicated above, the figures for the 91st Congress showed somewhat less cohesion.

The interviews indicated: there had been an unusual amount of DSG dissension in that Congress, most of it related to the Indochina War and the related questions of the balance of powers between President and Congress and the matter of national priorities. Indeed, a minority of DSG members in the 90th Congress organized as a group with the primary objective of pressing for a policy of U.S. withdrawal from the Indochina military conflict. Labeling themselves "the group," these 15 or so members had by the beginning of the 91st Congress contributed substantially to the growing visibility of the priorities issue in the House, at no small cost to the internal harmony of the DSG.[26]

Analysis of the votes of the 91st Congress disclosed that the noncohesiveness that existed was related strictly to the war and priorities issues. When these matters were removed from the data set, it was clear that the trend toward greater unity was still present.

Among the DSG members most disturbed by the DSG's lack of attention to Vietnam were Phillip Burton and Don Edwards of California, William Ryan of New York, and Robert Kastenmeier of Wisconsin. The DSG majority did not want to take on Vietnam because it feared that introducing the foreign policy issue would split them so badly that DSG effectiveness on domestic issues would be eliminated. In 1971, Burton and James Corman, both of California, tied in a vote for the chairmanship. Burton was elected after a third candidate, Henry Reuss of Wisconsin, withdrew. This served to cover over some of the dissatisfaction of the war opponents.

As the DSG has matured, there has been a growing split within its ranks on some elements of reform which a few years earlier would have been unanimously supported. Seniority is one such issue. In its early years, the DSG was composed primarily of newly elected Democrats. By the time of the 92nd Congress, though, the average DSG member had spent sufficient time in Congress to have some seniority. Now that they were assured of leadership positions, these DSG members were less interested in weakening the seniority process.

Nevertheless, at the 1973 Democratic Party Caucus and on the House floor the DSG took the lead in reforms. It was aided by outside pressures provided by organizations such as Common Cause, Ralph Nader's public interest groups, and the League of Women Voters. Some of the key new rules were:

1. A separate vote requirement on each nominee for committee chairman at the start of every Congress. Such votes are to be kept secret on demand of one-fifth of those present. If a chairman is not renominated, the next Democrat in seniority will be voted on for the post.

2. A legislative four-day notice is needed to approve a closed rule, and if fifty members request it, the Democratic Caucus must meet to consider whether the Democratic members of the Rules Committee should be instructed to permit amendments.

3. After the 93rd Congress, members of exclusive committees must give up their other committee positions.

4. The Speaker, Majority Leader, and Democratic Caucus Chairman are added to the Democratic Committee on Committees.

5. Caucus officers are limited to two terms.

6. Committee meetings can be closed only by a majority roll-call vote and only for reasons involving national security and defamation of character.

7. A Democratic Caucus is created on each committee with power to determine jurisdiction, budgets, ratios, and chairmen of subcommittees. The full Democratic Caucus must ratify appointment of all subcommittee chairmen and members.

8. The delegates representing the District of Columbia, Guam, the Virgin Islands, and Puerto Rico are to have committee seniority and voting rights.

After the Caucus on February 21, 1973, Speaker Carl Albert said, "We are trying to improve the image of Congress. That is difficult to do unless it is as democratic and open as possible."[27]

The Democratic Research Group and the United Democrats

By the 93rd Congress non-DSG Democrats recognized they would have to do something to coordinate their people. The DSG had a stronger research arm than the party leadership. The DSG's strong voice in the Democratic Caucus, and the suspicion that it had too much influence over Speaker Carl Albert, led to dissatisfaction among the more moderate Democrats in the House.

The southern conservative bloc announced that it was forming the Democratic Research Group in an attempt to recoup some of its lost influence in the House. Since 1960, that bloc has lost seats steadily to both Republicans and liberals, so that by 1973 only 76 of the 263 Democrats were from the eleven states of the Confederacy and at least twelve of them were considered liberals. Furthermore, in 1973, for the first time in a century, there was no southerner in the House Democratic leadership, and Carl Albert refused to appoint an acceptable southerner to fill any one of the three Democratic vacancies on the Rules Committee. The southern group protested the appointment of Gillis Long of Louisiana, who is considered a liberal. Southerners hoped that by organizing this new group they might gain the ear of the leadership. Sonny Montgomery of Mississippi, a member of the Steering Committee of the Democratic Research Group, stated: "The liberals have the DSG, the Blacks have the Black Caucus. Maybe if we organize, the leadership would listen to us a little bit."[28]

The moderates' hopes of checking the growing split in the Democratic Party—particularly in the House—between the liberals and the more conservative wing resulted in the formation of the United Democrats. It is a centrist group and its fifty charter members hope to attract under one wing the moderates who do not wish to belong to the DSG or to join the new Southern conservative version of a DSG. Organized in 1973, the group elected B. F. Sisk of California as its chairman. Sisk had served in the House nearly nineteen years and was a charter member of the DSG who moved away from the DSG in the 1970s. Gillis Long of Louisiana was selected as Vice Chairman and Robert Giaimo of Connecticut as Secretary-Treasurer.[29] Basically the group consists of members standing to the right of George McGovern and to the left of George Wallace. The United Democrats have no full-time staff and members pay no dues. The group plans to meet periodically to shape views on legislation, using staffs of members as needed.

The Republican Wednesday Group

In comparison to the large, well-organized, and very vocal DSG, the Wednesday Group is shy and retiring. Anonymity is its motto. Formed in January of 1963 by seven liberal Republicans in the House, the Wednesday Group had a membership of twenty-nine in the 93rd Congress. It is the most liberal and the largest of the informal groups on the Republican side of the House.

Founders of the Group included F. Bradford Morse, John Lindsay, Charles Mathias, Abner Sibal, Robert Stafford, and Stanley Tupper. Mathias and Stafford have since gone on to the Senate and Lindsay became Mayor of New York City. The original seven could be characterized as activists, and most had voting records well to the left of the average Republican in the House. They were issue oriented and "wished to combat the negativism of the Republican Party in its role of the opposition."[30]

Since all were liberals, they were a minority in a minority party, and had a distinct need for an exchange of information that could not be obtained through regular Party channels. The purpose of the Wednesday Group was to facilitate that exchange and to broaden communication among the members. The liberal bias of the Group, while dominant, was never rigid.

During its first year the Group expanded its membership to fifteen, including some who were moderates. However, before it could formalize itself, conflict developed over the nomination of Barry Goldwater as the standard-bearer for the Republican Party in the 1964 presidential election. Some of the members totally dissociated themselves from the Goldwater campaign, while others maintained that party unity was important. The Wednesday Group became linked with anti-Goldwater statements, and several of the more conservative members resigned.

The second big squabble within the Group was the result of the fight between Charles Halleck and Gerald Ford for the House Minority Leadership post. The Group took no formal position because the members were split on their support for the Ford and Halleck candidacies. There was even a proposal among some of the members to force through the candidacy of Robert Stafford, with the idea of preventing any candidate from being able to obtain a majority of the votes, so that a choice more acceptable to the liberal wing of the House Republicans could emerge as a compromise candidate. The tactic was newsworthy and several newspaper columns discussed it. This only served to upset members in the Group who were already supporting Ford. The ploy never developed any strength and was quietly dropped by its proposers, as the majority of the Wednesday Group voted for Ford.[31]

The Group did come together to back Peter Frelinghuysen in his bid to oust Melvin Laird as chairman of the House Republican Conference. Frelinghuysen lost by a narrow margin, but his showing proved that the Group could work as a unit.

Two of the founders of the Wednesday Group, F. Bradford Morse and Robert Stafford, were co-leaders until the end of the 92nd Congress. Morse served as the principal catalyst, the innovator, and the one who coordinated the research topics of the Group. In mid-1972 he left to become Under-Secretary-General of the United Nations. Stafford, now in the senate, had been the Group's executive handling the administrative problems and facilitating the meetings.

The Wednesday Group's membership expanded steadily from twenty in 1965 to twenty-nine in 1973. While broadening communications among the members and generating support for research this expansion diluted the activist attitude of the original Group, most of whom had further political ambitions. The conflict point was whether members should use the Group as a springboard for other political offices. The early activism subsided because of the belief that activism had been costly in terms of cohesion. By the end of 1966, half the membership consisted of men who had joined the Group after the activist period had been superseded by a research and issue period.

Another recurring issue is the Group's size. By 1973 the Group consensus was that it should not grow larger than twenty-nine members. A procedure was adopted to fill vacancies based upon an appraisal of the Group's needs and the corresponding qualifications of the possible candidates. Concerns ranged from gaining members from certain committees or from freshmen and sophomore groups, to providing representation to geographical areas.

Membership in the Wednesday Group during the 93rd Congress included thirteen from the East, nine from the Midwest, six from the West, and one from the South. California, Michigan, Ohio, and Pennsylvania each had at least three members. No Group member served on the Rules Committee, but it had representatives from all of the other twenty standing committees except Agriculture, Public Works, Internal Security, and Standards of Official Conduct. The committees with the greatest representation were Appropriations, Education and Labor, Foreign Affairs, and Merchant Marine and Fisheries. Four Wednesday Group members were the ranking minority members on their committees.[32]

The average age of the Group in the 93rd Congress corresponded closely to that of the legislative party as a whole, but its education level was above average. It included five former professors and a majority of the members held graduate degrees. The median member was in his tenth year in the Congress. It is interesting that most members represented suburban districts or districts with an urban-suburban or suburban-rural mix. Generally, one might characterize the members of the Wednesday Group as being moderate and liberal. What makes the Group cohesive is its willingness to explore and promote new ideas and new approaches to solving problems. This approach and attitude is completely consistent with the New Politics.

The primary attraction of the Group to its members is that it provides the opportunity to communicate. The problem-solving research is a secondary consideration. Generally those leaning further to the left in the political spectrum become more involved with initiating research, but the more conservative members also attend meetings and are very supportive by contributing office space, equipment, and supplies.

The Group, never wealthy, operated with deficits in 1966 and 1968 (campaign years). There are no membership fees or dues, but the Group receives contributions from members and from outside sources. Its small staff consisted of three researchers and a secretary. It was first funded through the Committee for Republican Research and through a campaign group, Republicans for Progress, which ceased operations in 1967. (The Committee for Republican Research later changed its name to the Institute for Republican Studies.[33]

The staff develops position papers based on suggestions from the members as well as on its own initiative. The Group has published a variety of papers, some critical of Democratic Administrations, but others of a long-range research nature. For example, in 1967, the Group issued a report on "Organized Crime and the Urban Poor." The thrust of the report was that a 50 percent drop in Justice Department prosecution of racketeers had occurred since 1964, and that the war on organized crime had come to a standstill. The paper also argued that the Johnson poverty program had been undermined by racketeers preying on the poor. The report recommended that the personnel in the Organized Crime Division of the Justice Department be quadrupled and that racketeers be pursued aggressively.[34] This report culminated with the introduction of nine bills, one of which eventually became the act which outlaws loansharking.

Other important Group publications include a book published in 1967 on "How to End the Draft, the Case for the All Volunteer Army"; "Crises in Urban Education," advocating massive federal assistance, published in 1968; "A Study in Air Safety," published in 1969; and a 1967 booklet by nine members, "Parallel Steps to Peace in Vietnam." This outlined a plan for staged de-escalation of American bombing, and received editorial comment from more than eighty newspapers. While proof of impact is difficult to obtain, it appears to have been instrumental in the Secretary of Defense's decision to order a study of a two-stage bombing reduction; it was the formula with which President Johnson finally drew the North Vietnamese into negotiations.[35]

"CBW and National Security," published in 1969, a theoretical evaluation of the strategic and tactical purposes served by chemical and biological weapons, was endorsed by sixteen members. This report was acclaimed by the chairman of the Senate Foreign Relations Committee, and went a long way toward broadening congressional receptivity to President Nixon's subsequent ban on biological weapons.[36]

The Group's procedure for passing on papers usually includes setting up a four- or five-member study group to hold meetings and criticize drafts. Finally the chairman of the study group or someone who has established himself as a spokesman will draft the final product.

The method of release of this type of project varies. Twice members have published books, but in most cases the chairman of the study group presents the study on the floor of Congress. Sponsorship of the finished paper is open to all Group members and to selected Republican nonmembers who have indicated an interest in the topic. The Wednesday Group name is never mentioned in the presentation of the project because the members believe explicit use of the name would inhibit endorsement by nonmembers and limit the Group's impact.

In pursuing its anonymity, the Group will not discuss the location of its office, or the nature of its staff. The membership of the group is not made available to anyone. Nevertheless, Sven Groennings, a former staff director, considers it surprising that the group has remained as anonymous as it has. Since 1963, more than twenty study groups within the Wednesday Group have issued approximately fifty releases, which have been endorsed by many congressmen.[37]

Since the advent of the Nixon Administration, the Wednesday Group has changed its tactics somewhat. This same kind of gear shifting was undertaken by the DSG when John Kennedy succeeded Dwight Eisenhower. In addition to lowering its critical profile, it has extended invitations to discussions at its meetings to select members of the Administration.

Group members have become increasingly involved in organizations such as the House Republican Research Committee (chaired by then Congressmen Robert Taft, Jr., a member of the Group). F. Bradford Morse suggested in 1970 that a research committee within the group be created. That same year the staff began circulating a weekly legislative summary outlining the salient points in leading bills. The Democratic Study Group had been providing a similar service, and members have found it to be very useful.

The Wednesday Group is in a dilemma with its party dominating the Executive Branch. If it focuses on an issue that is of concern to the Administration it is likely to have no real impact, since the Administration can address itself to the problem more quickly and with greater resources at hand. If it decides to tackle a problem not considered significant by the Administration, it may be viewed as criticizing the Administration for ignoring a problem that the Group considers important. This would breach the strong party loyalty within the Group.

The actual impact of the Wednesday Group on the legislative responses of its own party has been minor. Groennings believes that it is misunderstood by the more conservative members of the Party, and is regarded as a bunch of mavericks.[38] However, as the members of the Group have gained seniority and have become more involved in partywide task forces, its influence has increased. As far as the members themselves are concerned, the research operations of the Group broaden their expertise, and assist them in gaining favorable publicity and in building constructive records.

In five elections since the Wednesday Group's formation only three members lost their bids for reelection, and one of them ran far ahead of his party's presidential candidate at the time. The Group does not prepare campaign literature like the DSG does, nor does it engage in campaign fundraising. Members have, however, utilized the Group's research papers extensively in campaigns.

The Wednesday Group will never equal the Democratic Study Group in size, staff, or financing, unless the Republicans should become the majority party in the Congress. In that case it might expand and develop into a DSG type of operation. However, in its early years it has been a small nucleus of congressmen who tend to swing to the left of the average Republican member of the House. While serving basically as an information exchange, it has had a problem with the type of research it should be doing while the Republicans control the Presidency. It flourished best as part of the "constructive" opposition, one of the principal reasons for its founding.

House Republicans have also had a few other subgroups. Although begun primarily as a social group, the Chowder and Marching Society does more than socializing. At its weekly Wednesday meetings, its fourteen permanent members meet with junior Republicans who have been invited. The group provides an invaluable opportunity for younger Republicans to meet the leadership, and such distinguished alumni as Rogers Morton and Melvin Laird who became members of the Nixon Cabinet. Other social groups formed by senior Republicans in the House include the Acorns and the SOS. Members value these groups for the relationships formed, and for the opportunity provided to meet with party leaders on an informal basis.

In 1969 the conservative Republicans in the House organized an informal group called the Republican Regulars. Their principal concern was to express the conservative side of legislative and political issues to the leadership and the Administration. One effort to assert their power was made in 1971, when one of their members Samuel Devine of Ohio unsuccessfully challenged John Anderson for the chairmanship of the Republican Conference.

Conclusion

Political parties in the Congress have established formal machinery to assist the leaders in their endeavors to pass desired legislation and to establish a record to present to the electorate. Aside from the social groups and the freshmen "class" groups that form, particularly among members of the House, informal groups formed along ideological lines are almost inevitable. Discontent with the leadership and a sense of powerlessness among certain "disaffected" groups in the House led to the forming of the DSG in the late fifties, and the Wednesday Group in 1963. More recently dissatisfaction with the DSG has led the moderate and more conservative Democratic elements in the House to form their own informal groups. The results of this splintering of the Democrats in the House cannot yet be evaluated.

The Senate, as a smaller group with longer terms of office and larger staffs, does not feel the same need to organize into these informal groups. At present a small Republican Wednesday Group is operating but a minority of a minority is not in a position to be very powerful. Perhaps the only powerful informal group in the Senate was the "Inner Club," and whether that was a myth perpetuated by Lyndon Johnson or actually existed as a cohesive group has not been proven. There are, however, a group of senators who have considerable seniority, who consider the Senate to be the focal point of their political careers, and who cooperate to uphold the traditions of the Senate. There are also elaborate rules and courtesies practiced by all senators to enable the diverse body to function and perform its duties. Some senators, such as Joseph Clark of Pennsylvania, have felt locked out by the Inner Club, and perhaps like all groups there has to be a center of power, so it was easy to identify as members of an Inner Group those who had been there the longest, held committee chairmanships, and were close to the majority leader.

With the diminishing power of the southern bloc and the influx of a more liberal type of legislator both on the Democratic and Republican sides of the aisle, the power center in the Senate is no longer as identifiable as it was during Johnson's tenure as Majority Leader. Whether the Senate will ever again contain that kind of concentrated power remains to be seen. But informal groups within the Senate and the House will continue to surface from the members' need for informal communication. This is especially true in the House, due to its larger numbers and higher turnover.

Part III
Changing External Pressures

8

Public-Interest Groups: The New Lobbying

In the early 1960s, a young Harvard Law School student suddenly concluded, "All the courses trained us how to defend corporations. I wondered where the lawyers for the ordinary people were being trained, and discovered that they weren't."[1] That moment of decision was to spark one of the most remarkable movements in contemporary American history—Ralph Nader's one-man campaign for "consumer protection." It would take its place with the other monumental movements that dramatically changed the tenor and quality of American life in the twentieth century and thereby paved the way for the expression of the New Politics through the public-interest lobby.

John Gardner, the founder of Common Cause, has indicated the importance of such movements as follows:

There is a folk cynicism about the impact of citizen movements, but the record does not bear out the cynicism. Citizens' movements brought the vote for women, abolished child labor, foisted Prohibition on the nation (and later repealed it), launched the civil rights movement, made the environment a national issue, placed family planning on the national agenda and so on. Citizen movements have proven, over and over, that they are among the hard political realities of American life.[2]

Public-Interest Lobbying and the New Politics

While lobbying has been part of the American governmental scene since the nineteenth century, public-interest lobbying is new. Lobbying practices have been a special concern of reformers throughout the twentieth century. In 1946, Congress passed the Federal Regulation of Lobbying Act requiring lobbyists to register and indicate the source of their funding.[3] However, numerous reporting loopholes in the law have made it ineffective and misleading. The laundering of Nixon campaign funds in Mexico discovered during the Watergate scandals was not a Republican invention.

The organizations reporting the greatest lobbying expenditures since the law went into effect are the AFL-CIO, the American Legion, the American Farm Bureau Federation, the American Medical Association, the United Federation of Postal Clerks, the National Association of Letter Carriers, and the National Housing Conference. The National Association of Manufacturers and the United States Chamber of Commerce were among the top spenders in the early years of the reporting program. The American Medical Association (AMA), which has consistently had one of the largest lobbying budgets, is the only organization that has ever reported spending over a million dollars for lobbying in a single year. Its expenditures exceeded the million-dollar mark in 1949, 1950, and 1965, primarily as a result of AMA's effort to delay the development of national health insurance programs. Only since the emergence of the New Politics of the 1960s has there been any substantial spending by public lobbies.

The total amount of lobbying expenditures *reported* by all organizations between 1960 and 1970 ranged from $3.8 million to $5.8 million per year. In 1971 and 1972 they were $6,525,000 and $6,139,000.[4] Table 8-1 indicates the reported lobbying expenditures of the top twenty-five lobbyists in 1972. This is only a fraction of the total. Much of the lobby spending is disguised as public relations or legal expenses funded by individual businesses and union, industry, labor, and farm lobbies. A congressional committee which investigated lobbying in 1950 concluded that lobbying was at least a *billion-dollar-a-year* industry.[5] It is hard to believe that inflation alone would not have doubled that figure in over twenty years.

Despite these impressive statistics, Congress has found it difficult to enact legislation imposing tighter reporting requirements. Each time a major lobbying scandal has broken into the headlines, a new investigating committee has held hearings and recommended a new lobbying bill—which has died in committee, partly because of the effectiveness of those lobbying against such bills.[6] The widespread use of campaign contributions by lobbying groups is not unrelated to congressional inaction on this issue. One significant question is whether the New Politics will bring about any changes in this practice. The movement for public financing of federal elections has received increasing support as a result of the Agnew resignation and the Watergate investigation.

Lobbying has developed as a governmental influence partly because of the increasing impact of government in our lives. The First Amendment to the Constitution provides for the right to petition the government for a redress of grievances, and lobbyists use this provision as the constitutional justification for their activity. Every effort to control lobbying, therefore, must deal with this question of restricting freedom of speech and petition under the First Amendment. Controlling excesses without jeopardizing legitimate lobbying is a difficult task.

Although difficult to control and impossible to rid of all improprieties, lobbying is legal, and can even operate in the public interest. Lobbyists are useful specialists who can provide information on the impact government programs may have on specific affected groups. This kind of expertise is sorely needed in a complex society.

However, unbalanced lobbying is a serious problem. Big industry has the resources to tell its story, but many other interests, especially the public interest, are frequently unrepresented. The 1972 ITT-Kleindienst affair involving ITT's offer of a $400,000 guarantee (out of a total fund-raising target of $600,000) for the 1972 Republican convention is a case in point. The convention was scheduled to be held in San Diego, where a large new Sheraton-ITT hotel was opening. The offer was made at the same time that ITT was involved in the biggest antitrust case of the century. The case was settled out of court by the Justice Department and Attorney General John Mitchell.

Table 8-1
The Twenty-five Largest Lobbying Budgets

Organization	1972	1971	1970
Common Cause	$558,839	$847,856	$79,347
American Federation of Labor Congress of Industrial Organizations (AFL-CIO)	216,294	205,101	197,493
Veterans of World War I of the U.S.A. Inc.	213,743	308,946	341,244
American Postal Workers Union	208,767	257,093	228,325
United States Savings and Loan League	191,726	158,727	149,794
National Council of Farmer Cooperatives	184,347	60,000	94,307
Disabled American Veterans	159,431	129,831	117,134
National Association of Letter Carriers (AFL-CIO)	154,188	135,334	277,125
The Farmers' Educational and Cooperative Union of America	113,156	97,438	80,738
United Mine Workers of America	110,045	93,352	59,657
American Nurses' Association Inc.	109,643	no spending record	21,872
National Association of Home Builders of the United States	99,031	125,779	151,605
American Medical Association	96,146	114,800	96,064
Brotherhood of Railway, Airline & Steamship Clerks	88,540	91,642	75,056
Recording Industry Association of America Inc.	88,396	41,875	123,286
American Insurance Association	82,259	65,812	52,766
National Federation of Federal Employees	82,080	67,856	63,536
National Housing Conference Inc.	77,906	99,924	92,549
International Brotherhood of Teamsters	76,897	63,716	72,626
National Limestone Institute Inc.	75,777	3,278	9,084
American Civil Liberties Union	73,131	23,853	21,998
National Association of Real Estate Boards	70,941	74,952	33,748
Liberty Lobby Inc.	70,019	56,125	66,531
New York Committee of International Committee of Passenger Lines	66,636	100,342	not listed

Sources: Data compiled from the *Congressional Quarterly,* August 6, 1971, pp. 1682–92; August 19, 1972, pp. 2069–71; June 9, 1973, p. 1425.

Shortly thereafter Mitchell resigned to direct the Nixon campaign, which benefited from the ITT contribution. This serves as a pointed example of how industry can play for big stakes when its interests are at issue.

Since the lobbying process is most compatible with representative government when all sides of an issue have a spokesman, the emergence of a variety of public, or at least nonprivate, interest lobbies is a most significant development. The successes of the evironmentalists, the Council for a Livable World, Common Cause, and the Ralph Nader consumer lobbies show that groups dedicated exclusively to the general public interest rather than to some more specific interest can also use lobbying effectively.

The emergence of public-interest lobbying is closely linked to the ascendancy of the New Politics, for the issues with which the New Politics is so deeply concerned—governmental responsiveness, citizen participation, accountability, the public's right to know, "consumerism," commitment to urban and human development, and the quality of life—find their expression in the goals of the public interest lobbies.

A case in point concerns the recent fight over federal funding to develop the supersonic transport (SST). One of the most powerful lobbying coalitions in history, a combination of the aerospace industry, labor unions, the U.S. Department of Transportation, and the White House, was handed a stunning defeat by public-interest groups under the leadership of environmental organizations such as the Friends of the Earth, Sierra Club, Wilderness Society, Environmental Action, and Citizens Against Sonic Boom. This coalition was aided by opponents of the "military-industrial complex," Senate liberals, and broad-based public-interest lobby organizations like Common Cause and the Federation of American Scientists. United by their concern for the environment and their advocacy of a reallocation of national priorities and increased spending for urban affairs, human development, and the environment, this new coalition succeeded in defeating the attempt of the business-labor-government troika to secure additional federal funds to develop the SST.

Still another example of the close association between the New Politics and public-interest lobbying can be seen in the public interest lobbying for the Women's Equal Rights Amendment, for the twenty-sixth Amendment, which lowered the voting age, and for reform of the "seniority system" within Congress. Each of these issues reflects the New Politics concern for representation, participation, and accountability.

It would seem that conditions are favorable for the expansion of New-Politics-oriented public interest organizations. The average education level, the amount of leisure time, and the annual income of the American people are increasing. There have never been so many citizens with the opportunity to contribute time and funds to public interest organizations.

The prospect that the private lobbies will be balanced at least in part by public-interest lobbies is heartening, but it should not lead to complacency. The existence of a few new public-interest lobbying groups is insufficient to accomplish all the balancing that is necessary. Government action affects too many issues and too many areas of private interest. Also, public-interest groups can still not be assured of long-term support from a public that is still notoriously fickle in its concerns. In contrast, business groups can assume that their economic interests will continue to justify spending money for lobbying.

It is for these reasons that the public interest has often been shunted aside, and will continue to have difficulty sustaining itself. Even with the advantage of national communications media it is difficult to mobilize community spirit on any particular issue. Ordinarily, the chances are not great that an innovative idea will receive massive public support, if only because too few citizens will become aware of the opportunity to resist the vested interests. The public-interest lobby's batting average improves whenever the negative effects of private interest lobbying can be well publicized. This was the case when the campaign was mounted against the SST.

Additional relief from the burdens of unbalanced private interest lobbying is coming from another new category of nonprivate lobbying groups—lobbies for cities, counties, and states. While they are not *general* public-interest lobbies, the issues on which they are able to secure the support of their national membership are all related to the functioning of state and local government in an era of New Politics and New Federalism. From their local perspective they can be extremely helpful in building public-interest coalitions.

These national associations—the National League of Cities, the United States Conferences of Mayors, the International City Management Association, the National Association of Counties, the National Governors' Conference, the Council of State Governments, and the National Association of Regional Councils—lobby Congress for legislation, and in addition represent their membership to federal agencies and the White House,[7] These groups are becoming much more aggressive and have banded together as the Big Seven Public Interest Groups—colloquially known as the PIGs. Their research organizations have received substantial federal grants and contracts to study state and local government problems. The member governments of these organizations undertake pilot projects related to New Politics goals, such as consumer safety and protection; day care; neighborhood health delivery; treatment for narcotics addicts; air, water, and noise pollution; outreach projects for hard-core unemployed; halfway houses and visitation privileges for the convicted; scattered public housing; and citizen-based community development programs.

The federal agencies and the White House represent still another important classification of the nonprivate-interest lobby.[8] Much, though not all, Executive Branch lobbying is compatible with public interest lobbying objectives. The Great Society programs of the Johnson Administration—the poverty program, model cities, manpower training, truth in lending, medicare, and many other New-Politics-oriented programs—were lobbied through the Congress by a coalition of public interest groups and federal departments. On the other hand, Executive Branch lobbying for the SST was one good example of potential incompatibility between the public-interest groups and the Executive Branch. In 1970, the cost of lobbying by the

Executive Branch exceeded the total *reported* amount of lobbying expenditures by all the industry, union, medical, veterans, and public interest groups combined.[9] In the stiff competition for scarce resources, federal agencies are as active as cities, counties, states, and private organizations in attempting to influence Congress to protect their "vested" interests.

The SST struggle shows that there has been a tremendous growth in public interest group lobbying for "public" or "collective" goods and that, at least occasionally, its influence is powerful enough to counterbalance private interest lobbying—even when it is allied with the Administration. The "arrival" of meaningful public interest lobbying is partly attributable to and partly necessary for the success of the New Politics. To understand how, it is essential to study the growth of public interest lobbying from Ralph Nader to Common Cause.

Ralph Nader and the Public Interest

Few Americans living today have not heard of Ralph Nader, the one-man consumer lobby. Nader, as the archtype of the new public-interest lobby, advocates policies that in the past may not have been considered serious possibilities. His chief concern is to increase public awareness of the issues and to create a new majority interest—a "public" interest—that can have an impact upon the quality of American life in the future.

Certainly the effect Ralph Nader has had upon such diverse but vital areas as automobile safety, meat processing, food additives, air pollution, regulatory agency efficiency, and safety within the energy industries will assure him lasting fame. It has also demonstrated the potential power of public-interest lobbying in the New Politics era.

Starting out as a one-man crusade, Nader has been so successful in making both government and industry reform their practices that he has attracted funds to operate over twelve different centers and research groups dealing with consumer problems. Nader emphasizes the following basic objectives:

1. To provide a counterforce to unscrupulous business practices or to special interests generally;
2. To provide adequate consumer representation and promote the rights of the individual; and
3. To professionalize the expression of *public* need and *public* interests when government decisions are being made.

Nader's own feelings about the current state of public-interest lobbying were revealed in an interview with the *New York Times Magazine* in which he pointed out the need for citizens to have some recourse against federal and corporate officials who fail to protect the public interest. The Nader concept is that members of such government and business organizations must develop a public interest conscience and become "whistleblowers"—

people who will blow the whistle on their own organization when responsibility to society requires it. Nader even sponsored a conference of "Whistle-Blowers" in Washington in 1971 where individuals who had placed the public interest above their own job security were honored.[10]

Ralph Nader's organizations have been reasonably effective and highly visible to the general American populace, and he has had an impact on Congress. In many cases enterprising legislators who have recognized a heavy vote potential behind the dissatisfactions of ordinary people have made their own consumer-oriented reform proposals. Nader is welcome as a witness before most congressional committees and, as might be expected, he is best received by the New Politics congressmen.

An indication that the emerging consumerism of Ralph Nader would become a priority issue was provided by President Kennedy's March 1962 special message to Congress on "Protecting the Consumer Interest." This address set forth four basic consumer rights upon which governmental actions in the field of consumer affairs were to be based:

1. The right to safety—to be protected against the marketing of goods which are hazardous to health or life.
2. The right to be informed—to be protected against fraudulent, deceitful, or grossly misleading information, advertising, labeling, or other practices, and to be given the facts he needs to make an informed choice.
3. The right to choose—to be assured, wherever possible, access to a variety of products and services at competitive prices; and those industries in which competition is not workable and Government regulation is substituted, an assurance of satisfactory quality and service at fair prices.
4. The right to be heard—to be assured that consumer interests will receive full and sympathetic consideration in the formulation of Government policy and fair expeditious treatment in its administrative tribunals.

The legislation outlined in President Kennedy's special message did not meet with any substantial congressional interest, partially owing to the existence of more important foreign and domestic matters. However, other legislation was forthcoming during the Johnson administration. Many consumer bills were passed during the 89th and 90th Congresses. Automotive safety, truth in packaging, cigarette labeling, meat and poultry inspection, and truth in lending were among the many concerns of the new public-interest lobby that found their way into legislation.

One of Nader's most notable achievements was his one-man campaign against the General Motors Corvair. This campact car had an instability problem which investigation showed could be a serious safety hazard. His book *Unsafe at Any Speed* generated tremendous publicity and ultimately forced the auto manufacturers to show more responsibility by recalling defective cars when weaknesses became known.

Nader is not without his detractors, however. Profound differences of opinion exist regarding the merits of "consumerism." In the first place, no one can identify with accuracy the boundaries, or even the content, of that which is labeled "in the public interest." At the individual level of concern, each of us may in fact belong to opposing interest groups. We may, for example, champion auto safety as consumers, while working for an automobile manufacturer. How does one determine where the public interest lies when safety is pitted against jobs?

A second objection to public interest crusades lies in its inability to standardize its goals. Those who must respond to policy changes are often given no firm guarantees that further, and even conflicting, actions will not be necessary at a later date. For example, many manufacturing companies have been required to purchase pollution control equipment to meet quasi-permanent standards. However, there is no assurance that the regulations will not be changed two years later, making the equipment obsolete and requiring new capital outlays.

A third point is that business (or labor, or government) may fear that the competition will take unfair advantage of consumerism. Thus, investor-owned utilities chafe at the hint that consumer cooperatives, which already receive special low-interest loans from the federal government, may be given additional competitive leverage through the activities of consumer lobby organizations.

A battle royal is forming between the consumerists, who wish to have a "strong" and "independent" organization, and business groups. Those who want to deemphasize consumerism argue that the consumer groups mask an antibusiness prejudice, that they unduly favor consumer cooperatives, that the representation of consumer interests within an agency independent of presidential coordination with executive departments is unworkable, that public funds should not be spent for the recommendation or disapproval of products that actively compete in the marketplace, and finally that the regulatory agencies have done a reasonable job of ministering to consumer needs.

Nader disputes these contentions of the business interests. He especially resents the supposition that class action lawsuits should be limited to cases successfully prosecuted against consumer law violators by the Justice Department, a major point in proposals endorsed by the Nixon Administration. Not only does Nader maintain that consumer fraud has a low priority in the Justice Department, he further maintains that the department is subject to a conflict of interest in representing both consumers and the regulatory agencies, which Nader maintains are controlled by their respective industries.

Instead of the Administration proposals, which he declares to be calculated to mollify business, Nader proposes an independent office for consumer affairs be established. Specifically, he states:

I would have an Office of Consumer Protection as the first major proposal.... It would not have any regulatory powers, and as a result would be institutionally as free as possible from the network of lobbyists and special interest pressures that would surround it immediately after it assumed the regulatory functions dealing with consumer protection that are now under other departments. I don't think that is advisable. I think we should envision an Office of Consumer Protection which is unabashedly partisan to the consumer, of the consumer, for the consumer, and by the consumer, just as partisan as the U.S. Department of Agriculture is for the meat and poultry interests or the other regulatory interests are for their particular clientele group.[11]

Although he has been the advocate for greater governmental assistance on behalf of the consumer, Nader is also the most damning critic of the government's past record in protecting the consumer:

Government agencies haven't been doing their job. There hasn't been adequate competition for quality. There has been too much collusion, price fixing, too much conscious parallelism in the private sector. There are no private consumer groups with adequate countervailing power. There aren't more than a handful of lawyers who represent less than 1 percent of the buyers, or represent poor people against sellers and manufacturers.

The lack of representation has permitted this distortion in the legal system. Those who write the laws are those who benefit from them; namely, the large well-organized lobbyists at State legislatures and at Congress.[12]

Ralph Nader's rise to prominence coincided with the rise of New Politics. The two movements served to reinforce each other during the 1960s. His movement did not evolve so much from an ideological standard as it did from a practical concern for people and their affairs. He did not so much try to show people what was *possible* through a "consumer lobby," although that was the effect of his efforts, as he tried to arouse their anger and indignation by exposing corporate greed, shoddy workmanship, governmental laxity, and hazards to the public's safety. More than that, he firmly established the principle of "the public's right to know." In this sense, Nader captured the spirit of the times.

Fortune magazine's assessment of the probable outcome of the consumer movement suggests the complexity of its organizational problem. The chiller comes with its reflection on the transient nature of consumer movements:

But can a movement like consumerism, powerful and yet amorphous, really be institutionalized? Certainly the passion and craft of a Nader cannot be. Nor would the director of a consumer agency enjoy Nader's complete freedom of action. A Senate aide who helped draft the bill predicts that the new office might "have its time in the sun, like the Peace Corps or OEO. Then it will carve out a rather cautious domain of its own and become part of the bureaucracy."[13]

Not only must consumerism and other public-interest efforts survive the comings and goings of mortal champions, such as the early muckraking journalists and Nader, but they must also contend with the vagaries of bureaucratic aging. If "the public interest" is ever to become institutionalized, then it must somehow surmount this hurdle. The answer may lie in adoption of the movement by the New Politics Congress, and perhaps this is what Nader had in mind in 1972 when he launched an extensive evaluation both of Congress and the performance of individual Congressmen, whose profiles were printed and distributed in time for the 1972 elections.

Common Cause and the Public Interest

The National Urban Coalition was founded in 1967 by Dr. John Gardner, former president of the Carnegie Foundation, to focus national attention on the urban areas. He established the organization after resigning as Secretary of Health, Education and Welfare. This development was significant in that his resignation was accompanied by reports that he felt he could do more to influence government policy from the *outside* than he could as head of the cabinet department with a budget second only to that of the Defense Department.

Gardner soon discovered that the real barriers to progress were political, and that a major lobbying effort would be necessary to accomplish the organizations's objectives. Since nonprofit groups lose their tax exemption if they engage in lobbying activity, Common Cause was formed in 1969 to lobby for the issues identified by the Urban Coalition. In just over a year, 200,000 Americans paid fifteen dollars to become members of Common Cause, making it the best-funded public-interest lobby in American history. Through newspaper ads, television shows, and mailings, Gardner urged members of the "silent majority" to join his public lobby to help force a reordering of national priorities and counterbalance the special interest lobbies.

Common Cause, therefore, is essentially a national citizen's lobby that recognizes the extreme importance of lobbying in today's American political process and tries to represent the public interest on a broad range of issues. Many political commentators believed that Common Cause was merely a prelude to a new political party. But after half a decade of operation, it is clear that Common Cause intends to remain a nonpartisan citizen group, drawing strength from both parties as well as from those people not clearly associated with either party.

As Gardner observed, as few as a million people may be enough to turn the tide toward the public interest, and although winning the allegiance of even that number may prove to be a difficult task, he is optimistic that a million people can be reached and will respond because, in his words:

In every field of special interest there is a percentage of people who understand that if the nation fails, their special interest fails too. You find this at all levels; in unions, in minority communities, as well as in the professions. I don't think of it in liberal-conservative terms so much as in practical terms. These are the people who want to get going and solve our problems.[14]

While Ralph Nader began by challenging specific abuses directed at consumers by the business and governmental bureaucracies, Gardner began challenging some of the basic assumptions of American politics regarding representation and political financing. He planned to use the communication and educational revolutions to bring about a political reassessment and reevaluation of our priorities, and our means of accomplishing them. Because the Congress stands at the very center of the processes these movements seek to change, it will be the first institution to feel the full force of their effort.

Common Cause maintains that certain issues transcend politics, and so it focuses attention on issues rather than candidates. It teams up with other groups concerned about solutions to these problems. Issue leadership has come from its Washington office directed by President Jack Conway, formerly a top policy lobbyist with the United Auto Workers. Conway described that role as follows: "The citizens of the country have to have someone they can trust who is involved in the mechanics of government. We can't call all the members and ask what we should do on an amendment. They have to have confidence in the leadership to judge the situation."[15]

The scope of Common Cause positions is reflected in the following basic issues which it considered vital in recent years:

1. Making national, state, and local government more responsive to the people through reorganization of the legislative and executive machinery at all levels;
2. Withdrawing American military forces from Indochina, negotiating a nuclear nonproliferation treaty with the Soviet Union, and reducing defense spending;
3. Attacking the roots of poverty through sufficient income maintenance, job training, social security, and early childhood education programs;
4. Providing equal opportunities in all aspects of American life—including education, housing, employment, and voting;
5. Providing decent housing to every American family to fulfill the commitment made during the Truman administration;
6. Creating public-service employment through federal funding of jobs in both public and nonprofit agencies which provide services all citizens need such as public education, health, safety, and pollution control;
7. Equalizing and improving education in rural, urban, and suburban areas;
8. Overhauling the national health system;
9. Protecting the consumer from fraud and deceptive practices;
10. Stabilizing prices to protect earnings, savings, and fixed incomes;
11. Dealing more quickly and effectively with crime, including not only street crime but also corporate crime, organized crime, and official corruption;
12. Adopting no-fault auto insurance to remove one-third of the load on the court system;
13. Developing effective mass transportation;
14. Planning new cities and resources so that the "quality of life" will be improved.[16]

The methods to be used to attain these objectives are guided by some realistic rules for action. For example, Gardner contends that much citizen effort is wasted because the participants become disappointed by the lack of immediate success and quit too early. His group recognizes that the forces of the status quo which they fight are deeply entrenched. Therefore, the lobbying effort must be sustained over a long period of time. For the same reasons, Common Cause plans to strike at a limited number of targets rather than taking a "shotgun" type of approach over a wide area.

Gardner appreciates the importance of alliances. Many lobbying efforts are unsuccessful because they are perceived by legislators as representing a minority opinion or interest. If, however, a widebased coalition made up of several varied and dispersed interest groups faces a legislative struggle as an alliance, the chances of success are greatly increased.

The Common Cause leadership has attempted to exploit the communications revolution. In the past lobbyists have often operated behind closed doors. Common Cause operates on the principle that the public's right to know must be served in order to overcome the vested interests. Politicians who are exposed as dealing with special vested interest groups, it is hoped, can no longer afford this luxury.

Common Cause has been in the thick of a number of crucial historic congressional battles during its first years of operation. In addition, it has actively lobbied various state legislatures and filed many lawsuits on public interest issues. For example, it has attempted to have the laws concerning campaign spending rigorously enforced, as well as to have Congress legislate the loopholes out of the existing laws. As a result, Common Cause filed suit against both major political parties for allowing alleged violations of the present law to occur by evading spending ceilings. Common Cause also urged Congress to override the President's veto of a bill placing limits on political broadcasts.

It played an active role in urging congressional reform, especially in changing the seniority system in committee selection. One of the reasons for this concern is that certain congressional districts do not have effective two-party competition. Therefore, these "certain" seats can control the Congress by dominating the committee system where the seniority system has put representatives of competitive districts at a great disadvantage.

Common Cause has waged the battle for equal employment, hoping to curb job discrimination against minority groups. In 1970, Common Cause also worked for an expanded food stamp program, which is still short of its original goals. Although most of its issues are necessarily anti-status quo and by inference anti-Administration, Common Cause favored the President's Family Assistance Plan, which included the federal standards for welfare eligibility, minimum uniform payment in all states, and aid to the working poor. Common Cause also favored the creation of public-service jobs for the general welfare in order that everyone might have the opportunity to work, and it opposed certain proposed tax regulations that would have given private industries from $3 to $5 billion annually in tax writeoffs.

Another issue on which Common Cause was one of the participating lobbies was the constitutional amendment to change the minimum voting age from twenty-one to eighteen. After congressional passage, Common Cause then put additional pressure upon state legislatures for final ratification. In addition, the state legislatures have been lobbied regarding certain barriers that limit popular participation in the primary or general state elections. Targets here include short registration hours and dates, early filing deadlines, lack of absentee privileges, and certain types of delegate selection processes.

Despite all these apparent accomplishments, Common Cause must face two critical areas of attack. First, it has been alleged that the causes championed by Common Cause would have been successful anyway. The issues that they supported, it is argued, were already on the road to victory, with or without the help of Common Cause. In some cases, such as the SST votes, other forces in the lobbying process have been more significant.

A second challenge to Common Cause is from congressional leaders who are somewhat skeptical of the Gardner-inspired letter-writing campaigns, since they feel that the effort may not be nonpartisan, as is claimed. There is a feeling among Republicans that Common Cause is just a front group for liberals and Democrats. For example, the Republican National Committee's publication *Monday* ran two articles in April 1971 labeling Common Cause and Gardner as "purveyors of the radical Democratic line." In challenging the group's claim to nonpartisanship, *Monday* said that when Common Cause and Americans for Democratic Action were asked to identify their differences, "Neither could think of one major issue on which the other differed substantially."

Given this objection, can Common Cause ultimately succeed? One lobbyist has remarked: "The value of Common Cause is that it has awakened a lot of Americans to the fact that they can participate in the system. It will hurt the whole public interest movement in environment, civil rights, consumerism, you name it—if they fail." [17]

The importance of that question, and of Common Cause itself, to the future of American society is underscored by Dr. Gardner:

Today all experts on government accept lobbying as a legitimate part of the political process. Lobbying activities in Washington are carried out not only by commercial interests but by groups representing the unions, the cities, the universities, the various professions, religious groups and so on.

Then there are those who accept the idea of lobbying but say in effect that it must be left to the special interests. The theory is that each special group pursues its own selfish concerns but taken all together they balance one another out and the public interest is served.

The only trouble is it isn't true.

First, the public interest is neglected. All the special interests clashing in the urban setting have not somehow balanced out to produce wise and far-seeing urban solutions. The public interest in clean air and water has not been automatically served by the clash of special interests in the environmental field.

Second, the quality of life for individual Americans is affected. Most of the things individual Americans want come to them through the mediation of large institutions—industrial companies, government agencies, school systems and so on. And large-scale organizations tend to ignore the individual's right to have his say, ignore the fact that he isn't a statistic.

We must design our institutions so that they do not affront the self-respect of individual Americans. [18]

Conclusion

Given the constraints of limited funding, the transient nature of its public support, and its reliance upon the media to dramatize its meaning to society's power elites and to the voting public, public interest lobbying is faced with a situation somewhat similar to that of "community power" proponents in the mid-sixties. To hold the needed attention of the media, public interest lobbying must increasingly dramatize its message. To obtain tangible results in the public policy-making process, it must be able to engage in give and take with power elites without giving the appearance of selling out its constituency. Thus, the inherent tension between strident demand and sophisticated bargaining is part of the price to be paid for a media-oriented movement. Public-interest lobbying, let us hope, will be spared the fate which that tension created for the community power movement.

To be effective in legislation a lobby must engender some loyalties among congressmen. This means a lobby group must remind the congressman periodically of all the actions taken to help him win elections, to get his name before the public in a favorable way, and to support legislation affecting his district.

The major public-interest lobbies have some special ways of doing this that are particularly appropriate for New-Politics-oriented groups. Common Cause has even had a fair degree of success in lobbying legislators opposed to its objectives. One reason for this is that it has been able to identify persons in the home district who have aided the recalcitrant congressman with contributions and other support. These people are phoned, briefed on the issue and the congressman's position, and requested to make their position known to him. Very often they do so—and with surprising effectiveness. The funds collected by Common Cause and Ralph Nader are not handed to candidates as contributions. Instead, they are used to publicize their endorsement of politicians favorable to their views. Such publicity is circulated to the organization's membership as well as to the public media. This is intended to encourage not only contributions but also campaign work in support of their candidates. In addition, particularly aggressive groups may organize registration drives to help influence specific elections.

Once in office, public officials supported by the public interest groups are expected to introduce and work for the adoption of legislation the groups favor. The candidates' reaction to these responsibilities is also fully reported to the membership and to the media.

While this is a traditional part of the lobbying process, there is some difference when the public-interest groups do this. Various groups brief their membership on the voting records of members of Congress. However, an evaluation or rating of a congressman by the Americans for Democratic Action, the AFL-CIO, the American Medical Association, the Veterans of Foreign Wars, or the National Farmers' Union is not in the same category as a similar rating by Common Cause or Ralph Nader. The other organizations have a clear economic, professional, or ideological bias.

To the extent that the public-interest groups can maintain a reputation for objectivity in the public interest their ratings will continue to receive favorable treatment by the media. The approach to date by Common Cause and Ralph Nader has tended to meet these criteria. Both have found that their problem-solving and public interest orientation—as opposed to an ideological, professional, economic, or special interest orientation—has been a great asset. It is difficult to ignore an organization that singles out a social problem such as health, indicates that there is no Democratic or Republican solution, effectively argues its position in the media, and maintains an experienced lobby staff to harvest the grassroots pressures so generated. The problem orientation, the effective use of communications, the concept of public interest, and the public-interest lobbies' new activism in its behalf are all keystones in the further development of the New Politics Congress.

9

Checks and Balances: Congressional Perspective

The separation-of-powers and checks-and-balances system provided for in the Constitution has the effect of making the President and Congress joint decision-makers on the major decisions affecting the nation. That does not mean they are *equal* decision-makers, either in terms of their total power or in terms of their relative power on a particular kind of issue.

For example, with regard to legislation, the Constitution provides Congress with the power to pass bills that may or may not be favored by the President. At the same time it gives the President the authority to veto such bills, and in turn Congress has the authority to override the veto of the President if two-thirds of the members of each house disagree with him. Theoretically, Congress has the ability, if it has sufficient internal agreement, to bypass the President and establish the law of the land. But it is the President who has the power to execute the laws, and in doing so he must make numerous policy decisions not specified in the legislation. The effect may be substantially different than Congress intended, and in such cases the President may be challenged in the court system.

This basic Congress-President relationship has been operating since the Constitution was ratified. However, some informal and extra-Constitutional changes have occurred that have an impact on policy outcomes as well as on the relationship between the President and Congress. The Constitution did not anticipate the development of the American political party system, or the likelihood that the man elected President would have enough electoral power to ensure that a majority, or at least a substantial number, of the members of Congress would be from his political party.

The President can use his appointment powers over judgeships, ambassadorships, or indirect influence over jobs, contracts, grants, the location of federal facilities, and numerous other administrative decisions to persuade key members of Congress to support him. He can also mobilize the public- and private-interest lobbies when his objectives coincide with theirs. In more recent years he has had the option of taking his case directly to the people on nationwide television.

Who really has the last word, then? It is hard to say. In 1972 Ralph Nader committed a large staff to investigate how Congress operates. The book published after the project concluded: "No matter how hard the Congress may struggle on one issue, it is overwhelmed by the vastly greater forces of the Presidency. Whether Congress wins or loses, the President ends up on top."[1]

A different perspective was provided by a former member of both the House and Senate who became President, John Fitzgerald Kennedy:

155

The fact is, I think, the Congress looks more powerful sitting here than it did when I was there in Congress. But that is because when you are in the Congress you are one of a hundred in the Senate or one of 435 in the House. So that the power is so divided. But from here I look at a Congress, and I look at the collective power of the Congress, particularly the bloc action, and it is a substantial power.[2]

Careful distinctions must be made in discussing the relative power of the President and Congress. Confrontations between the President and Congress can occur on a variety of levels. When the matter in dispute is a detailed technical matter, or where confidential information is required to make decisions, Congress is at a great disadvantage. In some areas, it is not the whole Congress or the President who are really involved. The various subcommittees in Congress can become so expert in their particular area of the total congressional role that their decisions may be rubber-stamped by the full Congress. Likewise, the experts in many specific fields within the federal government can operate unchallenged by the President or his staff. Very detailed matters are usually settled in negotiations between these executive and legislative bureaucrats without full participation by either the President or Congress, who often act through proxies.

On the other hand, when major national issues affecting all the people must be debated, the full Congress is likely to become involved, and because of that the President will be more directly concerned with the matter. A major civil rights bill or one establishing a military draft system must involve the President. Here again, there is often a difference of opinion within the Executive Branch, that must be considered. The President, his cabinet officers, and the political people in his administration may not be fully supported by the bureaucracy when it comes to the implementation of some policies.

To reduce the likelihood of this the Nixon Administration carried out extensive purges of federal employees in the regional as well as in the national offices of federal agencies in Nixon's first and second terms. Some of the extreme measures taken by H. R. Haldeman and John Ehrlichman to gain control of the bureaucracy caused political embarassment when the tactics, procedures, and ethics of some of the political people appointed by Nixon were examined in the light of Watergate.

One of the powers Congress can resort to in attempting to control the Executive Branch is its appropriations powers. However, even this is rarely effective, because it is essentially a negative power and cannot force the President to adopt a positive approach in the opposite direction. Appropriations controls can, however, force the President to negotiate with Congress. Often it is Congress rather than the President that is trying to increase the total budget, even while reducing some appropriations favored by the President. Fortunately for Congress, the President does not have the power to veto items instead of entire bills, or it would lose whatever leverage the appropriations process provides it.

Even if Congress should win a budgetary war and succeed in passing legislation calling for a higher expenditure than the President requested, the

President can resort to the practice of impoundment; that is, he can instruct the Executive Branch not to spend more than he requested despite the fact that Congress made more money available. Congress is reacting to these challenges with specific legislation that attempts to reduce the president's impoundment options. In some instances the courts have backed Congress by requiring Nixon to make some appropriated monies available in situations where it was clear to the court who the recipients would be and who was being hurt.

The Constitution establishes several other situations where there is a need for joint action and where the Senate has a veto. The President is required to have Senate approval of his nominations for the Cabinet, ambassadorships, as well as for treaties. Very few appointees have actually been rejected, but the existence of the approval process has caused presidents to avoid nominating clearly unqualified people. At times of real confrontation, as in recent years, the Senate can use this power to influence national policy, as it did in rejecting two Nixon Supreme Court nominees, and a Johnson nominee.

The ultimate congressional sanction is one which is used so infrequently as to be virtually nonexistent—impeachment. All the political and social forces in our political culture work against impeachment. At the lowest point in Nixon's popularity in 1974, when only 26 percent of the American people thought that he was doing an effective job as President, it still was not possible to get a majority of the American people to agree that he should be impeached.

Even in a Congress dominated by the Democratic Party, there was not that much impeachment sentiment. Political people are more aware and tolerant of the temptations present in campaigns. They knew that some of the transgressions committed by Nixon campaign staffers had been committed by earlier campaign staffs, though it is unlikely that any went so far as to compromise the integrity of the Central Intelligence Agency (CIA), the Federal Bureau of Investigation (FBI), or the Internal Revenue Service for partisan electoral purposes. They also knew that impeaching Nixon would have placed Gerald Ford in the White House two years prior to the 1976 elections. This would not only create the possibility of an incumbent President seeking reelection, but would also tend to deprive the Democratic Party of the opportunity of using Watergate in their campaign.

From time to time Congress has used its investigative powers to good advantage. While occupants of the White House have tried to counter by developing the doctrine of executive immunity or privilege, the scope of that barrier to congressional scrutiny is still not resolved. Congress has a legislative function and effective legislation requires information. One way or another Congress usually gets it, often aided by the press, which has a similar interest in finding out and reporting the facts.

These instruments of congressional control and oversight of the Executive Branch are discussed below. The next chapter will deal with the extent of presidential powers to relieve congressional pressures and maintain the balance-of-powers system.

Investigating Committees and Executive Privilege

Although the House and Senate share a common lawmaking function and getting the facts is an essential part of legislation in the twentieth century, the Senate has come to dominate the investigations process. George Haynes found that during the first forty years following the adoption of the Constitution "the House conducted seven or eight times as many investigations as did the Senate."[3] That situation has been reversed in modern times, due in part to the difference between House and Senate rules and procedures. While the strong tradition of majority rule insures that no House investigation comes into being without the blessing of the dominant party, in the Senate important investigations can be initiated by critical minorities.

A broad interpretation of germaneness, sanctioned by the Senate and complemented by its tradition of unlimited debate, guarantees that a single member can introduce and argue the case for investigation. Because of its preeminence in the investigative field, the task of investigating the Executive Branch seems to fall to the Senate. As early as 1871 the Senate created a Standing Committee on Privileges and Elections to oversee and investigate the elections of its own members, and senatorial investigations of presidential campaigns predates Watergate.[4]

The Teapot Dome scandal spawned several investigations by the Senate into activities of the Executive Branch. The Senate's authority to investigate the Executive Branch and to compel testimony from private citizens who might refuse to testify was upheld by the Supreme Court during this time. The case that established this authority was that of oil tycoon Harry F. Sinclair, who was involved in the scandal. He had been advised by counsel to refuse to answer questions of a Senate investigating committee. Five years later Sinclair's conviction for contempt of Congress was upheld by the Supreme Court, and Mr. Sinclair served a three-month jail sentence.[5] In 1929 the Supreme Court again confirmed a Senate committee's authority to compel testimony to aid in the exercise of its lawmaking powers.[6]

The era of the Teapot Dome scandal also brought out the contrast between the House and Senate's ability to initiate investigations. Democrats in the House wanted to investigate whether Attorney General Harry Daugherty should be impeached in 1923. The House Judiciary Committee recommended to the full House that no grounds for impeachment had been found. In a House composed of 298 Republicans and 130 Democrats, the Chairman of the Judiciary Committee, Andrew Volstead, successfully moved to forestall an investigation. The no-impeachment resolution then passed 206 to 78 with a party line vote, and a potentially embarrassing inquiry was quashed by the power of majority rule.[7]

In contrast to the House, a vociferous minority in the Senate would have been able to debate a proposal for an investigation at length, and could probably have initiated one. Senator James Reed, a Democrat from Missouri, obtained the necessary authority, even though his party was in a minority in the Senate, to investigate Senate campaign practices. His investigation was authorized by a vote of 59 to 13 in a Senate comprised of fifty-six Republicans and thirty-nine Democrats.[8] Known as the Reed "Slush Fund Committee," the investigation continued for four years concentrating much of its effort on campaign practices in the Republican-dominated states of Illinois and Pennsylvania. There were other Senate investigations in the 1920s highlighting campaign expenditures for presidential nominations as well as elections. Although the House and Senate have contrasting approaches to investigations, once the House moves boldly, its hearings reflect the imprint of the majority party and its leaders more than is customary in the Senate.

The major investigations of the past twenty years and the headline grabbers have been conducted by the Senate rather than the House. In 1941, the Senate Special Committee to Investigate the National Defense Program was chaired by Senator Harry S Truman, and an inquiry into postwar military preparedness was conducted by Senator Stuart Symington.

In the 1950s the major issue was communism and three committees investigated various aspects of it. The House Committee on UnAmerican Activities and the Senate Subcommittee on Internal Security coordinated lengthy hearings and compiled an extensive record, but it was the Permanent Subcommittee on Investigations of the Senate Government Operations Committee, chaired by Senator Joseph R. McCarthy, that investigated communism in the Army and attracted national attention due to television coverage.

The most intensive investigation to date of the drug industry occurred in the late 1950s, under the direction of Senator Estes Kefauver. Also in the late 1950s and early 1960s labor racketeering was investigated by a Select Committee of the Senate Labor and Public Welfare Committee, with daily television coverage. Teamster President Dave Beck was the chief villain of the first investigation, Robert Kennedy was the staff counsel, and Senator John McClellan was the chairman. The next major labor investigation by McClellan occurred while Robert Kennedy was Attorney General. This time the target was the new Teamsters President, Jimmy Hoffa. Both Beck and Hoffa were eventually convicted and served time in jail.

During the Johnson Administration the most notorious investigation involved the President's former Senate assistant and Secretary to the Senate Bobby Baker, who resigned when he was charged with misusing his position for private financial gain. The Senate Committee on Rules and Administration, chaired by Senator B. Everett Jordan, conducted that investigation.

From Immunity to Privilege

Although Congress has the clear right to conduct investigations into matters about which it can legislate, there are some clear limitations when that investigation involves securing information from the President. The basis for these limitations is contained in the separation-of-powers doctrine. The doctrine is not often the source of major confrontation between Congress and the President, but whenever a major confrontation occurs, it becomes an important element. In recent years, an increasing number of conflicts between the Democratic Congress and President Nixon have occurred on the question of executive privilege. The term "executive privilege" was first used in the Eisenhower Administration.

The separation-of-powers doctrine provides the President with immunity not only against congressional inquiry but also from judicial process. There are numerous precedents for this, dating from George Washington's Administration. Constitutional specialist Edward S. Corwin quotes a summary of a discussion involving Vice President Adams where several key statesmen felt that "a President in Office was answerable to no judicial process except impeachment. The President . . . was above 'all judges, justices, etc.,' and, secondly, that judicial interposition involving the President personally was liable to interfere with the operation of the governmental machinery."[9]

Corwin states that despite the hundreds of investigations conducted by Congress since the days of Jefferson, he knew "of no instance in which a head of department has testified before a judicial committee in response to a subpoena or been held for contempt for refusal to testify. All appearances by these high officials seem to have been voluntary."[10]

One of the questions then seems to be how far the protection of the President extends. It became traditional practice that high executive officials were not bound to testify on matters that involved the President directly. Clearly, then, executive privilege is something which belongs to the President but which he can extend to certain members of his administration when he considers it necessary, except when the matter involves his impeachment.

In *Marbury v. Madison,* the question of executive immunity arose.[11] The distinction made in this case is clearly shown in the following citation.

The duties of a Secretary of State were two-fold. In discharging one part of those duties he acted as a public ministerial officer of the United States, totally independent of the President, and that as to any facts which came officially to his knowledge, while acting in the capacity, he was as much bound to answer as a marshall, a collector, or any other administerial officer. That in the discharge of the other part of his duties, he did not act as a public ministerial officer, but in the capacity of an agent of the President, bound to obey his orders, and accountable to him for his conduct. And that as to any facts which came officially to his knowledge in the discharge of this part of his duties, he was not bound to answer.[12]

In 1948 a Committee of Congress subpoenaed the FBI report on the loyalty of Dr. Edward U. Condon, Director of the United States Bureau of Standards. There was a House of Representatives resolution calling for the President to make this report available. President Truman refused, on the basis that as a matter of principle Congress did not have any right to confidential records of his office. The House responded by passing a bill requiring executive departments and agencies to produce information demanded by Congress. The bill, which called for jail sentences and fines and specified that they would apply to cabinet officers as well as their subordinates, finally died in the Senate.[13]

In 1953, during the McCarthy investigations of the United States Army, President Eisenhower wrote to Secretary of Defense Wilson:

Because it is essential to efficient and effective administration that employees of the Executive Branch be in a position to be completely candid in advising with each other on official matters, and because it is not in the public interest that any of their conversations or communications or any documents or reproductions concerning such advice by disclosed, you will instruct employees of your department that in all their appearances before the subcommittee of the Senate Committee on Government Operations regarding the inquiry now before it, they are not to testify to any such conversations or communications or to produce any such documents or reproductions.[14]

As the doctrine developed, it generally became standard practice that none of the assistants in the White House staff would be required to testify to Congress regarding matters that were part of their official duties. In this respect, these persons, who were not confirmed by the Senate and were direct Presidential appointees reporting directly to the President, were in a stronger position even than cabinet officers, who were appointed with the advice and consent of the Senate. In Senate confirmation hearings, nominees were often asked questions as to their attitudes on specific matters of public policy.

This distinction became a matter of some controversy when Presidential foreign affairs assistant Henry Kissinger was nominated as Secretary of State. The White House announced that Kissinger would continue to be a presidential advisor as well as Secretary of State. In prior administrations, as well as up until this point in the Nixon Administration, the presidential advisor on foreign affairs had never been the same person as the Secretary of State, and it was understood that the presidential advisor would not be called to the Senate for questioning, whereas the Secretary of State was often invited to appear and frequently did so. The Nixon move with regard to Kissinger was viewed as an attempt to make him totally immune from giving an accounting of his stewardship to the Senate. During his confirmation hearings, Kissinger testified on this point, and promised that matters falling in the administerial category, as opposed to direct presidential confidential discussions, would be treated as in the past.

In 1973 the Senate Committee on the Judiciary held hearings on executive privilege. Professor Raoul Berger testified that the term "executive privilege" was first used in a 1958 memorandum by Attorney General William Rogers, who was later to become Secretary of State in the first Nixon Administration. Professor Arthur Schlesinger agreed that the memorandum entitled "The Power of the President to Withhold Information from Congress" was the first official document to use the term.[15]

The opponents of executive privilege have used the Supreme Court decision in *McGrain v. Daugherty* (1927), which stated that the legislative power was regarded by the founding fathers as an attribute of the legislative power of Parliament as a basis for disputing it. They assert that Article 1 of the

Constitution conferred this power upon both the House and the Senate. Since the House of Commons was viewed as the grand inquisitor of the realm, and since the legislative function of "the grand inquest of the Nation" was specifically mentioned in both the Philadelphia and State Ratifying Conventions, "there isn't a smidgen of evidence that anyone sought in any way to curb it."[16]

President Nixon issued a statement on March 12, 1973 regarding executive privilege. He took the position that it "will be exercised only in those particular instances in which disclosure would harm the public interest."[17] By itself the statement is nearly a direct quote from Thomas Jefferson's notes of the advice given by Washington's cabinet about an investigation of General St. Clair's unsuccessful expedition into the Northwest in 1792; however, Washington gave the documents to the House. The Nixon statement further maintains that the tradition of previous administrations to refuse appearance of personal staff members before Congressional committees will continue. Based on the separation-of-powers doctrine, a President cannot be subject to congressional questioning. According to Mr. Nixon, his personal staff is immune as well because they are "in effect an extension of the Presidency."[18] Finally, Nixon designated his Attorney General as the final conduit through which a cabinet request for involing executive privilege must be approved before the presidential decision is made.

On April 10, Attorney General Richard Kleindienst testified before the Senate Committee, and in his opening presentation argued that "executive privilege is squarely founded in the separation of powers doctrine."[19] Senator Muskie challenged the Attorney General to indicate when the doctrine of executive privilege had been established. Kleindienst replied, "I really don't know Senator. It is immaterial to me. . . . President Washington, as an executive, invoked privilege, as I indicated in my former remarks." Senator Muskie responded that Washington "did not use the words 'executive privilege'" and that the origin of the term had been in the Eisenhower Administration.[20]

In a further exchange with Senator Muskie, Attorney General Kleindienst attempted to assert that executive privilege extended far beyond the immediate White House staff, beyond the cabinet officers, and that in fact it could apply to all federal employees. Muskie challenged him on this and asked if he meant that it applied to everyone of the employees of the federal branch of the United States. Kleindienst replied, "I think if the President directs it, logically, I would have to say that is correct."[21]

Senator Roth, a Republican from Delaware, inquired as to whether executive privilege, in the view of the Nixon Administration, would apply also to an impeachment proceeding. Kleindienst replied, "If you are conducting an impeachment proceeding based on high crimes and misdemeanor and you want to subpoena someone from the President's staff to give you information, I believe that, based upon the doctrine of separation of powers, the President would have the power to invoke executive privilege with respect to that information."[22]

The Attorney General's time before the bar of the Senate came to a close with an unexpected exchange. Senator Ervin made the point that a President's main duty according to Constitution was to "take care the laws be faithfully executed," and this did not mean he had the power to take care that they were *not* executed. As a remedy, Mr. Kleindienst noted that impeachment was the ultimate cure for a President who abused his powers. Senator Ervin countered that the President might forbid members of the Executive Branch from testifying, thus leaving the Senate without evidence to make a judgment. The Attorney General replied, "You do not need evidence to impeach a President. You get the resolution passed by the House and trial by the Senate and if the Senate votes on that trial, and if the Senate agrees, he is impeached. That is the end of it."

Senator Ervin objected, "You cannot try cases without evidence, even in impeachment trials." As the Kleindienst testimony ended, Senator Muskie commented, "You are tossing around proposals rather recklessly, Mr. Attorney General."[23]

On June 8, 1973 Senator Ervin introduced Senate Concurrent Resolution 30, "to establish a procedure assuring Congress fully and prompt production of information requested Federal Officers and employees." Senator Ervin's remarks from the floor clearly indicate that Attorney General's testimony was in part responsible for the resolution. "I am sure that many Senators and other American citizens were shocked on April 10, when then Attorney General Richard G. Kleindienst testified that the President could extend the doctrine of executive privilege to prohibit any and all of the 2.5 million employees of the executive branch from testifying or providing information to Congress."[24]

The resolution purposely refrained from using the term "executive privilege," to avoid either "expressly or by implication" putting a stamp of approval on such a concept. In brief, the resolution vests in Congress the determination of whether to accept a Presidential refusal of requested information. If a joint committee or a subcommittee of either house decides a refusal is improper, it can take action through passage of a concurrent resolution (Joint House Senate Committee) or resolution.

Watergate

The most recent and most Constitution-shaking confrontation involved the questions developed in the Watergate investigation. This inquiry started out as an investigation of election abuses by the Committee to Reelect the President (CREEP). Subsequently a long list of other illegal and questionable activities came to light as the White House tried to cover up. President Nixon refused to make information available to the Senate Select Committee on Presidential Campaign Financing (Watergate Committee), to a special prosecutor whom he had selected under an Act of Congress, and later to the House Judiciary Committee charged with considering whether he should be impeached.

Impeachment was not the outcome of the Teapot Dome scandals, but comparisons between it and Watergate are instructive. President Harding's Secretary of the Interior, Albert Fall, first testified before the Senate investigating committee probing the Teapot Dome affair, but later refused to continue. In this instance the committee relented and decided to let the courts act. Testimony was not sought through granting immunity on the ground that it might detract from successful prosecution. This cautious approach, uncharacteristic of the Senate's Watergate investigation, which granted widespread immunity, was proved correct by subsequent events. In 1931, seven years after his refusal, Fall was sentenced to a year and a day in the New Mexico state penitentiary and fined $100,000 for his activities in the Teapot Dome affair.[25]

To a certain extent history repeated itself in the Watergate affair. This time two Nixon Cabinet secretaries—Maurice Stans, Secretary of Commerce, and John Mitchell, the Attorney General—were implicated and compelled to testify before the Senate investigating committee. (The Justice Department and the Attorney General were also under suspicion in the Senate investigations of the 1920s, when the Attorney General admitted publicly that he destroyed evidence.)

However, the posture of the President was decidedly different in the two periods. In 1924, one of the senators favoring investigation of spending in the behalf of presidential candidates responded as follows to a query of what would happen if candidates and their managers would refuse to testify: "They will not! Coolidge will make them! His stand in this matter is all right!"[26] President Coolidge demanded and recieved Attorney General Harry Daugherty's resignation because he refused to cooperate with the Senate investigation. In contrast, President Nixon employed and threatened "executive privilege" and the vaguely defined doctrine of "confidentiality" to impede the Senate probe of Watergate.

The dilemma in the Watergate case was well phrased by Clark Clifford, former legal counsel to President Truman and Secretary of Defense for President Johnson, when he testified immediately after Mr. Kleindienst at the "executive privilege" hearings in April 1973. Clifford raised an issue regarding President Nixon's use of executive privilege before John Ehrlichman and H. R. Haldeman resigned and ultimately appeared before the Watergate Committee. He pointed out that since the President took the position that he knew nothing about Watergate, executive privilege could not legitimately be claimed. Privilege is said to protect the relationship between the executive and his aides. If no relationship existed, no privilege could be claimed. In Mr. Clifford's words, "I do not see how a President can have it both ways."[27]

The Special Prosecutor's Office under Archibald Cox pursued other aspects of Watergate with vigor. Finally in November 1973 President Nixon asked Attorney General Elliott Richardson to resign for refusing to fire Cox, and then had a new acting Attorney General fire Cox. This fueled suspicion that the President was personally involved in Watergate. Finally a new special prosecutor, Leon Jaworski, was appointed by the Attorney General.

Meanwhile, after all the Watergate Committee documentation was published and several related court cases were in process, a resolution was introduced in the House to have the Judiciary Committee undertake an investigation of whether or not Richard Nixon should be impeached. An attempt to set a deadline of the end of April for its report failed to pass. Obviously, House Republicans were interested in having the matter resolved, one way or the other, long before the November elections. Their fears were intensified when a special election was held in Grand Rapids, Michigan in February 1974 to elect a replacement for former congressman Gerald Ford. The Democratic candidate who based his campaign on moral corruption in high places, won in a district represented by Republicans since 1910.

In January 1974 the Ervin Watergate Committee decided to discontinue its hearings because it had sufficiently alerted the public to the illegal and questionable activities of the White House staff and other Nixon confidants and because the judicial process and the House Judiciary Committee seemed ready to finish the job. In March of 1974 the grand jury handed down indictments of several top Nixon aides, including H. R. Haldeman, John Ehrlichman, Gordon Strachan, Charles Colson, Robert Mardian, former Attorney General John Mitchell, and Kenneth Parkinson, a lawyer. The indictments were based on information developed by the Special Prosecutor's Office.

Impeachment

Article I, Section 2 of the Constitution states that "the House of Representatives . . . shall have the sole Power of Impeachment." Section 3 adds, "the Senate Shall have the sole Power to try all Impeachments. When sitting for that purpose, they shall be on Oath of Affirmation. When the President of the United States is tried, the Chief Justice shall preside: And no Person shall be convicted without the Concurrence of two thirds of the Members present." Section 4 provides: "The President, Vice President, and all civil Officers of the United States shall be removed from Office on Impeachment for, and Conviction of, Treason, Bribery, or other high Crimes and Misdemeanors."

The power to impeach is the most awesome and least used power of the Congress. The impeachment process dates back to fourteenth-century England, when a very weak Parliament in its infancy sought to make the advisers to the King accountable for their actions. The framers of the Constitution were also interested in limiting executive power, so they incorporated an impeachment process into the Constitution.

Essentially, the House of Representatives is the prosecutor, the Senate chamber is the courtroom, and the Senate is the judge and jury. The proceedings have been initiated by various means, including the introduction of a resolution by a member of the House, a letter or message from the President, a charge forwarded to the House from a state or territorial legislature or a grand jury, or a resolution reported by the House Judiciary or even by another House committee. However, the five cases that have reached the Senate in the twentieth century were based on resolutions emanating from the House Judiciary Committee.

If the Committee finds the charges justified, it reports a resolution to the House, which generally includes the articles of impeachment. This resolution is subject to adoption by a majority vote of the House. If it adopts the resolution, the House then selects managers to appear at the bar of the Senate to present the articles of impeachment. After the impeachment of President Andrew Johnson in 1868, the Senate adopted rules for an impeachment trial, which is conducted like a court trial for criminal offenses.[28] Both sides—the House and the officer to be impeached—may present witnesses and evidence, and the defendant is allowed counsel and the right to cross-examine. Senate practice has been for the Vice President or the President pro tempore of the Senate to preside, except that if the President is on trial the Constitution requires that the Chief Justice of the Supreme Court preside. Procedural questions are decided by the presiding officer but can be overruled by a majority vote of the senators present. Conviction requires a two-thirds approval of the Senate. A vote on a single article of impeachment is sufficient to convict the accused.

Despite the terms used (counsel, witnesses, defendants), the comparison of the House procedure to a grand jury, and the Senate considerations of charges to a trial, an impeachment trial is not a criminal proceeding. Officials convicted can later be tried for criminal offenses, but penalties for those found guilty by the Senate are limited by the Constitution to removal from office and disqualification from holding "any Office of Honor, Trust or Profit under the United States."[29] There is no appeal.

Since 1868 the Congress, remembering the bitterness caused by President Andrew Johnson's impeachment and subsequent acquittal by one vote, has not until the present time seriously considered presidential impeachment. Impeachment efforts in the House in the past one-hundred years have been confined to federal judges with lifetime appointments, with one exception. This was when Secretary of War William W. Balknap was charged with graft in connection with the appointment and retention of an Indian post trader at Fort Sill, Oklahoma. Balknap was impeached by the House but acquitted by the Senate.[30]

President Nixon, a Republican president faced with a Democratic majority, has had at best an uneasy relationship with Congress. Impoundment of funds by the President, the "arbitrary" use of presidental power as commander-in-chief of the armed forces, and strong differences of opinion over national priorities have kept the executive and legislative branches of the government in conflict. This already uneasy relationship was aggravated when the President won reelection in 1972 by an overwhelming majority. It seemed as if the expansion of presidential power would continue.

Talk of impeaching the President was muttered about in the back rooms in the early stages of the Watergate scandal, and by September 1973, when the Senate Watergate Committee finished its nationally televised hearings, it was being discussed openly. When, after much resistance, the President turned over secret tape recordings to Judge John J. Sirica on October 31, 1973, it was with the hope that pressure for impeachment would subside. However, several key tapes had large blank spots and some parts were just missing. Expert testimony suggested that there had been between five and nine deliberate erasures. Members of the White House staff offered various reasons for the gaps but there has been no satisfactory explanation.

Pressure mounted, and on February 6, 1974 the House Judiciary Committee received mandate to consider impeachment of the President. The vote on the House floor was 410 to 4.

One of the fruits of the New Politics was the defeat of Emanuel Celler, Chairman of the House Judiciary Committee and the most senior Democrat in the House by a young woman lawyer, Elizabeth Holtzman, in 1972. As a consequence, Peter Rodino, now Chairman of the Judiciary Committee, was charged with the impeachment investigation. Interestingly, the Judiciary Committee had been one to which New Politics congressmen gravitated. It included liberals, women, and blacks, such as Robert Drinan, Paul Sarbanes, Elizabeth Holtzman, Barbara Jordan, John Conyers, and Charles Rangel. The chief counsel selected was John Doar, who had served Attorney General Robert Kennedy as his on-the-scene representative in civil rights actions in the early 1960s. Albert Jenner, the minority counsel, was a moderate to liberal Republican.

The Judiciary Committee announced that the scope of its investigation would include acts of the President not indictable under criminal law. This was in direct conflict with the President's interpretation of impeachment, and the White House lawyers sent a sixty-one-page analysis of the constitutional standards for presidential impeachment to the Judicary Committee for its consideration. James D. St. Clair, chief lawyer for the President, argued:

The use of a predetermined criminal standard for the impeachment of a President is also supported by history, logic, legal precedent and sound and sensible public policy which demands stability in our form of government. In American history, only the impeachment of President Andrew Johnson should be looked to for guidance. Other impeachments, dealing almost exclusively with Federal judges, are not enlightening because judges are not removable by the elective process, as are Presidents.[31]

The dispute in the House Judiciary Committee over the grounds for impeaching a President is not a new one. Impeachment is a political process and the ambiguous part of Article I, Section 3 of the Constitution which allows that impeachment can be for other "high Crimes and Misdemeanors" has been the cause of endless debate. However, constitutional law professor Raoul Berger believes that the grounds for removal lie somewhere between the English jurist Sir William Blackstone's assertion that an impeachment "is a prosecution of the already known and established law" and the position taken by the minority leader of the House of Representatives when he proposed the impeachment of Justice William O. Douglas in 1970.[32]

Then Representative Gerald Ford argued that "an impeachable offense is whatever a majority of the House of Representatives considers it to be at a given moment in history."[33] Ford contended that conviction results from whatever offense or offenses two-thirds of the other body considers sufficiently serious to require removal of the accused from office.[34] In a variation of the Ford formulation, former Attorney General Richard Kleindienst once cynically defined the politics of impeachment: "You don't need facts. You don't need evidence. All you need is votes."[35]

The problems caused by Watergate have left the President very vulnerable. It is in this area that a case for impeachment becomes strong. Included in the charges that are being bandied about by various groups are: Establishing within the White House an irregular personal secret police that engaged in sich criminal acts as burglary, illegal wiretaps, espionage and perjury; Personal approval of a plan authorizing illegal domestic political surveillance, military spying on civilians, mail covers and espionage against dissenters, political opponents, journalists, and federal employees; The dangling of a high federal post to the judge in the Ellsberg-Pentagon papers trial; and The attempted use of FBI investigations, income tax audits by the Internal Revenue Service and other threats to harass political enemies.[36]

The questions that this list raises are many. How deeply was the President involved? He has the power to fire his assistants and is responsible for their conduct. If he permits them to perpetrate with impunity high crimes or misdemeanors against the United States, or neglects to superintend their conduct so as to check their excesses, he raises questions about his personal capacity to govern. The cumulative evidence of abuse of office might be decisive—especially if it is proved that the President was personally involved in the cover-up of the original break-in at the Watergate headquarters of Democratic Party.

Perhaps the most powerful defense against impeachment in the end may not be by the President himself. Many congressmen may vote against it because of the effect that impeachment may have upon the nation. If the evidence is not sufficiently "hard," it will be difficult for the full House to vote to impeach the President of the United States. It will be even more difficult to get a two-thirds vote for conviction in the Senate. The senators are conscious of the fact that they would be highly visible during the trial proceedings.

Nominations

Under the provision of Article II, section 2, of the Constitution the President has the power to nominate an amazingly large number of Federal officers, but only with the advice and consent of the Senate. The provisions of Article II, section 2 read:

. . . and he shall nominate, and, by and with the Advice and Consent of the Senate, shall appoint Ambassadors, other public Ministers and Consuls, Judges of the Supreme Court and all other Officers of the United States, whose appointments are not herein otherwise provided for, and which shall be established by Law; but the Congress may by law vest the Appointment of such inferior Officers, as they think proper, in the President alone, in the Courts of Law, or in the Heads of departments. The President shall have power to fill up all Vacancies that may happen during the Recess of the Senate, by granting Commissions which shall expire at the End of their next Session.

The advice and consent role of the Senate, although originally designed to be that of a screening agent, has since the Constitution was written developed into a very influential one.

Traditionally the Senate has recognized the presidential prerogative to appoint, and has balked at relatively few nominations. However, Senate scrutiny of nominees is particularly critical when a President sends to them potential members of the Supreme Court and potential members of his Cabinet. Quite a few nominations have been controversial, and some have been rejected.

Many factors enter into the Senate's consideration of an important nominee. Partisan politics, the major political and social issues of the day, the nominee's own personality, conflict of interest; any one or all four can play an important part in a nominee's acceptance or rejection by the Senate. The position of the president himself can be of importance, especially if he is a lame duck.

Presidential nominees sent to the Senate for consideration can be grouped into four categories:

1. Nominees to the Supreme Court, Courts of Appeal, independent boards, commissions, and some subordinate agencies of regular departments.
2. Nominees for department secretaries, under-secretaries, high diplomats.
3. Nominees for field services of departments or other administrative agencies and district court judgeships. These are political patronage nominees, and the President must obtain prior consent of a member of the Senate before the nomination is sent to the Senate.
4. Nominees for positions in the military and lower positions in the agencies. This group makes up the majority of Presidential nominations and is based on recommendation of a department or agency. Here the actions of the President and Senate are mere formalities, due to the large number of this type of nominee.[37]

In recent times the nominations that have caused the most controversy and raised the most intense opposition in the Senate have been nominations to the Supreme Court. Thurgood Marshall, who had served on the U.S. Second Circuit Court of Appeals since 1962, was the center of debate in 1967 when President Johnson nominated him to the Supreme Court. Marshall was questioned repeatedly by southern Democrats about his opinion on Court decisions concerning the rights of the accused. He refused to answer on the grounds that it would be improper for him to discuss matters before the court. Despite the heavy criticism from the southern contingent in the Senate, Marshall was confirmed by a 69-to-11 vote and became the first black to serve on the Court.[38]

However, President Johnson triggered bitter Senate debate in 1968 when he nominated Justice Abe Fortas for the position of Chief Justice. Here was a case of partisan politics versus a lame-duck president. The Republicans wanted the position of Chief Justice left open until after the election when, they hoped, a Republican president would make the nomination. Because Johnson was due to leave office at the end of 1968, he had no real power to marshal the votes for his nominee. Questions also arose as to the depth of Fortas's involvement with the White House. Allegations were made that he had assisted in drafting legislation for the Administration, and that he had advised the President on Vietnam and the handling of urban riots. It was also disclosed that he had accepted a $15,000 fee for conducting a law seminar at a local university. The fee was paid by five former business associates, one of whom had a son involved in a federal criminal case.

Led by Republican Whip Robert Griffin of Michigan, the Republicans pressed relentlessly for rejection of Fortas. The debate grew into a filibuster. Mansfield finally called for an end to the filibuster by reading a cloture motion. The motion was rejected by a roll-call vote of 45 to 43,[39] fourteen votes short of the fifty-nine needed to shut off the debate. Fortas, realizing that he would not be confirmed, requested President Johnson to recall the nomination. He then resigned from the Supreme Court. He was the first justice in history to resign under charges of misconduct.

President Nixon faced heavy opposition from the Senate with two of his Supreme Court nominations. In 1969 he nominated Clement F. Haynsworth, Jr. to fill the seat left vacant by Fortas. During the course of the battle over Haynsworth's nomination, tremendous pressure was applied to the Senators, both by the Administration and by groups lobbying against the nomination. Senator Richard Schweiker, a Republican from Pennsylvania, stated that he had not experienced such pressure in the nine years he had served in the Congress. Schweiker had announced early that he would vote against Haynsworth. Senator Hugh Scott, who had just become the new minority leader upon the death of Senator Everett Dirksen, was quickly put to the test by the nomination battle.

Leading groups lobbying against the nomination included the AFL-CIO and the National Association for the Advancement of Colored People (NAACP) who believed Haynsworth was hostile to both workers and blacks. While they and other opponents did not question the nominee's honesty, there was a question of the ethical propriety of some of his judicial decisions. The battle for and against the nomination was a bitter one. In a crucial vote of 45 to 55, Clement T. Haynsworth, Jr. became the first Supreme Court nominee to be formally rejected by the Senate since 1930.[40]

Table 9-1
Haynsworth Vote

For:	45—26 Republicans + 16 southern Democrats + 3 northern Democrats	
Against:	55—17 Republicans + 3 southern Democrats + 35 northern Democrats	

Source: *U.S. Congressional Record* Vol. 115, 91st Congress, 1st Session, November 21, 1969, p. 35396.

In 1970 President Nixon sent an even more controversial nomination to the Senate. At first glance it seemed as if the second nominee for Fortas's seat, G. Harrold Carswell, a judge from the Fifth Circuit Court of Appeals in Florida, was just another "strict constructionist." It was soon revealed that he had extreme views on segregation. Worse, he was a man of only mediocre legal and judicial abilities. But the most effective opposition was the rejection of Carswell by his own colleagues in the legal profession. However, the opposition was slow to mount because the Senate wished to avoid another bitter struggle with the Administration. Senator Birch Bayh, a Democrat from Indiana who had led the floor fight against Haynsworth, repeated his efforts. He claimed that Carswell's legal credentials were too threadbare to justify appointment. On April 8, 1970 the Senate rejected the Carswell nomination by a vote of 45 to 51. It was the first time since 1894 that a president had had two nominees for the Supreme Court rejected by the Senate.[41]

Table 9-2
Carswell Vote

For:	45—28 Republicans + 14 southern Democrats + 3 northern Democrats
Against:	51—13 Republicans + 5 southern Democrats + 33 northern Democrats

Source: *U.S. Congressional Record*, Vol. 116, 91st Congress, 1st Session, April 8, 1970, p. 10769.

The President attacked the Senate for its handling of the Carswell nomination. He said he respected the right of any senator to differ with his selection of a nominee, but

the fact remains under the Constitution it is the duty of a President to appoint and of the Senate to advise and consent. But if the Senate attempts to substitute its judgment as to who should be appointed, the traditional constitutional balance is in jeopardy and the duty of the President under its Constitution impaired.

Majority leader Mike Mansfield replied, "the Senate in advising and consenting shares the appointive power with the President."[42]

In a letter to then Senator William Saxbe, a Republican from Ohio, the President also stated: "The question arises whether I, as the President of the United States shall be accorded the same choice in naming Supreme Court Justices which has been freely accorded to my predecessors of both parties."[43]

Because of the bitter controversy over the Haynsworth and Carswell nominations, a prospective nominee for the Court, Representative Richard H. Poff, a Republican from Virginia, withdrew his name fron consideration. Poff was a respected conservative who had voted against every civil rights bill during his nineteen years in the House. He had signed the 1956 "Southern Manifesto" opposing the 1954 Supreme Court school desegregation decision.

Finally in 1971, the Senate confirmed the appointment of Harry A. Blackmun to fill the vacant Fortas seat on the Court. Nixon also sent two more nominations to the Senate for the Court—William Rehnquist, Assistant Attorney General, and Lewis F. Powell, Jr., former president of the American Bar Association and a practicing lawyer in Virginia. The last two were confirmed by the Senate, although there were grumblings about Rehnquist from the more liberal element in the Senate concerning his handling of protest demonstrations while he was at the Justice Department. But the opposition was so mild in comparison to previous nominations that Linda Charlton, writing about the nominations in the *New York Times* in September of 1973, noted that the attitude seemed to be that the President has the right to appoint people he wants to appointed positions. The party versus party and liberal versus conservative clashes over presidential appointees has been deemphasized.

Nominees to a President's cabinet have generally been approved by the Senate, but some have been quite controversial. In 1959 the Senate rejected Eisenhower nominee Lewis Strauss for Secretary of the Department of Commerce. Strauss was a controversial person.

He had previously served as head of the Atomic Energy Commission, and during the hearings on the nomination he was accused by opponents as having acted with personal vindictiveness in that position. Despite opposition, the Senate Interstate and Foreign Commerce Committee voted 9 to 8 to recommend confirmation, but the Democratic leadership refused to take a stand. President Eisenhower, angered by the Senate opposition to Strauss, threatened to use every single influence he had to win the confirmation. However, his wings were clipped because he was a lame-duck president, and he was faced with a Democratic majority in the Senate. The nomination was rejected by a roll-call vote of 46 to 49 (Democrats, 15 to 47; Republicans, 31 to 2).[44] Two outspoken and independent Republicans, William Langer of North Dakota and Margaret Chase Smith of Maine, joined forty-seven Democrats in voting down the nomination. This was the first time since 1925 that a Cabinet nominee had been rejected by the Senate.

While Cabinet nominees and nominees for heads of agencies seldom cause the excitement generated by the Strauss nomination, they have caused considerable debate in the Senate. In 1961, for example, Robert C. Weaver was confirmed as Administrator of the Housing and Home Finance Agency. Weaver was the first black to hold such an office, and therefore he was subject to close scrutiny by southern Democrats. They criticized Weaver's "extreme" views in favor of racially integrated housing and were highly suspicious of Weaver's belief that federal programs were an instrument to integrate housing. However, the Senate Banking and Currency Committee ultimately approved Weaver's nomination and the Senate confirmed it. In 1966, Weaver was nominated by President Johnson to assume the post of Secretary of the newly formed Department of Housing and Urban Development. This time Weaver's confirmation was confirmed by the Senate with no argument. He was the first black to hold a Cabinet post.

President Nixon has faced two Senate battles over his nominees for Cabinet positions. In 1969, the Senate had confirmed by voice vote all of his Cabinet nominations except that of Walter J. Hickel for Secretary of the

Interior. Hickel's nomination had been challenged by conservation groups, who questioned his dedication to environmental protection. He was also criticized for his ties to oil companies. As a result, Hickel faced four days of hearings by the Senate Interior and Insular Affairs Committee, during which he was questioned about his various activities including some $1 million worth of gas pipeline stock. He promised the committee he would sell the stock. Many senators expressed doubts as to Hickel's qualifications but said they would vote for him as it was customary to let the President select his first Cabinet members. Hickel's appointment was confirmed in the Senate by a 73 to 16 roll-call vote.[45]

In 1972, Richard G. Kleindienst was nominated for the position of Attorney General. Kleindienst's nomination was reported favorably out of the Judiciary Committee on February 29. However, charges were made by a nationally syndicated columnist that the nominee lied to the Judiciary Committee when he disclaimed any role in the Justice Department's out-of-court settlement of antitrust cases against International Telephone and Telegraph Corporation (ITT). Kleindienst requested that the Judiciary Committee re-open its hearings on his nomination to settle the charges. After twenty-two days of hearings, the Committee voted to reconfirm its prior recommendation of Kleindienst. His nomination was confirmed by a 64 to 19 roll-call vote.[46] The hearings on Kleindienst were described as "the longest confirmation hearings" in the history of the Senate. The Democratic majority in the Senate had prolonged the hearings in an attempt to substantiate the charges concerning the 1971 ITT antitrust settlement. He has since pleaded guilty to a charge that he had lied to the Senate Judiciary Committee concerning some aspects of ITT's dealings with the Republican party.

Mr. Kleindienst's confirmation problems were really the result of partisan politics, whereas Mr. Hickel's problems arose from groups of environmentalists challenging his conservation philosophy. Robert Weaver and Thurgood Marshall were challenged primarily because they were black. However, Clement Haynsworth and G. Harrold Carswell were challenged principally because their philosophy of interpretation of law was basically conservative and strict constructionist. Liberal senators, spurred on by various groups such as the AFL-CIO and the NAACP, questioned the last two nominations which were eventually rejected.

However, the Watergate scandal caused unique problems for some of Mr. Nixon's nominees for high jobs. L. Patrick Gray III was nominated in 1973 to become director of the Federal Bureau of Investigation. Gray's nomination was haunted by controversy and tragedy, and he was never confirmed by the Senate. He had the misfortune to come before the Senate in March of 1973 when the Watergate scandal was gaining momentum. He showed considerable lack of judgment in telling the senators that he was willing to release FBI files to them concerning the Watergate scandals in order to establish his own innocence in the entire affair. The Senate wanted to put off the nomination until the Watergate matter had been resolved, but Gray rejected that saying the FBI needed a leader.

White House support for Gray dwindled, and finally his nomination was withdrawn two days before the Senate was scheduled to vote on it. Gray was a victim of his own incompetence, the Watergate scandal, and of White House staff intrigue. He eventually resigned as acting director of the FBI on April 27, after he testified to destroying documents belonging to convicted Watergate conspirator E. Howard Hunt on the orders of presidential aide H. R. Haldeman.

Richard Kleindienst resigned as Attorney General early in 1973 because of the Watergate scandal. Nixon nominated Elliot Richardson, then Secretary of the Department of Defense, to take Kleindienst's place. It was not the man himself and his competence that was debated, but Kleindienst's eventual role in having the chief responsibility for the work of the special prosecutor who would be assigned to gather evidence on those involved with the Watergate scandal. Richardson's confirmation came only after he pledged to the Senate that he would allow the special prosecutor true independence. At the same time he was confirmed by the Senate, Richardson named Archibald Cox to fill the post of special prosecutor. So it was in a sense a dual confirmation by the Senate.

His concern with the independence of the special prosecutor caused him to resign in October of 1973. His resignation, coupled with that of his Deputy Attorney General William Ruckelshaus, was part of the so-called "Saturday Night Massacre." President Nixon asked Richardson to fire Cox, and Richardson refused, as did Ruckelshaus. Both Richardson and Ruckelshaus then submitted their resignations.

Badly in need of an attorney general to calm the cries of outrage that the Saturday Night Massacre provoked, Nixon chose William Saxbe, an outspoken Republican Senator from Ohio. Saxbe had recently announced he was not going to run for a second term in 1974, a fact that aided his routine confirmation by the Senate.

Aside from the controversial appointments engendered by the Watergate scandal, the Administration has had other appointments rejected that normally would be passed upon by the Senate. Robert H. Morris was nominated to become a member of the Federal Power Commission (FPC). Morris immediately became the subject of a lobbying campaign which contended that he was too closely tied to the oil industry, and would represent industry and not the consumer. Unfortunately, his nomination to FPC followed that of former Congressman William L. Springer, who was also believed to be business oriented. Consumer lobbyists wanted a consumer-oriented person on the FPC. Morris's rejection by the Senate was the first time since 1950 that a nominee for a regulatory agency post had been turned down.

Even career foreign service officers ran into Senate opposition. On July 11, 1973, the Senate Foreign Relations Committee rejected President Nixon's nomination of G. McMurtrie Godley to be Assistant Secretary of State for East Asian and Pacific Affairs. The 9-to-7 vote in the committee to postpone the nomination in effect killed it. Godley had been, prior to his nomination, serving as Ambassador to Laos.[47]

Chairman J.W. Fulbright stated that the nomination was rejected because Godley was too closely tied to a policy of U.S. intervention in South Asia to serve as the chief policy official for the East Asian area. Rejecting a career officer for nomination to a higher post because of disapproval of the government's foreign policy was unusual. In fact, Foreign Affairs Committee staff members said they could not recall a similar occasion in the past fifteen years.

The confirmation procedure used in considering House Minority Leader Gerald Ford for the vice-presidency established precedents as it went along. Back in 1965 when the Congress approved the Twenty-Fifth Amendment, language in that amendment gave it a role in filling a vacant vice-presidency. The amendment read: "Whenever there is a vacancy in the office of the Vice President, the President shall nominate a Vice President who shall take office upon confirmation by a majority vote of both Houses of Congress." However, there was no procedure for confirmation written into the Amendment. What was unique in the Twenty-Fifth Amendment was that both houses of Congress had to approve the President's choice of a vice president.

The House decided that the Judiciary Committee would have jurisdiction over the nomination proceedings. In the Senate there was vigorous debate between members who wanted to create a special committee to consider the nomination and those who wanted to refer it to the Rules Committee. Democratic and Republican leadership finally decided that the Rules Committee should have the jurisdiction.

Considering the scandal surrounding the resignation of Vice President Agnew, members of the Senate Rules and House Judiciary Committees asked for a sweeping investigation into Ford's background, covering his income tax returns, his voting record in the House, and followed up possible hints of influence peddling. The hearings moved quickly, and six weeks after his nomination he was confirmed by the House and Senate.

Ford's confirmation by both houses of Congress is unique in our history. The advice and consent on nominations has hitherto been the exclusive property of the Senate, and for the most part is likely to remain so. However, in writing the Twenty-Fifth Amendment, members of the House obviously believed that confirmation for such an important office as the vice-presidency was too important to be left to the Senate alone, and the Senate agreed.

10 Checks and Balances: Presidential Perspectives

While the Constitution has proved to be an enduring document, it has been expanded and informally amended by precedent and personality. The two greatest expansions have involved the growth of the scope of federal responsibilities and, in part because of that growth, the opportunity and need for more presidential leadership and policy initiative.

In the preceding chapter it was pointed out that many issues do not involve either the whole Congress or the President, in that both of them act upon the advice of their specialists. But even where the issue is of such a nature or significance that the whole Congress *is* the actor, it may not have a major impact. Because of the constitutional grants of authority to the President in foreign affairs, Congress plays a subordinate role in that arena. Congress has had difficulty influencing presidential policy in matters of defense and war. When it comes to influencing the detailed operations of the Department of Defense, Congress clearly lacks the expertise and the information necessary to evaluate most of what is happening. Congress may slow up appropriations for a weapons system but it lacks the expertise to substitute one of its own. A great opportunity in legislative influence would presumably be in the decision to enter into a state of war—and yet even here it has been called upon for an ex post facto judgment. The fact is that the United States has military and foreign policy commitments throughout the world that require a unified and timely response. Congress is not in a position to provide this. The need in the twentieth century to have instant response to a nuclear attack and the intertwining of foreign affairs and military policy has therefore worked to the disadvantage of Congress in terms of power. The juxtaposition of the President's commander-in-chief power and foreign relations powers have led to general acceptance of another presidential power—the so-called war power.

The increasing importance of informal foreign relations, as well as trade policy involving technical teams from various nations, make it difficult for Congress to participate or to make any changes. The decreasing use of treaties and the increased use of executive agreements, many of which are kept secret at the option of the President, have put the President in command of foreign affairs.

The interdependence of the world economy has given the President enhanced powers in the economic field, and the Employment Act of 1946 has led to further delegations of power to the President by Congress, as for example in the economic legislation of 1971. Ironically, President Nixon opposed the legislation, considered vetoing it, and indicated he would never use it. Yet not long thereafter he was making use of it in establishing wage and price ceilings, and even directed two dollar devaluations.

177

Impoundment—the process of withholding federal expenditures at presidential direction despite favorable congressional action is related to the President's economic powers. One way to meet the requirements of the Employment Act is to reduce federal spending in times of inflation. However, the determination of which spending to reduce becomes a significant policy decision, and presidential impoundment denies Congress a voice in that decision. The gradual expansion of impoundment therefore generated serious confrontations during the Nixon Administration; most of which the courts settled in favor of Congress. However, the President still has ample powers to delay action, and even unfavorable court decisions may not totally reverse the effect he intended.

Another major presidential power in coping with Congress is the veto. Overriding a veto is a difficult undertaking, since the issue may involve conflicting philosophical, political, social, or economic differences. Thus, Congress may be split and fail to muster a two-thirds vote in the House *and* the Senate. Usually a fairly solid vote in the President's own party is enough to block a veto. In a sense, it might not be necessary to use the veto. The mere threat of its use is a lever that friendly congressional leaders can employ to secure changes at the committee level or on the House or Senate floor. Nevertheless, the veto will sometimes be overridden, especially if a strong and broadly based interest group feels intensely about the issue. President Eisenhower, for example, was overridden on a pay raise bill for federal employees, and President Nixon suffered a similar fate on the War Powers Act in 1973.

All things considered, though, these exceptions in terms of overriding a veto, stopping an impoundment, or questioning a defense appropriation serve to point up how rarely Congress can prevail in a confrontation with the President. Some of these areas will now be discussed in more detail, to see why the President has so much power in these decisions.

The "War Power" of the President

The Constitution of the United States does not refer to anything called the "war power," but provides the President with two authorities which, taken together, were used by President Lincoln to justify the extraordinary measures he took after the fall of Fort Sumter, when he called a special session of Congress on July 4, 1861.

Article II, section 1, states: "The executive Power shall be vested in a President of the United States of America," and Article II, section 2, states, without further elaboration: "The President shall be Commander in Chief of the Army and Navy of the United States, and of the Militia of the several States, when called into the actual Service of the United States."

In contrast to the brief delineation of power given to the President relating to national security, the Constitution expressly details war powers for the Congress. Article I, section 8 enumerates the following: "provide for the common Defense; to define and punish . . . Offenses against the Law of

Nations; To declare War . . . To raise and support Armies . . . To make Rules for the Government and Regulation of the land and naval Forces; To provide for calling forth the Militia to execute the Laws . . . and repel Invasions."

While desiring a more national government than they had experienced under the Continental Congress or the Articles of Confederation, the Founding Fathers bestowed general executive authority on the President in Article II of the Constitution. But they also desired less centralized authority than they had known under the British crown. They restricted the President's treaty-making power by giving the Senate the power to vote on acceptance or rejection. They also restricted his right to declare war. As Alexander Hamilton explained in *Federalist Paper 69*, the President's power as Commander in Chief

would be nominally the same with that of the king of Great Britain, but in substance much inferior to it. It would amount to nothing more than the supreme command and direction of the military and naval forces ... while that of the British king extends to the *declaring* of war and to the *raising* and *regulating* of fleets and armies— all of which, by the Constitution, under consideration would appertain to the legislature.[1]

Arthur Schlesinger, Jr., writing in *Foreign Affairs* magazine in 1972, stated that war power has historically involved a competition between the power of the Congress to authorize war and the power of the President as Commander in Chief.[2] The issue is not declaration of war in the strict sense. Though the United States has engaged in a number of armed conflicts in the last two centuries, it has made only five formal declarations of war. The real issue is congressional authorization—whether or not by formal declaration—of the commitment of American forces in circumstances that involve or invite hostilities against states.

It is understandable that the prolonged conflict in Vietnam should raise in the minds of Congressmen the need to reexamine the basis for presidential war-making powers. Interest in the unilateral capability of a president to commit American troops in foreign states increased in direct proportion to the opposition to the war in Southeast Asia.

The first discussion of the use of presidential war powers arose when President George Washington issued a Proclamation of Neutrality in the Napoleonic Wars. However, the real expansion of the presidential war powers began in the presidency of John Adams, and suffered reverses in the late nineteenth century, but with the advent of strong presidential figures in the twentieth century has steadily grown. An article in the *American Bar Association Journal* in 1972 cites 199 actual instances in which the President ordered troops to take action in foreign countries without declaration of war.[3] The first occasion was in 1789, when President John Adams attempted to negotiate a settlement with France, which was routinely seizing American merchant ships. When that failed he went to the Congress and requested power to arm merchant ships and take other defensive measures. Congress responded by creating a Navy Department, voting appropriations for new warships, and authorizing enlistment of a "Provisional Army" for the duration of the emergency. While neither France nor the United States declared war on each other, there was fighting between the U.S. Navy and French privateers and warships and a treaty was signed in 1800.

While Adams had congressional support, he still had to take the initiative in order to protect American lives and property on the high seas. Throughout the early nineteenth century, U.S. presidents found themselves in similar positions of having to protect American shipping interests against Barbary pirates in the Mediterranean, and of convincing European powers that their footholds in the New World were not excuses to encroach on United States territory.

Demonstrations of the unilateral capability of the President to confront the Congress with *faits accomplis* were amply illustrated by Presidents Polk in Mexico and Pierce in Japan. Lincoln, of course, in conducting the Civil War, greatly expanded presidential war powers. However, in the years after the Civil War, a generation of what Arthur Schlesinger calls "Congressional Government" was established. Congress had harassed Lincoln and impeached his successor, Andrew Johnson. This shifted the presidential-congressional conflict from war power to treaty power. The Senate freely exercised its option to rewrite, amend, and reject treaties negotiated by the President. But during these years, the Congress made no attempt to assert itself on the question of war power or to encroach on the President's power as commander-in-chief of the armed forces. Troops were sent to Cuba, the Philippines, Haiti, and the Dominican Republic in support of American interests.

President McKinley set the tone for the twentieth century when he sent five thousand American troops to China, ostensibly to protect American lives and property during the Boxer Rebellion. Prior to the China intervention, military forces committed unilaterally by presidents were typically used in police actions against private groups. In this case American troops went into action against a sovereign state without congressional authorization.

Nevertheless, the Senate reasserted its prerogative by twice rejecting the Treaty of Versailles, on November 19, 1919 and on March 19, 1920.[4] In the 1930s the Congress passed several rigid neutrality laws limiting the executive's ability to join another world war. When Germany struck in 1939, President Roosevelt was restrained by the neutrality laws and by an isolationist Congress. Roosevelt stretched presidential powers to the limit in aiding Germany's opponents. He issued a "shoot-at-sight" order to the Navy to protect convoys in the North Atlantic. On September 3, 1940 the "Fifty Destroyer Deal" was announced. According to this executive agreement the United States traded fifty reconditioned destroyers to Britain for British naval bases in the West Atlantic. This agreement violated statutes and constitutional powers specifically granted to Congress. A defense by Attorney General Robert Jackson asserted that as commander-in-chief the President had the authority to "dispose" the armed forces. Consequently, the Attorney General interpreted this as the power to *dispose of* them.[5] In effect he put the United States into an undeclared naval war with Germany, without congressional authorization. In August of 1941 the House had renewed the Selective Service Act by a one-vote margin. After the attack on Pearl Harbor the nation was thrust into World War II and Congress had no alternative but to support the President.

The emergency aura that surrounded the Cold War in the late 1940s and 1950s enabled President Truman to use troops to prevent a Communist takeover in Korea in 1950. President Eisenhower acted unilaterally in committing American troops to Lebanon and the Pacific fleet of the Navy to Taiwan when it was being threatened by Communist China.

During the Cuban missile crisis, President Kennedy sent naval units to blockade Cuba and prevent Soviet missiles from being delivered. He also committed a small number of American troops and specialists to Vietnam. The trend continued with President Johnson, who increased the number of troops in Vietnam. He also secured passage of the Gulf of Tonkin Resolution (H.J.Res. 1145), which passed the House 410 to 0 and the Senate 82 to 2 on August 7, 1964.[6] The resolution gave the President sweeping authority "to take all necessary measures to repel any armed attack against the forces of the United States and to prevent further aggression."[7] President Johnson always claimed he had the power to send troops to Vietnam without congressional consent. However it was, politically, a judicious move on his part to obtain the resolution from the Congress.

The extremely unstable situation in the Middle East caused presidents Johnson in 1967 and Nixon in 1970 and 1972 to activate the Sixth Fleet in the Mediterranean to prevent conflict from spreading. A good case can be made for presidential prerogative in foreign affairs. Detailed diplomatic negotiations cannot be left to a diverse body like the Congress, with its multiple political commitments and conflicting personalities. One voice is needed in delicate diplomatic negotiations. The President is the logical figure to take charge of an ever-expanding military, diplomatic, and intelligence establishment necessary to the major American role in world affairs. With annihilation of the nation a genuine possibility in the nuclear age, only the President was in a position to develop and manage policy crucial to the nation's survival.

Such tremendous power is an ever-present temptation. The President in the twentieth century has unilaterally committed American forces numerous times, and once a president has made a commitment of troops he may be compelled to send more to protect the original investment. Vietnam is the tragic example, and the prolonged war is the reason the constitutional basis for the war powers of the President have come under close scrutiny by the Congress.

The rising opposition to the war in Vietnam caused several legislative attempts in the Senate to limit American involvement. Most senators felt we were committed to finishing what had been started, so that no formal action against Johnson was successful. However, the issue was a live one and enabled Senator Eugene McCarthy to put on a surprisingly successful campaign in the 1968 primaries. This opened the door for other challengers, such as Robert F. Kennedy, and eventually President Johnson withdrew from the race. Hubert Humphrey, who received the nomination, was defeated largely because he was associated with the Vietnam issue. When President Nixon would not end the Vietnam War, Senate opposition increased as he increased the scope of it. The first real expression of Senate opposition in terms of legislation came with the adoption of the National Commitments Resolution in 1969. The measure, while not having the force of law, was an attempt to reassert a congressional voice in decisions committing the U.S. to the defense of foreign nations. The resolution defined a national commitment as "the use of the Armed forces on foreign territory, or a promise to assist a foreign country, government or people by the use of the armed forces or financial resources of the United States, either immediately or upon the happening of certain event," and declared that "such a commitment results only from affirmative action taken by the executive and legislative branches of the United States Government."[8]

The second concerted effort on the part of members of the Senate to limit the President's "war powers" came in 1970, after the surprise invasions of Cambodia by American troops. An End the War Amendment was introduced by Senators McGovern, Hughes, Cranston, Goodell, and Hatfield in September. Senators Church and Cooper also introduced an amendment to the Foreign Military Sales bill to prohibit military assistance to Cambodia and to bar funds for U.S. military operations in Cambodia. Debate lasted seven weeks. In order to co-opt the opposition to the war, Senator Robert Dole of Kansas introduced a resolution to repeal the Gulf of Tonkin resolution. The Senate voted to repeal the Act and was momentarily diverted from more specific legislation.[9]

However, later that year, Senator William Fulbright, Foreign Relations Committee Chairman, introduced his own resolution to repeal the Tonkin Resolution, and the Senate again voted to repeal it. The McGovern-Hatfield Amendment, which had originally sought to cut off funds by the end of 1970, had been modified to limiting the troop strength in Vietnam to 280,000 men by April 30, 1971. It also proposed to limit funding after that date to finance the complete withdrawal of remaining troops by December 31, 1971. The proposal was rejected by the Senate by a vote of 39 to 55.[10]

The House was also in the throes of debate over the role of Congress in the declaration of war. Congressman Dante Fascell of Florida introduced a bill that would make certain that any future war would only be undertaken after serious consideration. The House Foreign Affairs Subcommittee on National Security and Scientific Developments held hearings intermittently in the summer of 1970 on Fascell's bill. As a result of these hearings, the House Foreign Affairs Committee reported Fascell's bill as a joint resolution. The resolution reconfirmed the power of the Congress to declare war, and defined the war-making powers of the President. On November 16, 1970 the House passed the resolution, but it died in the Senate.

With some modifications, the resolution was reintroduced as a bill by Congressman Clement Zablocki in early 1971. It passed the House in early August. The Senate Foreign Relations Committee also opened hearings on three war-powers bills: S. 731, introduced by Senator Jacob Javits; S.J. Res.

59, introduced by Senator Thomas Eagleton; and the Zablocki bill. During the committee's hearings, S. 731 was reintroduced as S. 2956, and this bill was later reported out of the committee with some amendments.

Reflecting congressional concern over the way the United States entered into such a costly commitment, S.2956 defined emergency conditions in which the President could commit forces in the absence of a declaration of war by Congress. It also prescribed procedures by which the Congress could terminate the emergency use of American forces if it disapproved of the President's actions. However, the bill exempted United States participation in the Indo-China fighting. It was designed primarily to reassert congressional power in future wars. The bill passed the Senate and an amended version passed the House. However, the Senate rejected the House version in the conference committee and the bill died.

In 1973, Senator Javits again introduced a bill—S. 440. In presenting their arguments for limiting the President's war powers, Senator Javits and others, such as constitutional law scholar Alexander Bickel and historian Henry Steele Commager, argued for a strict interpretation of the Constitution. In a statement before the Senate Foreign Affairs Committee, Senator Javits states that the purpose of S. 440, titled *The War Powers Act of 1973,* was to end the practice of presidential war.

Senator Javits believes that a dangerous imbalance in the constitutional system of checks and balances has occurred particularly with the "undeclared" war or Presidential war that has been waged in the past ten years. Senator Barry Goldwater and others believe that the undeclared war was waged with congressional consent and that there is nothing constitutionally illegitimate or even dubious about "undeclared wars." We and other nations have fought them frequently.

The modern controversies over the division of constitutional authority between Congress and the President with respect to military operations have a special intensity which reflects the scale of American involvement in world politics since 1940 and the shock and controversy resulting from Korea and Vietnam. The nation faces foreign policy problems today altogether different from those it faced in 1800 or even 1900. After World War II, the United States for the first time took direct responsibility for protecting its primary security as a nation, by a system of eight Collective Security treaties which involved forty-three nations. Among them were the North Atlantic Treaty Organization (NATO), the Southeast Asia Treaty Organization (SEATO), and bilateral treaties with Japan, Korea, the Philippines, and Nationalist China.

The treaties uniformly provided to the Chief Executive as commander-in-chief broad powers to involve the armed forces of the United States in hostilities. In fact, amendments to prohibit the use of the armed forces of the United States without congressional approval were offered in the Foreign Relations Committee and on the floor of the Senate during the consideration of several of these treaties, as well as during consideration of resolutions on Formosa, the Middle East, Berlin, Cuba, and the Tonkin Gulf. They were consistently opposed and rejected in the Committee and in the Senate. In

April 1972, supported by the House leadership, the Democratic Caucus voted 144 to 58 to ask the Foreign Affairs Committee to report out legislation terminating U.S. involvement in Indochina. House Majority Leader Tip O'Neill aided the cause by offering an amendment that made the final resolution acceptable to a majority of the members without altering the intent. The Committee reported out H.J.Res. 542, June 1973; the Senate Foreign Relations Committee had produced its own bill (S. 440) one day earlier.[11]

After passing both the House and Senate, H.J.Res. 542 was sent to conference to resolve the differences. In October, the House (238 to 123) and Senate (75 to 20) approved the conference report. The House passage of the conference report totaled only three votes short of a two-thirds majority of those present and voting; the number that would be needed to defeat a presidential veto. There were two kinds of opposition to the bill—those who supported the President's privacy in this area, and those who argued that the bill actually gave the President new powers that he did not already have. Senator Thomas Eagleton of Missouri called the bill "an open-ended blank check for 90 days of war-making anywhere in the world by the President."[12]

The general feeling among the members of the Congress was that something, no matter how imperfect it was, had to be done to redress what they perceived as grievous loss of influence over foreign policy. The War Powers Act was an attempt to restore balance between the Executive and Legislative Branches. The provisions of the bill are:

That the President could commit U.S. armed forces into hostilities or situations where hostilities might be imminent, only pursuant to a declaration of war, specific statutory authorization or a national emergency created by an attack upon the United States, its territories or possessions, or its armed forces.

The President "in every possible instance" should consult with the Congress before committing U.S. forces to hostilities or to situations where hostilities might be imminent, . . . and to consult Congress regularly after such a commitment.

That the President report in writing within 48 hours to the Speaker of the House and President Pro Tempore of the Senate on any commitment or substantial enlargement of U.S. combat forces abroad, except for deployments related solely to supply, replacement, repair, or training; and that the President be required to give supplementary reports at least every six months while such forces were being engaged.

That the troop commitment be terminated within 60 days after the President's initial report was submitted unless Congress delcared war, specifically authorized continuation of the commitment, or was physically unable to convene as a result of an armed attack on the United States; and that the 60-day period be extended for up to 30 days if the President determined and certified to the Congress that unavoidable military necessity respecting the safety of the United States forces required their continued use in bringing about a prompt disengagement.

That Congress, at any time U.S. forces were engaged in hostilities without a declaration of war on specific congressional authorization by concurrent resolution, is allowed to direct the President to disengage such troops.

And that congressional priority procedures be set up for consideration of any resolution or bill introduced pursuant to the provisions of the resolution.[13]

President Nixon's message accompanying his veto of the bill stressed the need for the President to conduct foreign affairs, and declared that the congressional intervention was both dangerous and unconstitutional. The terms, "foreign affairs" or "foreign policy" appeared in the text eight times, while "war powers" was mentioned once near the end.

Overriding the Nixon veto required a two-thirds majority (280) in the House. On November 7, 1973, the House voted 284 to 135 to override the veto—a slim four-vote margin. Republican support was necessary, and 86 of the 189 Republicans voted to override. The vote among northern Democrats was 143 to 9 and among southern Democrats 55 to 23. Four hours later the Senate concurred with the House, 78 to 18. In the Senate all three groups voted as follows: Republicans 25 to 15; northern Democrats 36 to 2; and southern Democrats 14 to 1. This was the first successful override of a Nixon veto in 1973, after eight prior attempts had fallen short.[14]

Perhaps in the statement of Supreme Court Justice Robert Jackson in his 1952 concurring opinion in the case of *Youngstown Sheet and Tube Co. v. Sawyer* one can find a reason for the overriding of the President's veto of the war-powers bill by the Congress. Jackson stated:

Presidential powers are not fixed but fluctuate, depending upon their disjunction or conjunction with those of Congress. . . .

When the President acts pursuant to an express or implied authorization of Congress, his authority is at its maximum, for it includes all that he possesses in his own right plus all that Congress can delegate. . . .

When the President acts in absence of either a congressional grant or denial of authority, he can only rely upon his own independent powers, but there is a zone of twilight in which he and Congress may have concurrent authority, or in which its distribution is uncertain. Therefore congressional inertia, indifference or quiescence may sometimes, at least as a practical matter, enable, if not invite, measures on independent responsibility. In this area, any actual test of power is likely to depend on the imperatives of events and contemporary imponderables rather than on abstract theories of law.

When the President takes measures incompatible with the expressed or implied will of Congress, his power is at its lowest ebb, for then he can rely only upon his own constitutional powers minus any constitutional powers of Congress over the matter. Courts can sustain exclusive presidential control in such a case only by disabling the Congress from acting upon the subject. Presidential claim to a power at once so conclusive and preclusive must be scrutinized with caution, for what is at stake is the equilibrium established by our constitutional system.[15]

President Nixon's action in Cambodia in 1970 belongs in the last category. Coming on top of an unpopular war, his unilateral action in committing American troops to Cambodia certainly played a key role in convincing hitherto supportive representatives and senators that he had indeed usurped the constitutional power of the Congress. This was a catalyst to the passage of the War Powers Resolution, limiting the President's ability to commit troops without congressional consent.

Solutions to this controversy are not simple. There must be a greater awareness of the joint possession of constitutional powers in the area of war-making. However, Congress and the Senate in particular must assure itself of a steady flow of information about foreign affairs. Senator Vandenberg, one of the architects of bipartisan foreign policy during the 1940s, stated in 1948 that he hoped that intervention by senators in foreign affairs was not

too contagious because . . . only in those instances in which the Senate can be sure of a complete command of all the essential information prerequisite to an intelligent decision should it take the terrific chance of muddying the international waters by some sort of premature and ill-advised expression of its advice to the Executive.[16]

Congress needs to assure itself of the information necessary if it is to maintain its equilibrium with the executive in the field of foreign affairs. But above all a recognition of the balance between the executive and legislative branches is needed. Perhaps that will not come until the wounds caused by Vietnam are healed.

Presidential Economic Powers

The initiative for developing and presenting to the Congress legislation regarding foreign trade, domestic taxes, and legislation necessary for "tuning" the national economy belongs to the President. He is assisted by a battery of civil servants in the Council of Economic Advisers, the Office of Management and Budget, the Export Import Bank, the departments of Treasury, Commerce, and Agriculture, and, to some extent, by the Federal Reserve Board.

However, legislation in this vital economic area also has to pass the scrutiny of such congressional committees as House Ways and Means Committee, the Joint Economic Committee, and the Senate Committees on Finance and Banking and Currency, which are not always in agreement with the Administration about the state of the economy, and actions needed to direct its course.

Conflict arises over the legislation necessary for "tuning" the economy. It can prove costly to the nation, as was well illustrated in the battle over the tax surcharge. It can also prove beneficial to the President, as in the case of the Economic Stabilization Act of 1970, which the Congress passed over the strong objections of President Nixon. He ended up utilizing the power the Act gave him to slap wage-price controls on the economy in August of 1970. Despite the need of the President for enabling legislation, he is the one who must take the initiative to remedy whatever is ailing the economy. It is he who must make the first move utilizing the powers at his disposal, as he did in his wage-price control action and tax relief for businessmen. The Congress can only follow.

When President Nixon entered the White House in 1969, Congress had recently enacted a surtax on the federal income tax, as requested by President Johnson, in order to dampen the results of demand inflation. It had taken Johnson two years to get the surtax and it came too late; demand inflation had carried the wholesale price index up at rapid rates. While the surtax did balance the federal budget by the last quarter of 1968, it really came too late to be effective in stopping inflation.

Nixon wanted a renewal of the tax surcharge in 1969, but the Congress was unwilling to renew it unless it was accompanied by a tax reform. In this case it was congressional initiative; taking advantage of the clear need for a surcharge, Congress instituted the most massive overhaul of the nation's tax statutes since the birth of the Republic. The Tax Reform Act of 1969 passed over the threat of a presidential veto.

Despite the President's efforts inflation mounted in 1969. The wholesale price index rose 4.8 percent, more than twice the rate of the years from mid-1965 to the end of 1968. President Nixon announced that the way to take the heat out of the inflation was to slow down the rapid expansion of demand for goods. This also called for increasing the unemployment rate to about 6 percent. According to economist Gardiner Means, while demand declined, inflation continued because it was an "administrative inflation" which arises from the exercise of market power. Administrative inflation can be initiated by business managers in an effort to widen profit margins, or by labor leaders seeking excessive pay increases. It does not rely on the classic supply-demand forces. This type of inflation occurs whether employment is full or less than full and whether we are in a recession, a period of stagnation, or a recovery period. It shows up particularly in price rises for autos, steel, machinery, and other products of the concentrated less-competitive industries.[17]

Congress had already granted the President authority to impose controls on consumer credit in 1969, and in 1970 it had approved the Economic Stabilization Act authorizing the President to place controls on wages, prices, rents, and salaries. In order to halt runaway inflation, the President suddenly instituted a mandatory ninety-day wage-price freeze on August 15, 1971, using this discretionary authority. This became known as Phase I.

The President replaced temporary Phase I with the more flexible Phase II, which set wage guidelines to a cost-of-living rise and price guidelines to contain profit margins. Businessmen were allowed to increase profits by producing more, but not by increasing prices relative to costs. It was generally argued that Phases I and II were quite successful in preventing administrative inflation, and they were substantially fair to both labor and capital. It looked as if the Nixon administration economists had found a fairly effective tool for cooling inflation.

The shift to Phase III in 1973 was a mistake. The economy was speeding up at a blistering rate in late 1972, and with the shift into Phase III the President lost what little chance he had to control it. Efforts to reinstate this control led to the disastrous freeze on beef prices and subsequent shortages. In August of 1973 Phase IV, voluntary controls, was launched, but it was ineffective.

In 1971 an inflationary economy became coupled with a definite recession. To offset this the President used his administrative authority to give businesses a tax break worth more than $3 billion a year, by allowing them an accelerated tax write-off of their depreciation costs. This came despite the growing budgetary deficit. In August of 1971 he also called for additional tax cuts averaging $5.7 billion a year over the next three years and indeterminant amounts after that to stimulate the economy. Congress modified the depreciation provision, wrote it into law, and provided a tax cut of $8.6

billion a year.[18] In so doing, it provided for more tax relief than the President had requested for individuals and less than he had sought for business.

However, as the economy started to overheat in 1972, the President again shifted his fiscal strategy and made an all-out effort to hold the federal budget in line and avoid an excessive deficit. This was the underlying cause for the constant battle between the President and the Congress over the excessive increases in appropriations for domestic-social programs. Impoundment of these funds by the President was frequent, and served to heighten the antagonism between the two branches of government.

August 1971 might be called Mr. Nixon's month of economic reckoning. He was forced to put controls on wages and prices, something his conservative soul rejected; he was forced to go to the Congress and request tax breaks for business in spite of mounting budget deficits; and he had to suspend the controvertibility of the U.S. dollar to protect it. The President was facing serious problems with the U.S. balance of trade and the devaluing of the dollar on foreign money markets.

At the historic meeting of finance ministers at the Smithsonian Institute in December of 1971, the United States agreed to devalue the dollar by 8.5 percent. The effect was to decrease the value of the dollar, making the price of American goods more competitive. The Administration also presented to the Congress in September of 1972 proposals for a complete overhaul of the international currency system. The proposals continued the Administration's efforts to diminish the importance of gold and replace the dollar as the standard measure of world monetary relationships. However, in early 1973 the U.S. trade deficit climbed radically, and the dollar ran into serious trouble in foreign money markets. On February 12, 1973, the Administration requested the Congress to authorize a 10-percent dollar devaluation, which it did.

Foreign trade policy in the Nixon Administration has suffered from disagreement among high administration officials as to which agency in the Administration would have the principal influence in formulating U.S. trade policy. In addition, the President, who had supported freer trade during his election campaign, was indebted to southern protectionists for substantial help during that campaign. This caused conflict in 1971 over an omnibus trade bill sent to the Congress when conservatives amended it by writing in strong protectionist language. The bill was killed by a mini-filibuster in the Senate at the end of the session. Congress and the President remained at odds over omnibus trade legislation, but Congress passed several other bills designed to improve the balance of trade by increasing exports, liberalizing restrictions on goods sold to Communist countries, raising the limit on Export-Import Bank loans, and removing some restrictions on the Bank's operations in order to increase U.S. trade. Congress was active in passing legislation concerning balance of payments and authorizing further U.S. support for several international banks. The results of all the activity to liberalize trade, particularly with the Soviet Union, resulted in a favorable trade balance in 1973, and a record high balance of payments in the fourth quarter of 1973.

The President's effort to obtain a most-favored-nation status for trade with the Soviet Union caused a great deal of controversy in the Congress. There was considerable debate, which was exacerbated by the harsh treatment of Jews and intellectuals by the Soviets, and the Mid-East War between the Arabs and Israelis. The large wheat deal consummated between the USSR and the United States in 1971 and cries that the deal drove up the price of wheat for the domestic consumer did not help the case for most-favored-nation status. Reacting to this political pressure, Congress has inserted itself between the President and his trade negotiations with the Soviet Union, and is preventing the Soviet Union from gaining most-favored-nation status for trade with the United States.

One of the most important problems facing the United States in the mid-1970s is the energy crisis. It could have devastating effects on employment and industrial production that determine the gross national product. Because the problem is international in scope and since this country has among the largest domestic oil reserves of the industrialized Western world, there could also be significant repercussions in United States relations with traditional allies. Looking backwards, it is clear that a shortage of oil had been looming on the horizon for some time; the Arab cutoff in 1973 merely provided rapid illumination of that point, compelling an immediate search for alternative energy sources.

The search for an overall policy on energy did not really begin until the spring of 1973 when John A. Love, former governor of Colorado, came to the White House to direct the Office of Energy Policy. The Administration had reached the conclusion in 1972 that the nation should become less dependent upon foreign supplies of oil, but the proposed program emphasized price and tax incentives to encourage private industry rather than the federal government to do the job. Between the time Love took office and his resignation in early December 1973, the Congress and the President batted around various legislative proposals concerning the handling of a crisis which was sure to grow, particularly when the full impact of the cutoff of Arab oil was felt. In December, the President announced that a federal energy agency would be established pending congressional approval. As a temporary measure he was issuing an executive order to establish the Federal Energy Office with William Simon, Deputy Treasury Secretary, as director.

Charged with handling what has turned out to be a series of crises, Simon and his staff in the Federal Energy Office attempted to smooth out the allocation of gasoline to the states; to quash mini-revolutions of truck drivers and gas station owners; to pacify governors who are running for office and using the crisis to gain publicity; to deal with concerned senators and congressmen who want to roll back the price of oil; and to generally keep a lid on a boiling pot. They also tried to formulate long-term strategies for United States independence of foreign oil.

On February 27, 1974 Congress sent the Emergency Energy bill to the President. While wanting the authorizing legislation very badly, Nixon vetoed it because it required a rollback on the price of oil. This rollback, the administration and its economists contended, would cause an even greater scarcity of gasoline and extend the already long lines of cars at the gas pumps and bring gas rationing. The Congress itself was divided over that issue and could not override the veto. Revised legislation that would include authority for the President to impose gas rationing if he deemed it necessary is under consideration.

The energy crisis has jolted the economists, who are already in retreat over their failure to visualize the disastrous inflation of 1973. Economic forecasting, at best a chancy business, has fallen on hard times. While the economists are searching for new tools to deal with a crisis-ridden economy, the politicians, including the Chief Executive, are struggling to maintain not only the nation's equilibrium but their own.[19]

Some of the underlying reasons for the fluctuating economy can be attributed to deep structural changes that have been taking place in it. Unemployment rates have been increased by the tremendous number of women, blacks, and teenagers looking for work. Often poorly educated and unskilled, they have problems finding jobs in the best of circumstances. Inflation is imbedded in an economy committed to using full spending powers of the government to avoid a deep recession; thus, we forego the breaks in the price spiral that recessions used to produce. Wages go nowhere but up. Manufacturers can offset this by higher production, but a growing service industry finds this difficult to do.

One of the most important reasons for the present difficulties of the economy is the increasing dependence of the United States on world commodity markets for raw materials. American inflation was greatly aggravated by events far beyond the control of the government, including the Arab-Israeli War; a low Soviet grain harvest; copper industry strikes in Africa; and even a change in the ocean currents off the coast of Peru, which wiped out the catch of anchovies. The lack of anchovies eliminated a key source of protein in animal feeds and caused panicky foreign buyers to bid up the price of soybeans in the United States. The issue of supplies of vital raw materials in the foreign market place has become most important, and is reflected in the comprehensive foreign trade legislation being considered by the Congress during the first and second sessions of the 93rd Congress.

The comprehensive foreign trade legislation that the President sent to the Congress in 1973 was conceived in a world largely concerned with tariffs, quotas, and other measures for protecting the domestic market. The overall purpose of the legislation is to enable the United States to negotiate effectively in new multilateral bargaining, and to manage the domestic impact of lowered tariffs and barriers. But the Arab embargo on oil radically changed that concern to a far different one—that of the effective use of the supply and production boycotts curtailing shipments of a vital raw material. This convinced the Nixon Administration that aggressive economic measures must be adopted to deal with actions such as the oil embargo.

Treasury Secretary George Shultz told the Senate Finance Committee that the Administration needs clear authority to withdraw the benefits of trade concessions from countries that impose illegal or unreasonable restraints on sales of commodities in short supply. So the Administration has formally approved the initiative taken by Senators Walter Mondale of Minnesota and Abraham Ribicoff of Connecticut to amend the Trade Reform bill in a way that will help the nation to respond to artificially created shortages of crucial materials.[20]

Foreign trade has become increasingly meshed with our domestic economic situation. The increasing dependency on world commodity markets, the necessity to deal with Arab-type boycotts or embargoes, and the possible havoc of such embargoes on the national economy open a new era in economics. There is a need for investing the Chief Executive with the necessary power to deal with problems of this type. Hopefully the trade bill now in Congress will give him some of the necessary tools.

New tools also will have to be devised to deal with an inflation that does not respond to the tried-and-true methods. An expanded labor market and a shrinking job market is another cause for concern. The tried-and-true methods of dealing with today's crisis-ridden economy just are not working. Close cooperation between the President and Congress is necessary as the Chief Executive attempts to develop solutions which must deal with far more than just the domestic economy.

Impoundment

Impoundment is used by the President of the United States to prevent the expenditure of funds for federal programs that have been authorized and appropriated by the Congress. While the Congress appropriates the funds, the President and the Executive Branch enjoy considerable discretion as to how those funds are spent. In the past fifty years, since the passage of the Budget and Accounting Act of 1921, which established the Bureau of the Budget and the executive budget, the President has gained more and more discretionary power over the spending of federal funds. Of the many means available to the President in his management of the federal budget, impoundment has become one of the most controversial.

The debate on impoundment has a tendency to generate more heat than light. One of the difficulties is the variety of the kinds of impoundment and the different reasons used to justify impoundment. Louis Fisher, an analyst with the Library of Congress and an expert on congressional activities, has divided the types of impoundment into four categories:

1. Efficient management impoundments. This covers instances in which funds are withheld either to effect savings, to accommodate changing events which make an expenditure unnecessary, or to satisfy basic managerial responsibilities. Impoundments of this type are of a common sense variety, evoking few protests from members of Congress.

2. Impoundment actions based upon statutory authority. Some statutes provide a routine delegation of impoundment power, requiring the expertise and managerial talents of the Executive Branch to determine if specified conditions have been met. For example, Title VI of the Civil Rights Act of

1964 requires that the President impound funds intended for areas which have not met the federal requirements with regard to discrimination. The authorities differ as to whether such a mandate from Congress is providing the President with a new power or is merely making explicit the power which he already has.

3. Impoundments based upon the general constitutional powers of the President, particularly his duties as the Commander-in-Chief of the armed forces. These impoundments are generally highly controversial, bringing the President into direct conflict with Congress and its responsibility to provide for the common defense.

4. Executive policy-making impoundments. In pursuing such goals as curbing inflation or rearranging budget priorities, the President sometimes uses impoundments to further his own objectives rather than those of the Congress.[21]

Historical precedents for impoundment of appropriated funds by the President go as far back as 1803, when President Jefferson did not spend the $50,000 allotted by Congress for the purchase of fifteen gunboats. However, as the country grew and the federal government expanded, the congressional control over spending power declined. In the years following the Civil War, the committees in Congress with control over spending fragmented. The House Ways and Means Committee split apart in 1865, retaining jurisdiction over revenue legislation but surrendering responsibilities over appropriations and banking and currency to two newly formed committees. The House Appropriations Committee jurisdiction also was splintered in those turbulent years and its autonomous spending powers were parceled out to separate committees. The President, instead of the Congress, gradually became the guardian of the public purse.

The Antideficiency Act of 1905 introduced the technique of monthly or other allotments "to prevent undue expenditures in one portion of the year that may require deficiency or additional appropriations to complete the service of the fiscal year."[22] In the Antideficiency Act of 1906 Congress stipulated that apportionments could be waived or modified in the event of "some extraordinary emergency or unusual circumstances which could not be anticipated at the time of making such apportionment."[23] This constituted an admission by the Congress that regardless of spending patterns anticipated when passing appropriation bills, or even after apportioning funds, conditions might necessitate a different pattern for actual expenditures.

However, it was not until the passage of the Budget and Accounting Act of 1921 that procedures for a new national budget were actually set down. The Act established the Bureau of the Budget and the General Accounting Office, and gave the President the responsibility for developing a national budget and transmitting it to Congress for consideration.

The Bureau of the Budget set forth procedures for establishing reserves and effecting savings. Appropriations from the Congress were to be treated as a mere ceiling on expenditures, rather than as a directive to spend the full amount. Executive departments and bureaus were expected to determine the portion of appropriations considered indispensable for carrying out activities. The remainder was to be carried as a general reserve, which was to be added to during the year if additional savings were possible. As a result of the Bureau's policy, the allotment technique now had two objectives: to prevent deficiencies and effect savings. The Antideficiency Acts were treated as containing an implied power that the Executive Branch in its budgeting procedures should make provisions for savings as well as for preventing deficiencies.

In the depths of the depression President Hoover asked for authority to effect savings through reorganization of the executive departments. He received authority to make partial layoffs, reduce compensation for public officials, and consolidate executive agencies in order to effect savings. Funds impounded by this economy were returned to the Treasury Department. Before he left office Hoover signed two more economy measures authorizing his successor to effect further reorganization and to reduce military spending.

Citing these precedents, Hoover's successor, Franklin Delano Roosevelt, requested authority to reduce veterans' benefits and the salaries of federal employees. Despite opposition within his own party, he obtained this authority in the Economy Act of 1933. Acting under the authority granted in this Act, Roosevelt reorganized, transferred, and abolished certain executive agencies and functions. This same executive order also transferred the functions of making, waiving, and modifying apportionments of appropriations from departmental heads and bureau chiefs to the budget director.[24] Unexpended balances for abolished agencies or functions would be transferred to the successor agency or to the Treasury Department by the director of the Budget Bureau. Thus, instead of permitting individual bureau chiefs to adjust apportionment schedules to satisfy their constituencies, this decision was centered in the Budget Bureau and the President.

Acting on recommendations of the Committee on Administrative Management (the Brownlow Committee), Roosevelt also proposed that the Congress establish general principles by which the President could reorganize the executive branch on a continuing basis. This reorganization proposal, though not originally intended as a cost-saving move, acquired that reputation.

After much debate a reorganization bill finally passed in 1939, which stated that continuing deficits made cutbacks desirable and directed the President to effect savings by consolidating or abolishing agencies for more efficient operation. Reorganization would take effect after sixty days unless voted down by a concurrent resolution in the Congress. The bill also strengthened Roosevelt's control over the budget by creating an Executive Office of the President and transferring the Bureau of the Budget here from the Treasury Department.

With the advent of World War II, the leverage for presidential impoundment increased. In a 1941 budget message FDR told Congress that it was appropriate to defer construction projects that interfered with the defense program, and recommended reductions for rivers, harbors, and flood-control work.[25] Later that year the President declared a state of unlimited national emergency. When Congress passed a public works bill, he appealed to the Senate to amend the bill so as to restrict new construction work to projects having defense significance. Congress refused to give the President that discretionary power, but followed Budget Bureau recommendations and included in the public works appropriation bill the provision that flood control projects "shall be prosecuted as speedily as may be consistent with budgetary requirements."[26] Throughout the war Roosevelt continued to carry out his policy of withholding allocations from public works projects that were not defense related. Some members of Congress attempted unsuccessfully to reassert legislative authority over public works spending in 1943.

In the Employment bill of 1945, Congress acknowledged that to assure full employment the President could vary expenditure levels in whatever manner he determined to be neccessary. The bill did not pass, and this mandate was conspicuously absent from the Employment Act of 1946, which is frequently cited as a basis of presidential authority. The 1946 Act delegated the responsibility for maintaining full employment to the entire government, and not to the President alone. But the assumption by the Executive Branch that it has the power to adjust levels of spending to assure full employment has never been challenged by the Congress.[27]

In the postwar period, Congress took an unusual approach of shifting from being an adversary of defense spending to a promoter. This was done by setting floors or minimums instead of the traditional ceiling on spending levels. One reason for this adoption of "floors," below which the Administration could not go, was to remedy the withholding of funds by the President.

In 1949, the Congress voted to increase President Truman's request for funds for the Air Force. The President had stated that he only wanted forty-eight air groups in the Air Force, but Congress decided there should be fifty-eight and added the extra funds to the request. Truman signed the measure but announced that he was directing his Secretary of Defense to place the extra funds in reserve. The impounded funds totaled $735 million.[28] Truman asserted that his prime reason for impounding these funds was to control federal expenditures and to reduce inflation. He had been unsuccessful in persuading the Congress not to pass tax-reduction bills; in fact his veto of one of the bills had been overridden. With revenue now lost through tax relief and receipts down as a result of the 1948–49 recession, Truman was redoubling his efforts to control expenditures.

President Truman was involved in another major impoundment dispute, which concerned the cancellation of the giant aircraft carrier the U.S.S. *United States*. The cost of this carrier, which was designed to accommodate long-range bombers equipped with atomic bombs, was estimated by the Navy at $189 million. Other estimates placed it closer to $500 million for the vessel and another $500 million for planes to fly from it. A bitter feud developed between the Air Force and the Navy over the carrier and the prerogatives of each service. The keel-laying of the ship took place as scheduled in 1949, but within a few days Defense Secretary Louis Johnson canceled the project with the support of the chairmen of the House and Senate

Armed Services committees, and two of the three members of the newly formed Joint Chiefs of Staff.

The military tendency to bypass the President and go directly to the Congress caused problems for President Eisenhower and his Secretary of Defense Hugh McElroy, who were opposed to additional funds for the Nike-Zeus antimissile system. They insisted that more basic research was necessary before the missiles could actually be produced. Congress, however, appropriated an extra $137 million for initial procurement of the necessary hardware. The Administration impounded the funds while awaiting further test results. In January 1960 President Eisenhower stated that funds would be released for continued research and development, but not for production. Robert McNamara, Defense Secretary under Kennedy, later estimated that deployment of the Nike-Zeus missile system would have cost an estimated $13 to $14 billion—more than double the original estimate of $6 billion—and that most of it would have had to be torn out and replaced almost before it became operational to make way for more advanced missile and radar systems.[29] It was not until September 1967, some eight years after Eisenhower impounded the funds, that the Johnson Administration agreed to deploy a light antiballistic missile system against a possible Chinese bombing threat.

The Eisenhower decision in impounding the original Nike-Zeus funds falls into the first Fisher category—efficient management. Truman's exercise of impoundment in the case of the additional Air Force funds belongs in the fourth category—executive policy-making. His impoundment of funds for the supercarrier was done with support of the powerful Chairmen of the Armed Services Committees, who believed that the carrier was unworkable and impoundment of funds was just good sense.

President John F. Kennedy and Defense Secretary McNamara also experienced trouble with Congress appropriating extra funds for a military project. Kennedy had requested $200 million for the B-70 manned aircraft project, but Congress added an extra $180 million. McNamara refused to release the unwanted funds. This aroused the ire of the powerful chairman of the House Armed Services Committee, Carl Vinson. The Committee voted to direct the Secretary of the Air Force to spend the full $491 million during fiscal year 1963 toward the production of the B-70.

President Kennedy wrote to Chairman Vinson urging that the word "authorize" be substituted for "direct." The President contended that this was more suitable for an authorization bill since funds had not been appropriated. Moreover he thought the change in language would be "more clearly in line with the spirit of the Constitution and its separation of powers."[30] The House acceded to the President's request, and the Administration went ahead with its plan to complete two prototypes of the B-70 before considering full-scale production. The bomber was a total flop. Of the two prototypes developed, one crashed and one is in the Air Force museum in Dayton, Ohio.

With some maneuvering Kennedy managed to prevent the confrontation with Carl Vinson from becoming a full-blown constitutional crisis. However, in refusing to release the extra funds for the bomber, he and Secretary McNamara were exercising the managerial responsibility of the Executive Branch for the spending of federal funds.

The fourth category of impoundment—exercising presidential discretion to curb inflation or to manipulate priorities—is the most controversial. This highly subjective category was involved in most of the impoundment disputes between President Nixon and the Congress.

Federal responsibility for economic stability was demanded during the 1930s, and received formal acknowledgment in the Employment Acts of 1945 and 1946. The Employment Act of 1946 in particular included the promotion of maximum employment, production, and purchasing power. Though control of inflation was not specifically mentioned, price stability could be inferred from the goal of maximum purchasing power and the development of policies to avoid economic fluctuations. All postwar presidents have interpreted the Act to include federal responsibility for combating inflation. The question is whether this responsibility is primarily that of the President or of the Congress.

The Omnibus Appropriations Act of 1950 amplified and gave legal status to the apportionment authority of the Bureau of the Budget. Initially, such authority was inferred from the BOB's interpretation of the Budget and Accounting Act of 1921 and Executive Order 6166, issued in 1933 by President Roosevelt. Section 1211 of the Act stated:

In apportioning any appropriation, reserves may be established to provide for contingencies, or to effect savings whenever savings are made possible by or through changes in requirements, greater efficiency of operations, or other developments subsequent to the date on which such appropriation was made available.[31]

Section 1211 resulted from an investigation by the Senate Appropriations Committee concerning the Post Office Department and the unwise apportionment of its funds in 1947. The Department had spent the majority of its funds in the first half of the year, and then announced that it needed supplemental appropriations or it would not be able to deliver mail the rest of the year. This prompted the Senate to request a study of apportionment of funds, and Section 1211 was then included in the 1950 Omnibus Appropriations Act. However, the phrases "changes in requirements" and "other developments" have been broadly interpreted to include inflationary pressures.

President Johnson utilized this power in 1966 in an attempt to curb inflation and keep the federal budget within limits. In late 1966 he ordered that a $3.5 billion reduction in federal programs be effected. The major item affected was the withholding of $1.1 billion in highway trust funds. Budget Director Charles Schultz justified the withholding of highway trust funds as a means of combating inflationary pressures and as good management. When funds were withheld, the construction cost index dropped about 3 percent for several quarters.[32]

Further efforts to check inflation were made in 1968, when Congress passed the Revenue and Expenditure Control Act. This combined a surtax with a spending ceiling and required a $6 billion reduction in the Administration's budget. However, even with the efforts of Presidents Nixon and Johnson, the ceiling on spending did not work. Congress granted several programs exemptions from the ceiling and the budget ended up being some $4.8 billion over the original ceiling of $180 billion.

Again in 1969 Congress set a spending ceiling for fiscal year 1970, at $192 billion—$1 billion below President Nixon's request. No exemptions were to be allowed, but they gave the President some flexibility by authorizing him to raise the ceiling by as much as $2 billion to cover certain uncontrollable items such as interest on the public debt, farm price supports, medicare, and other social insurance funds. When the House persisted in voting more funds than Nixon had requested, he stated his determination to stay within the budget.

Nixon also ordered all federal agencies to reduce new contracts for government construction by 75 percent. He announced plans to reduce research health grants, defer model cities funds, and reduce grants for urban renewal. This opened the President to the charge that he had allowed his anti-inflation policy to fall most heavily on the cities and public services, while at the same time backing such costly projects as the supersonic transport plane, manned space flights, a larger merchant marine fleet, a new manned bomber, and the Safeguard Anti-Ballistic Missile system. Impoundment was used here, it was charged, not simply as an anti-inflation technique but to shift the scale of priorities from one administration to the next.

During the fall of 1970, while signing an authorization bill for sewer and water lines, President Nixon warned that appropriations in excess of his budget would have a disastrous fiscal effect. He added that if Congress refused to exercise restraint he would act to avoid harmful fiscal consequences by withholding any overfunding. He warned the Congress again as he signed a public works appropriation bill that he would consider all means possible to minimize the impact of these inflationary and unnecessary appropriations, including deferment of the proposed starts and the withholding of funds. The Administration went ahead with public works projects that it had recommended, but it also deferred without exception all of the additional projects that Congress had added.

Nixon vetoed a Labor-HEW appropriation bill on January 26, 1970 which provided $1.1 billion more than he had requested. After the veto was sustained, Congress agreed to reduce appropriations from $19.7 billion to $19.3 billion. The bill included a provision limiting expenditures to 98 percent of appropriations, and specifying that no single appropriation could be cut by more than 15 percent.[33]

However, the President lost a round in June of 1970 when Congress overrode his veto of the Hill-Burton hospital construction bill authorizing direct grants of more than $300 million in excess of Nixon's fiscal 1971 budget. The President attacked the Congress on what he called its "rubber ceiling" budget. Legislative actions increased the budget and Nixon said that uncontrollable spending had been increased far beyond the congressional allowance. These efforts on the part of the President to force Congress to discipline itself were only skirmishes.

In 1972 the nation witnessed a real Battle of the Budget. In July the President asked Congress for authority to trim federal spending as he saw fit to meet a $250 billion ceiling on fiscal year 1973 outlays. If it denied him such power, the President stated, Congress would be blamed if taxes had to be raised in 1973. Congress refused to go along, but it also created a special joint committee to study the congressional appropriations process. Congress also tacitly conceded that the President could overrule it by refusing to spend money previously appropriated.

The President then turned to other tools at his command to limit spending—the veto power and impoundment of funds appropriated by enacted legislation. By the end of 1972, the President had vetoed sixteen public bills, the greatest number since President Eisenhower vetoed eighteen in 1954. But it was the wholesale impoundment of funds that caused the most uproar.

In 1971, the Nixon Administration reported that it was withholding more than $12 billion in funds, most of which were for highway and for various urban programs. It was becoming evident that part of the withholding was tied to the Administration's wish to drop the system of categorical grant-in-aid programs in favor of block grants and general revenue-sharing.

In 1972 again the Nixon Administration impounded funds in several programs. It made wholesale reductions in farm programs, including the Rural Environmental Assistance Program (REAP) and the $10 million water-bank program. It also terminated the emergency disaster loan program of the Farmers Home Administration, the rural electrification program, and the water-and-sewer-grant program. In 1973 President Nixon declared a wholesale eighteen-month moratorium on subsidized housing programs, low-rent public housing, rent supplements, homeownership assistance, and rental housing assistance.

Strong congressional reaction was raised to President Nixon's wholesale impoundment of funds and vetoes of such bills as day care and assistance for the elderly. In March of 1971 the Senate Subcommittee on Separation of Powers held hearings for the purpose of establishing better legislative control over impounded funds. Senator Sam Ervin, chairman of the subcommittee, introduced several bills to require the President to notify Congress within ten days whenever he impounds funds appropriated for a specific purpose or project, and to give Congress sixty days to pass a joint resolution disapproving the impoundment.[34]

Senator Hubert Humphrey proposed an amendment to the Revenue Act of 1971 requiring that whenever any funds are appropriated by Congress and then impounded by the President, the President "shall promptly transmit" to the Congress and to the Comptroller General of the United States a report containing the following information:

1. The amount of funds impounded;
2. The date on which the funds were ordered to be impounded;

3. The date the funds were impounded;
4. Any department or establishment of the Government to which such impounded funds would have been available for obligation except for such impoundment;
5. The period of time during which the funds are to be impounded;
6. The reasons for the impoundment;
7. To the maximum extent practicable, the estimated fiscal economic and budgetary effect of the impoundment.[35]

The Humphrey amendment to the Revenue Act of 1971 was adopted by the Senate, but deleted by the House because it was considered nongermane under the House rules. However, the Humphrey Amendment was finally incorporated into the Public Debt Limitation bill, which became law on October 27, 1972.[36] Prior to the enactment of the Humphrey amendment there had been no existing requirements for the President to report impoundments to the Congress.

George Mahon, chairman of the House Appropriations Committee, introduced a bill in the House in 1973 to prohibit impoundment if both houses of Congress adopted a resolution of disapproval within sixty days. Replying to President Nixon's claim that he had the constitutional right to impound funds to prevent an increase in prices or taxes, Mahon insisted that Congress could not concede such broad authority without destroying its coequal status.[37]

After extensive modification by the House Rules Committee, the Mahon bill was reintroduced by Representative Ray J. Madden, Chairman of the House Rules Committee. The new bill called for disapproval by only one house instead of two; reliance on the expertise of the General Accounting Office; a provision to discharge from the Appropriations Committee any impoundment actions referred there; and a spending ceiling of $267.1 billion for fiscal 1974. The bill passed the House on June 25, 1973.[38]

The response of many local and state governments to the wholesale impoundment of funds for highways, housing, water pollution, health grants, and nursing homes was to go to court. Impoundment of funds evoked more than sixty lawsuits in 1972 and 1973. Of those which have been decided, the administration has won only one, while losing more than thirty.[39]

One of the principal suits, *Missouri v. Volpe*, involved the government's impoundment of highway funds for Missouri. The State of Missouri brought suit against the Nixon Administration in 1971 in order to gain the release of impounded highway funds. Chief Judge William H. Becker of the U.S. District Court for the Western District of Missouri reviewed the legislative history and language of the Federal-Aid Highway Act. In his decision handed down in August of 1972, Chief Judge Becker noted that the effect of impoundment "has caused great and incalculable injury to Missouri because of continuing inflation of highway costs and interruption of efficient obligation of the funds apportioned to Missouri. Missouri has provided proof of this injury beyond the customary burden of proof by a preponderance of the evidence."[40]

The judge concluded that the reasons advanced by the Administration were "foreign to the standards and purposes" of the Act and the Highway

Trust Fund. Nothing in the statutory language on highways allowed for impoundment. The U.S. District Court then enjoined the Secretary of Transportation and the Office of Management and Budget to stop withholding from Missouri any authority to obligate its apportionment of highway trust funds for fiscal 1973. The decision was carried to the U.S. Court of Appeals for the Eighth Circuit, where Becker's decision was upheld. The government declined to appeal the case to the Supreme Court.

Despite the defeats the Administration has suffered in the courts and its gradual retreat in the battle over impoundment of funds, Solicitor General Bork stated in January 1974 that the administration will ask the highest court to overturn a ruling by the U.S. Court of Appeal in Washington, D.C. that it unlawfully impounded $6 billion in clean-water funds.[41]

The President decided on November 22, 1972 to withhold funds provided under the Federal Water Pollution Control Act Amendments of 1972 (FWPCA). His action raised fundamental political and legal questions regarding congressional intent and the constitutional separation of powers, since the bill became law when Congress overrode a Nixon veto on October 19, 1972. Nevertheless, the President directed the Administrator of the Environmental Protection Agency (EPA) not to allot among the states the maximum amounts provided for under the Act. Instead, the President requested that no more than $2 of the $5 billion be allotted for fiscal 1973 and not more than $3 of the $6 billion be allotted for fiscal 1974.[42]

In May 1973, Judge Oliver Gasch of the U.S. District Court for the District of Columbia handed down a decision. He focused his attention on two sections of the Act—Section 205, which stated that sums authorized by Section 207 "shall" be allotted, and Section 207, which authorized maximum levels for fiscal years 1973, 1974, and 1975. Judge Gasch found that the discretion implied in the language "not to exceed" referred to obligation and expenditure, not to the allotment. According to Gasch the language of the Act, read in the light of its legislative history, clearly indicates the intent of Congress to require the Administrator to allot, at the appropriate times, the full sums authorized to be appropriated by Section 207.[43]

Similar decisions were reached against the administration in New York City, Minnesota, and Virginia. However, in Los Angeles in July of 1973, Judge Hauk of the U.S. District Court held that the plaintiffs—Congressman George E. Brown and the citizens of the State of California—had failed to show that either had been injured or impaired by the EPA's refusal to allot the entire $11 billion amount for fiscal years 1973 and 1974.[44]

Later in 1973 the State of Texas, joined by Oklahoma, Missouri, and Wisconsin, brought suit as a class action for all the states entitled to the allotment of appropriations under the FWPCA Amendments of 1972. The U.S. District Court for the Western District of Texas decided against the administration.

With the exception of *Missouri v. Volpe* all of the court actions brought against the Nixon Administration concerning impoundment of funds have been at the U.S. District Court level. Certain general patterns are emerging in these decisions.[45]

Constitutional Issue:

Impoundment decisions have generally shied away from the larger constitutional questions, preferring to treat each case as one of statutory construction. Typically, the approach of the courts has been: Does the statute confer the discretionary authority claimed by the Executive Branch? Viewed in this light, it becomes a matter of interpretation for the courts, rather than a "political question" in which courts should not intrude.

Anti-inflation Policy:

The courts have uniformly dismissed the argument that funds may be impounded as part of an Administration's anti-inflation policy. Judge Becker in the 1972 Missouri Highway Case ruled that Executive Branch policy foreign to the expressed standards and purposes of the Highway Act was void, and the Court of Appeals agreed with him.

Other Statutes:

Administration efforts to go outside the "four corners of a statute," for example, drawing support from other legislative authority, have been unsuccessful. Judge Oliver Gasch could not find anything in the language of the Anti-Deficiency Act, the Budget and Accounting Act of 1921, or the Employment Act of 1946 to support the Administration's contention that school construction funds could be withheld.

Budget Proposals:

In several cases impoundment was justified on the ground that the President's budget had requested that the funds be rescinded. In two recession cases, the veteran's-cost-of-education program and Indian education, the fact that the President had proposed a recession was considered an inadquate reason for failing to carry out the programs.

Mandatory Language:

Several courts have handed down decisions against impoundment when mandatory clauses were present in the legislation. But the unsettled nature of the impoundment issue with regards to mandatory language is underscored by the various decisions regarding the clean-water funds. Three courts concluded that the Act mandated allotment of all funds. In contrast, Judge Merhige in a Virginia decision was persuaded that the language of the Act, together with its legislative history, granted the Executive Branch some discretion in allotting funds.

Congressional Intent:

In the absence of mandatory language, does a judicial remedy exist? In most decisions the courts have consistently rejected the notion that the Executive Branch may suspend or cancel a program—even in the presence of nonmandatory language—simply because the Administration finds that the program lacks merit. The Administration possesses spending flexibility, but that discretion is bounded by the larger objectives of the legislation. It must also be consistent with the policy and provisions of an act, and the Administration cannot substitute its sense of budget priorities for that of Congress.

Expenditure and Obligation:

Many of the decisions pushed the Administration one step closer to spending, without actually ordering that the funds be spent. For instance, ordering that the Administration allot the clean-water funds is an example of a step toward spending, but is not necessarily synonymous with it. Three court decisions specifically disavowed any effort to force the obligation of expenditure of funds. Only in the Virginia decision did the court venture to suggest that excessive withholding at the obligation-expenditure stage would also contravene the letter and spirit of the FWPCA amendment.

Several decisions ordered that funds be obligated, to prevent lapsing at the end of the fiscal year, with no assurance that the funds would actually be spent. But these decisions, while in effect ordering the Administration to release impounded funds, did not directly address the impoundment issue.

Although the history of impoundment is extensive, the authority for it is questionable and open to challenge. Impoundment has been one of the tools the Executive Branch could utilize with discretion, and get away with it; depending upon the time frame in which it was operating, the funds it was impounding, and the reasons given for the impounding. Thus, Franklin Roosevelt was able to impound public works funds, citing the importance of keeping those funds for the war effort, although this was challenged by Congress in 1943. Harry Truman was able to impound funds for extra Air Force units because of the deadlock between the House and Senate over the funds. His impoundment of funds for the supercarrier had the backing of the chairmen of the Senate and House Armed Services Committees. President Kennedy was able to ease his way gracefully out of a confrontation with Carl Vinson over the RB-70 because Carl Vinson was pretty much alone in his challenge.

Impounding funds to curb inflation became more common under President Johnson. Responding to tremendous pressure from the Congress to cut the budget, Johnson, in order to show cuts, impounded funds in some areas and delayed the spending in other areas. However, Congress was still dissatisfied with the President's efforts, and set a spending ceiling. This too was ineffectual, and was violated largely by the Congress itself in giving exemptions and exceptions to various programs.

With the election of President Nixon, congressional budgetary practices that had been long in need of repair were exposed by a President trying to keep within a budget ceiling, determined to curb inflation, and in the process reordering some of the priorities set by the previous Administration. Utilizing the veto, and the impoundment of funds, Nixon has forced the Congress to reconsider its authorization and appropriations process. When impounding funds to prevent deficiencies or to effect savings, few legislators would contest the President's authority. On the other hand, because of legal obligations and political restraints, relatively few items in the budget are subject to impoundment. And it is in periods of inflation, especially when Congress adds to the President's budget without making commensurate reductions elsewhere, that the President's power to impound gains greater legitimacy. Nixon has utilized this particular argument very effectively, and has gained the support of the American public.

A weakened presidency has resulted from the Watergate scandals. Thus it was not from a position of optimum strength that the President released some impounded funds, namely the health and education money and some housing money. At the same time the Administration retains a substantial amount of money in reserve, while awaiting the outcome of an appeal to the Supreme Court on the merits of impounding the clean-water funds.

Congress has set up committees to study the problems of the splintered authorization and appropriations process. A bill to reform the process is being considered. Meanwhile, the President is busy explaining Watergate and the Democratic Congress is intent upon imposing their spending priorities upon him. In the absence of Watergate, or if there were a Republican majority in Congress, or if Nixon had not been so brash in selecting programs for cuts, this headlong clash over impoundment probably would not have occurred.

Veto Power

The President's power to veto legislation was envisioned by the Founding Fathers as a check on the legislative branch of the government. To override a veto, the Congress must produce a two-thirds vote in both houses. However, the President does not have what is called an "item veto"—the ability to veto selected parts of a bill. He must either accept or reject the entire piece of legislation.

There are two types of vetoes: a regular veto, which is effected only when Congress is in session, and a pocket veto. The pocket veto occurs if the President fails to sign a bill within ten days after Congress adjourns, excluding Sundays, from the time he receives it. If he fails to sign a bill within the ten-day period while Congress is in session, the bill automatically becomes law. In the case of a regular veto, the President returns the bill he vetoes to the chamber in which it originated.

Use of the veto power varies. It also depends on whether or not the President's party has a majority in the Congress. During his two terms in office President Eisenhower vetoed approximately 181 bills including 93 public and 88 private bills. He is ranked fourth in the number of vetoes, behind four-term President Franklin D. Roosevelt (631 vetoes). Grover Cleveland was second with 584, and Harry S Truman ranks third with 250 vetoes.[46]

Eisenhower principally vetoed bills that authorized federal expenditures for items he felt were more properly handled at state and local levels. Bills affected by his approach were rivers and harbors bills and area redevelopment bills. For example, he vetoed an amendment to the Federal Airport Act and the Federal Housing Fund bill calling for less federal spending and a search for alternate financing.

He also would not accept a bill that he felt raised constitutional questions. Several times he sent a vetoed piece of legislation back to the Congress outlining his views as to why the bill violated the Constitution. Often the Congress would rewrite the offending provision and send it back to the President for his approval.

The Congress was successful in overriding only two Eisenhower vetoes. The first successful attempt came in 1959, when it voted to override a veto of a public works appropriation bill. The second time was in 1960, when it successfully overrode a veto of a federal pay raise bill.[47]

President Kennedy was elected with his own party in control of the Congress. During his three year term of office he vetoed only twenty-one pieces of legislation mostly minor bills. Thirteen of the bills were public bills. Because his own party was in control of the Congress he was able to work closely with the leadership to avoid conflict over the vetoed legislation.[48]

President Johnson, too, had his own party in control of the Congress. In the five years he was in office, he exercised his veto power only thirty times. Only thirteen public bills were vetoed. Johnson's vetoes were made primarily to curb inflation.[49] The Congress never overrode any of Johnson's or Kennedy's vetoes. (Table 10-1 illustrates the number of presidential vetoes from 1953 to 1973, including the number of public and private bills.)

President Nixon, faced a Democratic majority in the Senate that was committed to the social legislation initiated in the 1960s. During his first term in office he vetoed a total of twenty-eight public bills. Fifteen of these were pocket vetoes. Only four of the President's vetoes were overriden by the Congress.[50]

The President vetoed many bills, describing them as inflationary, wasteful of the taxpayer's money, or "budget-breaking." However, in his veto messages to the Congress he would detail why specific provisions in a vetoed bill were unacceptable, or were administratively faulty. For instance, in vetoing a bill to establish a national environmental data system he stated that the bill would "lead to the duplication of information or would produce results unrelated to real needs."[51] When he vetoed the bill to establish the National Institute for Aging he contended that its establishment was unnecessary as research was already being done and this new institute would disrupt existing units unnecessarily.

Table 10-1
Presidential Vetoes, 1953–73

Year	Veto Total	Public	Private[a]
1953	10	3	7
1954	42	18	24
1955	11	7	4
1956	23	14	9
1957	12	4	8
1958	39	12	27
1959	20	11	9
1960	24	13	11
1961	28	5	3
1962	12	4	8
1963	3	1	2
1964	6	0	6
1965	7	2	5
1966	7	5	2
1967	3	2	1
1968	5	3	2
1969	0	0	0
1970	9	9	0
1971	3	3	0
1972	16	16	0
1973	10	10	0

[a] Private bills are introduced by members and deal with such matters as claims against the government, immigration, and land titles.
Sources: *Congress and the Nation, Vol I, 1945-1964; Congress and the Nation, Vol II, 1965-1968; Congress and the Nation, Vol III, 1969-1972; Summary of Major Achievements, 93rd Congress 1st Session, Dec. 22, 1973*

It was not until the second session of the 91st Congress that he began to veto legislation passed by the Congress. In that session he vetoed nine public bills. These included appropriations for the Departments of Labor and Health, Education and Welfare, appropriations for the Office of Education, appropriations for the Department of Housing and Urban Development and Executive Offices, and authorization of additional funds for the Hill-Burton hospital construction program. Congress failed to override his veto of the HEW/Labor appropriations, but did manage to override the veto of the hospital construction program authorization. This was the first time in ten years the Congress had managed to override a veto.[52] The legislators were also successful in overriding the veto of the education appropriations. They could not override the veto of the appropriations for HUD and Executive Offices. Instead they sent the President a compromise appropriation bill just prior to adjournment.

Other bills vetoed by the President included a bill to limit campaign spending for political broadcasting by political candidates; a bill to authorize money for federal manpower training and public service employment programs; a bill to authorize money to assist hospitals and medical schools; a bill to establish a procedure for fixing and adjusting pay rates of federal blue-collar employees paid at prevailing wage rates for comparable work in private industry; and a bill to provide special retirement benefits to federal firefighters.

The most controversial presidential veto in the 92nd Congress was S. 2007, which authorized some $6.3 billion for the Office of Economic Opportunity and the establishment of day-care centers for children of working parents. The President objected to the bill's comprehensive child development programs, particularly the day-care section. He also objected to a provision that stated that he could appoint only six of the seventeen members of the board of directors of the National Legal Services Corporation authorized by the bill.[53]

In the 92nd Congress, Nixon exercised his veto power to the fullest. A total of nineteen public bills were vetoed. While the majority were authorization bills, the President twice nixed appropriations for the Departments of Labor and Health, Education and Welfare for fiscal 1973. Because of these two vetoes the funds for the two departments were appropriated at a lower level than either the Senate- or House-approved appropriations bills.

However, it was his pocket veto of nine bills after the 92nd Congress had adjourned that angered Congress the most. Included in these nine bills were two bills related to the aged—one which would establish a National Institute of Aging and another which would establish a federal level council to promote the interest of older Americans and represent them in planning federal programs and policies. Congress had passed these two items of legislation in response to an intensive lobbying campaign by interested parties. Nixon's pocket veto effectively killed this legislation.

During the early months of the first session of the 93rd Congress the President was dealing with the Congress from a position of strength engendered by the tremendous electoral mandate he received in 1972. Vetoes of legislation such as the $2.6 billion Vocational Rehabilitation Act and the Rural Water and Waste Disposal Grant Program were sustained. However, as his strength melted away in the face of the growing Watergate scandals, Congress passed such legislation as a bill requiring Senate confirmation of the director and deputy director of the Office of Management and Budget, which the President vetoed. The Senate voted to override him but the House could not muster enough votes and the bill died.

A true indication of the weak position of the President was the passage of the War Powers Act, which he also vetoed. Both the House and Senate voted to override the veto. The House vote was 284 to 135, four more than necessary. Voting to override the veto were 198 Democrats and 103 Republicans. The Senate vote was 75 to 18, with 50 Democrats and 25 Republicans voting to override; voting to sustain were 3 Democrats and 15 Republicans.[54] It was the only presidential veto in 1973 that was not sustained.

Another challenge to his veto power came when Judge Joseph C. Waddy of the U.S. District Court ruled that President Nixon's pocket veto of the Family Practice of Medicine Act (S. 3418) during the 1970 Christmas recess was unconstitutional. The judge ordered the government to publish the Act as law. The bill had been sent to the President eight days prior to the beginning of the Christmas recess. He exercised the pocket veto in that he failed to sign the bill ten days after the Congress adjourned *sine die*.[55]

The decision of Judge Waddy stemmed from a suit filed challenging the President's action under Article 1, section 7, clause 2 of the Constitution. The suit contended that a temporary recess does not prevent the President from returning a bill to Congress so that there would be an opportunity to override the veto. The judge declared in his decision that senators had been deprived of their right to vote to override the veto when the President withheld his signature from the bill. It was ordered that the administration must comply with the ruling or appeal the decision.

The President's threat to veto the Alaska pipeline bill was disregarded because of his weakened leadership. He had stated that he was unhappy with provisions in the bill that granted regulatory commissions powers which enabled them to circumvent the Office of Management and Budget in certain areas. However, the threat to veto was ill timed, coming on the heels of impeachment talk. The President was forced to tone down his veto threat and approve the bill.

Unlike the case of the Alaska pipeline legislation, when the President threatened to veto emergency energy legislation in February he made good on his threat, in March. Nixon said that a provision of the bill calling for price rollbacks on domestic crude oil would not provide the oil companies with sufficient capital to fund new exploration. At the same time, Democratic Senator Henry Jackson of Washington said that oil producers told him the price prescribed in the legislation would provide adequate exploration financing. This time the Presidential veto was upheld by the Senate, eight votes short of a two-thirds majority.

The President's victories in terms of sustained vetoes outnumbered his defeats in the first session of the 93rd Congress. In essence his veto of legislation has been a weapon to prod the Congress into reforming its own appropriations and accepting some fiscal responsibility for its actions. He did manage to maneuver them into forming a joint committee to study the problem. Congress is making a serious effort to reform its procedures. Legislation is being considered by both houses.

In Retrospect

The relationship of Congress and the President is a dynamic one, with turnabouts in power depending in part upon the presence or absence of an external threat to the nation, the need for immediate action, the kind of issue, and the information base on which it can be decided. Wilfred E. Binkley wrote a book referring to the relationship between Congress and the President, with stress on the period from Lincoln to Roosevelt. He characterized it as an ebb and flow of power.[56] That process has not changed, but even as the total scope of the federal government has grown exponentially in the years since Binkley was writing, certain areas of that total policy have been handed over almost totally to the President. In other areas Congress still has a major voice, *provided* it can organize itself effectively to express it. This is not always possible, because of political, structural, and personality situations within the Congress. These difficulties constitute a special challenge for New Politics proponents, since fuller participation and openness in decision-making are considered essential. The inability of the Congress to thwart vetoes is an especially difficult barrier for the New Politics during Administrations that do not share the zeal for New Politics socioeconomic legislation.

11

Urbanization, Suburbanization, and the New Politics

The growth of the New Politics is, in part, a response to the transition of the United States from an urban nation to one of metropolitan areas. For just as the earlier rural life style was buttressed by governmental support and attention to its problems, the New Politics has demanded that government pay increasing attention to urban and metropolitan social problems.

With the shift from a rural to an urban-suburban society there were increasing pressures for greater equity in the allocation of state and federal legislative seats. Malapportionment, in the form of over- or underrepresentation of select "interests" within the political community, had been an accepted tactic in the struggle for political power. This practice was geographically widespread and racial discrimination was one motivation. Cities and suburbs were underrepresented and the value of their votes was proportionally diminished through the overrepresentation of rural areas in state legislatures. This effect was achieved simply. The rural-dominated legislatures just failed to correct for shifts in population because doing so would reduce their political power.

Tennessee was a representative case. By 1961, it had been sixty years since the legislature was reapportioned. Minority domination was evident in that 27 percent of the voters could elect a majority of the upper house and 29 percent could elect a majority of the lower chamber. Even so, Tennessee was not the worst offender. According to Andrew Hacker, "In California, 11 percent of the voters could elect 51 percent of the state Senate; in Florida, 12 percent could elect the majority. In Kansas, 19 percent of the electorate could select more than half of the state's lower house; in Vermont it took only 12 percent of the voters to choose the majority."[1]

The situation was sufficiently grave for the Supreme Court to intervene. Justice Clark's majority decision in *Baker v. Carr* charged that "Tennessee's apportionment is a crazy quilt without rational basis," and further that "Tennessee is guilty of a clear violation of the state constitution."[2]

Although the decision directly affected only Tennessee, it served as a warning to states with similar practices and conditions. *Baker v. Carr* broke an impasse in the legislative-political sphere of government which was responsible for the fact that, as Justice Clark wrote, a "majority of voters were caught up in a legislative straight jacket."[3] It also brought apportionment laws under jurisdictional protection of the federal courts by virtue of the "equal protection clause" of the fourteenth Amendment. Within twenty months of this decision, most states were under civil suits challenging their current districting schemes and some states reapportioned so as to be more in harmony with the Supreme Court's ruling.

One of the fundamental questions left unanswered by *Baker v. Carr* was whether "fairness" required all kinds of legislative districts within a state to be "equal" in population and, if so, how much deviation from that equality would be allowed. The Court sought to answer that question with respect to congressional districts in *Wesberry v. Sanders*. In the majority opinion, Justice Hugo Black interpreted the language of the Constitution as supporting the principle that "as nearly as practicable one man's vote in a congressional election is to be worth as much as another's."[4]

The impact of the one-man-one-vote decisions reduced rural representation in Congress. At the same time, some rural emphasis disappeared because nonurban areas in America today, regardless of their population or area, are simply less rural than the hinterlands of past years. Instant media and improved transportation have helped to reduce area differences.

The 1970 Census demonstrated that the heaviest growth rate occurred in the suburban areas and in the Sun Belt states: California, Florida, Arizona, and Texas. Each of these states gained additional representation in the House. Only two of the fifty states added more than one seat. Reapportionment gave California an increase of five seats and Florida three. The 1970 Census also showed that 68.6 percent of the population lived in metropolitan areas, and that metropolitan growth was continuing so that city and suburban dwellers now outnumber those living in rural areas.[5]

The logical conclusion might be that metropolitan areas could act as a unified block to win almost anything from Congress that they want, but this was not the case. Core areas of the metropolis do not have the same needs or the same constituents as the suburban areas. Central-city residents are oriented toward basic service needs or problems such as welfare, housing, crime, and health. Suburbanites, often more economically secure than their city counterparts, seem to be more concerned with the education of their children, the "quality" of their life, suburban growth, and the preservation of their status within society. These different demands create a built-in tension between demand for change and the desire to preserve the status quo.

The two sectors of a metropolitan area often have different economic and racial constituencies. In many respects their interests are in conflict, as when interstate highways are being routed through central cities. Many suburbanites desire easier access to their jobs, but the *costs* of that access are often borne by central-city people, who are displaced from their homes, usually without adequate provision for alternative housing.

The popular impression of metropolitan areas is that the wealthy commute to work from homes in the suburbs while the poor and black live in the central city. While most of the poor and minority groups *are* found in central cities of older metropolitan areas in the Midwest and Northeast, many rich people live there, too. On the other hand, some poor people live in predominantly wealthy or middle-class suburbs, and ethnic groups are scattered, usually in clusters, throughout the entire area. This is true not only in the West and South, where there are fewer disparities in income and social status between city and suburb, but also in some of the old metropolitan areas. These differences in wealth, race, and heritage have considerable impact upon the political behavior of the suburbanite, and also upon his orientation toward his city, school district, region, and county.

Metropolitan areas differ from one another, as do their central cities. In most smaller metropolitan areas, the residents with high status and high incomes live in the central city. Even in those areas where the general impression of central-city poverty and suburban affluence is true, however, a wide range of suburbs exists. There is no such thing as the "average suburbanite" unless one compresses very wide ranges into a meaningless average.

In an effort to find some way to generalize about the suburbs social scientists have tried to classify them according to their functions, economic levels, demographic characteristics, and their types of local government. These frameworks make the suburbs more easily explainable but they do not reduce the actual diversity, and so they must be used with care.

One man-one vote was hailed as a victory for the cities against the rural domination of Congress. However, much time passed before the new representation process gained acceptance. Meanwhile, the dynamics of the demographic revolution altered the anticipated results. Reapportionment based on the new principle produced an expected decrease in rural-dominated districts. But suburban areas gained as many new seats as the central cities did. The net result was that the rural interests lost, but the central-city bloc did not really gain. In the next two decades, these relationships and constituencies will evolve toward more homogeneity, because the suburban population densities will increase and the older suburbs will be affected by the same urban problems now afflicting the central cities. Presently the shifting power balance is resulting in a revision of policy outcomes and of coalition alignments.

Impact on Rural Programs

The food stamp programs exemplify the shift in policy due to the reduction of rural political power. When World War II ended, the nation experienced problems of farm overproduction and poor distribution of agricultural goods. The rural-oriented Congress dealt with the problem by voting to pay cash subsidies to farmers to take some of their land out of production and try to support commodity prices at certain minimums. If the market price fell below these minimums the federal government purchased the crop to create demand and raise the price. By the Eisenhower years, the large amount of money being spent on support of commodity prices resulted in governmental stockpiling of huge food surpluses.

Because of the oversupply and the concurrent needs of poor families for more food, Secretary of Agriculture Ezra Taft Benson expanded the existing program of direct distribution of surplus food to the needy. However, distribution of bulk surplus flour and other commodities had at least three major drawbacks: it was not conducive to a balanced diet; it resulted in much waste, because the recipients could not make effective use of the commodities in their raw form; and many of the poor felt that lining up for a dole of surplus food was dehumanizing.

Several proposals came before the Congress between 1957 and 1964 concerning a national food stamp program. Each time, however, they faced a variety of opponents. Republicans charged that these were partisan bills because they involved demonstration programs in urban areas that coincidentally were Democratic districts. Southern representatives called it civil rights legislation and argued that it would be discriminatory against the South because the food stamps could only be used in stores that did not discriminate! Some representatives claimed that the proposal was a general welfare bill concerned with nutritional needs and was not motived primarily by a desire to reduce agricultural surpluses.

In 1957, House member Mrs. Leonor K. Sullivan, a St. Louis Democrat, introduced an amendment to an agriculture bill that would have forced the Secretary of Agriculture to institute a food stamp plan, in which stamps to be used as a money substitute in local supermarkets could be provided to those needing food. The Department of Agriculture had had that power since 1935, but it had not been exercised in twenty years. Since any food-oriented legislation had to go through the Agriculture Committee, Mrs. Sullivan threatened to block every other piece of farm legislation that year unless the bill, with her amendment, reached the floor. Under this threat the bill was reported out, but was defeated by a narrow margin on the House floor.[6]

In 1959 Congress approved the food stamp idea for three demonstration projects, at least one of them to be in a rural district. This legislation was never implemented, yet in 1961 President Kennedy began a food stamp demonstration project under a 1935 authority. After several pilot programs were successful, Mrs. Sullivan proposed a new food stamp bill, and in 1964 the new program was reported to the floor by the Agriculture Committee as part of a trade involving a tobacco research bill. The wording of the Food Stamp Act stated clearly that it was intended to help dispose of farm surpluses, although its primary sponsors were chiefly interested in its social welfare implications.

On the floor, passage hinged on a wheat-cotton subsidy bill that rural interests wanted. When the two bills ended up in succession on the agenda, the trade-off was clear. President Johnson sharpened the deal even more when he called the Food Stamp Act an integral part of the War on Poverty, and prodded urban Democrats to let the wheat/cotton bill pass for the Food Stamp Act.[7] Table 11-1 compares the vote on this Food Stamp Act with the 1957 vote. The influence of the trade on rural Democrats is clear, and equally clear is that suburban and rural Republicans backed off in their support.

The increase in the number of urban and suburban congressmen reflects the changes that took place in the composition of interests in Congress during the period from 1957 to 1964, and this in turn acted to neutralize the opposition. What is important to note is that what started out in 1957 as an agricultural measure became, by the time of final legislative action in 1964, widely perceived as *urban* legislation, even though some rural poor also benefited from the passage of the Food Stamp Bill of 1964.

The Food Stamp bill set a precedent for rural representatives to actively seek urban support as a means of passing their own bills. Republican Senator Roman L. Hruska of Nebraska found it necessary to speak as follows

Table 11-1
Comparison of House Votes on Food-Stamp Bills

	1957 Bill		1964 Bill	
	Number of Reps. Voting	*Percentage Pro-Food Stamp*	*Number of Reps. Voting*	*Percentage Pro-Food Stamp*
Democrats[a]				
Urban	74	94.6	94	90.4
Suburban	22	95.5	28	96.4
Rural	110	70.9	120	86.7
	206		242	
Republicans				
Urban	46	13.0	34	11.8
Suburban	34	23.5	35	11.4
Rural	95	13.7	107	4.7
	175		176	

[a] These categories are defined in the *Congressional Quarterly Weekly Report,* February 2, 1962, pp. 153 ff.
Source: Frederic N. Cleaveland, *Congress and Urban Problems,* (Washington, D.C.: The Brookings Institution, 1969), pp. 285 and 305. Copyright © by the Brookings Institution, Washington, D.C.

about the farm subsidy bill for fiscal 1973: "Misconceptions are held by many that this bill is a narrow one for farm interest programs. That is not the fact. . . . It is truly the urban consumers who reap the bountiful harvest of these programs."[8] This plea contrasts sharply with the situation in 1958, when the *Congressional Quarterly* reported that no bill "involved so clear an issue as the Senate's passage, 50 to 43, of a bill barring any restriction in farm price supports indefinitely."[9] The rural representatives realize now that they need support from urban representatives.

By 1972 and 1973 the rural bloc was caught in a pincers movement. The Nixon Administration, pressured by its inability to control inflation of food prices, was ready to seek alternatives such as the billion-dollar Russian wheat deal to dispose of agricultural surpluses, *while at the same time encouraging expanded agricultural production.* The objective was both to improve the balance of payments through exports and to reduce prices at home as a result of the increased supply.

The Agriculture Act of 1970 set the per-farmer per-crop subsidy limit at $55,000. In 1972, both houses handily defeated an amendment to the act reducing the maximum payment to $20,000. But Title I of the 1973 Agriculture Act did reduce the limit to $20,000. The Secretary of Agriculture was given some minor discretionary powers over application of the limit.

The Impact on Urban-Suburban Programs

The shifting balance of power in Congress has affected the varying sectional interests not only through a reduction in rural priorities, but also through the development of positive new programs intended to ameliorate conditions in urban areas. The treatment of poverty offers a good example.

Although feelings of moral responsibility are usually at the root of welfare programs, the real basis for any governmental social programs lies in the Constitution, which authorizes governmental action to "promote the general welfare." Nevertheless, given the widespread acceptance of the so-called Protestant Ethic, many of the people who work hard to get ahead and succeed in doing so conceive of the poor as lazy and deserving of poverty. It is, after all, the workers who pay taxes to support the poor. Edward Banfield argues that to some extent poor people are poor because there is a "culture of poverty" which some of the poor find comfortable.[10] This "culture of poverty" is characterized by an inability to develop the self-discipline required for most jobs in a highly industrialized society, an inability to temper one's present appetite to make the sacrifices necessary to personal well-being in some distant future, and a reluctance to "fix up" one's dwelling to meet the esthetic tastes and moral expectations of a middle-class society.

Given this view, it is simple to understand why welfare and other programs aimed at alleviating poverty always face serious and intense debate in Congress and why, even when they are approved, they are never aimed at attacking the bottommost level of poverty. The assumption seems to be that those on the bottom can never make it and that there is no real alternative to putting them on the dole.

The enormous social changes of the postdepression period led to new political reaction to the problems of poverty. The New Politics Congress responded to Lyndon Johnson's attempt to wage "War on Poverty" by establishing an innovative new agency—the Office of Economic Opportunity (OEO). The new agency's programs represented a third wave of antipoverty efforts dating from the 1930s. The first comprehensive federal response to the problems of poverty were reflected in the Social Security, rural, and WPA programs during the crisis-laden depression years of the 1930s. The beginning of urban renewal in 1949 represented the next wave of federal activity, which carried through the early years of the Kennedy Administration.

These postwar programs to reduce poverty were largely due to the pressures of urbanization and suburbanization. The end of the war made rapid urbanization a reality. Returning veterans were buying suburban homes, the defense workers who had stayed at home had money to do the same thing, and aided by government help in the form of mortgage guarantees for suburban homes and road building, the cities soon stopped growing despite massive migrations of rural population to the city. All of a sudden, the poor, the aged, the ill, and the unemployable became a large proportion of those left in the cities.

These events combined to create an acute overall housing shortage that caused Congress to become involved in the housing business in 1949. The urban renewal program did not produce the needed new housing, as Congress never provided sufficient appropriations, and much of the money was used to build downtown office buildings. The dominant philosophy at that time dictated that if poor people had decent homes, they would be motivated to *work harder* to maintain them, and in turn would eventually find their way out of poverty through *hard work*.

That American perception of poverty survived well into the 1960s, and this view of the poor as black ghetto-dwellers, old people, or unemployable social deviants still persists. In reality, there is no average poor person, and poverty is no more urban than it is rural. "The poor" is not a homogeneous group at all. It includes the elderly, the dependent children from broken homes, disabled persons, unemployable youths, and even the working poor who do not make a living wage despite their effort.

The most recent federal initiative was manifested in the landmark Economic Opportunity Act of 1964. As never before, this new effort to end "the vicious circle of poverty" was tied to struggles for political power. While many viewed the effort to help the poor as the important point, others were as interested in mobilizing poor people's votes and in helping them to realize that they could have power if they could organize themselves.

On March 16, 1964 President Lyndon Johnson called for a War on Poverty so that every American would be able to share all the opportunities of his society, and to advance his welfare to the limit of his capacities. Even in his speech to Congress, Johnson was calling for a radical departure from the dole method of helping the poor. He asked for "an investment in the most valuable of our resources—the skills and strengths of our people." He was looking for something beyond the New Deal, and the Office of Equal Opportunity (OEO) legislation proved that he was.

Passage of the OEO Bill provides one of the best issues upon which to separate the New from the Old Politics. Its emphasis on minorities split the conservative southern Democrats from their big-city political allies and yet attracted New-Politics-oriented Republicans to support it.

The New Politics push for more participation coincided with the OEO emphasis on "maximum feasible participation": by area. It also provided that the community action agencies could be public or private, and so took them out of direct control by the Old Politics people in City Hall. These were new problem-solving approaches. Although it was essentially the power of the urban Democrats that put the program across, this was not a rural-urban fight. Rural areas were included in the program, and this explains the votes *for* OEO by numerous rural Republican congressmen.

The legislation also represented political liabilities for LBJ. However, it heralded real power for the poor, financed by government money. Community-action and legal-aid programs were feared by many legislators and community leaders. For example, the large number of poor blacks in the South are mostly rural, and the bill included rural areas in its definition of where the Community Action Program would operate. Thus, an amendment became necessary that would permit the governor of any state an unquestioned veto of any OEO project in his state.

This program was designed not only to give money to the poor, but to form programs to make them self-sufficient. While they were becoming self-sufficient they would have the opportunity to help construct their own programs, and be employed at the same time. Such "maximum feasible participation" offered hope that the results would be greater than in previous government programs. Along with the optimism came internal disputes among the poor, interference from those opposed to the program, and insufficient funding making fair evaluation of the results difficult.

The bill to establish the Department of Housing and Urban Development in 1962 was a clearer case of urban versus rural tensions. Realizing that their power was slipping away, the rural legislators opposed the establishment of the Department of Housing and Urban Development as a counterpart for the Department of Agriculture. Previously the rural legislators were able to divide urban legislators and defeat antirural legislation. Now they were concerned not with specific legislation of a threatening nature, but rather with the whole trend which would add to the power of urban legislators. It would be much harder to block urban-related legislation if it had a department coordinating the attack. Establishment of a new cabinet department would create a linkage with the Executive Branch that could provide urban legislators with greater leverage in Congress.

After President Kennedy's death Johnson redrafted the urban cabinet department bill, changing the name of the department to give the impression that it involved less of a change than the Kennedy Department of Urban Affairs bill. Aided this time by the personnel changes resulting from the 1962 congressional elections, legislation establishing the Department of Housing and Urban Development was passed by Congress in December 1963.

The trend toward authorizing more federal programs to aid cities continued with a vengeance in the 89th Congress—the Great Society Congress—where Johnson had a very large Democratic majority. This was the high point for the Democratic Study Group and much of the early New Politics legislation. A cornucopia of programs in manpower, health, housing, welfare, and social services resulted.

One of the most interesting of these programs was the Demonstration Cities Act of 1965, which was later retitled the Model Cities Program. The motivation for this program was the history of failures being experienced in the large number of categorical, single-purpose, urban programs. These programs demonstrated that housing alone was not sufficient to aid a family with serious health and employment problems. The endless variety of overlapping programs often failed to realize their full potential. They were like using bandaids to fix cancer. Model cities was an attempt to take a *comprehensive* approach to the total needs of a particularly depressed area within a city. The guidelines for the Model Cities program stated that each city accepted into the program must designate an area containing no more than 10 percent of the total city population, yet having the highest concentration of health, welfare, drug addiction, crime, unemployment, and housing problems in that total population. Model Cities money was flexible money which could be used for a variety of approaches geared toward effecting a drastic change in specific neighborhoods by attacking the multiple factors inhibiting improvement.

As in the OEO program, Model Cities called for a high level of citizen participation. However, it put the reins of control in the hands of the responsible city authorities instead of in a community action agency independent of the traditional city government. This was a response in part to the pleas of the mayors not to establish another organization with federal money able to work at cross purposes with the city administration.

In many respects the OEO program was too decentralized, and had stirred up expectations that were not achievable without continuous inputs of massive federal funding. Model Cities had the same problem. It was assumed that the presence of the federal money as a lever in the city budget would help to attract additional city, state, and private funds to bring about solutions to city problems from coast-to-coast. This process was derailed in part because it was not feasible to alter long-standing deficiences overnight; because urban riots diverted funds and split constituencies; and because the continued federal funding drain as a result of the Vietnam War did not permit the level of federal financial intervention that was originally envisioned.

For the purposes of this analysis, what is important is that the New Politics coalition in Congress was able to secure passage of the legislation by working with a President who derived his greatest strength from the large cities and urban metropolitan areas in the nation. The highwater mark for farm subsidies was reached in the 1960s, and the new massive federal spending was for urban programs.

The 1968 election of Richard Nixon did not overturn this new priority system. Nixon received substantial support in the cities and while he set about dismantling the OEO and Model Cities programs, as well as revising the subsidized housing programs, he also introduced a few new urban programs. For example, the establishment of the Law Enforcement Assistance Administration (LEAA) in the Department of Justice in 1968 provided federal funding to the cities for law-enforcement. While much of this LEAA money was used for hardware, substantial amounts were used for increased training and pay of police officers. Later, in 1972, the Nixon Administration added another program within the LEAA called the High Impact Crime Program, which provided special funding for the eight cities with the highest incidence of "stranger-to-stranger" crimes. Original funding for the special program was $160 million in discretionary grants and research funds. By November 1973, the following awards had been made to the High Impact cities:

Table 11-2
Awards Made to High Impact Cities

City	Projects	Awards
Atlanta	12	$ 6,209,810
Baltimore	23	4,482,507
Cleveland	31	13,088,445
Dallas	14	5,192,676
Denver	20	5,382,805
Newark	14	8,609,196
Portland	7	6,060,674
St. Louis	34	5,398,968
	155	$54,425,081

Source: Law Enforcement Assistance Administration, *Newsletter*, III, 8, November 1973, p. 21.

The Nixon administration also introduced major new programs in the area of narcotics control, and established the Special Action Office of Drug Abuse Prevention (SAODAP) in the Executive Office of the President. The agency was created by Executive Order under the Drug Abuse Office and Treatment Act of 1972. Prior to SAODAP there were at least nineteen federal agencies involved in drug-abuse-prevention activities.

In fiscal year 1969 the budgets for these functions in the Departments of Defense, Justice, Treasury, and Health, Education and Welfare; Veteran's Administration; Office of Equal Opportunity; and the others approximated $66.4 million. By fiscal year 1973 the figure grew to $791 million with SAODAP spending $54 million, almost as much as the total in 1969. Despite the huge increase in spending, the program emphasis stayed the same. The two major items were Treatment Rehabilitation ($279 million) and Law Enforcement ($226 million).

The New Metropolitan Era

New Politics, through its emphasis on greater participation and equality, has provided the organizing basis for urban power in Congress. That is, New Politics power is broader than urban power but there is a substantial interlocking of Congressmen representing these two blocs. To some extent, this is due to the increasing association of cities with the poor and the minorities who traditionally have had the greatest difficulty participating.

Urban power is now clearly evident in Congress, but it has not yet been able to institutionalize itself in quite the same way rural power did. The Department of Agriculture was set up to deal with rural problems. Likewise, the Commerce and Labor Departments were directly related to a portion of the national economy, but the departments established since World War II have not had as fixed a clientele. Instead, the new departments—Health, Education and Welfare; Transportation; and Housing and Urban Development—have been organized around a problem to be solved.

This difference is reflected in Congress as well. The Agriculture Committees in Congress are geared to dealing with rural issues, a holdover from the days when this was primarily an agricultural nation. There is no "Urban Committee" as such, since this function was assigned to the Banking and Currency Committee, where many of the members have no special interest in urban and metropolitan problems. Specific urban functional problems such as transportation, housing, law enforcement, education, or health are assigned to committees whose primary concern is with some broader focus than the urban aspect of these functional problems. The lack of an individual committee to specifically address urban problems and the greater diversity of urban constituencies as opposed to rural clientele make it more difficult for the urban interests to unite and secure approval of urban programs.

Most of Richard Nixon's support in 1968 and in 1972 came from the new suburban constituencies in the nation. The domestic program emphasis of the first Nixon Administration reflected that tie. It is most apparent in the revenue-sharing approach adopted by the Nixon Administration for aid to local governments. Putting the local governments on a formula basis for federal funding was an alternative to continuation of funding for categorical aid programs developed under the Johnson Administration. Revenue-sharing had the effect of spreading the federal money over a greater number of local jurisdictions, including smaller cities and urban counties. Under the general revenue-sharing provisions, counties (including rural counties) received about half of the $10 billion allocated in the first two years, with cities and states receiving the other half.[11] The urban programs of the Johnson administration had been oriented very heavily toward central cities, especially large central cities, many of which receive much less money under the revenue-sharing formulas than they received under the Johnson grant programs.

After general revenue-sharing was operating, the Better Communities Act was introduced by the Nixon administration to replace most of the HUD programs, including Model Cities. The definition of eligible jurisdictions included metropolitan cities with populations over 50,000 and metropolitan counties whose population exceeded 200,000, without counting the cental city population. This meant that eighty-five counties in the nation qualified for Better Communities Act funding. With the exception of a few counties such as Los Angeles, Miami-Dade, and Nashville-Davidson, these counties had not participated on any broad-scale basis in the programs of the Johnson Administration. Under the Better Communities Act, 6.7 percent of the total funding of $2.3 billion would have been allocated to county governments.[12]

Mass transportation for urban areas, as it is promoted by the federal government and Congress, is another area where new urban power is having an effect. When major road-building programs were first put into planning stages in the middle 1940s, they were seen as beneficial to cities and rural areas—reflecting the growing interrelationships among every sector of the nation's economy. But building roads to resolve problems of access to and from commercial and industrial centers often created more serious problems. As time passed, it is more apparent that roads alone are not the solution to urban transportation problems, and mass transportation must be part of a planned metropolitan system.

In 1956, Congress created a trust fund for highway construction based on federal gasoline tax. Fourteen years later, an Urban Mass Transit Administration (UMTA) was established with authorization to spend just over $3 billion between 1971 and 1975 for needed capital improvements to existing mass transit systems. But most mass transit systems in the cities date back to the turn of the century. Further, many cities that need new mass transit must fund not only the construction and equipping of such a system, but also the large expense of securing new rights of way. Therefore, the funding of the recently created UMTA is insufficient to meet current needs, and many proponents of urban mass transit began viewing the lucrative highway trust fund as a supplemental source of revenues.

There are many arguments surrounding the appropriate use of trust fund money for mass transit. The basic point, though, is that mass transit is not highway construction, and that was the purpose of the existing fund. The powerful highway lobby, which succeeded in pushing the original legislation through Congress, had argued for years that the gasoline taxes are collected from highway users and should be spent only for their collective benefit.

Meanwhile, the "bust the trust" forces claimed that the use of the fund only for highways has unbalanced the national transportation system because too many highways have been built while little attention has been paid to urban mass transit. Environmentalists joined in the argument by pointing to the negative effects of automobile pollution and damage to the natural environment as a result of highway construction.

Another significant element in the struggle was the argument that rural taxpayers realize no gain from the building of mass transit systems in cities. Rural legislators claimed that federal mass transit funding is merely a subsidy to the urban-suburban commuter. Central-city residents, displaced by controversial federal and state highway projects that took their land and homes for the benefit of suburban communities, were another source of disenchantment with the highway trust fund.

An urban-rural conflict was basic in this dispute. The rural interests would derive almost no benefit from the rapid transit expenditures, while they had profited immensely from the road building. The urban-suburban representatives had some mixed emotions, as rail rapid transit is not feasible in every urban area. It requires substantial density in the transportation corridor to be a worthwhile investment, and many urban areas are too small or too dispersed to justify it. The bus transit provision therefore appealed to a larger group in Congress.

The original idea of the trust in the 1950s was predicated not on urban needs but on providing a national highway system. The reluctance of the House to "bust the trust" is firmly tied to the rural needs. The initiative for busting open the trust fund therefore came from the Senate. It is logical that it should, since senators represent whole states and most states have a significant urban population. Representatives, on the other hand, respond to smaller districts, a larger percentage of which include specifically rural interests.

The House included no mass transit aid in its form of the 1973 Federal Aid Highway Act. Instead the House bill provided that a state which canceled a federally funded highway project would return the funds allocated for that project to the federal trust fund. Then, that state would be given a priority option for funding of other road projects. Meanwhile, if the state sought mass transit aid it would apply to UMTA. An attempt to add highway funds for mass transit was defeated on the House floor by a vote of 190 to 215, after heavy lobbying by the highway interests and unsuccessful efforts by the Highway Action Coalition of environmentalists and city mass-transit advocates.[13]

The highway bill reported to the Senate floor by the Public Works Committee included the possibility of funding highway-related improvements to mass transit systems with funds taken from the highway fund. That was primarily directed at construction of "bus only" lanes and some capital expenditure on bus lines. On the Senate floor, Edmund Muskie and Howard Baker amended the bill to include rail transit systems as potential beneficiaries of urban highway funds. The amendment passed by a vote of 49 to 44. The prior year, when the highway lobby was caught off guard, the amendment won by a vote of 48 to 26, but died in conference since the House bill had no provision of highway funds for mass transit.[14]

Under the Senate bill, two existing categories of highway trust funds would be treated differently. Funds intended for new highway construction could be used for that purpose, while the trust funds set aside for "urban systems roads" could be used for urban mass transit. Urban systems roads are intended to be used for improvement to existing urban routes, not for building new ones, and so diversion from this source was less likely to alienate supporters who were needed. The Senate proposal to authorize the expenditure of even a portion of highway trust funds for urban mass transit aid was a dramatic break with precedent, and meant that the conference committee would have to grapple with the issue.

The conference committee resolved all the differences except the Senate bill's provision on diverting money from the highway fund to mass transit. The composition of the conference was especially significant. The House sent nine members, seven of them opposed to any use of trust funds for mass transit. Senator Jennings Randolph, Chairman of the Public Works Committee, planned to send nine senators, five of whom were opposed to mass transit diversion. However, the Senate Democrats had passed a rule that Senate conferees had to favor the Senate's position. Muskie and Kennedy prevailed upon Senate Majority Leader Mike Mansfield to overrule Senator Randolph. Mansfield agreed and seniority lost a battle to the New Politics. The seven ranking senators were sent, and this gave the Muskie-Baker amendment a slim 4 to 3 edge.

In twenty-nine meetings in May, June and July, the Conference Committee considered many plans in an effort to resolve the basic difference between the two bills.[15] One proposal, dubbed the "California Plan," would have abolished the trust fund when the interstate highway system became complete. At that point, each state would be free to collect its own highway taxes and devote them to whatever purpose it wished. This would be of particular benefit to states like California where the automobile is most intensively used and more highway user taxes are collected by the federal government than are returned to the state for roadbuilding.

The proposal was not acceptable to the Senate conferees, since it would delay new mass transit and pump still more money into roads before the interstate system is completed. They countered it with a proposal that would have left the trust fund intact but with a stipulation that 20 percent of the funds collected from each state would be returned to it immediately for alternative transportation uses. The House trust fund protectors would not accept this proposal.

The California Plan had suggested some lines of compromise, however. The House side offered to allow $100 million of the urban systems money to be freed for bus-related highway improvements. Although that was almost identical to the Senate Committee version of the bill, it was not as far-reaching as the Muskie-Baker Amendment, which included rail transit subsidies from urban systems money. Since the Muskie-Baker forces dominated the Senate conferees, they rejected the House plan, but its very offering was significant because it represented the first time that the House agreed to permit any nonhighway use of the trust. It was the turning point of the conference.

Finally, the House considered a version of the Muskie-Baker Amendment. Republican William H. Harsha of Ohio proposed extending the authorization period of the highway bill from the original three years up to four. At the same time, he asked for a separate urban transportation trust fund, with its revenue coming from an additional one-cent gasoline tax. Harsha felt that if the Muskie-Baker plan could be kept from going into effect before 1977, the original bill could be set up before then and the need for taking highway funds for mass transit would be eliminated.

This was not acceptable to the Senate conferees. However, House mass transit foe Harold T. Johnson, a California Democrat, agreed to change his vote on the basic concept of trust-banking for rail transit. A new agreement emerged which provided that the Muskie-Baker amendment would be canceled if a mass transit fund were set up before the 1976 effective date. This satisfied Harsha and broke the long deadlock.

Ironically that summer of 1973, when the bill received final passage, was the first time since World War II that the nation experienced an acute gasoline shortage. It is unclear whether the shortage of gasoline that was occurring and the predictions of continued and longtime fuel shortages for the nation influenced any congressmen. But it is important to realize that in most urban areas the automobile is less efficient than mass transit in terms of energy usage. The current energy crisis makes it likely that there will be a further shift in congressional priorities from the less efficient uses of fuel to those with greater returns.

Despite the New Politics and changing demographic and representative patterns affecting Congress, it is not appropriate to conclude that the urban-rural conflict is over. The era of shortages—immediately in energy resources and potentially in foodstuffs—is sure to play an important role in the future, perhaps making the urban-rural conflict secondary to simple attempts at equal distribution and survival. Nevertheless, as long as there is legislation that will disproportionately favor or impede urban or rural interests, there will be urban-rural conflicts.

Common Problems

These federal social and economic programs influenced by urbanization and suburbanization, when linked with the rise of New Politics, have resulted in an eclipse of first rural and then some big-city interests in terms of federal programs. To some extent, the revenue-sharing programs have been a boon to rural counties, because such counties never had the professional staff necessary to write proposals effectively under the former grant programs. They had participated in many of the programs that funneled federal money through state governments only because, on a political basis, they were able to make their voices heard in such distributions. Nevertheless, the big gainers from the Nixon program have been the suburban areas, which are gaining political power.

Yet all these areas are interrelated. From its beginning, the poverty program recognized poverty as both a rural and an urban problem. It still is, although the problem differs in these two environments. The rural poor generally have more stable family life and a more understanding community willing to offer emergency services to them, whereas the urban poor, especially those who have migrated there from rural areas, have suffered anomie as new urban residents. Moving from a farm to a high-rise low-income housing project in a city already having an oversupply of labor for unskilled jobs causes many problems.

As federal programs have become more sophisticated and problems have been more carefully defined, the interrelationships of the urban and rural problems have become much clearer. For example, in its 1967 report "The People Left Behind," the President's National Advisory Commission on Rural Poverty pointed out the effect of rural migration on urban poverty. It recommended that it was actually in the interests of the urban areas to support legislative efforts to alleviate poverty in the rural areas so that the poor there would have less motivation to move to the city, where they would just add to the oversupply of unskilled labor and the demand for public housing.[16]

The Rural Development Act of 1972 was passed as one effort to make rural living more attractive. It made many of the urban comforts like sewage treatment and water service feasible in the rural areas as well. Senator Henry Bellmon of Oklahoma said:

The Rural Development Act . . . is one of the most important pieces of legislation that has come through Congress. . . . The proper implementation of the Act will solve not only rural problems, but a lot of our urban problems as well, because so many urban problems result from the tremendous out migration of people over the last 40 years.[17]

Urban advocate Hubert Humphrey of Minnesota speaks knowingly of the urban-rural interrelationship: "The problems of urban America are one and inseparable with the problems of rural America; the problems of economic blight, economic dependency, and economic difficulty in rural America are inseparable from urban America."[18]

Increased participation of urban and suburban areas in governmental decision-making and the recognition of the interrelationship of central city-suburban-rural problems is more likely in future years to lead to a more balanced problem-solving approach that will treat all these areas as a part of an interrelated national economic system. "The systems approach" of the New Politics is particularly appropriate to the resolution of these problems because of its emphasis on better documentation of problems, more openness in decision-making, and more participation by those affected by the programs. This new emphasis and "problem orientation" also make less political partisanship more feasible where clear problems of a substantive nature are involved.

The call for this kind of approach was sounded by Max Ways in a 1964 article, which pointed out how Lyndon Johnson's problem-solving approach was tending to co-opt the opposition and depoliticize federal programs.[19] Despite the fact that the actual implementation of those programs did not necessarily have this effect, the theoretical basis for the current problem-solving approach was defined then. With the advantage of the intervening years of experience and experimentation with community-oriented programs, the foundation has been set for institutionalized citizen participation in the form of greater power for general-purpose governments, like cities and counties that are supported by revenue-sharing funds. This will make it practical for them to do some of the things that they alone are able to plan for, and this will change the face of America. That, in turn, will generate new pressures for a New Politics Congress capable of providing the *federal framework* for these local programs.

12 New Politics and Party Realignment

With the election of John F. Kennedy and Lyndon B. Johnson, Congress began to respond favorably to experimentation with new large-scale programs to cope with the nation's problems. In the context of New Politics, leadership from the Executive Branch prompted a problem-solving approach in Congress. Yet in 1968 a Democratic New Politics Congress was returned to office at the same time a Republican Richard Nixon, captured the presidency. This is one of the fruits of the decentralized American political party system, which is built upon a confederation of state and local parties. Each party includes a spectrum of liberals and conservatives and the only national candidates are those who run for the presidency.

The President is the key variable in the functioning of Congress. In a real sense, the national constituency is *not* the simple sum of the local constituencies, and so the voters may simultaneously elect a President from one party and a Congress from the other. For this reason, the suggestion by nationally recognized political analysts that a party realignment is in process is significant to the future of Congress. If a major realignment should occur it would be an important external influence on New Politics in Congress, since it may determine not only who gets to Congress but also whether the President will share or thwart congressional efforts to influence national priorities and programs.

Another result of New Politics is that issues become more important than party loyalty. This is most obvious in the presidential elections since 1960, which have followed a somewhat schizophrenic pattern. John F. Kennedy squeaked into office, Lyndon Johnson won in a landslide, Richard Nixon won a close election in 1968 and then won by a landslide in 1972. Every other election since 1960 has involved a landslide, followed by a close race, but the landslides have occurred when an incumbent President has run.

Despite the belief of some political analysts that a major realignment of the political party structure is in process, it is difficult to account for the Nixon landslide in 1972. His dramatic trip to China and other apparent successes in the field of foreign affairs in the absence of aggressive congressional initiatives in domestic affairs put the President in a good light. The addition of a Democratic candidate who was excessively committed to the left wing of the New Politics was an unexpected bonanza that prompted many Democrats to vote for Nixon. However, this is not sufficient basis for concluding that they switched to the Republican party permanently.

As for 1976, Mr. Nixon is personally on the defensive because of Watergate. The Democratic Congress has not succeeded in solidifying its own claim to innovation and positive participation in setting national priorities. Thus, inter- and intraparty rivalries as well as the conflicts between the congressional and presidential institutions will come to a head in the 1976 presidential election.

Scammon-Wattenberg and "The Social Issue"

If one were planning the strategy for either party for the 1976 presidential election, there would be some serious questions as to how to proceed. As might be expected there are even conflicting opinions regarding what has happened since 1968. In a 1970 book titled *The Real Majority,* Richard Scammon and Ben Wattenberg argue that there was a basic change in the 1960s and that the Old New Deal coalition based on domestic economic issues came apart at the seams. Their explanation is that there was a *substantive* change in American politics and that a new factor, which they label "the social issue," had determined the outcome of recent elections and would be the dominant force for some time to come.[1]

Scammon and Wattenberg also theorized that a *structural* change occurred in American politics as the result of the new demographic composition of the population. The majority of Americans were no longer young and they were not poor, black, or uneducated. They were instead middle-aged, white, middle income, and middle educated.

The authors suggest that planning strategy for future campaigns will depend upon how the candidates deal with these substantive and structural factors. Their advice to any candidate is to aim for the "real majority," which is to be found among the middle people in American politics. They also caution candidates against attempting to run a campaign based upon the social issue (race, crime, and lawlessness).[2]

In reaching these conclusions, they are in essence saying that Vietnam was not the overriding issue in 1968 that many considered it to be. They take the position that Americans vote primarily on the basis of domestic rather than international issues. To that extent, disapproval by middle America of the Vietnam War protests of the leftists was just another element of the social issue operating in 1968. The social issue also included reaction against the deviant moral values of many of the young. In short, very few Americans perceive the social upheavals of the 1960s as beneficial to themselves or to America, and they attribute the confusion to crime, racial turmoil, and dissident youth.[3]

There are many demographic indicators that clearly support the Scammon-Wattenberg position. For example, seven out of every ten voters were between the ages of thirty and sixty-four in 1968. Those under thirty and those over sixty-five were evenly split. However, as documented in chapter 2, one of the realities of politics is that young people tend not to participate, due to apathy, problems with absentee ballots, residency requirements, or as a form of protest. For this reason, as well as for the reason that when they vote they do not vote as a bloc, those under thirty are actually the weakest segment of the American electorate.[4]

Another supporting plank in the Scammon-Wattenberg approach is that poor people do not constitute a major segment of the electorate. Only 22 percent of the populace eligible to vote in 1968 had incomes under $5,000. Only 56 percent of them actually voted. Eighty-four percent of those with incomes over $15,000 voted. Those with the lowest incomes were a very minor portion of the total electorate, and were specifically the portion of the electorate least likely to vote. At the same time, the most affluent segment is the group most likely to participate, because of its stake in the *status quo.*

In terms of race, the figures also support the real majority thesis. Blacks constitute only about 11 percent of the total national population and, like the young and the poor, blacks in this country are among those least likely to vote on election day. In 1968, blacks cast only 9 percent of the national vote and in 1972 only 11.5 percent.[5] There is one respect, however, in which the black voting response differs from that of the young and the poor. Blacks tend to vote as a bloc, and have therefore had substantial influence in determining outcomes of an increasing number of local elections. Their potential power in close national and statewide elections is obvious.

From the standpoint of religion, 68 percent of the voters are Protestant, 25 percent Catholic, 4 percent Jewish, and 3 percent unspecified.[6] Since the election of John F. Kennedy, a candidate's religion is less likely to be a critical or polarizing issue in a national election. However, it still can be extremely important in local elections. Analysis of the religious groups suggests that the Jews are the only religious group that still regularly votes as a bloc. This factor, combined with their disproportionate involvement in political financing and their generally higher economic level, makes this religious group a potent force. This was demonstrated during the 1973-4 Arab-Israeli conflict, when politicians of both parties rallied to the Israeli position even at the price of jeopardizing a significant source of energy and opening up the prospect of gasoline rationing.

The ethnic vote is becoming increasingly difficult to calculate, especially on the national level. Ethnic groups are becoming assimilated at a faster rate as a result of the greater mobility in the nation, thus ethnics are becoming a smaller percentage of total population and a less concentrated bloc. These bloc tendencies can still be extremely important in a close local election, however. One other charge occurring that may contribute to the electoral results since the 1960s is that in 1960, 26 percent of the American voters had completed four years of high school, in 1968 the comparable figure was 36 percent, and in 1972 it was 37 percent. At the same time the percentage of American voters who attended college increased and now stands at the highest level ever, 30 percent.[7]

At the same time that some ethnic bonds are becoming looser, the trend toward greater urbanization (which was discussed in chapter 11) has been a major factor in the election of New Politics congressmen. The concentration of black populations in city districts and the Supreme Court ruling that gave urban districts fairer representation resulted in the election of black candidates. This tendency is likely to continue for some time as districts now having close to a black majority gain black populations because of migration and develop the political sophistication to coalesce around a black candidate who appeals to them.

These demographic trends are significant not only in the incremental increase of minority congressmen, but also in the macropolitics of presidential elections. The increasing location of voters in the suburbs and the migration to California, Arizona, Texas, and Florida is crucial. Scammon and Wattenberg believe that this new clustering of voters is of great political significance. In proposing a strategy to the Democratic party, they argue that the heavily populated area comprised of the states from Massachusetts south to Washington, D.C. and west to Illinois and Wisconsin, when added to the votes from California, could provide sufficient electoral votes for victory in a presidential election.[8] Terming this area "Quadcali", they note that it would be possible to win elections without any electoral votes from the South, whose defection was one of the major reasons for the weak Democratic showing both in 1968 and in 1972. They call this the key electoral factor of the next decade, and argue that it has come about because the Democrats are perceived by southerners as the problack national party. Ironically, the Democratic party gained this reputation primarily during the administration of Lyndon B. Johnson, the only southern president since the Civil War.

At the Democratic Convention in Chicago in 1968 there were strong forces calling for a leftward movement under the banner of New Politics. The philosophy and strategy was that a coalition could be formed of the young, the nonwhites, the well educated, the socially alienated, and the intellectuals. The feeling was that Archie Bunker and middle America could be ignored if necessary. While moderate Hubert Humphrey was nominated, the split in the party caused him to lose the election. The leftist forces received their chance in 1972 when they were successful in securing the Democratic nomination for George McGovern, who then proceeded to ignore the Scammon and Wattenberg electoral strategy and thereby contributed to the Nixon landslide. The extent of Nixon's victory was surprising in view of his general nonpopularity, and has been attributed heavily to anti-McGovern feeling rather than to pro-Nixon sentiment.

Any discussion of how to frame national party strategy must take into account the traditional voting patterns of the various power blocs. The Democrats are still seen as the party of the working man, of the Jews, the blacks, the intellectuals, the ethnic Catholics and, until recently, the South. These are the people who have tended to favor active social and economic reforms conducive to the New Politics and who have feared big business, which is considered to be under the control of the Republicans, who are more interested in slower social change and lower taxes as well as less extensive federal powers.

These stereotypes are changing as ethnics, blacks, the Jews, and southerners are further integrated into the American melting pot. For example, many of the disaffected Democratic voters in 1968 who put Richard Nixon in the White House were urban ethnics or southerners.

The lesson of recent history is that despite the success of the New Politics in Congress, there is much reason to go slowly in attempting to run a New Politics presidential campaign.

Any attempt to build a political coalition comprised solely of the young, the nonwhites, and the poor seems to be electoral suicide. A successful voting coalition must include other interests as well.

Realignment with a Republican Twist

Consistent with the Scammon-Wattenberg thesis, Kevin Phillips views the repudiation of the Johnson Administration in 1968 as a result of its ambitious social legislation and its inability to handle the urban and black revolutions. Phillips envisions an emerging Republican majority centered in the South, the West, and the urban suburban districts populated by the middle Americans, attributing the turnaround in Democratic and Republican fortunes to the strategy each party adopted after the 1964 election. While the Democrats linked themselves even more closely to the black socioeconomic revolution and to the increasingly liberal Northeast, the Republican party disengaged itself from the northeastern establishment which had long been its strength. As a consequence of this change, the Republicans were able to take advantage of the rising insurgency of the South, the West, and the middle Americans in suburbia.[9]

Phillips considers the post-1945 migration of many white Americans to suburbia and into the sunbelt states of Florida, Texas, Arizona, and California to be very significant to the election outcome in 1968. He notes that this migration along with that of blacks to the principal cities of the North fractured the New Deal coalition by making the racial problem a national rather than a local issue.[10]

In support of this regional view, Phillips analyzes each of the major regions and develops the following political scenario: the eleven states north of the Potomac River and east of the Appalachian Mountains (the Northeast region) are "establishmentarian." This region has gradually become less significant in national politics as the population migrations have continued. Nevertheless, Democratic strength is concentrated here where Democratic liberalism is greatest. The establishment Yankee class, the blacks, and the Jews in the Northeast are expected to continue their allegiance to the liberal policies of the Democratic Party. At the same time, the Catholics, the non-Yankee northeasterners, and suburbanites will be increasingly inclined to support the new southern and western conservative Republican Party.[11]

In contrast to the Northeast, the political power of the South has been rising since 1932. Consisting of the eleven states of the old Confederacy divided into two regions—the Deep and Outer South—the South has seen a startling reversal of political support for the Democratic party. Between the beginning of the New Deal Era in 1932 and its alleged end in 1968, the Democratic share of the presidential vote dropped from 90 percent to 26 percent in the Deep South, and from 77 percent to 32 percent in the Outer

South. In 1968 the Democratic presidential candidate received no more than 15 percent of the votes of southern *whites*. The states in the Outer South are particularly susceptible to becoming permanent members of the Republican camp.[12] This change has also been reflected in House and Senate elections in the New South, as detailed in chapter 2.

Several factors operating in the South will support the push toward the Republican Party. The gradual increase of black influence in the Democratic Party apparatus in many blackbelt communities will squeeze many conservative whites out of the party. As the national Democratic party becomes increasingly alien to the South, the Republican party will become more appealing. A factor working in the other direction is that while the Democratic Party continues to control Congress, Democratic congressmen are reluctant to jump to the Republican Party, where they would have to give up their prestige and patronage in the national Congress, as well as their seniority, which gives them such disproportionate power there. Despite the moods of New Politics, seniority is likely to remain an important factor in congressional power.

Historically, the Northeast dominated national politics as the heartland power blocs split along Civil War lines. However, the new sociological forces tend to divide the Northeast and to unite the middle of the country. The heartland consists of twenty-five states, which cast 223 of the 270 electoral votes necessary to elect the President. In 1968 Nixon carried twenty-one of the twenty-five heartland states, and gained the rest of his victory in the South and in California. Prior to 1968, even when the heartland participated in supporting the winning candidate, it was generally doing so as an extension of the northeastern political strength, whereas in 1968 it was the major base of the Republican victory.[13]

Political trends in the Pacific region of the United States correlate closely with national political trends and California is, for analytical purposes, a national sociopolitical microcosm. In 1968 the Pacific electorate followed the national trend toward realignment and an emerging Republican majority. The political future of the Pacific region is essentially that of California, for the remainder of the area is gaining population at a much slower rate. The two major forces in the California political conflict are the liberalism of the northern Pacific coast and the conservatism of southern and interior California. The first area is similar to the Northeast bloc, while the second area is similar to the heartland.

The plain fact is that the South's share of the national population is increasing and the electoral votes being lost by the Northeast are going to the South and the West. In comparing Phillips's views with those of Scammon and Wattenberg, it is interesting to note that both of them consider California an integral part of their strategy. Where they differ, however, is that Phillips stresses the importance of the South, while Scammon and Wattenberg believe the traditionally liberal Northeast quadrant is the critical area.

In analyzing George Wallace's strength in later writings on the 1972 election, Phillips says that he was unable to gain any electoral votes outside the Deep South and that in the North his primary and general election votes came from Democrats who were quitting their party. He concludes that this represents an electorate in motion between the major parties, rather than a permanent third-party movement. However, he may have been overly optimistic about the movement to the Republicans. The Democrats still have the option of regrouping and becoming more moderate.

Scammon and Wattenberg are among a minority of political scientists in suggesting that a realignment is neither necessary nor in progress. They point out that the 1968 elections displayed a typical pattern of Roosevelt New Deal coalition voting, with most of the cities voting Democratic and most of the suburbs and northern country areas voting Republican.[14] The majority of the wealthy voted Republican, while the majority of the poor voted Democratic. The middle class was split. They make the point that realignment involves a sharp polarization on the dominant issues of the day, whereas this has not been the case in recent national voting. They also point to the effectiveness of pressure group politics rather than political parties in dealing with divisive issues that may confront the electorate.

In the 1972 election the Republicans again displayed great electoral power in the South, California, and the Midwest, as Phillips anticipated. This, and Nixon's 61 percent of the popular vote, along with 521 electoral votes, would tend to support his thesis. However, the very magnitude of the Nixon victory suggests that something is wrong. The Republicans took not only the areas that Phillips had predicted but also the Northwest and the Northeast, with the exception of Massachusetts. To evaluate the Nixon victory, therefore, requires explaining the disaffection of the supposed Democratic areas as well as the continued success in the Republican areas.

George McGovern never aimed his campaign at the attitudinal center of the electorate as recommended by Scammon and Wattenberg. Consequently, the 1972 election supports their position just as much as it supports Phillips's.

Parties and the New Politics

The regional realignment is clearly visible, and is related to the migrations discussed in chapter 11. However, some new factors are operating—perhaps New Politics factors. The post-New Deal generation of voters is now a majority of the electorate. This corresponds with an increase in the percentage of independent voters and ticket splitters in recent years. Further, almost one-half of the prospective first-time voters for 1972 refused to declare an affiliation with either the Democratic or the Republican party. This indicates that the appeal of the established parties has diminished substantially.

A second factor is the growing significance of issues for the electorate. It would be expected that an electorate which is more New Politics oriented as a result of higher levels of education would be both less prone to political partisanship and more likely to listen to the issues and take a problem-solving approach. A 1968 Gallup poll reported that 84 percent voters said they chose the candidate and not the party.[15] This is a drastic change from the pre-1960 patterns when electoral behavior studies pointed to the overwhelming potency of party identification and dismissed the salience of issues. These tendencies are greatest among the younger and better-educated voters—two groups that are necessary to a winning total.

In *The Party's Over,* David Broder indicates that Scammon and Wattenberg may be describing political parties and political behavior in the formless stage that generally exists prior to a realignment. He suggests that their electoral strategies would tend to maintain the status quo, and that the temper of the times seems to make this an unsatisfactory resolution. Broder argues that the party system itself is in a state of decay, which he attributes to the fact that the party organization has lost control over the candidates' election process and the campaign itself. In addition, Democrats have shown that they were unable to control their own party convention and regulate their internal processes in 1972.[16]

The Phillips position seems to assume that the Wallace supporters will be future Republicans when the realignment is finalized. However, many of these voters are low-income workers who continue to view the Republican party as unrepresentative of and nonresponsive to their economic interests. In addition, there is the evidence that most of the southern Democrats who voted for Nixon in 1968 as well as in 1972 are continuing to vote Democratic in congressional, state, and local elections. In fact, Nixon's 1968 victory was the first presidential election since the triumph of Zachary Taylor in 1848 in which an incoming president did not carry with him at least one house of Congress. This feat was repeated in 1972 despite the Nixon landslide, which again gives credence to the argument that Nixon won not because he was favored but because McGovern was so unacceptable.

Another factor in this entire trend may be the absence of fresh leadership in the two major parties. That Richard Nixon could have gained his party's nomination for President in 1968 was somewhat surprising. On the other hand, there do not seem to be any giants among the potential Democratic candidates. Instead, the Democratic party has fallen into a pattern of competition among a number of leading senators for the nomination. Even in the wake of Watergate, the Democratic leadership in the Senate did not unite to derive the greatest political benefit out of the scandals or even to provide alternative leadership to the nation. Instead, there was jockeying for the 1976 nomination dominated by the same faces that were present in 1968 and 1972—Hubert Humphrey, Edmund Muskie, George McGovern, Edward Kennedy, Walter Mondale, Henry Jackson, and Birch Bayh. While these men tend to be identified with New Politics (even if Humphrey's credentials were earned decades ago), they all seem to have a variety of disabilities that preclude their taking the needed leadership role. On the other hand, Richard Nixon overcame serious disabilities and eventually succeeded in winning the presidency.

Issues and Realignment

What issues could appeal to the electorate with an intensity sufficient to polarize the parties and lead to a real choice between them? James Sundquist notes that in America's two-party system, realignment on the basis of foreign policy issues has never occurred.[17] He adds that on the domestic scene the most likely candidate is the social issue identified by Scammon and Wattenberg. However, even that may dissipate as the Democrats, with a few exceptions, gradually move toward the middle ground and deprive the Republicans of that issue. Other issues such as the environment, welfare, and urban blight are also related to problem-solving and do not separate the parties on any significant partisan basis. The racial issue retains its emotional potency, but may have had its greatest impact in 1968 and 1972.

Instead, traditional economic issues may again come to the fore, as a result of the failure of the Nixon administration to provide effective economic leadership. Inflation, wage and price controls, unemployment, devaluations, and the Soviet wheat deal, as well as the energy issue, are sure to hurt any Republican candidate in 1976. Another factor is that a decreasing significance for party identification and increased significance for issues tends to diminish the prospects for party realignment. They indicate a higher level of political socialization which tends to be more nonpartisan. Therefore the New Politics pitch must be for more effective and responsible government, without regard for blind party affiliations.

Phillips's concept of the electorate may be much too traditional in an era of such voter enlightenment, where traditional politics is a less significant voting factor than in the past.

In a paper presented at the American Political Science Association's 1973 conference, professors Arthur and Warren Miller, Alden Raine, and Thed Brown of the University of Michigan Center for Political Studies argued that the 1972 election marked the third consecutive time that one of the major parties failed to cope with the polarization of policy demands among its supporters in the presidential contest.[18] McGovern followed Humphrey and Goldwater in losing significant numbers of ideologically distinct segments of their own party to opponents whose policy positions were closer to the moderate position.

Miller et. al. believe that twelve years of national leadership which focused on national problems and policy alternatives have led to a transformation of the American electorate. The traditional politics of the 1950s, which had its basis in the social and economic cleavages of the New Deal, has been replaced by a new issue-oriented politics appropriate to the New Politics movement.[19]

In 1972 Nixon obtained 94 percent of the vote among self-proclaimed Republicans, 66 percent among the independents, and a surprising 42 percent vote among self-identified Democrats. The largest prior inroads into the Democratic party occurred when Eisenhower pulled 28 percent of the Democratic vote in 1952.[20] Nixon was an incumbent who had all the advantages of public exposure and an impressive record in the field of foreign affairs. The sterility of his economic program was not yet evident, and it appeared at the time of the election that he had taken bold new initiatives. In the 1972 election the turnout was still only 55 percent of the eligible electorate—the lowest since 1948. It may be expected that this result reflected a growing mood of alienation and poll-induced cynicism regarding the inevitability of Nixon's victory.

The Miller paper argues that there was substantial issue difference in the election. Table 12-1 shows the leanings of the voters on issues such as Vietnam, amnesty, marijuana, campus unrest, minorities, standard of living, busing, and five other issues clustered as a policy orientation index. As the table indicates, McGovern supporters were from 19 to 40 percent more liberal than Nixon supporters. Looking at the five-issue policy orientation index, 50 percent of the McGovern voters favored a general policy of social change, and an equal percentage of Nixon voters were diametrically opposed to social control and what they perceive as federal manipulation. The large percentage differences between McGovern Democrats and Democrats who voted for Nixon indicates a total lack of party cohesion or consensus on issues. The McGovern supporters appear to be somewhat atypical of the Democratic party as a whole.

McGovern's success in the primaries was due in part to strong support from liberal Democrats, as moderates and conservative Democrats were dividing their votes among other candidates or staying home. While the Democratic party as a whole was perceived as shifting toward more liberal orientation, McGovern was viewed as further left than any other political figure.

Miller et al. concluded that for the first time in a national election party identification was slightly less important than issues. Perhaps the next election will yield confusing results, as Watergate will alter some of the voting patterns. Distrust of government and political cynicism can affect the way in which the electorate views the system as well as the candidates.

James Sundquist argues in *The Dynamics of the Party System* that realignments are precipitated by the rise of new political issues that cut *across* party lines, are powerful enough to dominate political debate, and are capable of polarizing the community. A realignment issue must also be one on which major political groups take distinctly opposing policy positions. He identifies four issues that have arisen and polarized the electorate: First, in the late 1940s and early 1950s, there was the specter of communism. The second issue, which developed in the 1950s, was race. In the 1960s, the issue was Vietnam, which was followed by law and order—a close match for the social issue described by Scammon and Wattenberg.[21]

While the major parties have responded to these issues in diverse ways, they have not involved intensely polar positions and so have not been sufficient to cause a major party realignment. Sundquist points out that communism failed to be a politically realigning factor because it was not an issue on which major political groups adopted opposing policy positions. However, even the other major issues—race, Vietnam, and law and order—are the essence of the social issue described by Scammon and Wattenberg, but have not yet caused a major realignment. At least, the issue is clouded at the national level, because George McGovern was an extremist presidential candidate in 1972 and the realignment did not occur at the local level.

The most cross-cutting issue of the last decade was law and order. Black violence as well as student Vietnam protesters taking the law in their own hands caused national anxiety, but did not cause a realignment. Sundquist says it was an issue too diffuse for the formation of critically important political groups. There was no simple solution, legislative or otherwise, to alleviate the problem, and the major parties did not adopt distinct and opposing policy positions. After 1970, the state and local Democratic candidates tried to separate the racial component from the social issue. That it was still a lively issue, though, was demonstrated by George Wallace's success in northern as well as southern primaries.

Realignment and the 1976 Presidential Election

The lesson of the last decade seems to be that the public is truly interested in greater participation, more openness, and fewer arbitrary decisions by political figures. However, adoption of support for ultraleft causes personified by George McGovern in 1972 seems to impress the voters as another kind of arbitrary behavior with which they choose not to identify. The lesson for the New Politics is to maintain some balance of reality and objectivity with regard to the issues that are critical at a particular time. The social issue identified by Scammon and Wattenberg continues to be important both to the supporters of New Politics and to those who fear its excesses. At the presidential level, the voters' decisions are clouded by the relevance of foreign-policy-related issues as well. This is one of the areas in which Richard Nixon received some good press, which contributed to his 1972 victory.

New Politics supporters might note that one of the prime tenets and strategies of old politics is effective use of incremental approaches in appealing to the electorate. The public is always suspicious of political appeals, and in the long run it may be more effective to bring about gradual social change than to take radical positions on issues such as marijuana, amnesty, and busing. These issues gain much of their intensity from accidental factors of the moment. In the long run, questions relating to the standard of living and the role of the federal government vis à vis the states as well as the role of the people in political decision-making is crucial. Any political movement that attempts to go too far too fast is likely to stub its toe with the American electorate. Scammon and Wattenberg show that middle America has most of the votes. This group is basically open-minded and willing to change, but it is not receptive to rushing off in new directions without a full discussion of the potential consequences.

The success of New Politics at the House and Senate level, and especially in the most urban states, is not accidental. In those states politics has been able to tie itself to specific socioeconomic programs whose need is obvious. A problem develops in the national constituency when crosscurrents of conflicting interests are introduced. The public is pragmatic and will react against being pushed too far or taken for granted. When George McGovern

Table 12-1
Issue Composition of the Candidates' Support

	McGovern Primary Voters	Other Primary Voters	Democrats Voting for McGovern	Democrats Voting for Nixon	All Democrats	McGovern Voters	Nixon Voters
(N)	(78)	(104)	(377)	(271)	(1092)	(566)	(1021)
Vietnam:							
Left	79%	34%	69%	30%	52%	69%	29%
Center	17	26	19	31	24	19	29
Right	5	40	12	39	24	12	42
Amnesty:[a]							
Left	52%	17%	49%	18%	34%	54%	15%
Right	48	83	51	82	66	46	85
Marijuana:							
Left	41%	19%	30%	10%	20%	37%	17%
Center	19	6	11	7	8	11	11
Right	41	75	59	83	72	52	72
Campus unrest:							
Left	b	b	40%	12%	31%	43%	11%
Center	b	b	18	24	22	20	23
Right	b	b	42	64	47	37	66
Minorities:							
Left	49%	18%	50%	25%	39%	52%	25%
Center	25	35	24	24	22	23	27
Right	26	47	26	51	39	25	48

Standard of living:							
Left	53%	28%	53%	21%	39%	50%	18%
Center	16	22	23	24	23	24	25
Right	31	50	24	55	38	26	57
Busing:							
Left	19%	4%	23%	2%	14%	22%	3%
Center	10	2	8	2	5	8	4
Right	70	94	69	96	81	70	93
Five issues:							
Left	51%	18%	45%	15%	34%	50%	16%
Center	30	42	30	33	31	29	34
Right	18	40	25	52	35	21	50
Liberal-Conservative:							
Left	48%	24%	50%	14%	33%	54%	13%
Center	38	33	36	44	41	32	37
Right	14	43	14	42	26	14	50

[a] The format for the amnesty question was suitable for collapsing into two categories only.

[b] Data unavailable because primary voting and campus unrest questions were on opposite half-samples in early design.

Source: Arthur Miller et al., *A Majority Party in Disarray* (Ann Arbor: University of Michigan Center for Political Study, 1973). p. 226.

strayed too far from the middle ground in 1972, Democrats in urban areas bolted the party. This does not prove that a major party realignment is in process. What it does prove is that the non-New Politics people have been influenced by New Politics to the point of abandoning traditional loyalties to flee the Democratic party when their support is not justified. This is legitimate political participation and should be heeded.

Under the New Politics blocs of voters may change sides more often when they feel ignored. What is really occurring is not a party realignment but a deemphasis of party in favor of personal interest. This means that unless the Democrats can come up with a candidate who recognizes the need both for social progress and for moving slowly enough to sell his program to the electorate, even the crisis of Watergate may not be sufficient to return a Democrat to the White House in 1976.

The relevance of the New Politics Congress to this discussion is that since 1960 every Democratic presidential and vice-presidential candidate has come from the Senate. To the extent that the collection of Democratic candidates in the Senate is unable to coalesce upon an action program with which to mobilize the Democratic majority, a pragmatic public may be skeptical, and elect another Republican to replace Richard Nixon.

**Part IV
Emerging Congressional Patterns**

13 Congressional Decision-Making and the Budget

Among the 1973 confrontations between President Nixon and Congress was the attempt of the congressional leaders to reassert the legislature's prerogatives in the field of resource allocation. If, after all the policy analysis dust has settled and Congress has passed bills based upon extensive hearings and negotiated consensus, the President is free to impound at will the funds provided by Congress to implement the programs, then Congress has a sterile role. This concept is unacceptable to the congressional leadership, which reads the Constitution as calling for a partnership between the President and Congress. The lingering question, though, is, what can Congress do to reorganize its own processes to be able to play a more effective role?

The history of budgeting has been characterized by an evolution from what were known as control or object class budgets based on a categorization of inputs, such as items being purchased, to performance budgets, and presently to planning and program budgets which purport to measure outputs on a comparative value basis. This process has taken approximately sixty years, and has involved such related reforms as the civil service movement, the growth of the city management form of government, and the trend in government toward program management that utilizes the resources of industry and universities to carry out many public programs.[1]

The transition that has occurred has been closely tied to technological developments. The development of systems analysis in military and space programs, the expansion of information theory, and the use of the computer to make systems analysis and comprehensive management information feasible from a cost and time standpoint were essential to the process. Most of these technological innovations resulted from such catalytic events as the depression, World War II, and Vietnam. Computer-based planning-programming-budgeting-systems are not feasible unless economies of scale are present. Regardless of their other efforts on society, therefore, wars have provided the scale, the clustering of resources, and the massive concentration of effort that have led to the development and use of hardware that would not otherwise have been produced. However, the attempt to adapt these innovations to smaller-scale situations after the theory is perfected may take decades.

Controlling the Budget Cycle

The federal budgetary cycle is such that the President presents the budget for the next fiscal year in January of each year. For example, the budget for fiscal year 1975, which begins July 1, 1974, was presented to the Congress with a budget message in January 1974. To enable the President to do this the departments and agencies submit their final budgets to the Office of Management and Budget (OMB) in the preceding September. Thus this budget, which represented the spending for a full year beginning July 1, 1974, had to be submitted to OMB by the federal departments and agencies at least ten months before the fiscal year began, and probably before many of the previous year's requests had been approved by Congress.

One of the best examples of this kind of procrastination on the part of the Congress was in 1967. As of November 1967, Congress had failed to approve nine of the fourteen major appropriations bills for fiscal year 1968. That meant that for at least five months, federal officials were unable to make sound decisions on their current year programs, which were delivered to the OMB (then Bureau of the Budget) in the fall of 1966 and presented to the Congress in January 1967. Eleven months later the bills had not yet cleared Congress, and the departments and agencies were operating for five months of the new fiscal year on the basis of so-called "continuing resolutions" voted monthly by the Congress.

The problem is further complicated by the fact that when Congress finally acts, there must be an administrative reaction to the changes that have been made. If a program has been cut by Congress, the cut must be carried throughout the allocations planned for various programs in the regional field offices, as well as at the national headquarters. A budget finally determined in November with major changes would not reach the field office until December or January, by which time the field offices of some departments have already been instructed to submit to headquarters planned programs for the next fiscal year.

The effects of delayed congressional action are particularly costly to the field offices. For example, the primary function of many federal field offices is to travel and inspect activities within their assigned areas. One of the normal effects of a delay in the budgets such as was experienced in 1968 is that headquarters must either put a moratorium on all agency travel or cut it back drastically because it cannot be sure how much travel money Congress will eventually approve. As a result, such an office may be virtually dormant for the entire period beyond July 1 that it takes for the Congress to act on its budget for that year. Employees are not totally idle, but often it is necessary for field supervisors to engage them in "busy work" that does not contribute significantly to agency objectives.

As table 13-1 shows, Congress has not completed action on the budget before the fiscal year has begun in *any* of the last fifteen fiscal years (sixteen counting FY 1974). Only one agency, the Department of the Interior, has had most of its appropriations on time. The trend is toward longer delays each year. Excluding Interior, the earliest approval of the agencies surveyed in fiscal year 1968 was September 1967. In fiscal year 1969 and 1970 the trend toward later appropriations becomes more startling; in fiscal year 1970 the Department of the Interior did not receive its appropriations until October 29, 1969.

From 1970 to 1973 the Democratic Congress and the Republican President have found themselves increasingly at odds about federal spending. This has led to serious and prolonged disagreements, vetoes, and attempts to veto. This situation reached something of a peak in 1972 when the President twice vetoed appropriations for the Departments of Health, Education and Welfare, and of Labor for fiscal year 1973. As a consequence, those two departments never received appropriations but existed throughout the entire fiscal year on the basis of continuing resolutions passed by the Congress. This is not good public management, and led to more uncertainty than usual within those bureaucracies. It is difficult to convince bureaucrats that they should be concerned with cost factors and with measuring outputs when their leadership and Congress cannot even agree on the value or content of the department's program in a whole fiscal year.

Apart from any considerations of managerial efficiency, or disagreements with the President, members of the House and Senate Appropriations Committees have their own views as to their roles and what factors should determine their pace.[2] Former House Appropriations Chairman Clarence Cannon used to state publicly that delaying action on appropriations until after the start of the fiscal year had the effect of saving the taxpayers money because agencies and departments receiving increases would have less time to spend the money. He underestimated the capacity of the bureaucracy to consume resources.

The Record of Budgetary Reform in the Congress

If Congress takes seriously Executive Branch efforts to set more specific objectives and evaluate its effectiveness, it will have not only to improve the timeliness of its budgetary deliberations but also to accept the potential change in power over appropriations. The distribution of influence over the budgets has had a colorful history. Early in the nation's history, the House Ways and Means Committee handled both revenue and appropriations legislation. The first Appropriations Committee was established in 1865, and by 1885 there were sixteen different committees—eight in each House—empowered to appropriate funds.

Budget procedures were not much better in the Executive Branch, and the Budget and Accounting Act of 1921 was the first legislation to require that the President submit a coordinated executive budget. The law created the Bureau of the Budget to help the President, and the General Accounting Office to aid the Congress by auditing the Executive Branch. It also established the present system of separate authorization and appropriations procedures, with separate committees responsible for each of those processes.[3]

Committees that could become knowledgeable and specialized in the programs of particular departments and agencies were established. These committees assumed responsibility for authorizing money, that is, deciding which proposed programs were to be pursued, and setting a ceiling on appropriations for them.

Table 13-1

Date Representative Department and Agency Appropriations signed by the President[a] (by Congress and Fiscal Year)

Department	85-2 1959	86-1 1960	86-2 1961	87-1 1962	87-2 1963	88-1 1964	88-2 1965	89-1 1966	89-2 1967	90-1 1968	90-2 1969	91-1 1970	91-2 1971	92-1 1972	92-2 1973
Dept. of Agriculture[b]	June 13, 58	July 8, 59	June 29, 60	July 26, 61	Oct. 24, 62	Dec. 30, 63	Sept. 2, 64	Nov. 2, 65	Sept. 7, 66	Oct. 24, 67	Aug. 8, 68	Nov. 26, 69	Dec. 22, 70	July 30, 71	Aug. 22, 72
Dept. of Defense	Aug. 22, 58	Aug. 18, 59	July 7, 60	Aug. 17, 61	Aug. 9, 62	Oct. 17, 63	Aug. 19, 64	Sept. 29, 65	Oct. 15, 66	Sept. 29, 67	Oct. 17, 68	Dec. 29, 69	Jan. 11, 71	Dec. 18, 71	Oct. 26, 72
Dept. of Housing & Urban Develop.[c]	Aug. 28, 58	Sept. 14, 59	July 12, 60	Aug. 17, 61	Oct. 3, 62	Dec. 19, 63	Aug. 30, 64	Aug. 16, 65	Sept. 6, 66	Nov. 3, 67	Oct. 4, 68	Nov. 26, 69	Dec. 17, 70	Aug. 10, 71	Aug. 14, 72
Dept. of Interior	June 4, 58	June 23, 59	May 13, 60	Aug. 3, 61	Aug. 9, 62	July 26, 63	July 7, 64	June 28, 65	May 31, 66	June 24, 67	July 25, 68	Oct. 29, 69	July 31, 70	Aug. 10, 71	Aug. 10, 72
Depts. of Labor & Health, Education and Welfare[d]	Aug. 1, 58	Aug. 14, 59	Sept. 2, 60	Sept. 22, 61	Aug. 14, 62	Oct. 11, 63	Sept. 19, 64	Aug. 31, 65	Nov. 7, 66	Nov. 8, 67	Oct. 11, 68	March 5, 70	Jan. 11, 71	Aug. 10, 71	*
Depts. of Post Office & Treasury[e]	March 28, 58	Aug. 11, 59	June 30, 60	Aug. 21, 61	Aug. 6, 62	June 13, 63	Aug. 1, 64	June 30, 65	June 29, 66	July 7, 67	June 19, 68	Sept. 29, 69	Sept. 26, 70	July 9, 71	June 30, 72
Depts. of State & Justice[f]	June 30, 58	July 13, 59	Aug. 31, 60	Sept. 21, 61	Oct. 18, 62	Dec. 30, 63	Aug. 31, 64	Sept. 2, 65	Nov. 8, 66	Nov. 8, 67	Aug. 8, 68	Dec. 24, 69	Oct. 21, 70	Oct. 5, 71	Oct. 25, 72
Dept. of Commerce[g]	June 25, 58	July 13, 59	May 13, 60	Aug. 3, 61	Oct. 18, 62	Dec. 30, 63	Aug. 31, 64	Sept. 2, 65	Nov. 8, 66	Nov. 8, 67	Aug. 8, 68	Dec. 24, 69	Oct. 21, 70	Oct. 5, 71	Oct. 25, 72
Dept. of Transportation[h]										Oct. 23, 67	Aug. 8, 68	Dec. 26, 69	**	Aug. 10, 71	Aug. 22, 72
NASA[i]	Aug. 27, 58	Sept. 1, 59	July 12, 60	Aug. 17, 61	Oct. 3, 62	Dec. 19, 63	Aug. 30, 64	Aug. 16, 65	Sept. 6, 66	Nov. 8, 67	July 3, 68	Nov. 26, 69	July 2, 70	Aug. 10, 71	Aug. 14, 72

AECi	Aug. 25, 72	July 9, 71	June 2, 70	Dec. 11, 69	Nov. 20, 67	Oct. 15, 66	Oct. 28, 65	Aug. 30, 64	Dec. 31, 63	Oct. 24, 62	Sept. 30, 61	Sept. 2, 60	Aug. 18, 59	Aug. 27, 58
Foreign Aid *** *****	Dec. 21, 70	Feb. 9, 70	Oct. 17, 68	Jan. 2, 68	Aug. 12, 68	Oct. 15, 66	Oct. 20, 65	Oct. 7, 64	Jan. 6, 64	Oct. 23, 62	Sept. 30, 61	Sept. 2, 60	Sept. 28, 59	Aug. 28, 58

a The actual number of appropriation bills has varied from 12 to 16 in this period as various agencies have been considered in separate or combined bills as a result of organizational changes in either the Executive Branch or the Congress. The total number of appropriation bills in any session would include supplemental appropriations and a variety of smaller appropriations for executive and legislative agencies, as well as special appropriations such as those for the District of Columbia.

b Appropriations for the Department of Agriculture have included funds for the Environmental and Consumer Protection Agencies since fiscal year 1972.

c HUD became a separate department in 1966, but it is still included in the Independent Offices Appropriations Act. The dates prior to establishment of HUD are based on dates for its predecessor agency Housing and Home Finance Agency, which was also included in the Independent Office Appropriations Act.

d Labor and HEW appropriations have been in the same bill since fiscal year 1955.

e Post Office Department and Treasury Department appropriations have been in the same bill throughout this period. The Post Office Department became the U.S. Postal Service in 1971.

f State Department and Justice Department have been in the same bill throughout this period.

g For fiscal years 1959 through 1961 Commerce Department appropriations were a separate bill. In fiscal year 1962 Commerce was combined with others in the General Government Matters Appropriation bill. Since fiscal year 1963 it has been in the same bill with the State and Justice Departments.

h Prior to fiscal year 1968, the Federal Aviation Agency was funded through the Independent Offices Appropriation bill. Other components transferred to the Department of Transportation include the U.S. Coast Guard (formerly in the Treasury) and the Federal Highway Administration (formerly the Bureau of Public Roads of the Commerce Department).

i NASA is normally included in the Independent Offices appropriation bill. In fiscal years 1968, 1969 and 1970 it was a separate bill. In fiscal years 1959 and 1960 it was part of a supplemental appropriations bill.

j The Atomic Energy Commission appropriations for fiscal year 1959 were included under the Supplemental Appropriations Act of 1959. In fiscal year 1960 it was a separate bill. Since fiscal year 1961 it has received its appropriations under the Public Works bill, which was retitled the Public Works and Atomic Energy Commission Appropriations bill in 1968. However, it was a separate bill in fiscal 1971.

* No law, vetoed twice

** Tabled never signed

*** No appropriation. Operated under continuing resolutions in fy 73

**** March, 8 1972, over presidential veto.

Source: Thomas P. Murphy, "Congress, PPBS, and Reality," *Polity*, Vol. 1, No 4, 1969; *Congressional Record*, 1969–73.

Under the new law, a single appropriations committee was established within the House and Senate, with authority to act on all appropriations. One of the aspirations of those responsible for the change was that having one appropriations committee with centralized responsibility would lead to improved congressional coordination of the appropriation process. While appropriations were centralized under the revamped system, new battles took place in the separately organized authorization committees. In addition, the subcommittees of the Appropriations Committees also developed considerable autonomy, so that the desired effect was not achieved.[4]

Under the present system, the Executive Branch puts together an integrated national budget, which the President presents to Congress with his annual Budget Message. However, when the budget reaches the Congress it loses its comprehensive character. It is introduced for action in the form of a number of authorization bills referred to the substantive or authorization committees having jurisdiction, and later, in the form of approximately fourteen appropriations bills, it is considered by the twelve subcommittees of the House Appropriations Committee. These authorization and appropriation bills are considered at varying rates of speed and at different levels of detail. Some appropriations are approved early in the year before it is known what the total budget figure approved by Congress will be. Others are held until later in the year and may receive disproportionately large cuts because of some event that occurred in the interim period necessitating a reduction in the total federal budget.

One attempt to revise the procedures was the Omnibus Appropriations resolution, introduced in 1947 and finally approved in 1949. In 1950 an Omnibus Appropriations bill, under which all appropriations were to be considered as one bill rather than as a separate and unrelated series of bills, passed both the House and Senate and was signed into law on September 6, 1950. The following year, however, a revolt developed within the House Appropriations Committee, and the majority of the membership refused to use the omnibus procedures. The reason clearly was that the bill centered too much power in the hands of the aged committee chairmen. Since that time, there has been no omnibus appropriation bill; the appropriations subcommittees have returned to managing their own discrete bills for the agencies under their supervision.[5]

This particular reaction is most relevant to the consideration of Planned Program Budgeting Systems (PPBS). The revolt against the omnibus appropriation procedure was led by the subcommittee chairmen because they lost power under the system which forced all decisions to the top in the person of the chairman. Speaking loosely, the Omnibus Appropriations bill did for the chairman relative to subcommittee chairmen much the same thing that PPBS was to do later for Robert McNamara relative to the military chiefs of staff. To the extent that the analogy holds, congressmen might be expected to have resisted PPBS for some of the same reasons that military leaders and civilian bureau chiefs resisted it—as a diminution of their authority.

Attempts to solve budgetary problems by procedural changes designed to produce comprehensive treatment of the budget have also been unsuccessful. The Legislative Reorganization Act of 1946 contained a section which created a Joint Committee on the Legislative Budget. The Joint Committee was to be composed of the total membership of both House and Senate Appropriations Committees, as well as the two committees responsible for revenue measures—The House Ways and Means Committee and the Senate Finance Committee. This Joint Committee was to meet early each session, and provide by February 15 a "ceiling on appropriations and a ceiling on expenditures, which were then intended to be binding on the work of the appropriations committee during the remainder of the session."[6] The committee was never established. In 1947 the Senate amended the resolution that was reported by the Joint Committee, and the two houses never agreed on how to settle the difference. In 1948 they agreed on a maximum figure for the budget, but the appropriations committees exceeded the maximum and were upheld by both houses. The system was then dropped.

Later the Senate agreed to the establishment of a Joint Committee on the Budget with a strong staff to study appropriations in detail, but in six separate sessions the House refused to take action because this would reduce its traditional exclusive power to initiate appropriation bills.[7] The plain fact is that procedural changes or organizational gimmicks that affect the power balance in terms of who controls allocation decisions have not been made acceptable to the Congress.

However, as the appropriations legislation is passed later and later in the fiscal year criticism has become more strident, and Congress has begun to move slowly toward reform of its handling of the federal budget. This fact can be seen in the Legislative Reorganization Act of 1970, which was a small but important step in the overall congressional method of handling the federal budget. Various congressional committees have held hearings and in one way or another considered the inability of the Congress to take a centralized, comprehensive view of the budget.

The establishment of the Joint Study Committee on the Budget in 1972 (P.L. 92-599) seems to be the most serious effort to date to reestablish the "powers of the purse" in the Congress. The Joint Committee on Budget Control is co-chaired by Representatives Jamie Whitten of the House Appropriations Committee and Al Ullman of the House Ways and Means Committee. Senators John McClellan and Russell B. Long are co-vice chairmen, representing the Senate Appropriations and Finance Committees respectively.

The Committee held hearings in 1973 and introduced H. R. 1730. The House passed the bill by a vote of 386 to 23 in December 1973. In essence the bill recommends that a Committee of the Budget be established in each House with the power to oversee and review the total federal budget as one decision process. In the report accompanying this bill the Joint Committee on Budget Control outlines the procedures these budget committees would use in overseeing the progress of the federal budget through the authorization and appropriating processes.

In summary, these budget committees would be empowered: (1) to establish overall limitations on budget outlays and new obligational authority; (2)

to direct the taxation committees to raise or lower taxes and debt limitation in line with the spending limits; (3) to allocate budget outlay and new budget authority to other standing committees and, after receiving recommendations from the committees, subdivide the allocations to these committees by program area or along the lines of the committees' subcommittees; and (4) to channel all budget outlays for new programs through the Appropriations Committees (except for trust funds created by new taxes). Provision is made for a wrap-up appropriations bill to take care of spending changes made during the year, and under certain conditions, a tax surcharge bill to cover budget deficits. Concurrent resolutions from the budget committees would be subject to floor amendments, but if an amendment called for increased spending the sponsor would have to designate the source of funds to support it. This "rule of consistency," plus a proposal barring amendments to the limitations on budget outlays and new budget authority from any legislation except budget committees' resolutions, make the proposed budget committees very powerful.[8]

The report also recommends closer relationship between the authorization and appropriations processes. The authorization of funds has become a drawn out process (as illustrated in table 13-1) and consequently agencies are not receiving funds until later and later in the fiscal year. The Joint Committee also recommended that multiyear advance appropriations be made in response to the need for long-range requirements and certainty of financing required for instance by state and local governments and by receivers of grants-in-aid programs. The bill also acknowledges the difficulty of Congress making final decisions by June 30, and so proposes starting the fiscal year on October 1 instead of July 1.

Congress and PPBS

"Brainstorming" the question of what an ideal resource allocation system is supposed to achieve might well produce the following list of items as especially helpful in budgeting as well as in evaluating management performance:

1. Facilitate the measurement of the *total* cost of accomplishing defined objectives;
2. Allow comparison of alternative ways of performing a function;
3. Identify future cost implications of the alternatives;
4. Provide a means of comparing cost inputs and achievement outputs;
5. Spell out objectives in such a way that cost utility and cost benefit analyses can be applied;
6. Aggregate related expenditures wherever they might occur in the government's administrative structure.[9]

Relating these budgetary objectives to the characteristics of the control, performance, and planning budgets, it is apparent that for large and complicated programs, only the planning budget can provide or make full use of the data necessary for an ideal budget.

Almost twenty years ago Edward Banfield described the budget process that until recently accurately applied:

Under present practice, the federal budget is hardly more than an accumulation of bits and pieces gathered up from the various bureaus. Each bit or piece is designed, at least in the main elements of its structure, by use and wont, by the pressure of special interests, and by decisions of bureau chiefs—decisions which, while by no means capricious, are for the purpose of national budgeting often, perhaps generally, irrational. That the bits and pieces which come from the bureaus are examined, sometimes reshaped, and to some degree arranged and assorted by cabinet officers, the Budget Bureau, the President, and the Congress does not alter their essentially discrete and unsystematic character.[10]

PPBS was not merely a different approach or technique for putting together a budget. Rather than merely shifting emphasis or the locus of management evaluation, it demanded substantive reorganization and the reshaping of analytical procedures. Programs could be revised, but not by convenient incremental techniques customarily used—taking 5 or 10 percent from here or there on the assumption that budgets are always padded in anticipation of cuts. Under a truly functioning PPBS system, a 5 percent cut would have substantially affected the outputs of one or more programs, or perhaps caused a different alternative to be selected to achieve the organization's objective.

The implications of PPBS went far beyond the internal effects of the system. As different budgetary decisions were reached, with knowledge of their implications for a future period of time, functions of the federal government over that period of time and well into the future were being simultaneously defined. This process would not be easily subject to logrolling and other political tactics traditional in the federal system, especially in the legislative branch. This is why the Congress viewed PPBS with very mixed emotions.

When Robert McNamara went to the Congress each year with the Department of Defense (DOD) budget, he did not present the program budget that was utilized internally by DOD. Instead the DOD staff recast the program budget along the lines to which Congress had become accustomed. After Congress finished its review of the budget, DOD then translated Congress's actions and decisions back into the program budget for implementation.

The incompatibility of PPBS approaches with traditional practices of legislative oversight was considerable. What contrast could be more abrupt than to envision McNamara going to Congress to testify on a budget that had been developed by an interdisciplinary team of economists, management analysts, and systems and mathematical modeling specialists trained in the techniques of cost-benefit analysis, and to find sitting on the other side of the table members of the Congress not even willing to examine the document on a program basis? In 1967, for instance, Congress refused to appropriate funds for several agencies, including the State, Treasury, and Post Office Departments, to implement PPBS inside the agencies. A Congress still concerned with personal prerogatives and pork-barrel politics would be understandably slow to adopt the program budgeting approach.

Each year as part of its consideration of authorization and appropriation bills, Congress demands to know how the line item cuts of the previous year were effected. Budget officials from the Executive Branch found themselves in the difficult position of explaining how a particular congressional decision was converted into a program budget with the resulting fiscal and program impact.

Richard Fenno explains why the Congress and more particularly the powerful House Appropriations Committee would never be fully converted to PPBS as promulgated by the executive side of the federal government.

One of the most important powers that the Congress holds is the power to appropriate funds for the operation of the federal government. This power of the purse is the key to the institutional power of the House of Representatives and the single most serious blow to the House as an institution and the Congress as a whole would be to reduce that power.[11]

Within the House, the appropriations decisions are made by the Appropriations Committee, whose recommendations are accepted in nine out of ten cases. Within this committee there are a dozen subcommittees, each with jurisdiction over a significant department of the Executive Branch. Their recommendations to the full committee are seldom challenged.

Fenno outlined what he believes are the characteristics of these powerful congressmen, why the appropriations system is what it is, and how it solves the individual career aspirations of the Appropriations Committee members as well as the institutional goals of the House of Representatives.

Each member has a view of the public interest which he seeks to implement through service in Congress. Like the rest of us . . . He favors certain programs, opposes others and in general tries to implement his set of values through legislation.

He wants to make a career in the Congress, thus he wants to be re-elected to further both his career and his version of the public interest. This desire for re-election, as we know, keeps him reasonably responsive to the wishes of his constituents. . . .

He not only wants a career in the Congress but he wants to be an influential member of the House. He wants power inside the House and it is this desire that led him to the Appropriations Committee in the first place. This desire for inside power distinguishes the members of the Appropriations Committee from the other members of the House. . . .

Finally the necessary condition for meeting these three individual goals is that the Appropriations Committee be powerful.

If the committee is influential as a collectivity, the individual member will be influential—or so, at least the members believe. . . .

To their colleagues in the House, Appropriations Committee members argue that the power of the House of Representatives depends heavily on the power of the Appropriations Committee. . . . This is accepted by and large by most members.[12]

Given these factors, it is easy to understand why the Congress was unlikely ever to wholeheartedly adopt PPBS. Briefly outlined here are what Richard Fenno considers the important characteristics of the existing appropriations system that Banfield scornfully castigates:

1. Committee members support almost all of the ongoing programs of the federal government. Their view of the public interest does not vary greatly from the national consensus that supports most existing programs. They are sensitive to changes in public support and register those changes in their appropriations decisions.

2. The Appropriations Committee makes incremental additions or subtractions to ongoing programs and does not make wholesale reallocations of national resources.

3. Within the larger budgetary and appropriations sequence which extends back into the executive branch and forward to the Senate, the House Appropriations Committee conceives of its job as that of guarding the federal treasury by eliminating all unnecessary federal spending. They must reduce executive budget estimates wherever possible.

4. Appropriations subcommittee members develop a great deal of expertise concerning executive agencies for which they appropriate funds.

5. Once a decision has been reached within a subcommittee the members stand together in support of the decision.

6. Appropriations Committee members believe that their control over the executive branch is exercised not only by their formal control over budget requests, but by the fact that executives anticipate committee reaction in drawing up their budget requests. It is this anticipated reaction that is especially important. Committees members believe that someone must let the executive bureaucracy know they are being watched. They believe that they are equipped to do this.[13]

The key question is, What kind of information do members of the House Appropriations Committee need to act, and what kind of information do other congressmen and senators need for their decisions? They cannot possibly know all there is to know about the activities of the various federal agencies they oversee. Unable to undertake a comprehensive analysis of agency programs, they make their decisions on the basis of what Fenno calls the "sampling process."[14] Decision making is based on sampling (in a very limited way) aspects of agency behavior and drawing inferences from those samples about total agency performance.

There are three kinds of information that committee members look for: program information, confidence information, and support information. They want to know about agency programs to see if these programs accord with their view of the public interest and to assess how effective these programs are. Confidence information, on the other hand, concerns the agency or department itself. Members want to know if they can believe what an agency administrator is telling them at a hearing. They want to know if he will do what he says he will do. So they sample for information that will determine the degree of confidence they can have in an agency by sizing up an administrator at hearings; by asking detailed and specific questions of witnesses to see if they know their jobs; by checking agency performance against last year's promises and committee directives. If they are not satisfied, they remain extraordinarily suspicious. "Confidence is the cumulative product of countless interchanges, formal and informal, between committee and agency personnel over extended periods of time."[15]

The third kind of information desired by the members of the Appropriations Committee, support information, pertains to the size, shape, and intensity of outside support for agency programs. Questions such as who is affected by the program; who is helped or hurt by the program; and the intensity of the opposition and the support for the program are important to the members. Answers provide valuable political information. Members sample their constituents, look for disagreement among officials in the Executive Branch, and in general keep their eyes open for any hint that might provide them with information on programs. This informal and highly refined method of doing business has served the purposes of the House Appropriations Committee well over the years. New budget theories developed in the executive branch of the federal government face an uphill battle to infiltrate the tried and proven methods used by the members.

Systems-oriented managers believe it is more appropriate for Congress to discuss program content than object expenditures, i.e. travel, personnel, and equipment. As it stands now, they can never be sure whether they will be questioned about object expenditures or program content. This leaves them at a certain disadvantage. From the manager's standpoint, much of this uncertainty would be reduced if he could structure his conversations along the lines of program content. Then the manager would have the upper hand in determining where he will go in his testimony before the Appropriations Committee. Congressmen tend to view PPBS as giving the manager this strategic upper hand in the annual battle of the budget.

Allen Schick and Richard Fenno agree that if PPBS were ever adopted great disparity would exist in its use by the Executive and Legislative branches. The President and program officials are willing to disclose the *outcomes* of their analyses and plans—that is, the programs to be funded in the budget—but they are reluctant to reveal the alternatives that were considered and rejected, the analytic calculations that underlie their policy decisions, or the future costs of their decisions. Congress, however, is as much interested in the alternatives as in the policies, and it looks to analyses and projections as a means of challenging the executive program and budget recommendations.

Fenno believes that PPBS would in no way change the traditional methods by which the House Appropriations Committee does business. It would be very useful if the Appropriations Committee looked at both program and administrative budgets. This would enable them to view the alternatives and the reasoning behind the selected programs, and give them another "uncertainty-reducing" device upon which to base their decisions.[16]

Congress has not totally ignored PPBS. The 1970 Legislative Reorganization Act calls for restructuring budget classifications throughout the federal government for budget purposes. It also mandates five-year cost estimates for new programs, and directs the Comptroller General to review and analyze the results of government programs and activities carried on under existing law.

Although Congress tends to pay lip service to its own mandates, there are signs that some are taking them seriously. For instance, the Family Planning Service and Population Research Act of 1970 delineates the types of information that Congress now wants. Section five of this act might have been written for an executive PPBS system:

It calls for a five year plan specifying the number of individuals to be served along with program goals and costs as well as annual reports which compare results achieved during the preceding fiscal year with the objectives established under the plan which indicate steps being taken to achieve the objectives of the plan.[17]

Otto Davis, an economist, has argued that in fact "Congress has not had any control over the budgetary process if one interprets control in any way other than following what the executive proposed."[18] After exhaustively studying appropriations patterns from 1948–63, Davis could predict annual budgets mathematically based solely on "creeping incrementalism." He argues that PPBS is an opportunity for Congress to regain (or *gain*) control over the budget, if only it develops the capability to evaluate objectives and long-term plans within the PPBS format. The success of New Politics program objectives depends upon Congress's ability to develop these talents.

In hearings before a Senate subcommittee on PPBS in 1969, Comptroller General Elmer Staats suggested three ways in which Congress could gear itself up to handle the new program approval process:

1. Retrain present congressional staff personnel, hire some additional people trained in analytic techniques, and/or rely on outside consultants at least until competent in-house personnel could be secured;
2. Make a greater effort to point out program issues at an earlier point in time rather than waiting for a hearing so that agencies could prepare more responsive budget presentations;
3. Encourage the United States General Accounting Office (GAO) to develop the capability to analyze PPBS budgets for the Congress.[19]

On this last point Staats had earlier stated that GAO should move from the prime role of auditor to one of cost-benefit analyzer, and suggested that such analysis should occur *prior* to passage of legislation rather than ex post facto. In this way, GAO would be drawn into the legislative process of analyzing programs while they are still being considered.

These considerations were fully discussed and reported to the Joint Committee on the Organization of Congress.[20] GAO did acquire the mandate from Congress to perform cost-benefit analysis of federal programs in the Legislative Reorganization Act of 1970. Congress intended that GAO would be used "in analyzing cost benefit studies furnished by any federal agency to

Senate and House committees, and in conducting cost benefit studies of programs under the jurisdiction of such committees."[21]

GAO also received a mandate to develop, establish, and maintain classification of programs, activities, receipts, and expenditures of federal agencies in order to meet the needs of the various branches of government; and to facilitate the development, establishment, and maintenance of the data processing system required under Section 201 of the 1970 Reorganization Act. GAO was to do this in conjunction with the Office of Management and Budget and the Department of the Treasury. However, the Comptroller General testified in 1973 before the Senate Subcommittee on Budgeting Management and Expenditure that while the classification of programs was necessary, it should be done by the Executive Branch. GAO can and does identify the needs of the Legislative Branch and will continue to do so, but the Comptroller General felt that it was beyond their capability to perform the classification as stated in the 1970 Reorganization Act.[22]

GAO has greatly expanded its program evaluation, and in his testimony Mr. Staats outlined the reasons why the GAO should be the sole evaluator. The problems involved in program evaluation are many and complicated. GAO has been slowly but surely solving them, and in the process developing highly specialized staff for such work. It is in this role that GAO best can serve the Congress and give it the information it needs to make decisions in the authorization and appropriations process.

The traditions of the Congress do not enshrine efficiency as a criterion for decisions. As Richard Fenno said, congressmen bring highly personal reasons to play in their decisions concerning appropriations. Positions on the Appropriations Committee are often sought for the specific purpose of being able to support projects and programs in which the member's district has vested interests. Such interests are not easily dissipated in the name of general schemes of efficiency or cost effectiveness. Budgetary decisions are still going to be made by political figures for political reasons within the context of our political system. This factor has led some to question whether any efforts to help Congress would serve less to enable Congress to participate effectively in a new decision-making process than to teach it how to pervert PPBS to support the more narrow interests that some Congressmen are inclined to emphasize. There is no easy answer. Perhaps the solution lies in keeping both sides knowledgeable as to the options available. Then those in either camp who are willing to work for national objectives will be able to maintain the floodlights on the deliberations and the basis for the decisions.

The challenge to administrators, journalists, and others whose role is to inform and assist the electorate in making good decisions is to make it good politics for a congressman to support a sound budgetary decision. The issue presented them is the need to find a modus vivendi that will make it possible for the administrator to do a professional job, and at the same time for the legislator to accomplish his representational and political objectives within the context of a rational budgetary decision-making system.

Meanwhile, PPBS, as it was promulgated by the Secretary of Defense Robert McNamara, is being replaced by what the Nixon Administration calls Management by Objectives (MBO). Essentially it represents a retreat from the comprehensive PPBS approach to a scaled-down version with more limited objectives. As presently touted by the Office of Management and Budget (OMB), MBO involves setting specific objectives for the federal agencies which will have the cumulative effect of satisfying the broad objectives of the President's program. OMB hopes that by spelling out objectives, and following up on the federal agencies' performance in terms of these objectives, it can eliminate the vast quantities of paperwork that eventually caused the demise of the larger-scale PPBS approach.

Development of Information Technology

Besides discussing the application of PPBS technology to budgeting, Congress has finally entered the computer age in other respects as well. With the introduction of the Electronic Voting System (EVS) in the House of Representatives and the work now being done in the development of information systems, Congress, particularly the House, has decided to utilize the electronic monsters for its own operational benefit. Currently twelve committees in the House and two in the Senate are using computer terminals in their offices to prepare current "on line" calendars. All Congressional committees and clerks are cooperating in the Bill Status System designed by the House Information Systems (H.I.S.) staff. This system will become fully operational in 1974 throughout the entire Congress. The Bill Status System is designed to track bills through more than 120 possible steps in the legislative process.

Another significant development is the new computer system being designed to assist the Parliamentarian in compiling a current volume of the precedents of the House. The system will have the capability of text editing and composition and so allow continual updating.

On a more select basis various committees have been utilizing the computer. For instance, the H.I.S. staff analyzed the welfare program data for the Fiscal Policy Subcommittee of the Joint Economic Subcommittee. They also undertook a study of the total information system requirements for the House Committee on Banking and Currency, and a study of analytical procedures such as modeling and simulation with the Joint Committee on Internal Revenue Taxation.

In the Senate, the Subcommittee on Computer Services of the Committee on Rules and Administration has installed computer terminals in six members' offices in a pilot project providing content and status information on legislation. The Congressional Research Services (CRS) of the Library of Congress is providing congressional committees and other congressional clientele with a "current-awareness" notification of recent literature acquisitions from a computerized file. The CRS is testing a special videoscreen connection to the New York Times Information Bank, which will give the Congress access to a vast data file, including some seventy newspapers and magazines from 1971 to the present. The CRS is also developing an "online" issue briefing that will provide current, concise information on more than two-hundred issues, which will be accessible to members via computer terminal. This could be the most important use of the computer for the members.

The House Information Systems staff, which has all the data-processing activities in the House under its control, has been far more successful in developing information systems support for the House than its counterparts in the Senate. Senate development has been slowed because there is no centralization of effort. Presently the responsibilities are split between the Senate Committee on Rules and Administration, the Secretary of the Senate, and the Sergeant at Arms. In September 1973, Wayne Hays, Chairman of the House Administration Committee and the congressman most responsible for the establishment of the H.I.S. staff in April 1971, and Senator Howard Cannon, Chairman of the Senate Rules Committee, announced that they were proceeding with a joint development of a congressional bill status system. This system should combine the best elements of the systems being developed by the H.I.S. staff and the Senate Subcommittee on Computer Services, which has been working in cooperation with the CRS.

Congress has decided to keep the development of information systems in-house, in lieu of letting the GAO or the CRS develop the systems. Both the House and Senate will most likely develop sizable central information services staffs to service the committees and members.

However, with all these impressive advances, the Congress has not solved the most pressing problem of all, the need for fiscal and budgetary information to support the development of congressional budget ceilings and program allocations. Dr. John S. Saloma thinks that there is a possibility that Congress may foolishly attempt to make radical changes in the budget process and its own committee system without first building such an information base.[23]

Another major deficiency is the lack of information support for the legislative oversight or review function. Presently the staff of the H.I.S., in cooperation with the Committees on House Appropriations and Banking and Currency, is attempting to define precise information requirements and suitable formats in these areas, but it may take several Congresses to have a noticeable effect on committee operations.

Saloma also points to the disappointment with the PPBS approach as one setback to the development of congressional information technology. Reforms in the executive budget which promised to give the Congress better information and incentive to build its own analytical staff have not materialized, because the Executive Branch has not had the data or the analytic capability.[24] The sophisticated computer modeling for social policy has not developed as rapidly as projected, but everyone is hopeful that with the strides being taken in the Congress today in the development of information systems, plus the move toward reform in the overseeing of the federal budget PPBS as originally envisioned, might return.

The Next Steps

When the Senate Subcommittee on National Security and International Operations opened its hearings on PPBS in 1967, it issued a memorandum that seems to provide a cogent summary of the prevailing congressional attitude. It stated:

Congress too, may not welcome all the implications of PPBS.

The experience to date does not suggest that the Department of Defense is likely to place before Congressional committees the analyses of costs and benefits of competing policies and programs on which the Department based its own choices. Without such comparisons, however, Congress will be in the dark about the reasons for selecting this policy over that. It may be that Congress will wish to improve its own capability for systematic analysis of public problems in order to compete on more even terms with the Executive Branch. Futhermore, the more centralized decision making becomes in the Executive Branch, the more important some competition of this sort from Congress might be. The centralizing bias of PPBS may be more important than the anticipated technical improvements of the budgetary process, because of a lessening of competitive forces within the Executive Branch. . . .If PPBS develops into a contest between experts and politicians it will not be hard to pick the winners. They will be the politicians in the Congress and the White House. It has been said and correctly, that as interesting as observing what happens to government when confronted with PPBS will be watching what happens to PPBS when confronted with government.[25]

How prophetic this memorandum was. The politicians did win in a sense. Members of Congress generally seem to feel that they have learned how to work with the existing budgetary system to achieve their objectives. But there is serious question as to whether the Congress has been able to affect the general trend of the total budgets and programs presented by presidents. Clearly some members of Congress have been more successful in gaining federal programs for their areas. Those who have been less successful have no reason to believe they would be more successful with a new system based on even more objective data. Few members of the Congress have really concerned themselves with the "macro" aspects of the budget.

Much of the difficulty, then, in securing changes in congressional attitudes toward PPBS or MBO is due not to any real consideration of the substantive merits of PPBS, but rather to the degree to which it may threaten members of Congress—even if their perception of their current influence on the process is out of focus. Achieving change in Congress has not been easy in the past. The Legislative Reorganization Act of 1970 was a long time in committee hearings, and full implementation will be slow.

Various committees, particularly the Senate Subcommittee on Government Operations and the Joint Economic Committee under the chairmanship of Senator Proximire, have held hearings and published papers concerning PPBS.[26]

Senator Hugh Scott of Pennsylvania introduced a bill to establish an Office of Program Analysis and Evaluation in Congress, along with a Joint Committee of Congress on Programs Analysis and Evaluation. In his statement introducing the bill, Senator Scott told the Senate:

As the Nation's complex problems—such as poverty, housing, urban blight, transportation, pollution, and health—continue to increase, the annual budget increases in size and complexity.

Congress has the responsibility of evaluating and appropriating the funds requested in the budget. The individual requests are considered by the various congressional committees and finally by the Appropriations Committees. However, Congress does not have the means to make an overall evaluation of the total budget structure, or to keep tabs on all the programs for which it votes to spend taxpayers' money, from the standpoint of priorities, duplication, and cost effectiveness.

My bill would provide a permanent, professional staff to assist in determining what we can afford, what must come first, where overlap can be eliminated, and how to get the most out of each dollar spent.[27]

The Scott bill was considered but never enacted. However, some action along the lines he suggested will eventually occur. "Crosswalks" of total agency budgets will become as outmoded in the budget process as green eyeshades have become in auditing and accounting. This is not to suggest that PPBS removes the need for controls. At lower management levels performance and workload data will still be related to the old object class categories for control and evaluation purposes.

If Congress is to consider the budget both in program terms and in line-item terms, as Fenno suggests, then it will need new staff mechanisms to enable it to participate. The GAO and the Legislative Reference Service, now upgraded and renamed the Congressional Reference Service, are being utilized more and more by Congressional committees to supply needed information. Over time the GAO, which *is* a legislative agency, has been upgraded from an audit and deficiency-control agency to one with the capability of conducting comprehensive management evaluations. It has offices throughout the nation, so it can easily make site verifications of questionable inputs from the executive branch. GAO has been expanding its operations and acquiring large numbers of interdisciplinary specialists who are teaming up with professional accounting staff to do the job that is required for program-budgeting decision-making.

A fully implemented Planned Program Budgeting System in terms of what was intended when McNamara first began to preach the word has been sidestepped for the time being, but the revolution has begun, and the scaled-down version—MBO—is an acknowledgment that setting national goals and keeping the agencies in line with those goals is the way government should be run.

Congress, if and when it reforms itself internally—and all indications are that it will soon—will be more involved than ever in the budgeting process. Its interest in program budgeting is growing, and is becoming more and more acceptable.

The present situation looks more hopeful now that Congress has begun to grapple with measures to reform its handling of the federal budget, and to regain control of backdoor spending and "uncontrollable expenditures." It is to be hoped that the recommendations of the Joint Committee on the Budget will be fully considered before the 93rd Congress becomes history.

The caliber of congressmen and their supporting staffs has been upgraded considerably over the past fifteen years, in response partly to the increased competence of the electorate, partly to increased competition for congressional seats as the two-party system has been extended into new areas, and partly to the New Politics. In turn, the new breed of congressman has resulted in pressures on chairmen who formerly ruled without any consideration of participation by the committee members. Chairman after chairman has been forced to establish subcommittees and permit more democratic committee procedures.[28] That the process has not yet run its full course is evident. If this trend continues it should lead eventually to a disappearance at least of the self-confidence gap in Congress. If the reforms recommended by the Joint Committee on the Budget are even partially implemented, and Congress begins to consider the federal budget in terms of both programs and line items, it will regain some of the power it has acceded to the executive branch. The bureaucrats will have to reconsider their role in the budget-making process considerably.

The application of new techniques in an administrative process that involves political decisions is a complex matter. More is involved than merely harnessing the technology and training of the people who are applying the system. The administrator must also make his peace with the elected legislative representatives of the people. There is no magic in PPBS or in MBO. Effective management utilization of such a budgetary system requires full cooperation from a responsive legislative body which accepts the goals of sound administration as the primary criteria.

14 Geopolitics and Federal Spending

Harold Lasswell's dictum that politics decides "who gets what, when, where, and how" is still true under the New Politics. Ideological and party interests are still important, but there are also regional and geographic interests to be advanced through the political system. In the end, House and Senate members must respond to district and state interests. The congressional appropriations process is an ideal setting for geographical competition as the various districts, states, and regions try to maximize their benefits from federal programs.

The distribution of large sums of federal money, therefore, has a serious geopolitical dimension. The New Politics has had substantial influence on the selection of national priorities and so on—the *purposes* for which money is spent. However, it has not reduced the level of geopolitics involved in deciding *who gets* whatever money is spent for the new priorities.

One of the interesting aspects of the federal system is the fact that governmental initiatives with regard to particular public needs usually come from more than one level of government. In some cases the distribution of federal program money has enabled the state and local governments to reallocate money for public purposes that would otherwise be underfunded. In other cases, the federal money has been conditional upon certain levels of effort or standards of performance by the state or local government, and so has stimulated more state and local government spending.

In some functional areas it is difficult to indicate which level of government is the predominant provider of the service. The federal approach, for example, can range from direct performance of the function to simply financing it through other governments, universities, nonprofit groups, or the private sector. The latter procedure is used most frequently when the federal government has the primary responsibility.

Health care provides a good example of the diversity in roles. The federal government furnishes direct services through the U.S. Public Health Service and the Veterans' Administration. The National Institutes of Health not only perform major research programs, but are also the major source of funds for university research projects and provide substantial services to the private sector for basic research on cancer, heart transplants, and kidney machines. Meanwhile, the U.S. Department of Health, Education and Welfare funnels public assistance to the states, which in turn match some of this money for distribution by their counties and cities. Direct federal medicaid and medicare payments are made to hospitals, doctors, and extended-care facilities.

Another type of federal involvement in health occurs through the U.S. Food and Drug Administration, which regulates pharmaceutical manufacturers. The states play a similar regulatory role through their medical boards, which license physicians, dentists, veterinarians, pharmacists, and other health specialists.

Hospitals are run by cities, counties, and states, as well as by the federal government. And a substantial number of hospitals are nonprofit and are operated by religious organizations. In more recent years doctors and even commercial hospital corporations have been growing rapidly. Since the Hill-Burton Act was passed in 1946, few major hospitals have been built without the assistance of federal funding.

On the other hand, two areas that are almost exclusively federal domain are foreign affairs and defense. The growth of federal expenditures for defense since the beginning of the Korean War is phenomenal. Figure 14-1 indicates that defense expenditures have increased from $13.1 billion in 1950 to $80.6 billion in 1974. While there has been a steady increase in the total dollars expended on defense over this period, defense expenditures as a percentage of total federal spending have been declining since the Korean War, with the exception of 1966-68 during the Vietnam War. Since then the downward trend has continued, and by 1974 it was almost exactly what it was in 1950—about 30 percent. Defense spending was not reduced, but as our national priorities were redefined, it grew more slowly than other governmental programs.

Specifically, New Politics influence has contributed to securing substantial increases in the socioeconomic programs of the federal government, such as housing, health, welfare, and poverty. In addition, the federal government has broken new ground by undertaking substantial financial responsibility in areas like elementary and secondary education and law enforcement, which have long been considered local governmental functions. New federal initiatives have also been taken in transportation, in environmental protection, and more recently in energy development.

Table 14-1 shows the growth in the size of the federal budget and changes in the percentages allocated for defense and nondefense purposes since 1950. The major shift, which occurs in 1965, resulted from a combination of cutbacks in Vietnam defense spending and the initial funding for the Great Society programs. The total effect was a drastic change in the mix of federal expenditures.

Essentially, there are two reasons for the new priorities reflected in the figures. First, the increasing demands for socioeconomic programs have exceeded the ability of local governments to pay for them. Because of the disparities in the capacity of cities in various parts of the nation to fund new urban programs, it has been necessary to turn elsewhere for funding. States were often slow to take aggressive action to relieve the situation, and cities were generally dependent upon the property tax as the major source of funding. At the same time, many of these cities were competing with their suburbs for new development and new jobs. Increasingly, the problems were located in the cities, which lacked the financial capacity to handle them. They were unable to raise new taxes because the existing taxes permitted by most states were regressive and would thus hurt those who needed help or

Figure 14-1

U. S. Defense Expenditures 1950-75

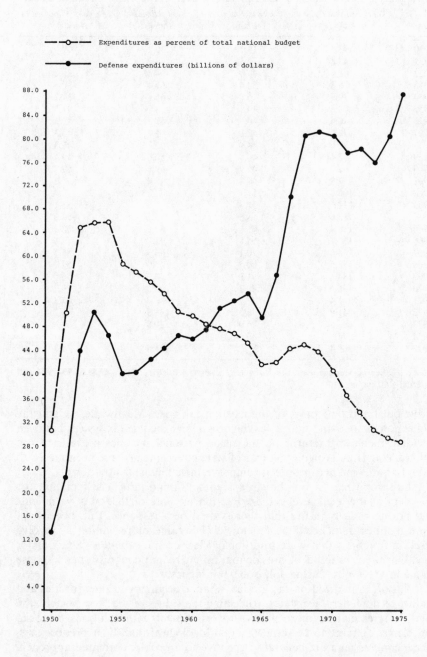

Table 14-1
Relationship of Federal Defense to Nondefense Expenditures

Year	Total Federal Budget (billion)	Defense Budget (billion)	Percent Allocated to Defense	Percent Allocated to Nondefense
1950	43.1	13.1	30.4	69.6
1951	45.8	22.5	49.2	50.8
1952	68.0	44.0	64.8	35.2
1953	76.8	50.4	65.7	34.3
1954	70.9	46.6	65.8	34.2
1955	68.5	40.2	58.7	41.3
1956	70.5	40.3	57.2	42.8
1957	76.7	42.8	55.7	44.3
1958	82.6	44.4	53.7	46.3
1959	92.1	46.6	50.6	49.4
1960	92.2	45.9	49.8	50.2
1961	97.8	47.4	48.4	51.6
1962	106.8	51.1	47.8	52.2
1963	111.3	52.3	46.9	53.1
1964	118.6	53.6	45.2	54.8
1965	118.4	49.6	41.9	58.1
1966	134.7	56.8	42.2	57.8
1967	158.3	70.1	44.3	55.7
1968	178.8	80.5	45.0	55.0
1969	184.5	81.2	44.0	56.0
1970	196.6	80.3	40.8	59.2
1971	211.4	77.7	36.7	63.3
1972	231.9	78.3	33.8	66.2
1973	246.5	76.0	30.8	69.2
1974	274.7	80.6	29.3	70.7
1975	300.4	87.7	28.8	71.2

Source: Office of Management and Budget, *U.S. Budget in Brief, FY75,* U.S. GPO-1974 and internal staff papers.

drive out important parts of the existing tax base. Meanwhile, federal tax collections were rising sharply as the progressive income tax system has been yielding increasing returns on the rising personal incomes prevalent since World War II. A growing number of state governments have been forced to adopt an income tax in order to improve their financial situations.

The second reason for the shift is equally important. The fact that the problem at the local level required action by state or federal governments did not necessarily insure that there would be a response. But, because of New Politics influences, the federal level became more willing to involve itself in functions that were traditionally local responsibilities. These major breakthroughs in terms of presidential initiative and congressional response came in the 1960s, during Johnson's presidency.

Johnson capitalized on the gradual change occurring in the attitudes and values of the federal legislator. Reflecting the values of the New Society, the new congressman is more willing to experiment with solutions to social problems. Tending to be somewhat less ideological than their predecessors, these congressmen are generally receptive to a problem-oriented approach, rather than one based upon artificial standards of states rights or theories of governmental nonintervention in the private sector.

Equity in Federal Grant Programs

Economist Murray Weidenbaum analyzed the impact of selected federal expenditures on the distribution of personal income by regions. He characterized such expenditures as "progressive" (tending to *reduce* inequality in regional income), "proportional," or "regressive" (tending to *increase* inequality in regional income).

He discovered that domestic programs, such as farm price-support payments, aid to education, public assistance, highway grants, and Corps of Engineer projects, were progressive. Regressive impact resulted from expenditures by the National Aeronautics and Space Administration (NASA) and to a lesser extent by the Department of Defense purchases in private industry. "The slightly less regressive overall position of military purchases arises from the inclusion of a large amount of medical, office, ordnance, and similar supplies which are provided by more traditional industries."[1] When the traditional purchases were excluded, Weidenbaum found that "for similar high technology programs, NASA and DOD geographic distribution patterns appear to be quite similar."[2] National competence for large-scale research and development is not evenly distributed across the country; therefore, expenditures tend to be clustered in a relatively few areas, and agencies that award such contracts are vulnerable to charges of inequitable distribution of their funds.

As total federal expenditures have become an increasing proportion of the governmental expenditures in various parts of the nation, it was inevitable that substantial imbalance, if not inequity, would develop in the distribution of those federal funds. On the average, the federal grants have ranged as a percentage of local government expenditures from 2 percent for Honolulu and Sacramento to 133 percent for Providence to 200 percent for Tulsa in fiscal year 1972–73. Table 14-2 documents the responses of other cities to a 1973 survey by the Muskie Subcommittee on Intergovernmental Relations.

In any federal program where funds are to be distributed on the basis of proposals and their evaluation by federal agencies, there is unlikely to be an even distribution of the funds. Indeed, as many federal programs are experimental, it would be unwise to implement such programs in every area of the nation until their value had been demonstrated in a pilot project. The likelihood of success in the demonstration would be directly related to the ability of the city or county receiving the grant. Unfortunately, there is no index of city and county management effectiveness, and agencies must do the best they can to evaluate the quality of the proposals submitted. The problem with that, of course, is that some jurisdictions are more effective than others in *preparing* proposals—yet they may be less capable of performing effectively.

In the discussion in chapter 8 of lobbying for federal programs by cities

Table 14-2
City Funding Provided by Federal Grant Programs in
Selected Cities, 1972-73

City-State	F.Y. 73 Budget (Local Funds Only)—(millions)	Approximate Amount of Federal Assistance— (millions)	Federal Assistance as a Percentage of Local Budget
Tulsa, Okla.	33.8	66.5	200%
South Bend, Ind.	15.8	20.0	125%
Flint, Mich.	7.0	8.6	123%
Cedar Rapids, Iowa	20.5	23.8	116%
Seattle, Wash.	87.5	100.0	115%
Springfield, Mo.	13.5	14.9	114%
Lubbock, Texas	30.1	29.3	97%
Tucson, Ariz.	60.0	57.0	95%
Phoenix, Ariz.	187.0	15.6	62%
Columbus, Ga.	24.4	14.3	58%
Bridgeport, Conn.	67.2	35.0	52%
Norfolk, Va.	131.0	60.0	46%
Oklahoma City, Okla.	39.4	18.2	46%
St. Paul, Minn.	58.9	27.4	46%
Fresno, Calif.	44.4	20.2	45%
Lansing, Mich.	21.0	9.0	42%
Wichita, Kan.	30.3	11.3	37%
Austin, Texas	97.8	32.7	33%
Denver, Colo.	117.6	37.0	32%
Boston, Mass.	243.0	70.0	29%
Cincinnati, Ohio	107.6	31.0	29%
Dallas, Texas	220.0	57.0	26%
Albuquerque, N.M.	64.5	14.9	23%
Montgomery, Ala.	22.9	5.3	23%
Dayton, Ohio	79.1	16.8	21%
San Jose, Calif.	54.0	11.5	21%
Fort Wayne, Ind.	22.7	4.9	21%
Little Rock, Ark.	13.0	2.6	20%
Fort Worth, Texas	68.7	13.3	19%
Youngstown, Ohio	29.0	5.2	18%
Chicago, Ill.	993.6	104.8	16%
San Diego, Calif.	145.0	19.2	13%
Providence, R.I.	76.0	10.0	13%
Savannah, Ga.	21.8	2.3	11%
Portland, Ore.	157.0	14.7	9%
Greensboro, N.C.	40.0	2.8	7%
St. Petersburg, Fla.	39.0	2.8	7%
Elizabeth, N.J.	43.1	2.4	6%
Worcester, Mass.	103.0	6.0	6%
Anaheim, Calif.	50.8	1.4	3%
Honolulu, Hawaii	142.0	2.8	2%
Sacramento, Calif.	60.0	1.4	2%

Source: United States Senate, Committee on Government Operations, Subcommittee on Intergovernmental Relations, *A New Federalism*, Washington, United States Government Printing Office 1973, pp. 514-580.

and counties, it was noted that some cities and counties took a very entrepreneurial approach toward the federal funds. They established Washington offices and took other management steps to enhance their ability to secure program assistance. In contrast, other cities and counties submitted few proposals for consideration.

In any competition where the funding is being provided through federal tax collections, it is obvious that residents of some states will provide more input to the central coffers than they will receive in grants. The political leaders representing these areas must justify that situation to their constituents. They are therefore under pressure to bring about a change in the system so that their jurisdiction would receive a large share of the total funding being provided by the federal government.

Regional arrangements are also beginning to take on greater importance in the federal system in dealing with local social and economic problems. Metropolitan planning commissions and councils of governments, for example, are gaining the power to ensure that regional planning occurs before federal money is made available to city and county governments in their areas. This practice serves to make metropolitan areas more aware of the value of regional cooperation in their attempts to secure a legitimate portion of available federal funds.

As a consequence of these types of pressures, the grant and contract processes of the federal government have evolved. The legislation for many programs calls for distribution of funding on per capita or other automatic formulas that essentially take away from the federal agencies the judgment as to where money for the program should be spent. Even under such formula programs there is room for dispute. Recognizing that some kind of formula must be employed, the issue is which one should be adopted. Under a straight per-capita formula, an area that has a high per-capita income will receive the same amount of funds as one with a low per-capita income. Therefore, the federal government is being used to collect money for local use without any reference to the needs that exist in those different areas. Since many of the federal programs were initiated *because* of the inability of local government to pay for what was needed, this does not make much sense.

On the other hand, having a relatively high per-capita-income level does not mean that a city or county will vote the taxes that such incomes would make feasible. For that reason many federal programs base some payments at least in part on the degree of local tax effort—the amount of taxes raised in a jurisdiction relative to tax potential. Examples include the highway, education, unemployment insurance, manpower assistance, medicare, income maintenance, and public-housing programs.

Federal funding can be a determining factor in the establishment of many state and local programs—as well as in the nature of the benefits to be provided under the program. The federal unemployment insurance program is especially interesting. It is based upon a federal payroll tax, 90 percent of which is used to fund trust accounts for the states establishing such programs. Not surprisingly, they all did. Even if they failed to do so, their contributions would have been used to pay for programs in the other states.

The federal government adds a payment of about 20 percent of the payroll tax, based on the level of benefits the various states establish.[3]

Revenue-Sharing

The general revenue-sharing program developed out of the experience of using grant, contract, and automatic formula payment programs to provide services that state and local governments were not effectively providing. Essentially, general revenue-sharing is another formula approach, except that it has a broad scope and replaces a variety of federal programs with one federal payment.

The nine uses on which general revenue-sharing can be spent by local governments are: public safety, capital improvements, environmental protection, health services, public transportation, recreation, financial administration, social services, and libraries. Local governments are prohibited from using revenue-sharing funds to reduce taxes by maintaining the same service levels but employing the new revenue to *replace* tax dollars previously collected. Revenue-sharing funds are also not usable as matching money for other federal government programs.

Revenue-sharing is not only a formula for distribution of federal monies; it is also based upon a different management philosophy—namely, that the local governments are in a better position than any federal agency to determine what their priorities ought to be. This element of political decentralization was very significant to the local governments. For example, under the previous formula programs, a government might stand a good chance of securing a federal grant for new sewers, but often its greatest need was to purchase park land and no money was available for that. Under revenue-sharing, local governments can establish their own priorities, and apply the money where it is needed.

The final formula that Congress approved for general revenue-sharing involved population, general tax effort, and relative income. Monies are allocated to the various jurisdictions depending upon the mix of these three variables in each area.

The special revenue-sharing proposals submitted by the Nixon Administration in 1972 and 1973 carry the revenue-sharing approach one step further. Special revenue-sharing, like general revenue-sharing, provides state and local governments with a payment that can be used according to local priorities. However, the scope of each of the four special revenue-sharing proposals is limited to a major functional area. Within those functional areas—law enforcement and criminal justice, education, manpower, and urban development—the local government is free to utilize the money to meet the needs it considers most pressing.

The proposed Better Communities Act, for example, which includes the urban development category, would cover the purposes of acquiring and improving real property, purchasing and developing open space, relocation of those displaced by community development activities, the building of neighborhood infrastructures, rehabilitation of residential and commercial properties, the elimination of harmful physical conditions, and the providing of community services necessary to carry out community development objectives.

These various needs are now served by seven different programs: model cities, urban renewal, basic water and sewer grants, neighborhood facilities, rehabilitation loans, public facility loans, and open space. Essentially, the special revenue-sharing is a bloc grant system, unlike the categorical grant systems previously used in these four major functional areas. Other grant programs in fields such as economic development, aging, and health would continue as categorical grant programs based upon the proposal process.

Proposed as a five-year program, the formulas for special revenue-sharing would result in large reductions in federal support for some cities and counties. For example, Newark, New Jersey was receiving about $17 million in federal grants in the urban development areas covered by the Better Communities Act but would receive less than $10 million under the formula for the fifth year. Other cities or counties that did not participate in the categorical program would receive millions of dollars in new revenue.

A partial cushion to the impact of the formulas was provided by the so-called "hold-harmless" provision. This mechanism would provide a city or county with the higher of its formula grant or the program level it previously enjoyed. However, the hold-harmless protection would fade away after two years and many jurisdictions with great need could ultimately fare even worse than they do now. Further, this approach would require many congressmen to vote their district interest regardless of what they really thought of the philosophy of the legislation in terms of more local control and priority definition.

A detailed analysis of the voting, especially within the House, on amendments to the formula to be used in various revenue-sharing bills would undoubtedly reveal efforts of congressmen to influence the formula in a way that would be most favorable to their constituencies. Obviously, such a survey would have to be limited to areas with reasonably large cities or counties, where the impact would be substantial.

A similar analysis of Senate votes would be much more complex because cities, counties, and states all participate in general revenue-sharing. A formula might be very favorable for the state but unfavorable for its major cities and counties, or the situation could be reversed. It would depend on how those governments had made out in the grant competition. It would therefore be difficult to know why a senator had voted a particular way, unless one of the formulas being considered would provide favorable results for all the jurisdictions (cities, counties, and state) he represents.

In either case, geopolitics entered into the decision to replace some grant programs with revenue-sharing as well as into specific formulas established to distribute the revenue-sharing money. The Senate formula favored states with smaller population and few large cities, while the House formula was more generous to large population concentrations. Considering the fact that House districts are distributed by population, Senate seats are not, and that the nation has become highly urbanized, this is not surprising.

Geopolitics of Federal Science and Technology Spending

The revenue-sharing controversies of the 1970s were not the first geographical distribution issues to be debated and resolved in Congress. The question of equitable distribution of federal money became one of the dominant issues in the 1960s, when major decisions were being made regarding federal research and development (R&D) budgets. The dollars being distributed amounted to as much as 15 percent of the total federal budget. The emphasis in this debate was on how much money was distributed within each state. The R&D controversy did not involve federal money for states, counties, or cities as such, but rather for universities, industries, and nonprofit research institutes located across the country.

The states and localities were affected insofar as the success or failure of proposals submitted by their R&D performers had a major impact on their economic well-being. The focus was on the use of federal contract money to provide jobs, stimulate growth, and strengthen the higher education systems of the various areas, many of which were competing with each other for economic or educational leadership. Further, it was felt very strongly that R&D business was of a higher quality than most other kinds of business because it usually involves smokeless industry, higher-than-average salaries, large numbers of employees with graduate and professional degrees, and specialized research facilities. All of these characteristics are potential magnets for other industries that could provide subcontractor services to the prime contractors.

Across the nation chambers of commerce are still trying to repeat the growth patterns made famous at Ann Arbor, Palo Alto, and Route 128 where unique combinations of prestigious Michigan, California, and Massachusetts universities and new R&D industries proved very profitable to the communities. In reality, a strong center of science and technology does not automatically result in local economic development. For every Route 128 or Palo Alto or Ann Arbor that can be cited there is also a Los Alamos, Brookhaven, or Tullahoma, where the economic impact of federal research facilities has not led to other kinds of community development.

The geopolitics of science consists of the competition over where the various projects will be conducted. However, the national political process sometimes raises this geopolitical question before rather than after the fact. In some cases the location decision is a requirement for congressional approval of the project. Thus, those which are acceptable on their merits may be rejected by Congress, while less acceptable projects have been approved by Congress because of where the work will be conducted.

Since research and development funding involved millions of dollars, it was not surprising that emotions were intense when federal research and development funds became concentrated in a few areas. Aside from stimulation of economic growth in particular regions of the nation, these expenditures also cause regional shifts of intellectual and industrial resources. For instance, political and business leaders in the Midwest alleged that their region experienced a brain drain—that is, a loss of talented scientists and engineers—because the region received a small share of federal research and development contracts.

Such complaints are predicated on the assumption that factors other than allocative efficiency should govern the distribution of federal research and development funds. It is frequently argued that since the tax monies used to fund federal projects are collected nationally and voted by the House and Senate, Congress has a duty to ensure that there is a geographically balanced distribution of such funds. The suggested emphasis on geographical distribution of research and development funds to the depressed and slow-growth areas for enhancement of their economic growth is in direct conflict with the philosophy that the government should buy from the supplier able to produce the best balance of quality, cost, and time factors, regardless of geographic location.

The extent to which an oligopoly exists in the military-industrial complex is evident when we consider that the annual expenditures of the Department of Defense alone are equal to the combined yearly sales of General Motors, Standard Oil of New Jersey, General Electric, Ford, and Chrysler. In the 1960s, NASA's annual expenditures were roughly the same as the budget of the State of New York. Since NASA and DOD are not able to produce the hardware they need themselves, they are in a sense "locked in" to the government-oriented corporations. Twenty-one of the top twenty-five contractors in 1966, were also in the top twenty-five in 1957.[4]

In *The Modern Public Sector,* Murray Weidenbaum wrote:

By reducing both the governmental orientation of these companies and the government's reliance on them, the nation might be able simultaneously to achieve several important objectives—reducing the geographic concentration of federal contracts, increasing competition for government business, protecting the interests of the taxpayers, and reducing the arsenalization of an important branch of American industry.[5]

This government support and influence is not limited to corporations. Much of the aid to higher education is in the form of research support. Seventy-five percent of all R&D work in the universities is performed with federal funds, even when state appropriations for university research are included in the total figure.[6] Historically, the mission agencies such as DOD, NASA, and AEC have provided more federal aid to universities than the Higher Education program of the U.S. Office of Education or the National Science Foundation (NSF).

It has been said that the government may be doing to the university structure what it has done to the defense industry—subsidizing and encouraging the growth of a relatively few giants. A House Committee on Science and Astronautics report pointed out that twenty-five universities produced two-thirds of the science Ph.D.'s in 1939, and that the same group (fifteen private and ten state universities) was still producing two-thirds of the Ph.D.'s in 1965. This group also received 60 percent of all federal expenditures on university science in 1965, and an even greater percentage of the research grants and contracts of mission-oriented agencies.[7]

The House Committee report provided some clear indication of concentration by size when it stated that:

While some 100 universities absorb 90 percent of the total federal outlay, the 10 largest on the list of Department of Defense contractors receive 70 percent of defense outlays. The 10 largest on the National Aeronautics and Space Administration list receive nearly 60 percent of that agency's outlays and the 10 largest on the Atomic Energy Commission list, nearly 50 percent.[8]

Because of the domination by mission agencies of university grants and contracts, there is also a major disparity in the geographic distribution of funds. The report noted that "the North Central and South Central States, which turn out respectively 31 and 14 percent of the Nation's Ph.D.'s, receive less than their share of . . . the total Federal flow: only 18 and 5 percent, respectively."[9]

Referring to the maldistribution of federal research funds, Dr. Fred Harrington, President of the University of Wisconsin, indicated that if the concentration of R&D continued, the "nation would be on the road to manpower chaos, economic chaos, social chaos, and defense chaos."[10] He failed to mention the political consequences of overconcentration, but Daniel Roman covered that point thus:

The concentration of government support in relatively few schools has political ramifications. Congressmen representing districts where there are no universities or where the universities are not recipients of lavish federal funds are concerned about the practice of giving money to established institutions with outstanding reputations. Should the government help build up the scientific capability of other schools? Does research effectiveness in heavily funded universities reach a level of diminishing returns?[11]

The heavy concentration of dollar expenditures in defense-related industries is only one manifestation of the balance problem. Commenting on an NSF survey (which is summarized in table 14-3), Dr. Ralph E. Lapp wrote that the five leading regional complexes, none of which are located in the Midwest, have attracted one-third of the national brain power and hold 58 percent of DOD's prime contracts for research and development. The study showed that every state in the Great Lakes and Plains regions suffered a net loss and the total was 22,415 scientists, including two Nobel Prize winners. The 22,415 represent the net difference (loss) of those scientists receiving their degree training in the Midwest but no longer living there and those gained by the Midwest from the rest of the country. The net loss of Midwest scientists represented gains particularly to California and New England. The effects also include industrial dollar loss. Former Governor Otto Kerner estimated the traceable loss to the Illinois economy as fifty thousand dollars per year for each scientist leaving the state.[13]

It is understandable that the Midwest should be concerned about its rela-

Table 14-3
Concentration of Scientific and Technical Personnel by Geographic Region

Regional complex or Metropolitan area	Research and Development		Management or administration	Total[a]
	Basic	Applied		
New York City complex (25-mi radius includes Newark, Paterson, Jersey City)	3,148	2,978	2,746	10,221
National capital area (25-mi. radius centered at Greenbelt, Md.)	2,863	2,252	2,707	8,298
Los Angeles complex (San Fernando, Pomona, Pasadena, Santa Ana)	1,504	1,548	1,479	5,552
San Francisco Bay area (Richmond, Livermore, Palo Alto, San Jose)	2,204	1,381	989	5,137
Boston complex Routes 128,495	2,031	1,037	779	4,257
Chicago complex (includes Gary, Indiana)	1,417	1,231	976	4,019
Philadelphia complex (includes Camden, N.J.)	1,035	1,020	791	3,309
Wilmington, Del.	386	581	431	1,579
Pittsburgh	573	468	368	1,626
Minneapolis-St. Paul	537	444	351	1,531
Total	15,698	12,940	11,599	45,529
Total in U.S.	35,700	30,250	24,500	102,000

[a] Total indicated here is more than the sum of the row; it includes development and design personnel.
Source: Ralph E. Lapp, "Where the Brains Are," *Fortune* (March 1966), p. 156. Courtesy of Fortune Magazine.

tive position in the competition for federal research and development contracts. This condition presumably will continue to exist until the region achieves the intellectual-industrial mix necessary for a successful research and development industry. Former Secretary of Defense Robert McNamara very succinctly made the point to a group of fifteen Midwest congressmen inquiring as to the reason their region lagged so far behind the others in winning significant research and development contracts. His statement was: "We seek the best brains and go where they are. And generally speaking, they are not in the Midwest."[14]

At the base of all the debate regarding the distribution of R&D funds is the question of whether research and development dollars should be concentrated in a relatively few "centers of excellence" or should be more broadly distributed among the fifty states. The implications are not simple. States with strong R&D programs and resources tend to grow stronger by attracting additional scientists and contracts closely tied to where the research minds are located. In a political context, R&D contracts are plums. Congressmen whose districts prosper tend to be reelected. Awards made on a basis of political expediency do not preclude scientific competence; however, they do not require it either. It is dubious whether such criteria would be in the national interest over the long run.

During the midsixties, Representative Ken Hechler of West Virginia was a most vocal critic of the unequal distribution of the federal government's research and development funds. Speaking on the House floor in 1965, Congressman Hechler stated:

Ideas are translated into action and production and economic expansion in the immediate areas where they are originated. What we are seeing now is that the continued concentration of funds for idea production in a relatively few areas is drawing off the trained scientists and engineers from other sections. We are seeing areas of equal or close to equal competence bypassed to some extent, their growth rate stunted.

The problem has now reached a stage so severe and the potential benefits to the entire Nation are so great that we can no longer ignore the importance of including geographic distribution among the factors to be considered.[15]

Congressional concern over geographic distribution was aptly described in an editorial titled "The Research and Development Pork Barrel," which appeared in *Science,* a publication of the American Association for the Advancement of Science. The editor, Dr. Philip H. Abelson, a distinguished scientist, questioned whether research funds were allocated on the best basis and why "congressmen from the underprivileged states have been so remiss" in defending their constituencies.[16]

House and Senate Studies

One congressional reaction to the concentration of R&D activity and the consequent economic imbalance was to document the problem. However, the first comprehensive congressional look at the government's expanding involvement in R&D occurred with the submission in 1964 of a report to the Subcommittee on Science, Research, and Development of the House Committee on Science and Astronautics. In response to a request from that Subcommittee, the National Science Foundation (NSF) prepared a report titled *Obligations for Research and Development, and R&D Plant, by Geographic Divisions and States, by Selected Federal Agencies, Fiscal 1961–1964.* Concurrently, five other reports were submitted by the Subcommittee, all dealing with federal involvement in R&D.

The findings of the NSF report were that approximately 70 percent of federal research and development funds for all performers were allocated to nine states and the District of Columbia in both fiscal years 1963 and 1964. California was the major recipient, with 35 percent of the federal total in both years, or over four times that of the next leading state, New York (8 percent). Maryland received 5 percent and only three other states (Texas, Massachusetts, and Pennsylvania) had as much as 4 percent. All of these states are either on the Atlantic or Pacific or the Gulf Coast, highlighting the concentration.[17]

The NSF study documented the percentage distribution of federal R&D obligations for educational institutions in 1963. Once again California led the way, capturing almost 31 percent of approximately 1.5 billion R&D dollars. The distribution to educational institutions of the major states was as follows:

Table 14-4
Distribution of Federal R&D Obligations to Educational Institutions

State	% of Total R&D Outlay, Educational Institutions	State	% of Total R&D Outlay, Educational Institutions
California	31	Maryland	5
Massachusetts	12	Pennsylvania	3
New York	9	Michigan	3
Illinois	7	Ohio	2
New Mexico	6	New Jersey	2

Source: Reprinted from Thomas P. Murphy, *Science, Geopolitics, and Federal Spending* (Lexington, Mass.: Lexington Books, 1971), p. 28.

Ten states had about 80 percent of the total federal obligations to educational institutions for R&D.

The NSF report also provided data on the geographic distribution of federal R&D obligations for profit organizations.

Representing almost two-thirds of the total, these obligations rose from approximately $5.8 billion in 1961 to almost $9.4 billion in 1964. Once again the largest recipient was California, with its share of the total around 40 percent. In order of funding magnitude for 1963, the leading states were:[19]

Table 14-5
Distribution of Federal R&D Obligations to Profit Organizations

State	% of Total R&D Outlay, Profit Organizations	State	% of Total R&D Outlay, Profit Organizations
California	44	New Jersey	3
New York	9	Maryland	3
South Carolina	4	Florida	3
Texas	4	Missouri	3
Washington	4	Massachusetts	3
Pennsylvania	4		

Source: Reprinted from Thomas P. Murphy, *Science, Geopolitics, and Federal Spending* (Lexington, Mass: Lexington Books, 1971), p. 28.

The Daddario Report substantiated the allegations of a very uneven distribution of contract dollars among the states. It suggested that steps be taken to assure a more geographic distribution of R&D funds, particularly in the long run. One response to this pressure was President Johnson's 1965 memorandum to the departments and agencies of the government, titled "Strengthening Academic Capability for Science Throughout the Country."[20] It called for aggressive efforts to reduce the funding disparities.

The studies were continued by other committees. At the conclusion of extensive testimony, the Senate Subcommittee on Government Research, chaired by Senator Fred Harris, reached four conclusions. First, given particular elements in a particular region or state, including the spirit of entrepreneurship, the availability of risk capital, and the interaction between academic research and industry, the expenditure of federal research and development funds in an institution of higher learning or in a state would have direct and immediate impact on the economic development and growth of that state or of the area served by the institution of higher education. Second, the presence of high-quality research in an institution of higher learning has direct impact on the quality of education received by the students in that institution. Third, for two reasons—economic impact and the impact upon the quality of education—the distribution of federal research and development funds, as a matter of national policy, should be made on an equitable basis throughout the country and among institutions of higher learning. And fourth, there is no easy way to provide a more equitable distribution of funds.[21]

In December 1965, the Subcommittee on Employment and Manpower of the Committee on Labor and Public Welfare, under the chairmanship of Senator Gaylord Nelson, identified some of the causes for the present distribution of R&D funds and made recommendations that sought to "increase the benefits from Federal research and development to the less developed regions of the Nation."[22] Senators Jacob Javits of New York and George Murphy of California, both Republicans, stated it was difficult to support the findings and recommendations. That the Senators were from states receiving the largest shares of federal R&D dollars may have had something to do with their dissenting view.

Senator Murphy expressed his position quite clearly: "I wish to disassociate myself from the findings and implications of this subcommittee report that the Federal research and development funds should be awarded with any objective in mind other than that of obtaining the best value for the dollar spent."[23]

Senator Javits pointed out that the "unique aptitudes of our population mix" as well as "the many advantages which New York State offers in the field of scientific research and technological development combined to offer unique capabilities in the fields of research and development."[24] The Senator was not sure that the state's R&D capabilities were being adequately recognized.

One additional significant event was the so-called Roush Amendment to the NASA Authorization Bill for fiscal year 1966. Congress in 1965 authorized $5.1 billion for the National Aeronautics and Space Administration for the following year. The bill authorizing these funds, H. R. 7717, included a provision in the form of an amendment submitted in committee by Representative J. Edward Roush of Indiana stating the sense of the Congress was that "it is in the national interest to distribute funds as widely as possible across the nation" and that the National Space and Aeronautics Administration (NASA) "should explore ways and means of distributing its research and development funds whenever feasible."[25] The provisions reflected concern in Congress that NASA funds were being concentrated in the coastal states. The NASA bill, including the Roush Amendment, passed the House by a roll-call vote of 389 to 11.

All eleven votes cast against H. R. 7717 were by Republicans. Melvin R. Laird of Wisconsin, Chairman of the House Republican Conference at that time, explained that he voted against the bill because from 78 to 80 percent of NASA funds were being spent in coastal states. Laird pointed out, "this is the only method available to those of us in the great central sections of the United States in expressing our deep concern and sincere disappointment over the failure of a national space agency to follow through on their earlier commitments to recognize our section of the country."[26] In addition to Laird, eight other midwesterners (Nelson of Minnesota, Clancey and Devine of Ohio, Michel, Reid, and Collier of Illinois, Cross of Iowa, and Skubitz of Kansas) and two Californians (Utt and Younger) voted against the NASA authorization.

During the Senate debate, William Proxmire of Wisconsin echoed Laird's concern. Proxmire stated that "as a Senator from the Midwest" he was troubled by the fact that "approximately 80 percent of the NASA budget is spent on the coastal states, in the well-known 'space crescent' extending from Florida around through Texas." Senator Proxmire went on to point out that the Senate Aeronautical and Space Sciences Committee had amended the House provision of H. R. 7717 to urge the distribution of funds on a geographical basis by dropping the geographical reference. He said the Committee had made "this innocuous but laudatory provision more innocuous and less laudatory," and that as the bill stood, NASA could distribute funds "perhaps upon some other criteria, like the size of the business."[27] Chairman Clinton P. Anderson of New Mexico responded that "the desire for wide-spread distribution is limited by other, more important considerations," such as the question of "who can best and most economically do the job on the basis of past performance records and bids."[28]

NASA—A Case Study of Bidding

While Congressman Roush was extremely bothered over the maldistribution of R&D contracts, the matter is really quite complex. At a minimum an area must *have* technically competent firms that *want* government contracts. If they do not bid they cannot win. Since Congressman Roush was most disturbed by NASA concentration, the author, while serving as Deputy Assistant Administrator for Legislative Affairs at NASA, planned and directed a survey of all major contract awards in the five-year period immediately following the approval of Project Apollo in May 1961 until June 1966.[29]

The seventy major contracts studied include all contracts in excess of five million dollars awarded by NASA during the five years. All of these contracts were considered by a Source Evaluation Board, which reviewed all proposals, ranked them according to a number of factors, and made a presentation to NASA's administrator, deputy administrator, and associate administrator. These three then selected the contractor. The contract awards were analyzed with attention to their geographical distribution, but also to develop information about the bidding patterns of the various regions. Since a bid is a prerequisite to an award, bid analysis may be a more realistic approach to the question of equitable distribution of contracts than a survey showing the geographic distribution of contracts.

The major contracts under review had substantial impact on the national and regional economy. They involved an expenditure of approximately four and one-half billion dollars, which represented 43 percent of NASA's research and development appropriations during the five-year period. Statistics gathered, by state, for these major contracts include the 4975 requests for proposals and the 570 bids submitted, so that only 10.5 percent of the invitations for proposals actually resulted in bids.

An examination of the regional average of contracts awarded versus bids submitted indicates that the Mountain region was first, being awarded 20 percent of the contracts on which its firms bid (1 of 5), followed by the East South-Central (8 of 44) at 18.2 percent. The Midwest (7 of 48) tied the Mid-Atlantic region (16 of 109) with 14.7 percent. Their firms were awarded a higher percentage of the contracts they bid on than the Pacific, New England, and South Atlantic regions, which together provided over 53 percent of the total bids, but were awarded only 44 percent of the contracts.

When the value of contracts awarded was analyzed, the Pacific region was awarded $3021 billion for seventeen contracts and dominated the entire competiton with 67 percent of the total contract dollar value. This unusually high average of $177.7 million per contract in the Pacific region was due to the California location of the giants of the aerospace industry, including North American-Rockwell, Lockheed, General Dynamics, Northrop, and the Douglas plants of McDonnell-Douglas. California was therefore always represented in competition for the largest contracts, and often the choice was between only two or three California companies.

However, not all of the $3021 billion represented by the prime contracts awarded to the Pacific region were retained by the contractor. Prime contractors pay other firms to execute subcontracts relating to various aspects of their contract. First- and second-tier subcontracts are distributed to firms located throughout the nation, including many that do not specialize in aerospace work. Many of these subcontractors are located in the heavily industrialized midwestern states.

A comparison of the bidding patterns of the individual states in table 14-6 reveals much greater inequity than the regional comparison. Clearly, the disparities among regions are due to the great differences in the effective bidding rates of firms located in the various states which happen to be included within those regions. Twenty-five states received 98.5 percent of the requests for proposals. Eighteen states never submitted a single bid, and six of these (Montana, Alaska, Rhode Island, Vermont, and North and South Dakota), received no requests for proposals. States receiving requests but submitting no bids were West Virginia, Hawaii, Oregon, Utah, Wyoming, Idaho, South Carolina, North Carolina, Arkansas, Delaware, Nebraska, and Maine. Of the thirty-three jurisdictions bidding, nineteen states and the District of Columbia were awarded contracts. Of the twelve Midwest states, nine bid and five were successful. Eight of the twenty successful states were awarded a contract only once. This means that eleven states and the District of Columbia were awarded sixty-two of the seventy contracts. Indiana made only one bid.

While California was awarded the greatest number of contracts (fourteen) and its contracts had the greatest dollar value ($2273 billion), it also submitted the greatest number of bids (134). In fact, its award average was 10.4

Table 14-6
Relative Success of Bidding States, 1961-6

State	No. of bids	Contracts awarded	Success (%)	State	No. of bids	Contracts awarded	Success (%)
New Hampshire	1	1	100	Louisiana	15	1	7
Washington	6	3	50	Massachusetts	19	1	5
Arizona	2	1	50	Florida	40	2	5
Wisconsin	2	1	50	Virginia	14	0	0
Tennessee	4	1	25	Georgia	6	0	0
New Jersey	27	6	22	Nevada	5	0	0
Alabama	36	7	19	Illinois	5	0	0
Maryland	41	7	17	Mississippi	3	0	0
Ohio	12	2	17	Connecticut	3	0	0
Minnesota	6	1	17	Colorado	2	0	0
Pennsylvania	33	5	15	Indiana	1	0	0
Michigan	13	2	15	Iowa	1	0	0
Texas	43	6	14	Kansas	1	0	0
Missouri	7	1	14	Kentucky	1	0	0
California	134	14	10	New Mexico	1	0	0
New York	49	5	10	Oklahoma	1	0	0
Washington, D.C.	41	3	7	Total	570	70	

Source: NASA contract files.

percent of the bids submitted—below the median success rate of 12.3 percent.[30]

The Midwest congressional delegation has often protested that contracts "due" the Midwest were awarded to "the two coasts." In the NASA case study, the Midwest was more successful than the two coasts *on contracts for which it competed.* If the Midwest could increase the number of its bids, maintain the same award ratio, and compete for the large dollar contracts, the NASA experience suggests that the disparity in the geographic distribution of contracts would be drastically reduced.

Locating Federal Laboratories and Facilities

One special category of federal action, which has been the object of numerous regional battles, has been the location of federal facilities and installations by the various agencies of the government. This is a very large category, since it includes post offices, navy yards, military training bases, and public health facilities, as well as space operations centers such as Cape Kennedy and atomic research centers such as Brookhaven and Los Alamos.

From coast to coast, cooperative community efforts were developed to compete for new federal research laboratories, especially those of the growing National Aeronautics and Space Administration. Contractors were wooed by cities and counties and their Chambers of Commerce. All these people put pressure on their representatives and senators to help them convince the federal agencies with large budgets to keep the contracts flowing.

Because of the substantial risk implicit in reliance upon contracts where cutbacks may be made, the competition for federal laboratories is bound to increase. Laboratories are generally spared the boom-and-bust characteristics of contracts and so often have more enduring value for the community and region. Elsewhere, the author studied the conflict over establishment of the NASA Space Centers at Houston and Cambridge, the National Environmental Health Sciences Center at the Research Triangle at North Carolina, the AEC Accelerator at Weston, Illinois, and the Coast and Geodetic Shipyard and Laboratory at Miami.[31] The final decisions were a result of a combination of agency desires, managerial considerations, economic considerations, political pressures, committee relationships, White House contacts, university flexibility, community responsiveness, and special state support.

When there are a variety of qualified areas, it becomes increasingly difficult to secure a decision on such a facility. NASA was held up for two years on its decision to establish the Electronics Research Center at Cambridge, and the Department of Health, Education and Welfare was delayed for a similar period in the establishment of the National Environmental Sciences Center in North Carolina. In the latter case, Congress actually went so far as to specify that the Center could not be built within fifty miles of Washington, as a means of precluding several of the sites preferred by the Department of Health, Education and Welfare. This is not a surprising congressional reaction. It is much easier for Congress to agree where the center should *not* be located than it is to agree on where it *should* be located. Supporters of the alternative sites, band together to prevent the establishment of a center at any particular location.

The Impact of New Politics on Geopolitics

The difficulty of defining the New Politics has been discussed several times. Taking the specific case of New Politics influence on geopolitics as a factor in federal decision-making is especially complex because the issue is a basic economic one, which tends to separate philosophy from the practical questions. The case for New Politics in this category can best be summarized as follows:

The New Politics congressman must be just as concerned as the Old Politics congressman about governmental economic decisions affecting his district. Because of the New Politics, Congress seems more willing than previously to consider more carefully whether the program should be approved in the first place. But once the decision has been made that a federal program or facility will be established, the New Politics representative must press for a fair share for his district.

The dilemma of regional versus national priorities was summed up nicely in a *Washington Post* editorial on the day of the key 1973 vote on the Alaska Pipeline. This was a case of the New Politics Senator Gravel—the man who read the Pentagon Papers into the Senate Record in protest against unwarranted governmental secrecy—attempting to bypass the National Environmental Protection Bill, for which he had voted. In this case the Senator's geopolitical interests outweighed his commitment to New Politics and environmentalism, when the issue became one of direct economic impact for his state. The vote ended in a 48 to 48 tie, which Vice President Agnew broke by voting for the Gravel amendment.

Despite this defeat, it is important to remember how much the situation had changed to make possible such a close vote. During the 1960s for example, the philosophy of technology assessment "a form of policy research which provides a balanced appraisal to the policy maker" and "a method of analysis that systematically appraises the nature, significance, status, and merit of a technological program," was adopted in Congress.[32] Before the New Politics Congress, property values were routinely given greater support than environmental and general interest considerations. Another key vote was taken on the Alaska pipeline in November 1973 after the Middle East War and oil shortage. It passed this time 88 to 5.

Another interesting impact of the New Politics relates to the struggle for facilities and installations. With increasing frequency, public interest groups are succeeding in making it clear that the interests of the local chamber of commerce in greater economic activity and increased population may be at variance with the interests of the public in the quality of life in their community.

For example, between 1961 and 1970, under Secretaries McNamara, Clifford, and Laird, the Department of Defense issued 1088 base closure actions.[33] Virtually every state was affected and the volume of congressional inquiries on these issues mushroomed beyond anything previously experienced. Senators and congressmen representing both the Old and the New Politics reaction agreed that there had to be cutbacks in defense costs, but questioned why it had to affect their states or districts.

However, the New Politics added a new twist. While traditionally local areas have been virtually unanimous in pressuring their congressional representatives to seek new facilities and to hold on to those which now exist, elements of some communities are becoming more selective as to the kinds of facilities considered desirable. In many areas there are pressures on the DOD to *release* urban land being used for military purposes, on the basis that there are civilian needs of a higher priority. Perhaps the best example is Bolling Air Force Base on the Potomac River in Washington, D.C., which DOD wants to use for a Little Pentagon. In the 1960s Bolling was deactivated as an operational airport because of increased civilian traffic at National Airport. After blocking the Little Pentagon for several years, in 1973 the City of Washington succeeded in getting the House District Committee to vote out a measure turning one-third of the base over to the city for urban housing.

Another segment of society turning up its nose at *some* types of federal largesse is the prestige university. Specifically, there are demands that the universities move away from their recent dependence upon government military contracts and devote more time and resources to socially oriented projects. Across the nation, pressure is being applied to force the scientific schools and the research institutes to reject DOD contracts, which, so the argument goes, compromise the academic freedom of the cooperating institutions and pervert the prestige and competence of the researchers.

As these arguments gain appeal among the academic institutions, antidefense feelings become institutionalized through the adoption of administrative restrictions against the acceptance of military contracts. An example of the consequence of new university pressure is the December 1970 decision by the arts and sciences faculty of Harvard. They amended their rules governing outside research support to bar research that would require the security clearance of university personnel or that would in any way preclude the general publication of experimental results. Presumably this action reflected, among other things, dissatisfaction with the Vietnam War and with the current high status of military budgets within our hierarchy of national priorities. In many respects, this is a far more sophisticated problem than the protests against the ROTC program or the resistance of recruiters from the military and the Dow Chemical Company, which were prevalent in the late 1960s. It threatens the basic supportive links which have existed between the various military and civilian institutions for decades.

Perhaps the most publicized incident of campus protest against present university science policies came with the so-called March 4th ("March Forth!") movement of 1969, which had its origin in a hastily planned voluntary research strike on the M.I.T. campus. The purpose of the strike, organized by both M.I.T. students and faculty into a nationwide effort involving some thirty universities, was to focus attention on how the "misuse of scientific and technical knowledge presents a major threat to the existence of mankind."[34] The consequences for the university so far have even been somewhat positive. M.I.T. physicist Bernard T. Feld, returning from a trip to Europe, claimed that March 4 "has done more to enhance M.I.T.'s reputation abroad than anything else; European scientists had formerly regarded M.I.T. as a narrow technological institute."[35]

Even in Congress there is a new mood. The Legislative Branch seems prepared to accept the fact that research and development expenditures of federal agencies will not be distributed to the regions on a proportional basis when the competence to perform such work is restricted to several regions. The federal research and development program is no longer looked upon as the only major vehicle for bolstering economically depressed or sagging regions. If a region wishes to develop the requisite concentration of specialized researchers, industrial support, investment capital, and risk-taking management, the patterns for doing so are clear. An attempt to induce an artificial balance between regions on research and development contracts might be a disservice to both industry and taxpayers.

There is now a considerable body of federal legislation and some corresponding program funding by a number of agencies and departments to help direct money to disadvantaged areas. As Weidenbaum indicated, the domestic programs tend to accomplish this equalization, whereas the research and development programs increase concentration because competence, quality, and reliability are the primary criteria for procurement decisions. The objectives of equal economic growth may be better achieved by applying the equity criteria to domestic programs that are not strongly dependent on industry location. Regional readjustments can be achieved through these mechanisms without perverting the efficiency and effectiveness of federal research and development programs.

The greatest geopolitical impact of the New Politics has been in the stress on reevaluating priorities and in responding to needs rather than pork-barrel considerations, whether scientific or otherwise. The federal government has been experimenting with various new approaches, organizations, and mechanisms to meet the demands for change that surfaced during the 1960s, when aspects of our political and governmental institutions were questioned to a degree unknown before.

The social desirability of much of the research and development expenditures is being reevaluated, not only by the public but by an increasingly budget-conscious Congress. The rapid growth in federal R&D expenditures since the beginning of World War II seems to have peaked, and science is no longer regarded as the sacred cow when it comes to appropriating funds. A shift in emphasis from defense to urban, environmental, and other social concerns is in progress. The debates over the termination of the Office of Equal Opportunity and the Alaska pipeline are some of the more dramatic recent examples.

A 1970 speech by Assistant Secretary of the Treasury Murray Weidenbaum to the American Institute of Aeronautics and Astronautics confirms the new mood. In serving notice on the R&D community that it could no longer hide behind its expertness nor unilaterally commit the nation to massive expenditures without considering other vital needs of our society. Weidenbaum stated:

The determination of the uses to which public resources, particularly money, are put is a matter for the general public to decide. Hence, if a professor or engineer wants to devote his leisure time to designing a commercial submarine or planning a linear accelerator, he should be entirely free to do so.

However, when he asks for $100 million of taxpayer money to start building the gadget, he should have to justify it—and not in the soft theological terms so often used by the natural scientists in such matters, but in the hard, objective manner of the social scientists.

He should have to answer questions such as these: Are the expected benefits worth the cost? How well can he measure the benefits? Has he omitted important elements of cost to society, such as polluting the environment? Finally and most crucial, are the returns from this use of public funds likely to be greater than from alternative uses?[36]

Since federal R&D programs were initiated, the levels of expenditure have been determined by the trend of contemporary political and economic events. Now in the 1970s the economic, social, and political climates are changing again. Based on demonstrated societal needs, more resources must be devoted to ameliorating the problems of urban and rural America. As geographic disparities in R&D have become an increasing concern for the politicians in Congress and the White House, the government has been forced to search for new mechanisms and approaches to help deal with the economic, social, and political consequences that have resulted from this uneven geographic distribution of R&D resources.

Regardless of which specific techniques evolve as the ones most useful to Congress in its role of legislating and appropriating funds, it is clear that science has used up all its blank checks, and that budgets for science as well as the military-industrial complex must be reviewed and balanced. Although the geopolitical struggles for a bigger piece of the federal pie will continue, the next era appears to be one requiring interest groups to demonstrate clearly how and why their areas fit into national priorities.

15 The Impact of the New Politics Congress

Thomas P. Murphy and Robert D. Kline

Since 1960 there have been drastic changes in the membership of Congress and in the nature of its legislative product. The various changes are summarized under the title "New Politics" because they involved a shifting and sharing of power and its fruits as a result of expanded political participation.

The reduction in the power of the Conservative Coalition in Congress is a fact. As late as the Kennedy Administration, the Conservative Coalition still ruled the Congress and its key switching posts, such as the House Rules Committee. This has changed in a number of respects. First, since the solid South is no longer so solid seniority is bestowed less automatically upon Southern Democrats; second, many Republicans now represent less conservative districts, many of which are located in the new suburbs; and third, the liberals have finally organized themselves better, as a result of New Politics influences.

There is more competition for seats in Congress than previously existed. While a substantial number of seats still go uncontested in the general election, a number of formerly one-party districts in the South as well as in the Midwest have become competitive. This means that even where, for example, blacks in a congressional district may represent 30 to 40 percent of the population and so lack the votes to elect a black candidate against an effectively organized white candidate, this group can hold the balance of power in a reasonably close election. By voting Republican they could deny reelection and the fruits of seniority to Democrats even in southern districts, which are still classified as safe districts. These tactical factors will become increasingly important as the minority electorate develops better leadership, becomes more truly integrated into the benefits of the New Society, and recognizes the relationship of political participation to its continued prosperity.

It would be a mistake to overlook the impact of the opening-up process that has occurred with regard to who votes. The Twenty-Sixth Amendment to the Constitution gave the vote to those eighteen through twenty years old, thus ending the traditional high-school debating issue as to whether citizens old enough to be drafted were also old enough to vote. The Amendment and related legislation also reduced artificial residency requirements and outlawed the poll tax as a condition for voting, so that those who were more mobile than others in our society and those for whom the poll tax was a barrier would be able to participate more fully in the political process. This is not a self-executing change. Experience has shown that the young and the poor are less likely to participate in politics, even when given the opportunity, because of lack of knowledge, fear, or a feeling of separation from the society and its political process. Nevertheless, the structural changes have removed legalistic barriers and opened up possibilities that can be mobilized with effective organization and leadership.

With the opening up of the voting process, it has become feasible for persons of more diverse backgrounds or personal characteristics to be elected to Congress. In 1974 there are sixteen black members of the House of Representatives and one in the Senate, whereas in 1960 there were five in the House and none in the Senate. Likewise, in 1960 there was one Spanish-speaking representative in the House, while in 1974 there are five, including the first congressman of Puerto Rican descent. Since the admission of Hawaii to the Union in 1959, persons of Asiatic descent have held seats in both the House and the Senate for the first time. While the number of women has not changed substantially since 1960, the kind of women elected to Congress has changed. In previous years women made their way to Congress as replacements for their deceased husbands; now women are being elected on their own merits as serious candidates. These changes are a reflection of the changing society that underlies the New Politics.[1]

The nature of constituencies has changed, partly as a result of the urban migrations of the 1950s and 1960s and the one-man-one-vote ruling of the Supreme Court, which resulted in the establishment of some districts with a preponderance of minority populations. A number of these districts with heavy black or Spanish-speaking populations (or a combination of the two) are still represented by whites. This is likely to change as the minority populations develop their own candidates.

Presently two black and two Spanish-speaking representatives are from districts where their own minority does not represent a majority of the population. Senator Edward Brooke of Massachusetts was elected by a white constituency, and as the freedom and openness of American society advances, there are likely to be more elections in which a black candidate will be selected over a white one by a predominantly white constituency.

Therefore, while the nonwhite male membership in Congress still amounts to about 8 percent, it is likely to increase. Moreover, since 75 percent of the nonwhite male members are Democrats, the percentage that this new group represents in the total House is a less significant indicator, while it is under Democratic control, than the percentage it represents in the Democratic Party in the House. An even finer point to make is that the Democratic Study Group (DSG) contains slightly more than a majority of the total Democratic House membership, and yet virtually all of the New Politics representatives are members of it. They amount to approximately 20 percent of the total membership of that liberal wing of the Democratic Party, and so have a stronger voice in the Democratic Caucus and in the House than it may appear.

With some effective leadership from within the Black Caucus, the Women's Caucus, or the Spanish-speaking congressmen, it is obvious that this entire group can enlist the support of numerous other Democrats as well as some Republicans on many issues, and this can make a difference in the legislation that Congress produces. Yet it is a mistake to assume that the minority delegation will be a monolithic bloc on issues where civil rights, discrimination, and urban questions are not involved. Such voting behavior would probably trigger a backlash that would reduce the effectiveness of the New Politics in Congress.

Another substantial change working to insure a more meaningful voice in Congress for New Politics positions has been the enhanced ability of public interests to express themselves. The rapid development of a number of public-interest lobbying groups organized specifically to offset the tremendous political power of the old private interest lobbies has occurred since 1960.

Ralph Nader came on the scene as a consumer advocate in the early 1960s. His personal drive and style of operation attracted numerous dedicated young people who felt isolated from the traditional political process but believed they could have an impact on where society was going through influencing the actions and opinions of legislators and bureaucrats. They have done so by using a combination of traditional lobbying techniques, and going into court when necessary to harness judicial pressures in favor of the public interest.

Dr. John Gardner, a former president of the Carnegie Foundation, resigned as Secretary of Health, Education and Welfare in the Johnson Cabinet when he felt that Vietnam expenditures were going to be so large that it would not be feasible to increase the human-resources spending he believed necessary to redress some of the economic and social ills in American society. Upon resigning his cabinet post in 1967, Gardner established the Urban Coalition. In 1969, he formed Common Cause, because the Urban Coalition, as a nonprofit organization, would lose its tax-exempt status if it engaged in lobbying activities. Common Cause quickly established itself as a force to be reckoned with because of the intellectual leadership it provided, the widespread grassroots support it developed, and its ability to raise money to establish an effective lobbying staff in Washington.

Starting with a lobbying expenditure of only $3754 in 1969, by 1971 Common Cause had become the organization reporting the greatest expenditure on lobbying. It even widened the gap in 1972, spending approximately $558,839 on lobbying, while such major lobbies as the American Federation of Labor reported $216,294, American Insurance Association $82,259, the American Medical Association $96,146, and the Farmers' Educational and Cooperative Union of America $113,156.[2]

This does not necessarily mean that the public interest is better represented in terms of lobbying and making its points with Congress than these other organizations. Common Cause reports its expenditures more conscientiously. An organization campaigning for more accountability and honesty in government would undermine its very purposes if it were to hide some of its lobbying expenditures as public relations or legal fees, as most of the other large lobbies traditionally do. Nevertheless, the clustering of resources exhibited by Common Cause enables that organization to concentrate on a number of key issues each year. Its campaigns have reached the Congress and have had an impact, often in combination with other nonprofit groups such as those under the leadership of Ralph Nader, or the Committee for a More Effective Congress.

Other organizations with a more narrow public interest grew up in the 1960s. In addition to the peace groups that tended to organize among youth and around universities, environmental groups became very important. Organizations such as Friends of the Earth, the Sierra Club, and Environmental Action had a major impact on the congressional decision to reject the President's request for additional funds to develop a commercial supersonic aircraft. They were also successful in lobbying for the establishment of the Environmental Protection Agency to initiate and oversee air- and water-pollution programs.

Democracy in Congressional Process

As new kinds of congressmen have been elected they also have had an impact on the internal environment of Congress. There is more internal democracy in Congress today than at any time since the two houses of Congress became large bodies. In the early years Congress was small enough that internal democracy was not the problem it became later, when a House of 435 members would be virtually dominated by 10 percent of that number who held all the key power positions as a result of the operation of the seniority process.

The liberalization of the rules for participation and the spreading of congressional power has occurred in both houses and in both parties. The famous Johnson Rule established by Majority Leader Lyndon Johnson in the Senate provided that no Democratic member of the Senate, no matter how powerful, could receive an appointment to a second major committee until all the members on the Democratic side had received at least one good committee assignment. Later the rule was extended to the point that no one could chair two committees, and there was even a limitation in the number of subcommittees that could be chaired by one member. This opened up more chairmanships and spread the leadership and ability to bargain among a larger number of senators.

Since there were so few Republican Senators, more discipline has been necessary to enable them to trade with the Democratic presidents and the majority leader. Everett McKinley Dirksen became a strong leader who could bargain for amendments or patronage with Lyndon Johnson because he could deliver his bloc of Republican votes. When he died and Hugh Scott became leader, the Republicans adopted a more collegial form of leadership with more widespread participation.

On the House side, the impetus for opening up the process and creating more meaningful participation by younger congressmen came from the Democratic Study Group (DSG). By gaining a strong voice in the Democratic Caucus the DSG was able to reduce the power of the Conservative Coalition of Republicans and Southern Democrats who had been frustrating the will of the majority of the Democratic Party. After throwing its weight around in the 89th Congress when it pushed through many new programs, the Democratic Study Group was cut back by election reverses in the years following the Johnson landslide. The DSG then turned to developing institutional reforms that would make it possible for a smaller group to have significant influence.

Consequently, in the 1970s they succeeded in getting agreement from the Democratic Caucus that chairmanships would not pass strictly on seniority but would require a secret majority vote within the Caucus when challenged by 20 percent of the membership. Perhaps even more important, each member was limited to one subcommittee chairmanship. This automatically increased the number of Democrats holding subcommittee chairmanships from 97 to 137, a 40 percent increase.

Also, now that the chairmen had to distribute the subcommittee chairmanships, more subcommittees were formed. Previously, some had used ad hoc groups which they chaired so they would have greater control over the various bills before their committees. A chairman could keep matters bottled up in a subcommittee by preventing a vote from being taken. Now it was possible for a subcommittee that did not agree with the chairman to force a vote in the full committee. All these changes followed revolts on a number of committees in the 1960s which resulted in the establishment of subcommittees which diluted the power of the chairman.

Other reforms related to activity on the House floor were also significant. The closed-rule authority of the Rules Committee was further limited so that members would have more advance notice and an opportunity to open a closed rule. Another openness reform was the new requirement for committee meetings to be public unless a specific committee vote closed particular meetings. The proposed requirement that the minority receive a fair share of committee staff resources will work to enhance the minority's ability to limit action by the majority.

The other changes on voting that occurred in the House were directed toward the accountability process. Much of the business of the House is done in the Committee of the Whole, where more informal rules exist than when the full House meets. Many major decisions relating to bills are worked out in the Committee of the Whole, where traditionally the vote was by voice or by unrecorded tellers. With the requirement for a recorded teller vote, weak-kneed congressmen who were subject to the pressures of the private lobbies and had previously voted against their constituents' interest in the Committee of the Whole were now required to go on record there as well as on the full House floor. This change in procedure was credited with the defeat of the SST appropriation in 1971 by a mere thirteen votes.[3] The recorded teller vote can of course also work to defeat good legislation when congressmen believe their constituencies will react negatively.

In the Senate much attention was directed to Rule 22, which governs votes on cloture. Since the Senate has unlimited debate, a minority could filibuster a bill to death. Rule 22 provided that if two-thirds of the Senate voted to terminate debate they could kill the filibuster. However, securing a two-thirds vote proved to be very difficult, and in 1959 this ruling was liberalized to provide that the two-thirds would be based upon those present and voting rather than on the total Senate. This made it somewhat easier to get cloture. Numerous attempts to reduce the voting requirement to 60 percent have been made at the beginning sessions of recent Congresses, but they have been unsuccessful.

The common thread in all these reforms in the House and Senate is that there were attempts by the majority to prevent a determined and united minority from blocking action. In the Senate this is usually achieved through a filibuster, but in the House the Rules Committee often prevented a bill from getting to the floor where the majority could take action. Once again, however, it is necessary to note that the procedure itself is ideologically neutral. During most of this century progressive senators have had more occasions than conservative ones to utilize Rule 22. The current Rule is probably a good compromise that prevents a very small minority from blocking action yet is sufficiently difficult to provide some protection for minority rights against the potential excesses of majority rule.

Changing Congressional Outputs

The change in the composition of Congress, in the kinds of interests represented there, as well as in the procedural openness and opportunity for participation by the new members, had very serious effects on the outputs of Congress during the 1960s and 1970s The first impacts were extensions of the kinds of liberal legislation voted during the New Deal Congresses in the 1930s. They were concerned with civil rights, the War on Poverty, voting rights, minimum wage and social security increases, manpower training, and housing legislation. However, medicare and the Elementary and Secondary School Act were also major extensions of federal involvement in local government and private sectors responsibilities.

This socioeconomic strain of legislation gave way later to more concern with legislation affecting the quality of life. The kinds of things sponsored by the environmentalists would fall into this category, as would much of the consumer-oriented legislation for which Ralph Nader was a prime catalytic agent. Even the Law Enforcement Assistance Act initiated by the Nixon Administration was concerned with reducing fear as a barrier to enjoyment of the quality life. The Twenty-Sixth and Twenty-Seventh Amendments to the Constitution are also related to the quality of the political system.

Consumerism

The increasing attention to the citizen as a consumer was spawned by the New Politics early in the 1960s, and as it grew it became more inclusive. Beginning with the Nader-inspired product-safety demands early in the sixties, this element of the New Politics moved progressively to consider many aspects of man's physical environment. Most recently it has come to view the citizen as *consumer* of governmental services. This in part helps to explain the increased demands for greater *accountability* in governmental decision-making, for greater *responsiveness* by the governmental bureaucracy as a whole, for *decentralization* of federal programs to state and local governments as a means to accomplish that responsiveness, and for *community power* as a necessary partner to that decentralization, and finally, for general revenue-sharing as a specific response by the New Politics Congress to help finance these demands.

The 1960s will be remembered by many as the decade of the "thalidomide baby." President Kennedy was seeking greater federal regulatory powers over the drug industry when the thalidomide scare occurred. A survey by the Food and Drug Administration showed that the drug appeared to be directly responsible for an increasing number of infants being born with "phocomelia"—seallike flippers instead of limbs. The public outcry that followed was directly responsible for congressional legislation that dramatically increased the regulatory powers of the Food and Drug Administration.

A 1964 report by the Surgeon General's Advisory Committee on Smoking and Health, established by President Kennedy, moved Congress to pass highly controversial legislation the following year requiring each package of cigarettes sold within the United States to bear a label warning of the potential health hazards involved in smoking. Finally, in 1970 Congress enacted legislation banning the advertising of all cigars and cigarettes on radio and television.

In 1966, Congress enacted a landmark "truth in packaging" law, which authorized both the FDA and the FTC (Federal Trade Commission) to establish standards and regulations for the identification of contents of packaged material. It was the passage of such legislation that subsequently allowed Robert Finch, then Secretary of HEW, to impose a ban on the use of cyclamates in all beverages and general purpose foods after January 1, 1970. The artificial sweetener, when given in large doses, had been found to induce cancer in rats.

Largely as a result of the efforts of Ralph Nader, Congress passed the National Traffic and Motor Vehicle Safety Act of 1966, which required manufacturers of new cars to recall defective vehicles. By 1974 over 20 million defective automobiles had been recalled as a result of this legislation. Later, tests conducted by the National Highway Safety Bureau, established under the legislation, showed that approximately 18 percent of the commercial tires tested failed to pass one or more minimum tire safety standards. Congress responded by extending the National Traffic and Motor Safety Act of 1966 for an additional three years and required tire manufacturers to notify consumers of safety-related defects in their products.

In related legislation, the Congress passed the Child Protection and Toy Safety Act of 1969, to protect children from harm due to toys that exhibited potential mechanical, electrical, or thermal hazards. The Coal Mine Health and Safety Act of 1969, which is considered to be the most comprehensive mine health and safety legislation in American history, expanded and strengthened safety regulations governing the mining industry, and allowed the U.S. government to make disability payments to miners suffering from "black lung."

Perhaps the most symbolic consumer effort by the New Politics Congress concerns the battle that began in 1970 to establish an independent Consumer Protection Agency within the federal government. The agency is intended to protect the consumer from abuses not only by "big business" but by governmental bureaucracies. Legislation to establish such an agency was introduced in both chambers of Congress in 1970. The Senate passed a bill, by a 74-to-4 roll-call vote, that would have created an independent Consumer Protection Agency with much the same status as other regulatory agencies in government. The bill proposed a Council of Consumer Advisors, which would be organizationally located within the Executive Office of the President. However, the House did not pass it. In 1971, the two chambers of the Congress reversed their earlier positions on the consumer legislation. This time the House of Representatives overwhelmingly passed the measure, but the Senate killed it by failing to invoke cloture.

Finally, after the previous unsuccessful attempts of Congress to create a broad-based Consumer Protection Agency, on October 28, 1972, President Nixon signed a bill establishing the Consumer Products Safety Commission (CPSC). Described as the most powerful regulatory agency, CPSC has the authority to act against hazardous products. It is unusual among independent regulatory agencies because the legislation creating it says it must submit its proposed budget to Congress and the Office of Management and Budget simultaneously. With a jurisdiction of from 1000 to 100,000 products that have been associated with at least 30 million consumer injuries yearly, the Commission can order the repair of defective items, ban their sale, or set up mandatory safety standards.[4]

Environmentalism

Environmental issues also received more attention in the New Politics Congress. A dramatic increase in the use of the automobile during the 1960s and the well-publicized effects of oil spills that often resulted from nothing short of outright neglect served as the primary forces in bringing the issue of man's pollution of his own environment to the forefront of the public's attention.

From the outset, this new ecology movement presented America with conflicting and difficult choices. In fact, it often presented the average citizen with a zero-sum game, where protecting the environment sometimes could only be assured by the loss of industry and the jobs vital to a given area's economy, or by federal regulations that ultimately created further strains upon the average citizen's pocketbook. Such was the case with federally mandated emission-control devices upon the production of new automobiles.

The increased use of the automobile in the past decade greatly increased the incidence of air pollution in the United States. California is often referred to as a present-day glimpse of the America of the future. Its most populous and polluted city, Los Angeles, offers frightening insights into the future of major American cities surrounded by high-density suburbs and mile upon mile of freeways designed for private commuter traffic. Eighty percent of the air pollution in Los Angeles is caused by emissions from automobiles.

Congress first responded with the Clean Air Act of 1963, detailing the initial steps to be taken in ending inter- and intrastate air pollution, and broadened this approach in the Clean Air Act of 1965. Both Acts were sponsored by Senator Edmund Muskie, and provided the Secretary of Health, Education and Welfare with the authority to establish and enforce newly created standards limiting the emission of hydrocarbons and carbon monoxide from new automobiles. The first such standards were issued in 1966, and they became effective in 1968.

In 1967, the Congress strongly asserted itself in this area by enacting the Air Quality Act of 1967 (PL 90-148). This Act authorized the Secretary of Health, Education and Welfare to establish "air quality regions" throughout the United States and to impose and enforce federal air quality standards in states that failed to act, and provided full funding for regional control commissions established under the law. The 1963 law was broadened again in 1970 by Senator Muskie's Clean Air Act amendments. The first National Air Quality Standards were promulgated by this legislation and car manufacturers, despite heavy lobbying by the auto industry, were given until 1975 to *produce* nonpolluting automobiles.

Air pollution is fundamentally different from other types of pollution hazards to man's environment. This fact is strikingly illustrated by the contrast between air pollution and oil spills. Air quality is more constant and measurable, therefore providing some reasonable basis for determining its immediate and long-term effects upon the environment. Oil spills, on the other hand, are isolated and sporadic incidents, making the measurable immediate and long-term damage to the environment much harder to calculate. Furthermore, because of the incremental nature of air pollution, public indignation is rarely aroused to the point where local, state, and federal officials feel compelled to act. Oil spills, though, are sudden and dramatic, often creating inexorable pressures upon governmental officials to act.

On March 25, 1970 the Congress passed the Water Quality Improvement Act. Its passage was delayed for nearly six months by controversy over its oil cleanup provisions. The law makes an owner of an oil facility liable for up to $8 million for cleanup costs and the owner of a vessel liable for up to $14 million for each oil spill, unless the owner can demonstrate that the spill resulted from an act of God, war, or the negligence of the government of a third party.[5]

Land-use planning has become an important priority in recent years. A report to the President's Council on the Environment stated that a quiet revolution in land controls is occurring throughout the nation. Many local communities have attempted to restrict development, or direct it in ways less costly to the community and its environment. Several states have legislated protection for areas of obvious environmental importance such as the wet-lands of Delaware and the Pacific coast. In his January 1974 State of the Union Message, President Nixon said that a national land-use policy is a high priority.

The National Land Use Policy Act was first introduced in the Congress in 1971 by Senator Henry M. Jackson, chairman of the Senate Interior Com-mittee. Senator Jackson's bill was designed to set up a new office in the Department of Interior which would administer some $100 million over an eight-year period to states agreeing to draw up and implement statewide land use plans in accordance with federal guidelines.

Under the Act every state desiring to become eligible for federal funds would submit a land-use plan to the Secretary of the Interior for approval. They would also be required to directly regulate, almost as a super zoning board, five kinds of land use defined in the legislation as being of "more than local concern." States would be required to oversee development in areas of critical environmental importance like beaches, wetlands, historic sites; regulate large-scale urban developments like subdivisions, shopping centers; monitor regional public utilities that in themselves have a major impact on land uses around them; and closely check other major projects such as air-ports, major highway interchanges, and recreational facilities.

Senator Jackson's bill passed the Senate in 1972, but remained bogged down in the House Interior Committee until the end of the 92nd Congress. It passed the Senate again in June of 1973, but was killed in the Rules Com-mittee in March 1974. Eventually some federal action will be taken to regu-late land use.

Participation and the Quality of Political Life

Congress also has been active in the area of constitutional amendments to increase individual participation in both voting and societal activities. In March 1971 Congress passed the Twenty-Sixth Amendment to the Constitu-tion, providing the vote to those eighteen years of age and up. It was ratified by the states in less than one hundred days after its passage—a new record. A year later and forty-nine years after it was first introduced, Congress passed and sent to the states what may eventually become the Twenty-Seventh Amendment to the Constitution. Popularly known as the "Equal Rights Amendment," the measure states: "Equality of rights under the law shall not be denied or abridged by the United States, or by any state, on account of sex." It is somewhat fitting that this amendment should be a capstone to more than a decade of activity to promote true equality within American society, because it expresses the credo of the New Politics.

Another output of the New Politics Congress has been more concern with citizen participation and citizen information so that participation can be meaningful. Citizen participation, as it evolved, became much more than merely a means to increase the feelings of political efficacy of the poor; it became an important *procedural* weapon against cumbersome bureaucracies which all too often were more occupied with procedure than with outcome. It was, as James Q. Wilson has suggested, not just "a way of winning popular consent for controversial programs. It is part and parcel of a more fundamental reorganization of American local politics," for which Congress was directly responsible.[6]

The concept of citizen participation was introduced into new areas, the first of which was a demand for greater "accountability" in government to combat the "secrecy" all too often enshrouding the decision-making process. The Freedom of Information Act of 1966 (PL 89-487) guaranteed public access to all government papers, opinions, records, policy statements, and staff manuals unless they were covered by one of the nine specific exemptions added to the Act by Congress. However, a review by the House Government Operations Subcommittee on Foreign Operations and Government Information in September of 1972 revealed that bureaucratic delays and excessive fees in the processing and publication of requests for documents, the very type of thing that the Act had sought to remedy, were major impediments to its implementation.

The governmental secrecy issue was made graphic for the public by Daniel Ellsberg's 1971 leaks to the media of data which later became known as the "Pentagon Papers." The *Washington Post* and The *New York Times* published lengthy excerpts from the still-classified documents and were challenged in court by the Department of Justice. On June 29, 1971, Chairman Mike Gravel convened a special session of the Senate Public Works Subcommittee and, before a room full of reporters and astonished colleagues, began reading still-unpublished and classified excerpts from the papers into the *Congressional Record*. The outcome of all this seemed to be an admission that the Pentagon was overclassifying its information. Ironically, the Ellsberg trial was terminated when it became known that Nixon assistants had violated the law by breaking into Ellsberg's psychiatrist's office in an effort to get evidence on him.

However significant the actions of Ellsberg and Gravel may have seemed at the time, the energy crisis captured national attention in the winter of 1973 and threatened to expose yet another ugly result of governmental policy-making that was surrounded by secrecy for reasons of national security. On January 15, 1974, Senator Frank Church charged that secret decisions, which had shaped the government's energy policy for twenty years, were largely responsible for the uniform shortages of energy in the United States in 1974. In making those charges, Senator Church requested the Justice Department to declassify thirty-eight sensitive documents written in 1954, which describe in detail how the oil industry was exempted from antitrust laws in the production of crude oil in the Middle East for reasons of national security.

Increasing concern about the accountability of public officials and alarm over governmental secrecy was accompanied by demands for greater decentralization of governmental decision-making and program implementation. As the nation had moved toward a New Politics Congress in response to the pressures of societal change, the federal government at the same time was accruing much additional power, and becoming involved in matters that were formerly local responsibilities.

Local school districts and local police departments were not part of the federal responsibility prior to 1960. Now there is heavy involvement in both these functional areas which were formerly reserved for state and local governments. As a result of this tremendous expansion of the scope of federal activities, most of which has involved the delivery of services, additional power has gravitated toward the President, because administration and management are his role. In addition, as indicated earlier, the power of Congress to force him to take positive action is very slight.

The nation's governors, county executives, and mayors—the spokesmen for the "other half" of the federal framework—used their New Politics lobby organizations to remind the President and the Congress of their need for financial relief to resolve local problems. Such disparate politicians as Richard Nixon and George Wallace asserted that the federal government was no longer omnipotent (not that it ever was), and that Washington seemed too distant from the ordinary citizen's problems. Congress took notice and enacted the State and Local Assistance Act of 1972. It is one of the most important pieces of legislation in the twentieth century, for revenue-sharing is a departure from the long trend of centralizing governmental power in Washington.

Revenue-sharing complements the earlier federal attempts to decentralize decision-making found in Lyndon Johnson's Community Action programs. It is a physical decentralization of the revenue expenditure process, accompanied by a physical decentralization to ten federal regions of many federal domestic program agencies. The decision-making power that accompanies these funds is being returned to state and local government.

Clearly, the problems of many high-density urban areas—crime, congestion, concentration of a dependent population, pollution, poor housing, unemployment or underemployment, health needs that outstrip the capacity of health care systems to deliver services—cannot be treated in isolation of one another. They interface, and any program established to deal with them will fall far short of its goals if it is not organized to deal with its effects on all of them.

Regionalism and regional development are important new concepts being utilized in Congress and elsewhere to define the complex web of those interrelationships, especially when they affect more than one governmental jurisdiction. But regionalism entails much more than an awareness of the physical interrelationships that bind geographic areas and individuals together. It also includes the more intangible interrelationships that bind individuals into a "community."

There is no institution within American society with greater innate potential than Congress to help establish the operating framework for such a community, as well as to reconcile the differences that will arise among many Americans in the years to come over the value, the efficacy, and the equity of regional government. Congress must anticipate this trend and provide the leadership essential to its success. It involves the lengthy and trying process of reclaiming authority it delegated to the President to meet the demands of an era in which the federal government found itself as the sole provider of needed social services. It entails the devolution of federal taxing and spending authority to local and regional units of government, which are structurally more capable of coping with a broad range of problems that differ in their intensity and priority according to local circumstance.

Adapting the Separation-of-Powers Doctrine

In evaluating the long-term significance of the New Politics Congress, it is necessary to review some other realities. Under the Constitution, the United States still has a system of checks and balances and of separation of powers at the federal level. It still has a two-party political system, and these two parties and their competition provide the political dialectic essential to citizen expression and to the organization of Congress to produce legislation. Members of Congress, whether adherents of the Old or the New Politics, urban or rural, Republican or Democratic, still face the need to run for reelection every two or six years. Congressmen still represent a pluralistic society whose values are evolving and changing emphasis. For some time the United States has been a postindustrial society, one which has established itself as an industrial power but is now concerned with the uses of that power, with the distribution of the fruits of the power, and with improving the quality of life itself.

With the best of intentions on all sides, there would still be problems. There are still violators of law and order in our society. The people still have a lack of sufficient facts to really know who is right when the parties, or different members of the same party, disagree on what policies ought to be followed. The nature of foreign relations and the constitutional powers of the President are such that Congress has to take a back seat in areas such as foreign affairs which are so crucial to national development and growth. Even here, though, Congress still has a significant role.

Providing the natural resources for a postindustrial society with its socio-economic sophistication and advanced technological systems in electronics, automation, communications, and transportation can be a problem. No nation's resources are infinite, and so choices must be made. For instance, in the 1970s it became necessary to choose in some cases between continuing to enhance the environment or switching to a different type of fuel that would have deleterious pollution effects but would ease the energy shortage. Such dilemmas will continue to haunt the national decision-making process, and in spite of all of the advances which can be catalogued, the nation still cannot afford to do everything simultaneously that the various public and private interest groups might identify as priorities. Therefore there must be a sorting out of priorities, and someone must be held accountable for the decisions that are made.

It is disturbing, however, that despite the New Politics Congress and despite the increasing level of education in the citizenry there is still a lack of public confidence in Congress. Congress has speeded up its decisions somewhat, has certainly opened up its deliberations, has cooperated with the media in telling the story of how legislation is made, and has provided for more accountability in voting. Yet the public does not seem to have accepted Congress as the key decision-maker it is in the total priority-setting process.

Perhaps the problem is that while Congress is now more representative of the electorate and has a more democratic framework, its capacity to act has also been weakened. As power has been diffused, the demands for aggressive leadership have increased. This is essentially a political party problem and the combination of growing heterogeneity among Democrats, greater fragmentation of political power in Congress, and weak leadership from the Speaker have created a new dilemma—a conflict between Congress's ability to represent and its capacity to govern.

Until the Nixon Administration, liberals were not too concerned with the public not giving high marks to Congress and looking upon Congress as an encrusted group plodding its way through its share of national decisions. There was confidence that the President was more important in providing leadership and setting directions, and that he had a program to communicate to Congress and to the nation. Some liberals actually felt that it was good that the public did not think highly of Congress because that weakened Congress's hand in confrontations with the President, who was expected to be more responsive to liberal implications and intellectual inputs.

The second Nixon Administration showed the hollowness of this attitude. For the first time in history, the public rated the President at an even lower level than it rated Congress. Such disillusionment was serious, as the public could look to neither Congress nor the President for leadership. The nation was suffering economic setbacks, it had not solved all its social problems, and it was existing in a world where atomic power could create a military crisis within hours. While the wounds over the unpopular war in Vietnam still remained, President Nixon made some advances in relations with China and Russia that eased some of the external threat to the national security. However, runaway inflation continued, and problems with the balance of payments and the international monetary system demanded action. A Republican President was forced to impose wage and price controls on the economy as well as direct two devaluations of the American dollar. Indirect involvement in the Arab-Israeli War was followed by a temporary but significant cutoff of Mideast oil shipments to the United States.

In many respects the people responded more negatively to these pocketbook issues than to the Watergate revelations.

From an institutional standpoint, Congress was forced to respond to the President. Nixon's use of the veto power threatened Congress, because it is difficult to override a veto. However, Nixon sometimes combined it with impoundment and utilized it to an extent and in a way that prior presidents had never attempted. He not only failed to spend money Congress had approved, but did so in accordance with his own subjective view of national priorities. If he had imposed an across-the-board 5 or 10 percent cut on *all* programs as a demonstration that there was a need to reduce federal spending to relieve inflation and get the economy under control, he would have had some basis for support in Congress. By singling out environmental projects, poverty programs, and housing funds, Nixon made it clear to all concerned that he was thumbing his nose at Congress and was insisting on having his own way even after he had failed to in the legislative process.

As the facts came out, the impact of Watergate as a challenge to Congress became clear. The Senate, and later the Judiciary Committee of the House, attempted to conduct investigations on the allegations regarding Watergate and White House involvement in it, but the President extended the doctrine of executive privilege as a cloak over his staff and Administration officials. He was challenging the very authority of Congress to investigate, and was doing so not solely to protect the separation of powers doctrine but presumably to protect himself and his closest associates.

In 1971 Nixon had been less than candid with Congress in discussing how soon the Vietnam action would be terminated. When he then proceeded to launch a new venture in Cambodia, American airpower was used in a way that looked to many like the development of a new Vietnam. When challenged the President—as had his predecessors—fell back upon the so-called "war powers" authority of the President. Congress found it necessary to respond to all these challenges to its authority.

The War Powers bill did not attempt to say that the President could not respond to an international emergency. Rather, it laid down some conditions he should consider, and provided that within 60 days, if Congress did not sustain his decision to enter into hostility, he would have to stop, with thirty days provided to work out the withdrawal of American military forces.

Congress required the President for the first time to report impoundments in a systematic way. Another piece of impoundment legislation being considered by Congress is a bill introduced by Senator Sam Ervin and Representative Ray Madden. It provides that impoundment of funds would be ineffective if Congress disapproves of the impoundment within sixty days.

It also struck out at President Nixon through Senate refusal to confirm two of his Supreme Court nominees, Clement Haynsworth and G. Harrold Carswell. Committee veto procedures that had been developed a decade earlier now were being used with more frequency. This involves writing into legislation a requirement that Congress be advised of certain decision steps and be given sixty to ninety days to veto the proposed action.

However, all of these that Congress was attempting to exercise over the President are essentially negative controls.

The traditional power of Congress over appropriations has been a rather effective control over the presidency, but having mechanisms for control and being able to use them in such a way as to cause positive actions to occur are two different things. In the first place, blocking a presidential action is easier than causing a president to take an action that he may not wish to take. His refusal to move and execute the laws of the nation can be challenged in the courts but this can be quite time consuming and provide only after-the-fact relief. In addition, Congress itself is not a monolithic body. Therefore, it will have difficulty in controlling a President who has the loyalty and support of his party. Even if it is a minority party in Congress, its power will almost always be sufficient to block the override of a presidential veto.

The challenge from Nixon was such that Congress began to discuss seriously the development of a congressional budget so that it would have positive alternatives to offer the President rather than be limited to carping at his own programs. Nevertheless, the attempt to create one major committee within each chamber of Congress that would combine some of the powers of the House Ways and Means Committee to raise revenue and of the House Appropriations Committee to allocate it raises serious problems. Members of the House have used their seniority to gain powerful positions on these two very important committees, and are not interested in having their power watered down and shared with the other members of the House. The proposals made involved compromising to the extent of permitting members of other committees to serve on the new Committee on the Budget that might be established. In other words, some of the members would come from the Ways and Means Committee, some from the Appropriations Committee, and the remainder from the rest of the House of Representatives. The same kinds of problem exist on the Senate side, where the Senate Finance Committee is in charge of raising revenue and the Appropriations Committee is in charge of allocating it, but no one is responsible for making a comprehensive decision on how revenues and expenditures are to be balanced in any particular year.

As if the intrachamber complications were not serious enough, whenever Congress attempts to get together on a joint approach to budgeting it leads to questions about the primacy of the House of Representatives in raising revenue and evokes the specter of the Clarence Cannon-Carl Hayden controversy of 1962, where the two aged appropriations chairmen could not even agree on where to hold conference committee meetings to work out differences in House and Senate appropriations bills. Congress has a long way to go to establish this kind of monitor committee, which would take a look at total budget and the income and the expenditure pattern of the federal government and come up with a comprehensive financial package based on a deliberate priority system. If it does not succeed in doing this, it will have little option but to be open to efforts by the President to use impoundments to balance the budget or manipulate funds for programs to fit with priorities he believes are important.

The leadership problem, therefore, continues to be a serious one. Institutions are important, and structural arrangements and organizations are also significant. However, it is not sufficient to have large federal programs on the books, to have rhetoric about citizen participation in poverty and model cities programs, to have manpower revenue-sharing, or a theory of New Federalism. All these things must be means to some end. Long-range goals and targets for reaching them are essential. To the extent that it is impossible to have a unity of goals in a pluralistic society, there must at least be a diverse package of goals based upon mutual accommodation with enough in it for everyone to justify working hard for the success of the total package.

In some respects Congress is well geared to help provide that kind of leadership, because most of what Congress does involves this kind of internal accommodation. But, it must demonstrate the capacity to do so on a sustained basis.

Recent history suggests that Congress functions best when supporting a person who is providing aggressive leadership. It did so especially in the 89th Congress while President Johnson was pushing forward with social programs, but it also backed Richard Nixon in his efforts toward the New Federalism through a decentralization of some federal functions to the ten federal regions he established as well as to the state and local governments. When such a relationship is not functioning, Congress can slow up or check a president who is overly arrogant in the use of his powers by dragging its feet on appropriations and passing bills that require that the President report certain kinds of action. However, this is a long way from providing aggressive Congress-based initiative and positive leadership.

From a political standpoint, the President has a fixed four-year term. The people can pressure Congress, when they find the President unresponsive— but the President may not respond to their resulting pressure upon him. This is especially true when a President, is serving the last term the Constitution permits him or for other reasons will not be running for reelection. Further, when there is a difference of opinion between Congress and the President and the public is divided or does not understand the issue, he still has the advantage in being able to appeal to public opinion.

The President can secure a televised press conference at any time. Direct television coverage of Congress, however, is generally limited to the sensational investigations that are conducted from time to time, usually in the Senate. The problem was demonstrated in 1974 when President Nixon gave his State of the Union Message in which he attacked Congress for inaction and called for an end to the Watergate investigations. The congressional response was essentially a talk by Senate Majority Leader Mike Mansfield. While Mansfield's sincerity undoubtedly came across in his telecast, he could not speak for the whole Senate and could not even speak for all the Democrats in the Senate—much less the House. The more sophisticated electorate is aware of this.

The people have an image of the presidency and a concern for it as an institution. Even while only 25 percent of the people felt the President was doing a good job and while fellow Cabinet officers and staff assistants to the President were being indicted, there was very little sentiment for impeachment. This is the ultimate congressional sanction but it is an almost unthinkable weapon.

One response might be that there should be a way short of impeachment to change the president when it is viewed to be as in the national interest. Perhaps there is a lesson in how easily the nation disposed of Vice President Agnew. No revolution followed, there were no major shock waves, and it was a bipartisan action. The new vice president was confirmed with a minimum of difficulty, despite the fact that it was the first time that the new Twenty-Fifth Amendment was being used and a number of key decisions and procedural relationships had not been sufficiently spelled out in the Amendment.

Some means of referendum short of impeachment is necessary with regard to the presidency. In the parliamentary systems of Western Europe, when the leadership is felt to be out of touch with the nation, or is unable to move its program because of recalcitrance in the party ranks, it is possible to call for new elections and to get a new signal from the electorate. That would not serve any useful purpose in a system where the House elections are already every two years and when, as during the Nixon debacle, the opposition Democratic Party already *was* the majority in Congress.

The problem therefore was not in changing a Democratic majority in Congress to a Republican majority which would be more responsive to where the nation seemed to be saying it wanted to go. The problem specifically concerned the incumbent of the presidency itself and his relationship to Congress. The only remedy available in the end was impeachment and this is a drastic matter which takes time, involves recrimination on both sides, impacts the electorate, and injects a leadership gap in foreign affairs as well as in domestic program development.

The only other means available to check the President is to have an effectively functioning Congress. The New Politics has done much to break down the artificial involvements, the initiative-stifling aspects of the seniority system, and the exercise of power by small and unrepresentative minorities. Rather than stopping to congratulate itself on its progress, Congress should redouble its efforts to improve its decisions by making more use of data processing, securing better staff analysis of the budget and program proposals of the President, establishing mechanisms for comprehensive economic policy-making, and improving its own linkages to the intellectual community.

It must also move even further to improve its image by giving the minority party the opportunity to participate more effectively, by finding some real solutions to the problem of political campaign financing, and by taking a less partisan and more problem-solving-oriented approach to the matters before it. This will not happen until most of the members of Congress decide that effective politics is good politics.

Notes

Chapter 1
The New Politics

1. Daniel Moynihan, "Youth and the Troubled Sixties," *Washington Post,* July 29, 1973, p. C-1.

2. *Washington Post,* July 12, 1973, p. A-12.

3. Austin Ranney and Willmore Kendall, *Democracy and the American Party System,* (New York: Harcourt, Brace, 1956), p. 65.

4. Max Farrand, *The Records of the Federal Convention of 1787,* Vol. I (New Haven: Yale University Press, 1966), p. 20.

5. Arthur Schlesinger, *A Thousand Days* (New York: Houghton Mifflin, 1965), pp. 63-64. Copyright © 1965 by Arthur Schlesinger, Jr.; reprinted by permission of Houghton Mifflin Company.

6. *Ibid.,* p. 14.

7. Martin Luther King, "Letter From Birmingham Jail," *Why We Can't Wait* (New York: Harper & Row, 1964), pp. 78-79.

8. Theodore White, *The Making of the President 1964* (New York: Atheneum, 1965), pp. 412-13.

9. Edward Banfield, *The Unheavenly City* (Boston: Little, Brown, 1968), p. 19.

10. "God May Be a Democrat: But the Vote Is for Nixon," *Time,* October 30, 1972, p. 20.

11. Frank Marini, *Toward a New Public Administration: The Minnowbrook Perspective* (Scranton: Chandler Publishing Company, 1971), p. 311.

12. Theodore White, *The Making of the President 1972* (New York: Atheneum, 1973) p. 30.

13. *Ibid.,* p. 178.

14. *Ibid.*

15. *Ibid.,* p. 161.

16. *Ibid.*

17. Interview by Glenn Gardner with Carol Casey, staff member to Committee on Party Structure and Delegate Selection and Credentials Committee, August 24, 1973 and March 5, 1974.

18. *The Party Reformed,* Final Report of Commission on Party Structure and Delegate Selection, July 7, 1972, pp. 7-8.

19. Interview by Glenn Gardner with Jerome Donovan, Executive Director of Credentials Committee, September 14, 1973.

20. Hunter S. Thompson, *Fear and Loathing on the Campaign Trail* (San Francisco: Straight Arrow Books, 1973) pp. 286-87.

21. *Ibid.,* p. 303.

22. Delegates and Organizations Committee, Republican National Committee, *The Delegate Selection Procedures for the Republican Party,* Part II, July 23, 1971, pp. 4–9.

23. Rules Adopted by Republican National Convention, August 21, 1972.

24. Richard C. Bain and Judith H. Parris, *Convention Decisions and Voting Records* (Washington, D.C.: The Brookings Institution, 1973), p. 340.

25. Senator James Buckley, "Testimony before the Rules Committee of the Republican National Convention," Miami, Florida, August 14, 1972.

Chapter 2
Representing the New Constituencies

1. Congressional Research Service, "Incumbency in Congress" (Washington, D.C.: U.S. Library of Congress, 1973), pp. 1–3.

2. Raymond Wolfinger and Joan Heifetz Hollinger, "Safe Seats, Seniority, and Power in Congress," *American Political Science Review,* June 1965, pp. 337–49.

3. Congressional Quarterly, *Guide to the U.S. Congress,* (Washington: Congressional Quarterly, 1971), p. 461.

4. Congressional Quarterly, *Congressional Quarterly Almanac* (Washington, D.C.: Congressional Quarterly Service Inc., 1960–73).

5. U.S. Bureau of the Census, "Voter Participation in November 1972," p. 20, number 244, December 1972, p. 2.

6. *Ibid.*

7. *Ibid.*

8. Sidney Hyman, *Youth in Politics* (New York: Basic Books, 1972), pp. 108–13.

9. Republican National Committee, *The Young Voters,* (Washington, D.C.: Republican National Committee, 1972), p. 3.

10. "National Student Votes," *The National Student Vote,* 1972 (Berkeley: University of California Student Lobby, 1972).

11. The Republican National Committee, *The Young Voters* (Washington, D.C.: Republican National Committee, 1971), pp. 5–7.

12. *Ibid.*

Chapter 3
Blacks, Spanish-speaking Americans, and
Women in Congress

1. Roscoe C. Brown, Jr. and Harry A. Ploski, *The Negro Almanac* (New York: Bellewether Publishing Company, 1967), pp. 453–54.

2. *Voting Rights Act of 1965, 79 Stat 437, 42 U.S. Code,* 1973.

3. Don Bonafede, "Black Vote Loses Cohesion, But Gains Sophistication," *National Journal,* June 24, 1972, p. 1061.

4. U.S. Bureau of the Census, *Congressional District Data Book, 88th Congress* (Washington, D.C.: U.S. Government Printing Office, 1963), data item number 41.

5. Congressional Quarterly, *Congressional Districts in the 1970s* (Washington, D.C.: Congressional Quarterly, 1973) 236 pp.

6. Joint Center for Political Studies, "Potential Black Voter Influence in Congressional Districts," (Washington, D.C.: Howard University, 1973).

7. *U.S. Congressional Record,* "Remarks by William Clay," February 19, 1971, p. 3352.

8. *Ibid.*

9. Mark R. Levy and Michael S. Kramer, *The Ethnic Factor—How America's Minorities Decide Elections* (New York: Simon and Schuster, 1972), p. 25.

10. "Black Caucus: 60 Recommendations for the President," *Congressional Quarterly,* April 2, 1971, p. 783.

11. "Nixon Responds to Black Caucus," *Congressional Quarterly,* May 28, 1971, p. 1173.

12. "A Salute to the Congressional Black Caucus," *Focus,* September 1973, p. 3.

13. Ronald Sarro, "LBJ Helps Jordan Get Committee Job," *Washington Star-News,* January 14, 1973.

14. "Women Office Seekers: This Year, More Than Ever," *Congressional Quarterly,* October 8, 1972, p. 2800.

15. Congressional Quarterly, *Guide to Congress* (Washington, D.C.: Congressional Quarterly Service, Inc., 1971), pp. 467-68.

16. *Ibid.,* p. 468.

Chapter 4
Freshman Power in the House of Representatives

1. This chapter draws heavily from Thomas P. Murphy, "Political Ethics in a Coattails Congress," *Ethics,* July 1967, pp. 291-96, and Thomas P. Murphy, "The Extraordinary Power of Freshmen in Congress," *Transaction,* March 1968, pp. 33-39.

2. Edmund Burke, "Speech to the Electors of Bristol," November 3, 1774, *The Works of the Right Honorable Edmund Burke* (4th ed.; Boston: Little, Brown, 1871), II, pp. 89-98.

3. Ross J.S. Hoffman and Paul Levack (eds.), *Burke's Politics* (New York: Knopf, 1949), p. 41. The full text of the statement containing this quote is available in Edmund Burke, "Thoughts on the Cause of the Present Discontents" (1770), *The Works of the Right Honorable Edmund Burke,* I, 4th ed. (Boston: Little, Brown, 1871), pp. 435-537.

4. Murphy, "Political Ethics in a Coattails Congress," p. 294.

5. In October 1966, just prior to the election, the author interviewed congressmen for two weeks, including the Democratic leadership and twenty-nine of the freshmen Democrats. Additional first-hand information was obtained through daily activity on Capitol Hill during the entire period of the 89th Congress as Deputy Assistant Administrator for Legislative Affairs, National Aeronautics and Space Administration.

6. Murphy, "The Extraordinary Power of Freshmen in Congress," p. 36.

7. See Jeff Fishel, *Party and Opposition* (New York: David McKay, 1973), pp. 125-68, for an insightful discussion of freshman congressmen.

Chapter 5
New Politics in the House of Representatives

1. Alexander Hamilton, *et al., The Federalist Papers* (New York: New American Library, 1961), p. 322.

2. *Ibid.*

3. U.S. Congress, *Preamble and Rules* Adopted by the Democratic Caucus (Washington, D.C.: U.S. Government Printing Office, 1973) Rule 7, p. 1.

4. Randall Ripley, *Party Leaders in the House of Representatives.* (Washington, D.C.: The Brookings Institution, 1967), p. 19.

5. *Guide to Congress* (Washington, D.C.: Congressional Quarterly Service, Inc., 1971), p. 42.

6. *Congressional Quarterly Almanac 1946,* Vol II, (Washington, D.C.: Congressional Quarterly Service, Inc., 1947), pp. 362 and 535.

7. James Robinson, *The House Rules Committee* (New York: Bobbs-Merrill Co., Inc., 1963), p. 78.

8. *Ibid.,* pp. 79-80.

9. *Congressional Quarterly Almanac 1961,* Vol XVLL (Washington, D.C.: Congressional Quarterly Service, Inc., 1962), p. 74.

10. Robinson, *op. cit.*

11. Robert D. Novak, "Anti-Kennedy Feeling in the House," *Wall Street Journal,* June 28, 1962, p. 1.

12. Editorial, *Wall Street Journal,* March 13, 1962, p. 14.

13. Novak, *op. cit.*

14. Robert Novak, "Young GOP Congressmen Buck Leadership," *Wall Street Journal,* January 9, 1963, p. 3.

15. "House Liberals Surprise Caucus," *Wall Street Journal,* January 15, 1963, p. 1.

16. "Republican Leader Halleck Seeks to Mollify Young Republicans in House," *Wall Street Journal,* February 19, 1963, p. 4.

17. *Ibid.*

18. *U.S. Congressional Record,* Vol. III, 89th Congress, 1st Session, 1965, p. H21.

19. *Ibid.,* pp. H21–24.

20. *Congressional Quarterly Almanac* 1965, Vol XXI, p. 1083.

21. "House Creates Group to Study Streamlining of Congressional Machinery," *Wall Street Journal,* March 12, 1965, p. 13.

22. Lyndon Baines Johnson, *Vantage Point, Perspectives of the Presidency, 1963–1969* (New York: Holt, Rinehart, Winston, 1971), p. 78.

23. Joseph W. Sullivan, "Big GOP Gains Signals a Spending Clampdown," *Wall Street Journal,* November 10, 1966, p. 1.

24. Joseph W. Sullivan, "House Republicans, They Are Out to Win," *Wall Street Journal,* March 1, 1967, p. 18.

25. Joseph W. Sullivan, "Democratic Discord," *Wall Street Journal,* February 16, 1967, p. 1.

26. *Congressional Quarterly Almanac 1967,* Vol. XXIII, p. 117.

27. *Ibid.,* p. 107.

28. "Maverick Democratic School Aid Plan Seems Likely to Pass The House," *Wall Street Journal,* May 23, 1967, p. 13.

29. *U.S. Congressional Record,* Vol 113, Part 22, 90th Congress, 1st Session, October 18, 1967, p. 29319.

30. "Poverty Fund Cut Fails," *Wall Street Journal,* November 1, 1967, p. 5.

31. *Congressional Quarterly Almanac 1969,* Vol XXV, p. 1055.

32. Norman C. Miller, "House Liberals, A Frustrated Majority," *Wall Street Journal,* September 4, 1969, p. 8.

33. Norman C. Miller, "Nixon Wins Fight to Keep Poverty Office Intact," *Wall Street Journal,* December 15, 1969, p. 5.

34. *U.S. Congressional Record,* Vol 116, Part 24, 91st Congress, 2nd Session, pp 3209–3210.

35. *U.S. Congressional Record,* Vol 116, 91st Congress, 2nd Session, July 15, 1970, p. H24484.

36. *Ibid.*

37. *U.S. Congressional Record,* Vol. 117, 92nd Congress, 1st Session, p. H61.

38. "House Democrats Vote Study Seniority System," *Wall Street Journal,* March 19, 1970, p. 26.

39. Norman C. Miller, "Republicans Shifting Towards the Left?" *Wall Street Journal,* January 1, 1971, p. 1.

40. *U.S. Congressional Record,* Vol. 117, 92nd Congress, 1st Session, 1971, p. H132.

41. *Ibid.,* p. H141.

42. *Ibid.*

43. "Both Parties in House Vote Reform on Naming Party Chairmen," *Wall Street Journal,* January 21, 1971, p. 5.

44. *Congressional Quarterly Almanac 1971,* Vol. XVII, p. 84.

45. Norman C. Miller, "More Congressmen with Seniority Finding This Is the Year to Quit," *Wall Street Journal,* January 26, 1972, p. 1.

46. *Congressional Quarterly Weekly Report,* January 27, 1973, p. 137.

47. *Congressional Quarterly Weekly Report,* October 20, 1973, p. 2793.

48. *U.S. Congressional Record,* Vol. 119, 93rd Congress, 1st Session, March 7, 1973, pp. H1442, 1443, and 1448.

49. *Congressional Quarterly Weekly Report,* July 14, 1973, p. 1893.

50. Mary Russell, "Lobby Says Secrecy Is House Rule," *Washington Post,* July 5, 1973, p. A-13.

51. *Ibid.*

52. U.S. Congress, House of Representatives, *Resolution: To Reform the structure, jurisdiction, and procedures of the committees of the House of Representatives by amending Rules X and XI of the Rules of the House of Representatives. Committee Print No. 2,* March 12, 1974, 93rd Congress, 2nd Session, House Select Committee on Committees.

Chapter 6
The New Senate

1. James L. Buckley, "Notes of an Earnest Freshman," *Washington Star,* February 11, 1973, p. B-3.

2. *Congress and the Nation, Volume I, 1945-1964* (Washington, D.C.: Congressional Quarterly, Inc., 1965), p. 20.

3. *Congressional Quarterly Weekly Report,* Vol. 17, No. 9 (Washington, D.C.: Congressional Quarterly, Inc. 1959), February 27, 1959, p. 339.

4. *Ibid.,* No. 15, April 10, 1959, p. 517.

5. "Johnson Replies to Critics of His Leadership," *Ibid.,* No. 23, May 5, 1969, p. 766.

6. *Congress and the Nation, Volume I, 1945-1964,* p. 21.

7. *Ibid.*

8. *Ibid.,* p. 16.

9. *Ibid.,* p. 21.

10. *Ibid.,* p. 17.

11. Alan Oten, "Dirksen, Smooth, Nimble and in Trouble," *Wall Street Journal,* February 28, 1968, p. 11.

12. Arlen Large, "A Test of Determination," *Wall Street Journal,* September 16, 1966, p. 16.

13. *Congress and the Nation, Volume II, 1965-1968,* p. 912.

14. *Ibid.,* p. 902.

15. Morton Mintz, "Defeated Senator Long Denies Bitterness," *Washington Post,* January 5, 1969, p. 1.

16. *Ibid.*

17. Arlen J. Large, "Dirksen's Death Left Leadership Gap," *Wall Street Journal,* September 9, 1969, p. 1.

18. "Three-Way Contest, Scott, Baker, Hruska," *Wall Street Journal,* September 15, 1969, p. 1.

19. *Congressional Quarterly Weekly Report,* Vol. 28, No. 6, January 6, 1970, p. 349.

20. *Ibid.*

21. *Ibid.*

22. Andrew J. Glass, "Congressional Report/Mansfield Reforms Spark Quiet Revolution in Senate," *National Journal,* March 6, 1971, p. 504.

23. *Ibid.*

24. *Congress and the Nation, Volume III, 1969-1972,* p. 97a.

25. "Senate Upset: Byrd Defeats Kennedy for Whip," *Congressional Quarterly Weekly Report,* Vol. 29, No. 4, January 22, 1971, p. 180.

26. *Ibid.,* p. 182.

27. "First Vote February 18, in Anti Filibuster Drive," *Ibid.,* No. 7, and "First 1971 Attempt to Modify Filibuster Rule Fails," *Ibid.,* No. 8, pp. 415-16.

28. Glass, *op. cit.,* p. 500.

29. *Ibid.*

30. *Ibid.,* p. 501.

31. "Senate Seniority Resolution," *Congressional Quarterly Weekly Report,* Vol. 29, No. 10, March 5, 1971, p. 512.

32. Mary Russell, "Academe's Varying Views Fail to Clarify Powers Issue," *Washington Post,* March 8, 1973, p. C-3.

33. *Ibid.*

34. A bill requiring Senate confirmation of future Directors of the Office of Management and Budget was signed by the President in February 1974.

35. *Congressional Quarterly Guide to Current American Government, Spring 1974* (Washington, D.C.: Congressional Quarterly, 1974), p. 75.

36. William S. White, *Citadel: Story of the U.S. Senate* (New York: Harper & Row, 1956).

Chapter 7
New Politics and Congressional Party Organization

1. "Ford Rebuffed by the Conservatives," *Wall Street Journal,* January 19, 1965, p. 4.

2. *Congressional Quarterly Almanac,* 1971, p. 10.

3. *Ibid.,* p. 25.

4. Leroy B. Rieselbach, *Congressional Politics* (New York: McGraw-Hill, 1973), pp. 104-5.

5. *Ibid.*

6. William S. White, *Citadel: The Story of the U.S. Senate* (New York: Harper & Row, 1956); and Nelson W. Polsby, "Goodbye to the Inner Club," *The Washington Monthly,* August 1969. Other references in the literature include Donald R. Matthews, *U.S. Senators and Their World* (Chapel Hill: University of North Carolina Press, 1960), and Joseph S. Clark, *The Senate Establishment* (New York: Hill and Wang, 1963).

7. Polsby, *op.cit.*

8. George B. Galloway, *History of the House of Representatives,* (New York: Crowell, 1961) p. 155.

9. *Congressional Record,* 85th Congress, 1st session, January 30, 1957, pp. 1324-26 and Kenneth Kofmehl, "The Institutionalization of a Voting Bloc," *The Western Political Quarterly,* June 1964, pp. 258-60. The four chairmen were Emanuel Celler of Judiciary, William Dawson of Government Operations, Wayne Aspinall of Interior, and James P. Richards of Foreign Affairs.

10. *Ibid.,* pp. 260-62.

11. *Ibid.,* p. 263.

12. *Ibid.,* pp. 264-66.

13. James Oberstar, "Toward an Open Congress": a speech for the League of Women Voters of Minnesota, October 11, 1971, p. 2.

14. Kofmehl, op. cit., p. 269.

15. *Congressional Quarterly,* October 10, 1969, p. 1943, and Thomas E. Mann, Arthur H. Miller, and Arthur G. Stevens, "Mobilization of Liberal Strength in the House, 1955-1970; a look at the Democratic Study Group," a paper read at the 1971 Annual Meeting of the American Political Science Association, September 1971, Chicago, p. 5; printed in the *American Political Science Review,* June 1974, pp. 667-681, as Stevens, Miller, and Mann, "Mobilization of Liberal Strength in the House, 1955-1970: The Democratic Study Group."

16. National Committee for an Effective Congress, *Congressional Report,* April 30, 1962, p. 1.

17. Mann, Miller and Stevens, *op. cit.*

18. John Bibby and Roger Davidson, On Capitol Hill, (Holt, Rinehart, 1967), p. 156.

19. U.S. *Congressional Record,* Vol. 107, 87th Congress, 1st Session, pp. 1589-90.

20. U.S. *Congressional Record,* 88th Congress, 2nd Session, October 2, 1964, p. 22926.

21. National Committee for an Effective Congress, *op cit,* pp. 3-5.

22. *Ibid,* p. 5.

23. *Ibid.,* March 15, 1973, p. 3.

24. Mann, Miller, and Stevens, *op cit,* p. 7.

25. *Ibid.,* p. 17.

26. *Ibid.,* p. 20.

27. Richard L. Lyons, "Democrats Vote to Open House Meetings and Rules," *Washington Post,* February 22, 1973, p. A-1.

28. Richard L. Lyons, "House Dixie Bloc Losing Clout," *Washington Post,* February 15, 1973, p. 6-11.

29. Mary Russell, "Divided House Democrats Feel Leadership Energy Crisis," *Washington Post,* July 9, 1973, p. A-2.

30. Sven Groennings and Jonathan P. Hawley, editors, *To Be A Congressman: The Promise and the Power* (Washington, D.C.: Acropolis Books, Ltd., 1973), p. 79.

31. Craig Peper, "The Minority Problem," unpublished paper (Washington, D.C., 1965), p. 39.

32. Groennings and Hawley, *op. cit.,* p. 83.

33. *Ibid.,* p. 85.

34. *Congressional Quarterly,* September 1, 1967, p. 1700.

35. *Op. cit.,* Groennings and Hawley, p. 93.

36. *Ibid.*

37. *Ibid.,* pp. 88-89.

38. *Ibid.,* p. 94.

Chapter 8
Public-Interest Groups: The New Lobbying

1. Mark Barry Sullivan, "Ralph Nader," *Britannica Book of the Year, 1972,* p. 143.

2. John W. Gardner, "The People Are Not Powerless," unpublished statement distributed in 1970 by Common Cause, a public-interest lobby, undated.

3. *Legislative Reorganization Act of 1946,* Public Law 79-601.

4. "Lobby Spending: Common Cause Leads Again," *Congressional Quarterly,* June 9, 1973, p. 1424.

5. U.S. Congress, House of Representatives, Select Committee on Lobbying Activities, *Hearings, Expenditures by Corporations to Influence Legislation,* 81st Congress, 1950, pp. 519-20.

6. *Legislative Reorganization Act of 1946,* PL 79-601; U.S. Congress, Senate, *Senate Reports,* Vol. 2, Miscellaneous Reports on Public Bills, II, 85th Congress, 1st Session, January 3-August 30, 1957, pp. 103-5; *Congressional Record,* 90th Congress, 2nd Session, 1967, p. S3272; U.S. Congress, House, Committee on Standards of Official Conduct, *Hearings on Lobbying,* 92nd Congress, 1st Session, March 16 and 24, 1971, pp. 1-16.

7. Suzanne Farkas, *Urban Lobbying: Mayors in the Federal Arena,* (New

York: New York University Press, 1971); Bernard Hillenbrand, "The Big Six—A New Force on the Washington Scene"; and John Garvey, Jr., "On Behalf of the Public Interest," *Public Management,* December 1971.

8. Thomas P. Murphy, "Congressional Liaison: The NASA Case," *Western Political Quarterly,* June 1972, pp. 195-96, and *Congressional Quarterly,* August 6, 1971, p. 1681.

9. *Ibid.*

10. Julius Duscha, "Stop! In the Public Interest!," *New York Times Magazine,* March 21, 1971, pp. 16 and 19.

11. U.S. Congress, Senate, *Federal Role in Consumer Affairs,* pp. 24-49, and particularly p. 27.

12. U.S. Congress, Senate, Subcommittee on Executive Reorganization and Government Research of the Committee on Government Research, *Hearings on Federal Role in Consumer Affairs,* 91st Congress, 2nd Session, 1970, pp. 43-44.

13. Richard Armstrong, "The Passion That Rules Ralph Nader," *Fortune,* June 1971, p. 228.

14. David C. Anderson, "Gardner's 'Temperamental' Imperative," reprinted from *The Wall Street Journal,* © Dow Jones & Co., Inc. 1970, August 31, 1970, p. 10.

15. Gardner, *op. cit.*

16. *Ibid.*

17. *Business Week,* October 23, 1971, p. 94.

18. Gardner, *op. cit.*

Chapter 9
Checks and Balances: Congressional Perspective

1. Mark J. Green, James Fallows, and David R. Zwick, *Who Runs Congress?* (New York: Bantam Books, 1972), p. 94.

2. Lewis W. Koenig, *The Chief Executive* (New York: Harcourt, Brace, 1964), p. 126.

3. George Haynes, *The Senate of the United States* (Boston: Houghton Mifflin, 1938), p. 551.

4. *Ibid.,* p. 281.

5. *Ibid.,* p. 521.

6. *Ibid.*

7. *Congressional Record,* Vol. 64, Part 3, 66th Congress, January 1923, pp. 2450-52.

8. Haynes, *op.cit.,* p. 537.

9. Edwin S. Corwin, *The President, the Office and the Powers, 1787-1957* pp. 112-13. Reprinted by permission of New York University Press. Copyright © 1957 by New York University.

10. *Ibid.,* p. 113.

11. *Ibid.,* p. 112.

12. *Ibid.,* p. 112.

13. *Ibid.,* p. 386.

14. *Ibid.,* p. 115, and U.S. Congress, Senate, Committee on the Judiciary, Subcommittee on Separation of Powers, *Hearings on Executive Privilege,* Vol. I, 1973, p. 249.

15. *Ibid.,* p. 247.

16. *Ibid.,* p. 240.

17. *Ibid.,* Vol. III, p. 196.

18. *Ibid.,* p. 197.

19. *Ibid.,* Vol. I, p. 19.

20. *Ibid.,* pp. 29-30.

21. *Ibid.,* p. 46.

22. *Ibid.,* p. 39.

23. *Ibid.,* p. 52.

24. *Ibid.,* p. 490.

25. Haynes, *op.cit.,* p. 519.

26. *Ibid.,* p. 547.

27. Senate, *Hearings on Executive Privilege,* Vol. I, p. 56.

28. Congressional Quarterly, *CQ Guide to Current American Government, Spring 1974* (Washington, D.C.: Congressional Quarterly Service Inc., 1974), p. 16.

29. *Ibid.*

30. *Ibid.,* p. 19.

31. Bill Kovach, "White House Moves to Narrow Grounds on Impeachment," *New York Times,* March 1, 1974, p. 1.

32. Congressional Quarterly, *op.cit.,* p. 17.

33. *Ibid.*

34. *Ibid.*

35. Thomas Griffin, "The Proper Grounds for Impeachment," *Time Magazine,* February 25, 1974, p. 23.

36. Andrew J. Biemiller, *Labor Looks at Congress 1973,* Publication Number 770 (Washington, D.C.: AFL-CIO, 1974), pp. 1-4; U.S. Senate, *Select Committee on Presidential Campaign Activities Hearings,* Vols. 1-13 (Washington, D.C.: Government Printing Office, 1973); Congressional Quarterly, *Watergate: Chronology of a Crisis,* Vol. I (Washington, D.C.: Congressional Quarterly, 1973), p. 24; Tom Braden, "The 'Impeachable Offenses' of President Nixon," *Washington Post,* December 8, 1973, p. A-19; George Lardner, Jr., "Former Nixon Aides Indicted in Cover-up of Watergate Case," *Washington Post,* March 2, 1974, pp. A-1, A-11; and Timothy S. Robinson and Lawrence Meyer, "Six Indicted in Ellsberg Break-in," *Washington Post,* March 8, 1974, pp. A-1, A-12.

37. Joseph E. Kallenbach, *The American Chief Executive* (New York: Harper & Row, 1963), pp. 391–95.

38. *Congress and the Nation Volume II, 1965–1968* (Washington, D.C.: Congressional Quarterly Service, Inc., 1969), p. 89a.

39. *Ibid.,* p. 90a.

40. *Ibid.,* Volume III, 1969–72, p. 97a.

41. *Ibid.,* p. 99a.

42. *Congressional Quarterly Almanac* 1970, Volume XVI (Washington, D.C.: Congressional Quarterly Service Inc., 1971, p. 160.

43. *Ibid.*

44. *Congress and the Nation Volume I, 1945–1964,* p. 109a.

45. *Ibid.,* Vol. III, pp. 97–98.

46. *Ibid.,* p. 100a.

47. "State Department Nominations." *National Journal Reports,* July 21, 1973, p. 1078.

Chapter 10
Checks and Balances: Presidential Perspectives

1. Alexander Hamilton *et al., The Federalist Papers,* No. 69 (New York: New American Library, 1961), pp. 417–18.

2. Arthur Schlesinger, Jr., "Congress and the Making of American Foreign Policy," *Foreign Affairs* October, 1972, p. 110.

3. U.S. Congress, Senate. Committee on Foreign Relations, *War Powers Legislation, 1973, Hearings,* before the Committee on Foreign Relations, U.S. Senate, on S. 440, 93rd Congress, 1st Session, April 11 and 12, 1973, p. 126.

4. Thomas A. Bailey, *A Diplomatic History of the American People* (New York: Appleton-Century Crofts, 1958), sixth ed., pp. 621–22.

5. Edward Corwin, *The President: Office and Powers* (New York: New York University Press, 4th ed., 1964) p. 238.

6. *Congressional Quarterly Weekly Report,* Vol. 20, No. 33, August 14, 1964, p. 332.

7. U.S. Congress, House and Senate, *A Joint Resolution to enable the President to take all necessary measures to repel any armed attack against the forces of the United States and to prevent further aggression,* H.J. Res. 1145, 88th Congress, 2nd Session, 1964.

8. U.S. Congress, Senate, *Report on War Powers,* S. Rept. No. 220, 93rd Congress, 1st Session, June 14, 1973.

9. *Congressional Quarterly Almanac 1970,* Vol XXVI (Washington, D.C.: Congressional Quarterly Service, Inc., 1971) p. 465.

10. *Congressional Quarterly Weekly Report,* Vol. 30, No. 17, April 22, 1972, p. 874.

11. *Ibid.,* p. 871.

12. *Congressional Quarterly Weekly Report.,* Vol. 31, No. 41, November 10, 1973, p. 2743.

13. *Congressional Quarterly Guide to the Current American Government, Spring 1974,* (Washington, D.C.: Congressional Quarterly, Inc., 1974), pp. 43-44.

14. *Congressional Quarterly Weekly Report, op. cit.* November 10, 1973, p. 2985.

15. U.S. Congress, Senate. Committee on Foreign Relations, *op. cit.,* p. 282.

16. Arthur Schlesinger, Jr., *op. cit.* Reprinted by permission; copyright 1972 by the Council on Foreign Relations, Inc.

17. Gardner C. Means, "Beware Phase Three," *Washington Post,* February 18, 1973, p. B-1.

18. *Congress and the Nation, Volume III, 1969-1972,* p. 79.

19. "Back to the Dismal Science," *Time,* January 14, 1974, p. 62.

20. Hobart Rowen, "The Threat of Foreign Embargoes," *The Washington Post,* March 7, 1974, p. A-31.

21. Louis Fisher, *Buffalo Law Review,* Fall 1973, reprinted in the *Congressional Record,* (daily edition) February 4, 1974, Vol. 120, No. 10, p. S1163.

22. Louis Fisher, "The Politics of Impounded Funds," *Administrative Science Quarterly,* September 1970, pp. 361-77, reprinted by the Congressional Research Service of the Library of Congress, July 21, 1971, p. 2.

23. *Ibid.* ·

24. *Ibid.,* p. 3.

25. *Ibid.,* p. 4.

26. *Ibid.,* p. 5.

27. Fisher, *Buffalo Law Review,* reprint, *Congressional Record,* p. S. 1164.

28. Fisher, *Administrative Science Quarterly,* reprint, Library of Congress, pp. 6-7.

29. *Ibid.,* pp. 8-9.

30. *Ibid.,* p. 9.

31. *Ibid.,* p. 10.

32. *Ibid.,* p. 11.

33. *Ibid.,* p. 12.

34. Sam J. Ervin, Jr. "A Brazen Seizure of Power," *Washington Post,* 1973, p. A-14.

35. Dennis M. Sherman, "Impoundment Reporting by the Office of Management and Budget: A Preliminary Analysis," *Congressional Record* (daily edition) January 29, 1974, Vol. 120, No. 6, p. 662.

36. *Ibid.,* p. S663.

37. Fisher, *Buffalo Law Review,* reprint, *Congressional Record,* p. S1171.

38. *Ibid.*

39. Fred Barnes, "Nixon Seeks Ruling on Funding," *Washington Star-News,* January 25, 1974, p. A-8.

40. *State Highway Commission of Missouri v. Volpe,* 347F. Supp. 950, 952 (W.D. Mo. 1972). Reprinted at 118 Congressional Record S14345-47 (daily ed.) September 8, 1972.

41. Fred Barnes, *op. cit.,* p. A-8.

42. *City of New York v. Ruckelshaus* (Civ. Action No. 2466-72, D.D.C.), reprinted at 119 *Congressional Record* S8604-07, daily edition, May 9, 1973.

43. *Ibid.*

44. *Brown v. Ruckelshaus* (Civ. Action Nos. 73-154-AAH and 73-736-AAH, D. Cal.) reprinted at 5 ERC 1803 (Environmental Reporter Decisions No. 22, September 28, 1973).

45. Louis Fisher, "Court Cases on Impoundment of Funds, A Summary and Analysis," Congressional Research Service, Library of Congress, Washington, D.C., August 22, 1973.

46. *Guide to the Congress of the United States* (Washington, D.C.: Congressional Quarterly Service, Inc., 1971), p. 583.

47. *Ibid.*

48. *Ibid.*

49. *Congress and the Nation, Volume II, 1965-1968* (Washington, D.C.: Congressional Quarterly Service, Inc., 1969), p. 92A-96A.

50. *Congress and the Nation, Volume III, 1969-1972,* p. 101A.

51. *Ibid.,* p. 104A.

52. "Hill-Burton Veto Overridden," *Congressional Quarterly Weekly Report,* Vol. 28, No. 26, July 3, 1970, p. 1680.

53. *Congress and The Nation, Vol. III.,* p. 615.

54. "Congress Votes to Override Nixon's Veto of Resolution Limiting Power to Make War," *National Journal Reports,* November 10, 1973, p. 1699.

55. "Recess Pocket Veto Ruled Unconstitutional," *National Journal Reports,* August 25, 1973, p. 1265.

56. Wilfred E. Binkley, *President and Congress* (New York: Knopf, 1947). 1947).

Chapter 11
Urbanization, Suburbanization, and the New Politics

1. *Baker v. Carr,* 369 U.S. 186.

2. Andrew Hacker, *Congressional Districting: The Issue of Representation,* rev. ed., (Washington, D.C.: The Brookings Institution, 1964), p. 26.

3. *Baker v. Carr,* p. 259.

4. *Wesberry v. Saunders,* 84 Supreme Court 526, p. 531.

5. U.S. Bureau of the Census, *Statistical Abstract of the United States: 1973,* 94th ed., Washington, D.C., 1973, table 19, p. 19.

6. Frederic N. Cleaveland and associates, *Congress and Urban Problems,* (Washington, D.C.: The Brookings Institution, 1969), p. 282.

7. *Ibid.,* p. 301.

8. *Congressional Quarterly Weekly Report,* August 5, 1972, p. 1971.

9. *Congressional Quarterly Annual Supplement,* August 29, 1958, p. 25.

10. Edward C. Banfield, *The Unheavenly City,* (Boston: Little, Brown, 1968), p. 125.

11. Public Information Office, Revenue Sharing Office, Department of the Treasury.

12. Richard Nixon, *Community Development Message* delivered March 9, 1973 and submitted to Congress on April 19, 1973.

13. Michael J. Malbin, "Transportation Report: Long Deadlock Ends in Compromise Opening Highway Trust Fund for Mass Transit," *Congressional Quarterly Weekly Report,* August 11, 1973, p. 1166.

14. "Highway Fund: Efforts to Open It to Mass Transit," *Congressional Quarterly Weekly Report,* October 7, 1972, p. 2605.

15. David Martin, "Heading the Highway Lobby Off at the Overpass," *The Washington Monthly,* November 1973, p. 54.

16. President's National Advisory Commission on Rural Poverty, *The People Left Behind,* 1967, p. 39.

17. "Congress Faces the Rural Challenge," *American County,* September 1973, p. 7.

18. *Ibid.* p. 7.

19. Max Ways, "The Two Lyndon Johnsons and the U.S. of 1964," *Fortune,* January 1964, p. 196.

Chapter 12
New Politics and Party Realignment

1. Richard Scammon and Ben J. Wattenberg, *The Real Majority* (New York: Coward, McCann, 1971), p. 19.

2. *Ibid.*

3. *Ibid.,* p. 43.

4. *Ibid.,* p. 48.

5. *Ibid.,* p. 55. Also *Congressional Quarterly Weekly Supplement,* February 3, 1974, p. 440, and Bureau of Census *Current Population Report Series,* 192, p. 20.

6. *Ibid.,* p. 56.

7. *Ibid.,* pp. 59-60. Also Bureau of Census, *1960 Census* and *Current Population Report Series,* March 1972.

8. *Ibid.,* p. 71.

9. Kevin Phillips, *The Emerging Republican Majority* (New York: Anchor Books, 1970), p. 26.

10. *Ibid.*, p. 38.

11. *Ibid.*, p. 175.

12. *Ibid.*, pp. 286-87.

13. *Ibid.*, p. 292.

14. *Ibid.*, p. 177.

15. David Broder, *The Party's Over* (New York: Harper & Row, 1971), p. 199.

16. *Ibid.*, p. 195.

17. James L. Sundquist, *Dynamics of the Party System* (Washington, D.C.: The Brookings Institution, 1973), p. 319.

18. Arthur Miller, *et al.*, *A Majority Party in Disarray* (Ann Arbor: University of Michigan Center for Political Study, 1973), p. 1.

19. *Ibid.*

20. *Ibid.*, p. 5.

21. Sundquist, *op. cit.*, p. 308.

Chapter 13
Congressional Decision-Making and the Budget

1. Allen Schick, "The Road to PPB: The Stages of Budget Reform," *Public Administration Review* (December 1966), pp. 253-58.

2. Aaron Wildavsky, *The Politics of the Budgetary Process* (Boston: Little, Brown, 1964), pp. 47-62.

3. Daniel M. Berman, *In Congress Assembled,* (New York: Macmillan, 1964), pp. 338, 349-50.

4. Richard Fenno, "The House Appropriations Committee as a Political System; The Problem of Integration," *American Political Science Review* (June 1962), pp. 310-64.

5. Robert Ash Wallace, "Congressional Control of the Budget," *Midwest Journal of Political Science* (May 1959), pp. 160-61, and Dalmas H. Nelson, "The Omnibus Appropiations Act of 1950," *Journal of Politics* (May 1953), pp. 274-88.

6. Jesse Burkhead, *Government Budgeting* (New York: Wiley & Sons, 1956), p. 328

7. *Ibid.*, pp. 328-31.

8. U.S. Congress, Joint Study Committee on Budget Control, *Recommendations for Improving Congressional Control over Budgetary Outlay and Receipt Totals,* House Report No. 93-147, 93rd Congress, 1st Session, April 18, 1973.

9. Melvin Anshen, "The Federal Budget As an Instrument for Management and Analysis," in David Novick, ed., *Program Budgeting* (Cambridge, Mass., Harvard University Press, 1965), pp. 10–11.

10. Edward C. Banfield, "Congress and the Budget: A Planner's Criticism," *American Political Science Review,* 1949, p. 1219.

11. Robert L. Chartrand, Kenneth Janda, Michael Hugo, eds., *Information Support, Program Budgeting and the Congress,* (New York: Spartan Books, (distributed by Hayden Book Co., Inc.), 1968), p. 176.

12. *Ibid.,* pp. 177–78.

13. *Ibid.,* pp. 179–80.

14. *Ibid.,* p. 183.

15. Allen Schick, "A Death in the Bureaucracy: The Demise of Federal PPB," *Public Administration Review,* March/April 1973; p. 154.

16. Chartrand, Janda, and Hugo, *op. cit.,* p. 183.

17. Schick, *op. cit.,* p. 154.

18. U.S. Congress, Joint Economic Committee, Subcommittee on Economy in Government, *Hearings, Planning-Programming-Budgeting System: Progress and Potentials,* September 1967, p. 208.

19. U.S. Senate, Committee on Government Operations, Subcommittee on National Security and International Operations, *Hearings, Planning-Programming-Budgeting,* August 23, 1967, p. 61.

20. U.S. Congress, Joint Committee on the Organization of Congress, *Hearings Organization of Congress,* 89th Congress, 1st and 2nd Sessions, and *Organization of Congress, Senate Report 1414,* 89th Congress, 2nd Session, July 28, 1966.

21. U.S. Congress, Public Law 91–510. *The Legislative Reorganization Act of 1970,* October 26, 1970, p. 29.

22. U.S. Congress, Senate Committee on Government Operations, Subcommittee on Budgeting, Management and Expenditures, *Hearings on Improving Congressional Control of the Budget,* Testimony of Elmer Staats, Comptroller General of the United States, May 1, 1972, Vol. 2, pp. 3–36.

23. John S. Saloma III, "The Quiet Revolution: The Development of Information Technology in the U.S. Congress," Paper for the American Political Science Association Study of Congress Conference, October 19–20, 1973, p. 2.

24. *Ibid.,* p. 8.

25. U.S. Senate Committee on Government Operations, Subcommittee on National Security and International Operations, *op. cit.,* August 11, 1967, pp. 7–8.

26. U.S. Congress, Joint Economic Committee, *The Analysis and Evaluation of Public Expenditures,* The PPBS System, 91st Congress, 1st Session. 1969.

27. U.S. Congress, "S-3322, Introduction of Bill to Establish an Office of Program Analysis and Evaluation and a Joint Committee of Congress," *Congressional Record,* 90th Congress, 2nd Session, April 11, 1968, p. S4085.

28. Thomas P. Murphy, "The Extraordinary Power of Freshmen in Congress," *Transaction* (March 1968), pp. 33–39.

Chapter 14
Geopolitics and Federal Spending

1. Murray Weidenbaum, "Where Do All the Billions Go?" *Transaction,* January/February 1966, p. 7.

2. *Ibid.*

3. Charles Culhane, "Labor Readies Stronger Jobless-Pay Plan," *National Journal,* June 9, 1973, pp. 821–30.

4. Murray Weidenbaum, *The Modern Public Sector—New Ways of Doing the Government's Business* (New York: Basic Books, Inc., 1969), pp. 38, 40, 43.

5. *Ibid.,* p. 60.

6. Michael D. Reagan, *Science and The Federal Patron* (New York: Oxford University Press, 1969), pp. 18–19.

7. U.S. Congress, House of Representatives, Committee on Science and Astronautics, *Government, Science, and Public Policy,* 89th Congress, 2nd Session, 1966, p. 25.

8. *Ibid.*

9. *Ibid.*

10. Philip H. Abelson, "The Research and Development Pork Barrel," *Science,* July 2, 1965, p. 11.

11. Daniel D. Roman, *R&D Management: The Economics and Administration of Technology,* (New York: Appleton-Century Crofts, 1968), p. 34, and Charles L. Schultze, *Setting National Priorities, The 1971 Budget* (Washington: The Brookings Institution, 1970), p. 48.

12. Ralph E. Lapp, "Where The Brains Are," *Fortune,* Vol. 23, No. 3, March 1966.

13. *Ibid.,* p. 155.

14. *Ibid.,* p. 154.

15. U.S. Congress, *Congressional Record,* May 6, 1965, p. 9659.

16. Dr. Phillip H. Abelson, "Editorial," *Science,* July 2, 1965.

17. Report on the Subcommittee on Science, Research, and Development of the Committee on Science and Astronautics, U.S. House of Representatives, *Obligation for Research and Development and R&D Plant by Geographic Divisions and States,* by Selected Federal Agencies, Fiscal Years 1961–1964, 88th Congress, 2nd Session (1964), p. 5.

18. *Ibid.,* pp. 13–14.

19. *Ibid.*

20. *Public Papers of the Presidents,* Lyndon B. Johnson, 1965, Vol. 2, Item 514, "Statement by the President to the Cabinet and Memorandum on Strengthening Academic Capability for Science," p. 996.

21. Senate Subcommittee on Government Research of the Committee on Government Operations, *Equitable Distribution of R&D Funds by Government Agencies,* part 3 (from testimony of Dr. Donald F. Hornig, then Special Assistant to the President for Science and Technology), 89th Congress, 2nd Session, pp. 540-56.

22. Report and Recommendations of the Subcommittee on Employment, Manpower, and Poverty of the Committee of Labor and Public Welfare, "The Impact of Federal Research and Development Policies on Scientific and Technical Manpower," 89th Congress, 2nd Session, 1966.

23. *Ibid.,* p. 63.

24. *Ibid.,* pp. 61-62.

25. H.R. 7717, 89th Congress, 1st Session, 1965.

26. U.S. Congress, *Congressional Record,* May 6, 1965, p. 9639.

27. *Ibid.,* p. 12251.

28. *Ibid.,* p. 12252.

29. Thomas P. Murphy, *Science, Geopolitics, and Federal Spending,* (Lexington, Mass.: Lexington Books, 1971), pp. 63-86.

30. *Ibid.,* pp. 77-83.

31. *Ibid.,* pp. 197-360.

32. U.S. Congress, House, Committee on Science and Astronautics, *Technology Assessment, Statement of Emilio Q. Daddario, Chairman,* Subcommittee on Science, Research, and Development, 90th Congress, 1st Session, rev., August 1968, pp. 1-10.

33. Murphy, *op. cit.,* pp. 435-36.

34. Bryce Nelson, "Scientists Plan Research Strike at M.I.T. on March 4," *Science,* January 24, 1969, p. 373, and "M.I.T.'s March 4: Scientists Discuss Renouncing Military Research," *Science,* March 14, 1969, pp. 1176-178.

35. *Ibid.,* p. 1178.

36. Murray L. Weidenbaum, Assistant Secretary of the Treasury for Economic Policy, "Government Investment in Technology," a speech before the annual meeting of the American Institute of Aeronautics and Astronautics, Houston, Texas, October 22, 1970.

Chapter 15
The Impact of the New Politics Congress

1. See chapter 3, table 3-3.

2. See chapter 8, table 8-1.

3. *Congressional Quarterly Weekly Report,* March 26, 1971, p. 729.

4. Judy Gardner, "Consumer Report: New Product Safety Commission Adopts Tough but Reasonable Approach to Its Job," *National Journal Reports*, September 22, 1973, p. 1391.

5. *Public Law* 91-224, March 25, 1970.

6. James Q. Wilson, *Urban Renewal: The Record and the Controversy* Cambridge, Mass.: MIT Press, 1966, p. 421.

Index

324

327

About the Authors

Thomas P. Murphy is Executive Director of the Institute for Urban Studies, and Professor of Government and Politics at the University of Maryland. He received the B.A. from Queens College in 1952, the M.A. from Georgetown University in 1960, and the Ph.D. in political science from St. John's University, New York, in 1963. His articles on Congress, politics, urban affairs, budgeting, and organizational structure have appeared in numerous professional journals. He is the author of *Metropolitics and the Urban County* (1970); *Emerging Patterns in Urban Administration* (Lexington Books, 1970); *Science, Geopolitics, and Federal Spending* (Lexington Books, 1971); *Pressures Upon Congress* (1972); *Government Management Internships and Executive Development* (Lexington Books, 1973); and *Universities and the Urban Crisis* (1974). Dr. Murphy has been active not only as a professor and an administrator, but also as a citizen participation, planning, management, organization, training, and budgetary consultant at the federal, state, and local levels. Since 1969 he has been Director of Governmental and Educational Services for the Lawrence-Leiter Company of Kansas City.

Robert D. Kline is a management auditor with the U.S. General Accounting Office. He formerly served as a graduate assistant with the Institute for Urban Studies and was an intern with Maryland State Senator Steny Hoyer and later served as Senator Hoyer's legislative assistant. His military experience includes two years active and five years reserve duty with the U.S. Air Force. Mr. Kline attended the University of Maryland-College Park, where he received the B.A. in government and politics in 1972 and the M.A. in political science with a concentration in public administration in 1973.

Elizabeth A. Knipe has been a lecturer and then an instructor with the Institute for Urban Studies of the University of Maryland-College Park since 1973. She was the Washington Research Representative for Chilton Research Services of Philadelphia from 1971-1973. During the two previous years she was a research assistant for the National Academy of Public Administration. While at the Academy, Ms. Knipe concentrated on education and training programs in the federal government, including the Federal Executive Institute, as well as in state and local governments. From 1963-1967 she worked as a staff assistant to the director of the Senate Juvenile Delinquency Subcommittee of the U.S. Senate. Ms. Knipe received the B.A. from Trinity College in Washington in 1959 and the M.P.A from the University of Missouri-Kansas City in 1969.